W. K. H ... MHCIMA, DipHot(Göt)

Department of Management Studies for Tourism and Hotel Industries

University of Surrey

The Larder Chef

Food Preparation and Presentation

Third edition

BUTTERWORTH HEINEMANN

Butterworth-Heinemann
Linacre House, Jordan Hill, Oxford OX2 8DP
A division of Reed Educational and Professional Publishing Ltd

A member of the Reed Elsevier plc group

OXFORD BOSTON JOHANNESBURG
MELBOURNE NEW DELHI SINGAPORE

First published 1969
Second edition 1975
Reprinted 1977, 1980, 1981, 1984, 1985, 1986
First published as a paperback edition 1987
Reprinted 1988
Third edition 1989
Reprinted 1990, 1992, 1993, 1995, 1996

British Library Cataloguing in Publication Data
Leto, M. J. (Mario Jack) *1910–*
The larder chef: food preparation and presentation
1. Food – for catering
I. Title II. Bode, W. K. H. (Willi Karl Heinrich) *1931–*
641.3'0024642

ISBN 0 7506 0943 5

Printed and bound in Great Britain by
Biddles Ltd, Guildford and King's Lynn

Preface

For some time now we have felt there was a need for a comprehensive and detailed book on the operation, administration, and instruction in the work normally carried out in the Cold Larder Department of a catering establishment.

It does not matter whether the establishment be restaurant, hotel or industrial. The process of buying, storing, and preparing perishable foodstuffs for cooking is of paramount importance and the efficient operation of this department can contribute, in no small measure, to the economy and to the sound and hygienic running of the establishment.

The Larder Chef, in the final analysis, is the person responsible for producing the food required by the kitchens in a sound and wholesome condition. He is further responsible for the various displays of cold foods which are very often the show windows of the establishment. Last but not least, he is the watchdog of the establishment, guarding by good storage and effective control some very valuable and very perishable items.

Despite these facts, there is hardly any book on the market dealing with this work and when we set up a specialist Larder Department in the Hotel and Catering Department of Bournemouth College of Technology, we had to carry out a great deal of research to enable us to teach the subject effectively to our students, and particularly to National Diploma Students.

This book was born of this research and experimentation and we are sure it will be of the utmost importance, not only to students of catering and apprentice chefs but also to managers of catering undertakings, particularly the very many small hoteliers, who are not in a position to employ specialist staff in this department.

We are, of course, well aware that many of the tasks described in this book have been taken over by manufacturers who, by applying mass production techniques, are able to supply many of the needs of the caterer in some form or other.

This trend may or may not be progressive, according to one's opinion, but even if so-called 'convenience foods' are in use in particular establishments, it is still of some importance to distinguish a rump from a sirloin, or a lemon sole from a dover sole. It is also useful to have some knowledge of how certain cuts of meat, poultry, fish, etc., are prepared for cooking and the most effective method of storing and controlling these foodstuffs.

We would like to take the opportunity here, to extend our thanks to Mr. G. Ransom, F.H.C.I.M.A., A.M.B.I.M., M.R.S.H., Head of the Faculty of Tourism, Catering and Hotel Administration at the Bournemouth College of Technology, as well as to all our other colleagues who have given us much help and encouragement during the three years in which this book was written. We would also like to thank Alison Orchard who drew additional illustrations for the third edition.

We hope that *The Larder Chef* will be of good use to young and old students of an industry to which we have, together, given seventy years of service here in England and in several countries on the Continent.

M.J.L.
W.K.H.B.

A Note on Metrication

With our entry into the European Economic Community or Common Market, and with most shades of opinion committed to changing to the metric system of weights and measures, the time has come to apply this system to cookery recipes in general and more particularly to *The Larder Chef*, as the larder department must of necessity have very close associations with the food trade, with purchasing, and with packaging in all its aspects.

Many industries have, of course, already adopted the metric system and, on the academic side, many examining bodies are considering setting their examination scripts in metric terms; we are sure that the same will be the case in the hotel and catering industry.

There is nothing very complicated in the metric system. Having mastered decimalization in our coinage and by now becoming familiar with the decimal point, the imagined difficulties are all but overcome. In fact as this system lends itself to the use of vulgar fractions as well as decimals we are given the best of both worlds.

In our opinion complications could arise if exact conversion were to be attempted for the comparatively small amount of ingredients which we use in the recipes listed in *The Larder Chef.* For this reason we have chosen to adapt the recipes to the metric weights and measures whilst at the same time retaining the nearest possible approximation to the overall volume or weight of the recipes recommended in our first edition and thus producing the same number of portions for each recipe. To simplify this operation we use a basis of 25 grams as the most convenient approximation to the ounce; we use one-eighth of a litre, or 125 millilitres, as the nearest approximation to the gill (quarter-pint).

Thus in this new edition we are presenting recipes in both metric and imperial weights and measures balanced as to the portions they will produce. They should be read in this light rather than as conversions ingredient against ingredient.

We recommend, however, that for quantities greater than 1 kilogram or 1 litre, exact conversions from the conversion tables below should be calculated to two decimal places. This situation often arises in the cold larder department when dealing with carcasses or joints of meat, whole fish or large quantities of foodstuffs or liquids.

The metric system works decimally, each multiple of a unit being ten times the preceding one and each sub-multiple one-tenth. A standard system of prefixes is used for multiples and sub-multiples. Multiplication is effected

by moving the decimal point to the right; division by moving it to the left.
The units of most concern in catering are:

(i) The *gram* (g), a measure of weight equal to 0.035 ounce.
(ii) The *litre* (l), a measure of capacity equal to 1.76 pints.
(iii) The *metre* (m), a measure of length equal to 39.37 inches.
(iv) The *cubic centimetre* (cm^3) or *millilitre* (ml), a measure of volume equal to 0.061 cubic inches.

The multiples when applied to grams are:

deca (dag) = 10 grams; *hecto* (hg) = 100 grams; *kilo* (kg) = 1,000 grams.

The sub-multiples when applied to grams are:

deci (dg) = 1/10th gram; *centi* (cg) = 1/100th gram; *milli* (mg) = 1/1,000th gram.

The same prefixes are applicable to the other basic units to multiply or divide them by 10; thus the decilitre (dl) = 1/10th litre, the kilometre (km) = 1,000 metres, etc. Fractions are indicated in the normal manner, thus $\frac{1}{2}$ litre; this is the same as 5 decilitres, or 50 centilitres, or 500 millilitres in decimal terms, or it could be expressed as 0.5 1 (5/10ths of a litre).

For temperatures the Celsius (or as it is more commonly known, the centigrade) scale is now in daily use. This scale reads from 0°C, freezing point, to 100°C, boiling point of water at sea level: this compares with 32°F and 212°F in the Fahrenheit scale. Thus if we start at the freezing point, 0°C and 32°F, and go to boiling point, 100°C or 212°F, it would require 180°F to equal 100°C. A Fahrenheit reading is therefore 180/100ths (or 18/10ths or 9/5ths) of the centigrade reading, after deducting 32. Hence to convert Fahrenheit to centigrade: subtract 32, then divide by 9 and multiply by 5, i.e.

$5 \times \frac{(F - 32)}{9}$. *Example*: converting 140°F gives $5 \times \frac{(140 - 32)}{9} = 60°C$.

To convert centigrade to Fahrenheit: divide by 5, multiply by 9, then add 32, i.e.

$\frac{C \times 9}{5} + 32$. *Example*: converting 60°C gives $\frac{(60 \times 9)}{5} + 32 = 140°F$.

As already stated, for simplicity the recipes in this book use approximations with little significant effect on recipe balance: 25 grams equal 1 ounce; $\frac{1}{8}$th litre (125 ml) equals 1 gill ($\frac{1}{4}$ pint). For more exact conversions the following table might prove useful:

Oz	*Fractions of lb*	*Decimals of lb*	*Grams*	*Practical approx.*	*Decimals of kilogram*	*Practical approx.*
16	1	1·0	453·5	454	0·4535	0·45
8	½	0·5	226·75	227	0·22675	0·23
4	¼	0·25	113·375	113	0·113375	0·11
2	⅛	0·125	56·6875	57	0·0566875	0·06
1	1/16	0·0625	28·34375	28	0·02834375	0·03

Pints	*Fractions of gallon*	*Decimals of gallon*	*Millilitres*	*Practical approx.*	*Decimals of litre*	*Practical approx.*
8	1	1·0	4,548	4,548	4·548	4·55
4	½	0·5	2,274	2,274	2·274	2·27
2	¼	0·25	1,137	1,137	1·137	1·14
1	⅛	0·125	568·5	569	0·5685	0·57
½	1/16	0·0625	284·25	284	0·28425	0·28

Grams	*Kilos*	*Oz*	*lb*
1,000	1	35·27	2·204

Centilitres	*Litres*	*Pints*	*Gallons*
100	1	1·76	0·22

Cubic centimetres	*Litres*	*Weight (grams)*	*Pints*	*Fluid oz*	*Weight (kilos)*	*Decimals of lb*
1,000	1	1,000	1·76	35·27	1	2·204

Contents

1. Le Garde-Manger

FUNCTION OF THE LARDER DEPARTMENT

The Cold Larder, or Garde-Manger, is a department set aside for the storage of perishable foods, both raw and cooked, and where foodstuffs such as Meat, Fish, Poultry, and Game are prepared and made ready for cooking. In this department, too, all 'cold' items found on the menu, such as Hors d'Œuvre cold fish or meat dishes, cold sauces, salads, salad dressings, etc., are prepared and 'dressed'.

For these functions to be effectively carried out, it is essential that:

(1) The room be separate from the kitchen, and located in a cool place. At the same time it must be close to the kitchen to avoid undue running about between the two departments, which are closely interrelated.

(2) It should be light, airy and well ventilated and sufficiently spacious to allow the staff to carry out their duties in a clean and efficient manner.

(3) It must be equipped with the necessary fittings, plant, machinery and tools, in accordance with the volume and/or quality of the trade of the catering establishment in which it is situated.

BREAKDOWN OF WORK

Taking the above into consideration, it naturally follows that the work is broken down into various fields such as Hors d'Œuvre, Salads, Butchery, Poultry, Cold Buffet etc. and, in effect, in large busy establishments each of these functions or duties are carried out by one or more men or sometimes women, who specialize in the work of that particular sub-department. As an example, the Butcher, Poulterer, or Fishmonger may be an expert in that particular field without being a trained chef or cook, and it sometimes happens that the salads or Hors d'Œuvre are prepared by female staff trained in those particular duties only.

More frequently, these various duties are allocated by the Chef Garde-Manger, who is in overall charge of the department, to commis or assistant chefs, and they are known as Commis Garde-Manger, whatever duties they are assigned to. Naturally, the busier the establishment, the more Larder-work it entails, therefore more commis are required to man the department. The smaller the volume of trade the fewer commis required, and so on. In many establishments the Chef Garde-Manger is single-handed and carries out all the various functions himself.

It should be mentioned at this stage that often quality rather than quantity, of trade is the determining factor in deciding the number of staff required in the Garde-Manger, or for that matter in the kitchen as a whole.

RESPONSIBILITIES OF THE CHEF GARDE-MANGER

The responsibilities of the Chef Garde-Manger, therefore, are many and varied. He is responsible to the Chef for the efficient running of his department and for the co-ordination of the work of his staff; for the training and discipline of larder staff; for the foodstuffs in the department, some of which may be stored in refrigerators or even in deep-freeze, or preserved by other means. The responsibility is his for keeping a record of such foodstuffs and a day-by-day record of issues to kitchen or other departments.

He must study the menus in advance, so as to be able to order meat, fish, etc., in time for the foodstuff to be prepared and cleaned and made ready for the kitchen in time for it to be cooked; and also all necessary stores for the various larder productions such as salads, Hors d'Œuvre, sauces, buffets, etc.

He is responsible for the efficient storage of food to avoid deterioration and wastage and for the cleanliness and hygiene in the department, to avoid any danger of contamination and possible food poisoning. He should also advise the Head Chef as to what items of foodstuffs require using to prevent eventual wastage.

LARDER CONTROL

If this department is to be run efficiently and economically, it is essential that the Chef Garde-Manger should exercise the strictest possible control over the foodstuffs received and stored in the department.

This involves: (1) Checking the quantity and quality of all goods delivered to the larder; (2) Ensuring that all foodstuffs are stored at the right temperature and that they can be easily checked; (3) That the food is protected from contamination by vermin, etc.; (4) That portion control is rigidly carried out e.g. a given weight of meat, or fish, or vegetables, etc., should always produce the required number of portions of steaks, fish fillets, salads, or Hors d'Œuvre; (5) That stocks of food are regularly turned over; (6) That food is *not* overstocked; (7) That a simple daily stock sheet be kept by each sub-department and handed to the Chef Garde-Manger at the end of each day's business to enable him to write out his order for the following day; (8) Obviously, every effort must be made to maintain the highest possible standard of hygiene, to prevent any deterioration in the foodstuffs under his control and every precaution should be taken to discourage pilfering.

The stock and order sheets should be made as simple and easy to keep up-to-date as possible. A complicated stock sheet, requiring too much writing, will defeat the whole object of the exercise, as it will be neglected during busy rush periods, the very time it is most needed.

For some sub-department stocks, the devising of a simple but effective list is reasonably easy. With others it is not quite as easy. For example, the keeping of the stock of food sent in and returned by the Cold Buffet can be complicated and time-wasting, if one is to measure every ounce or inch. Therefore, it is necessary to accept some rule of thumb, providing this is well supervised. Note that an experienced Chef du Froid or Chef Garde-Manger should be able to tell at a glance the weight, or number of portions of a given joint or cold dish, within very narrow margins.

The butchery department also presents some problems and the stock sheet for this department needs careful consideration. Fish, salad vegetables, canned foods, and dairy produce, on the other hand, are comparatively easy to control. Naturally, each catering establishment will produce its own system, taking its own problems into account, but the stock/order sheet given here should meet the requirements of most larder departments.

Department				*Day and date*	
Item	*Unit*	*Stock*	*Unit price*	*Cost* £ p	*Order*
Tomatoes	kg (lb)	2			12
Sardines	tins	4			8
Eggs	doz	1½			4
Oil	l. (gal)	½			1
Vinegar	l. (qt)	1			2

LIAISON WITH KITCHEN AND PASTRY DEPARTMENT

The larder or 'Garde-Manger' is both a storage department for most perishable foods, and a preparation department for such foodstuffs (Figure 1). The larder staff, under the supervision of the Chef Garde-Manger, are responsible for the ordering, storing and preserving of stores, keeping stocks up-to-date, and accounting for such items as meat, fish, poultry, game etc. which pass through the department on their way from the suppliers to the kitchen and eventually to the restaurant or banqueting rooms. The bulk of such foodstuff needs dissecting or cleaning, dressing, cutting into the required joints or portions, and generally preparing for cooking.

To function in an effective manner, the larder department must operate in harmony with the kitchen in particular, and in many cases with the pastry department, too, if confusion and wastage are to be avoided (Figure 2).

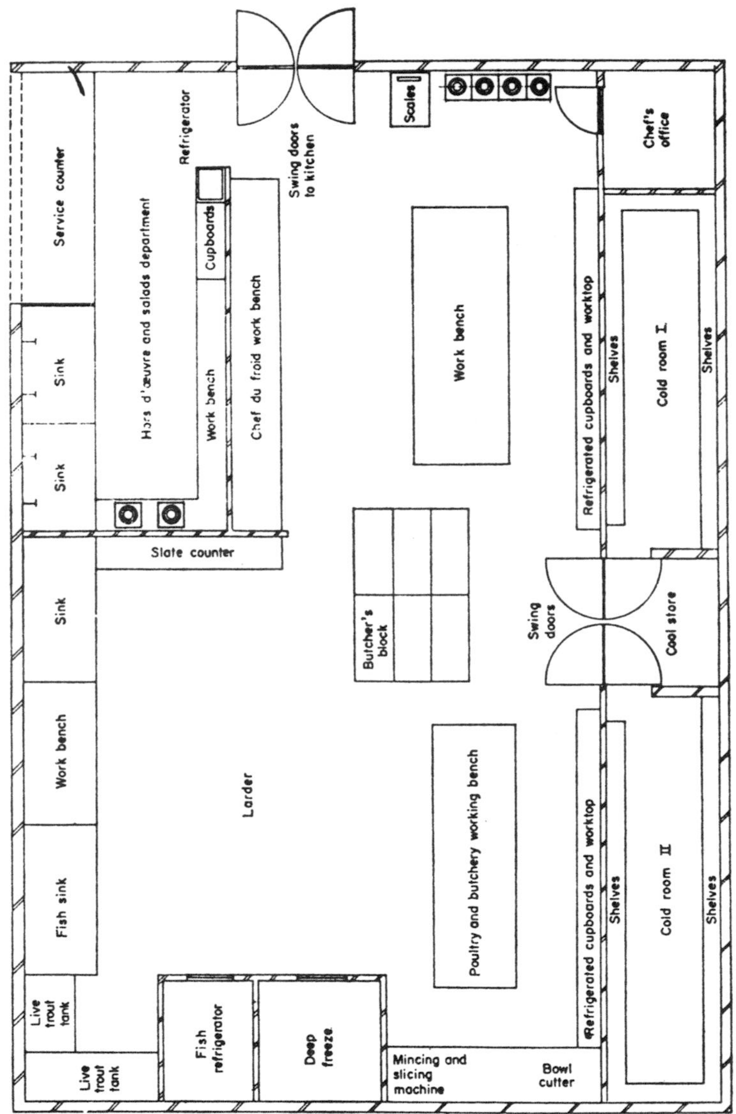

FIG. 1. *Layout of the larder in a medium-sized hotel*

Lack of liaison between the departments could result in duplication of work, or sometimes in certain processes not being carried out to the best advantage. As an example, certain foods intended for cold service are best

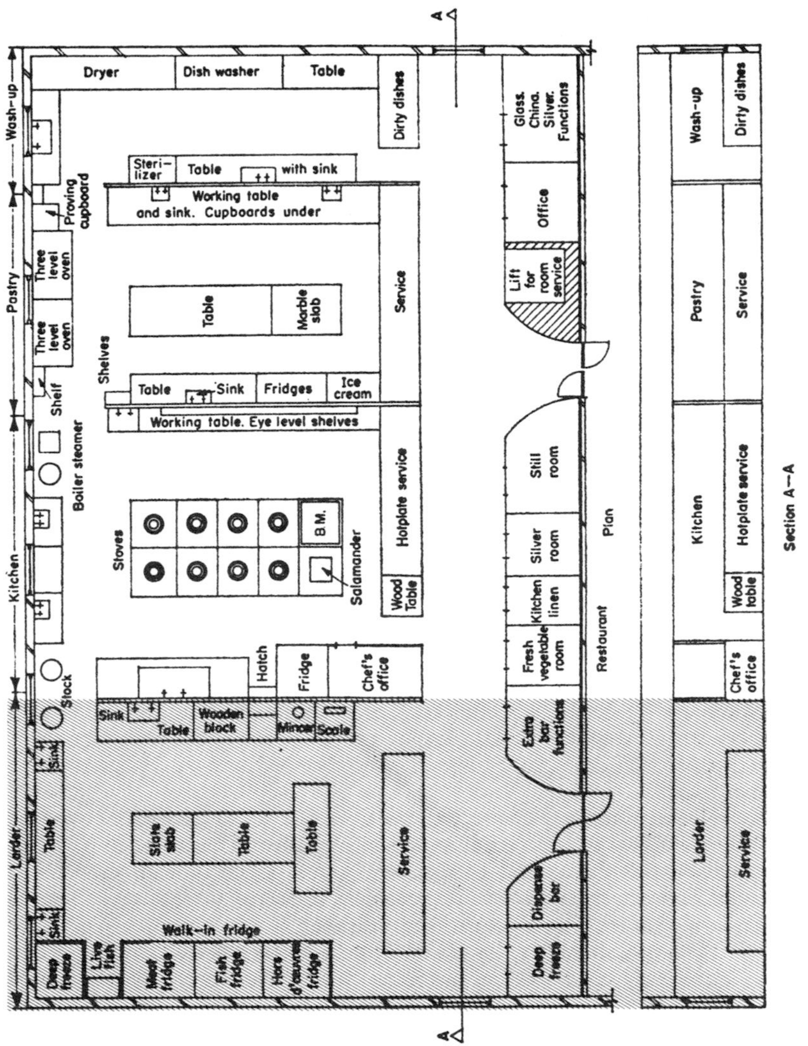

FIG. 2. *Layout of a medium-sized hotel kitchen in relation to the larder*

cooked in the kitchen where there are greater facilities for carrying out the operation, as well as being more closely supervised, thus obtaining the best results.

Likewise, pastry for pies or puddings, and various savouries served from the larder department are best prepared by the pastry staff who will be more skilful in such work, and who are equipped with the necessary apparatus and tools for producing such items for use by the larder department. Such tasks as the lining of pudding basins or the covering of meat pies, prior or after filling, by the larder staff – in readiness for cooking in the kitchen – are examples of such co-operation between the departments.

On the other hand, such savoury fillings as are required by the pastry chef for such items as sausage rolls, patties, or pasties, ravioli, etc., will be prepared in the larder and transferred to the pastry as and when required.

Another important function of the Garde-Manger is to process and utilize the 'leftover' element of any meal, and consequently parts of cooked joints, poultry, fish or even eggs, vegetables and potatoes will be transferred from the kitchen to the larder at the conclusion of every meal. Naturally, the Head Chef will seek to keep these left-overs to a minimum by careful ordering but, in a busy establishment with a varied menu, a certain amount of left-overs are unavoidable.

It is the task of the Chef Garde-Manger in consultation with the Head Chef to make the best possible use of these. Some will go to the preparation of Hors d'Œuvre or salads; others, suitably trimmed and dressed, to the preparation of cold dishes; and some will be used in 'made-up' dishes. All these factors should be, and usually are, taken into account by the Head Chef when planning his menus and the close co-operation of the Chef Garde-Manger can be of the utmost importance.

A number of garnishes or accompaniments to dishes served from kitchen departments are prepared by the Garde-Manger and a list is given at the end of the chapter. Such items as stuffings, forcemeats, lardons or bacon rashers, are naturally provided by the larder, as well as cold sauces for the accompaniment of hot dishes, such as tartare or remoulade for fried or grilled fish, *sauce menthe* for roast lamb, *sauce raifort* for roast beef, *sauce ravigote* or vinaigrette for calf's head, and many others which are dealt with in another section.

In some instances, savoury butters too are prepared by the larder department for use by the kitchen. But such preparations as dumplings and some savoury patties used by the kitchen for garnishes are prepared by the pastry department, with the savoury ingredients, chopped suet or fillings provided by the larder.

It will be seen from the above, that the Chef Garde-Manger *must be familiar* with the garnishes and accompaniments of *all dishes on the menu*, in particular the classical fish dishes and entrées and soups. Close liaison, therefore, is essential between these various departments if delays and complications are to be avoided at the time of serving these dishes.

It is advisable, therefore, for the student to make himself familiar with the more commonly used classical garnishes. There are some very good books on this subject, notably *Escoffier's Guide to Modern Cookery*, or *Le Répertoire de la Cuisine*.

USE AND CARE OF EQUIPMENT, MACHINERY AND UTENSILS

Refrigerators

These play a very important part in the function of the Garde-Manger as they enable perishable foods to be stored at a low temperature and thus prevent deterioration in the food and particularly the growth of harmful bacteria. It should be clearly understood that the refrigerators are not deep-freeze compartments and the temperature should be set at a little above freezing point or 0-1°C (32°F). A temperature of around 2-3°C (34-36°F) is desirable and, as too great a variation in temperature can be harmful to the food in store, an effort must be made to keep the temperature as constant, or as near constant as possible. The following principles must be observed.

(a) Ensure that the refrigerator is in good working order; check the thermostat to make sure it is functioning; have the refrigerator serviced regularly and the level of the refrigerant 'topped up' if necessary;

(b) Defrost regularly to enable the evaporator to function efficiently. This is done by switching off the motor and opening the doors to allow the warm air to melt snow, frost and ice which is clinging to the vanes of the evaporator and the coils. Never in any circumstances should one use an ice pick or a knife to dislodge the ice, as there is a danger of perforating the coils, thus allowing the refrigerant to escape.

(c) Use the door as little as possible and never leave it open longer than is necessary for depositing or withdrawing foodstuffs from the refrigerator. The atmosphere outside the refrigerator will be at a much higher temperature normally and will, therefore, be attracted into the colder temperature causing it to rise rapidly.

(d) Never place hot food into the refrigerator as this will raise the temperature and is harmful to the other foods in cold store.

When the refrigerator is being defrosted, it should be thoroughly cleaned. The racks and bars are removed and scrubbed with hot water containing a grease solvent, rinsed and allowed to dry. The walls, floor and doors should be thoroughly sponged down likewise, with hot water containing grease solvent, then rinsed and dried. During this cleaning and defrosting operation the foodstuffs will naturally have been removed and transferred to alternative storage.

Mincing Machine and Bowl Cutter

This is a combination machine and is used for a number of functions in the Garde-Manger e.g. mincing of meat for sausages, meat loafs, Galantine-Farce etc., minding of fats prior to rendering for dripping, mincing or chopping of cooked foodstuffs, as well as raw for various larder preparations.

The bowl cutter will mix as well as chop the foodstuff and is particularly useful for sausage meats. The mincer can also be used for breaking down bread and crusts, which have been *thoroughly dried first*, into brown bread crumbs, and the bowl cutter can be used for crumbing *fresh crustless bread* into white bread crumbs. It can also be used for chopping vegetables if required. Care must be taken to ensure that meat and fats are free from any bones or sinews, which would cause damage to the knives, and that fresh bread is not put through the mincer as this becomes packed tight in the barrel and can cause the motor to seize up. Seizing up can also be caused by over-loading the machine, which must be avoided.

Whilst every precaution is taken by the manufacturers to make the machine safe to use, it must be used with care to avoid accidents. Metal spoons or spatulas must not be used to push or stir the foodstuffs whilst the machine is in motion, as they are likely to get caught up in the blades with serious results.

Both the mincing and bowl cutting attachments can be dismantled for cleaning, which should be done with hot water containing grease solvent, then rinsed and dried before re-assembling. The bowl itself is not removable and must be cleaned on the machine. Some of the parts are of cast iron and care must be taken not to drop them on to hard surfaces as they will crack or break.

Finally, the machine must be lubricated at regular intervals with the lubricating oil provided. The operator should study the instruction chart so that he becomes familiar with the oiling points.

The Slicing Machine

This machine is used for cutting slices of cooked meats such as ham or tongue, or any other joint of meat which must, naturally, be boneless. It is also used for cutting bacon or gammon rashers which will of course be uncooked. A calibrated scale is fitted to determine the thickness of the slice or rasher and one must ensure that this is returned to zero prior to placing one's hands in the vicinity of the blade to remove or adjust the joint of meat or to clean the machine.

The slicer is the gravity feed type but other makes and types are available e.g. horizontal feed. They may be hand operated, semi-automatic or fully automatic, the latter having both blade and carriage mechanically operated.

For cleaning, the machine should be dismantled in accordance with the instruction chart provided by the manufacturers and all parts washed in hot water containing a grease solvent. They should then be rinsed and dried prior to re-assembly. The parts not removable should be cleaned on the machine and care must be taken to ensure that no foodstuffs are left clinging to any part of it as this could be the ideal breeding grounds for bacteria.

Cotton waste and a wooden palette are used for cleaning the edge of the blade.

Remember, the scale must be set at zero before undertaking any of these operations.

The blade should be kept sharp by using the grindstone attachment provided, when necessary, but care must be taken not to do this too often or for too long as it will cause wear to the blade.

The machine should be kept lubricated with the oil provided, in accordance with the instruction book.

Scales and Weighing Machines

There are several types, the uses of which are obvious. Large platform scales for weighing large joints of meat or other heavy weights are obtainable. For lesser weights there are smaller scales such as graduated scales fitted with a price chart showing at a glance the prices of the odd grams (ounces) and/or the price per kilogram (lb). The Inspector of Weights and Measures should inspect and set these periodically.

No maintenance is necessary other than keeping them in a scrupulously clean condition. This is done by sponging them over with a cloth soaked in hot water and then drying thoroughly. The pans of the small scales and the tray of the graduated scales are removable and should be washed in a sink of hot water.

Foodstuff should *not* be placed directly on to the platform or pans of the scales but should always be on a clean dish or tray or on a sheet of greaseproof paper when being weighed. Naturally, the weight of the container must be taken into account when reckoning the weight of the food.

Electric Grinding Machine

This machine is used for grinding an edge on knives and choppers, or cleavers, as and when required. It should not be abused and should be brought into use only when the steel or the hand carborundum stone fails to set a sufficiently keen edge to the cutting tools. The too frequent use of the grinding machine not only unduly wears the steel of the knives, etc., but has a detrimental effect on the steel itself, causing it eventually to lose its temper. The following instructions should be carefully observed:

(a) Make sure there is sufficient water in the well and that the water is being pumped on to the grindstone, before using. Never use the stone dry.

(b) Use the guides fitted to the machines for either knives or choppers, as this ensures the correctly set edge.

(c) Hold the handle of the knife, or chopper, in the right hand and draw the edge along the stone from the heel of the knife to the tip, with the stone revolving in the *forward* position. Now switch to *reverse* and reverse your drill; knife handle in the left hand, edge of knife from heel to tip, from right to left. Do not over-grind. Set the edge with a steel.

Keep the machine in a clean condition by sponging the stove enamelled parts with a damp cloth, then dry. Change the water frequently to prevent sediment from clogging the pump.

For lubricating, follow the instructions on the chart and learn the lubricating points.

Boiling Plate or Gas Rings

They are used to heat or cook foodstuffs as required, e.g. principally for cooking vegetables for Hors d'Œuvre, for rendering fats, and for the making of aspic jelly, sauces, pickles and other Larder preparations. The flame must at all times be controlled to avoid the risk of burning the food and the taps are adjustable to a range of settings to suit all purposes.

Spillings, or boil-overs, should be wiped down immediately to prevent them from baking hard on the hot surfaces. When bars are cooled, remove any crusted matter, then wash in hot water containing a grease solvent. Periodically, the burners will require the same treatment and must be carefully dried before replacing. The enamel surround should be sponged down with the water. Abrasives should *not* be used as they damage and scratch the enamel.

Griller/Toaster (Salamander Grill)

As the name implies, this is used for either grilling or toasting foodstuffs. It is used principally for toasting bread for making savouries and canapés, and for grilling sausages, chipolatas or other foodstuffs for savouries.

For cleaning, the burners should be lightly brushed to prevent the holes from clogging up. The metal reflectors should be carefully wiped clean as they are easily damaged. The fat drip tray must be emptied and cleaned daily. A little water in the tray will prevent the grease from baking on. *Do not* allow crumbs to burn in the tray. The stove enamel parts should be sponged with a damp cloth and wiped dry.

Gas Boiler

Used for cooking large joints such as hams, gammons, tongues, etc., and also for cooking lobsters or crabs. The pan interior must be emptied and cleaned, washed and dried *each time* it is used.

Butchers' Blocks

These are used for all butchery work: dissecting, jointing and cutting meat, as well as cutting fats, breaking and chopping bones, etc. They are composed of a number of sections of timber in block form, jointed together and framed around with a stout wooden frame, the whole secured with bolts which pass through frame and blocks and all secured together. They have the advantage of being reversible, so that when one surface becomes badly worn, the block can be reversed. They can also be re-surfaced when badly worn by having the surfaces cut by the large saw at a timber yard.

The block usually rests on a stout deal frame, into which may be fitted drawers to contain the butcher's tools.

A good general rule is to keep the surface as clean and dry as possible. The top *should never be scrubbed*. It should be scraped or brushed with the scraper or wire brushes provided and left to dry. Wet meat should not be allowed to lie on the block longer than is necessary, as brine or water can soften the joints or produce wet rot between the blocks. *Never wash the tools on the block*, as this can add considerably to the moisture content.

Steel Tables

These are used as work benches but foodstuffs must not be cut on them. Apart from scratching the surface of the table, such malpractice can also blunt the edge of the knife or tool being used. Boards are provided for such a purpose. The tables should be cleaned by sponging with a cloth soaked in hot soapy water, rinsed with clean water and dried. The chopping boards should be well scrubbed and dried after use. In particular, care should be taken not to leave any fish scales clinging to the surfaces. Formica top tables can be sponged down, as for the steel tables, but the wooden framework must be scrubbed and dried.

Saucepans and Lids

These are mostly aluminium and require the utmost care to keep clean. Certain foods cause bad discoloration of aluminium and the saucepans should be washed in hot soapy water, polished to a bright shine with wire wool and soap, thoroughly rinsed, and dried each time after use. *Soda must not be used*, as this causes pitting and discolouring. The same treatment is given to aluminium trays and other containers. Enamel trays are washed in hot soapy water, rinsed and dried as also are china and earthenware bowls and basins and plastic Hors d'Œuvre dishes.

Frying Kettles and Frying Pans

The frying kettles are used for deep frying and for rendering fats into dripping. The frying pans are used for a variety of shallow frying or sauté-ing operations. Both are made of wrought steel and are best cleaned, whilst still hot, with a heavy dry cloth.

Polythene Bins – Hygiene

Three is the minimum quantity required for daily use in the larder: (1) For brining meat (usually kept in refrigerator), (2) For swill (all waste foodstuffs, suitable for feeding to pigs), (3) For refuse (all waste unsuitable for pig feed; paper, tin, glass, floor sweepings, etc.).

The swill and refuse bins should be emptied daily and washed out with warm water. They must not be exposed to excess heat, otherwise they will lose their shape, or even melt. In particular, *no disinfectants must be used in the swill bin*, as this could poison the pigs. The bin for brining meat *must not* be interchanged with either of the other two.

Finally, at the end of each session, the sinks, counters and floor must be left in a clean condition, together with all the other items mentioned above. Porcelain sinks should be cleansed with scouring powder and rinsed out. Drains should be cleared, cloths washed and hung up to dry. Counters should be scrubbed, window sills sponged clean, and finally the floor well swept.

If these operations are carried out, the department will always be clean and fresh for the commencement of each session.

Other Larder Tools

The following tools are made of steel or tinned steel and are cleaned by washing in hot water containing grease solvent, then rinsed and dried:

Serving Spoons and Ladles:	For spooning or ladling foods.
Sieves:	For sieving various foods.
Colanders:	For draining foodstuffs.
Conical Strainers and 'Chinois':	For straining sauces, etc.
Meat Presses:	For pressing joints etc.
Pie Moulds:	For pork or veal and ham pies.
Whisks:	For whisking and stirring food.
Egg Slicers:	For slicing hard boiled eggs.
Steel Basins:	Containers, etc.
Graters:	For grating foods.

Knives, Choppers, Saws, etc.

All these tools are made of tempered steel and should be cleaned with scouring powder, prior to washing in hot soapy water, rinsing and drying.

Butcher's Boning Knives:	For jointing and boning.
Butcher's Steak or Cutting Knives:	For cutting meat.
Butcher's Saw (tenon):	For surface bones.
Butcher's Saw (bow):	For deep seated bones.
Butcher's Choppers and Cleavers:	For chopping bones.

Butcher's Chopping Knives:	For chining joints.
Cook's 30 cm (12 in.) *Knives:*	For poultry.
Cook's 20-24 cm (9/7 in.) *Knives:*	For vegetables.
Cook's 6-8 cm (4 in.) *Knives:*	For turning, etc.
Cook's 14-20 cm (7 in.) *filleting Knives:*	For fish filleting.
'Tranchelard' Knife:	For carving or bacon rashers.
Palette Knives:	For lifting or turning food.
Potato Peelers French or English:	For peeling vegetables.
Mandoline Vegetable Slicer:	For slicing vegetables, etc.

Wooden Utensils

Wooden spatulas and spoons are used for stirring foodstuffs to prevent burning. Wooden Mushrooms are used for pressing foodstuffs through sieves. These wooden utensils should be well scrubbed, washed, rinsed and dried after use.

Miscellaneous

The following tools are kept clean by washing in hot water, rinsing and drying. Care should be taken to prevent them from rusting or deteriorating.

Cutlet Bat:	For flattening cuts of meat.
Trussing Needles:	For poultry trussing.
Larding Needles:	For larding cuts of meat, poultry, etc.
Larding Pin:	For larding joints, etc.
Lemon Zesters:	For scraping of lemon peel.
Lemon Decorators:	For channelling lemon skin.
Vegetable Scoops:	For shaping vegetables and potatoes.
Butcher's Hooks:	For hanging joints etc.
Skewers:	For skewering meat, etc.
Brining Syringe:	For pumping brine into joints.
Brinometer:	For measuring density of brine.

2. *Hors d'Œuvre and Salads*

PREPARATIONS

This sub-department of the Garde-Manger is responsible for the preparation of all Hors d'Œuvre including single dish Hors d'Œuvre such as smoked salmon, caviar, fruit and fish cocktails, etc. Oysters are normally served by the Fishmongery sub-department.

Cocktail Hors d'Œuvre and savouries, likewise, are prepared by the Hors d'Œuvrier, as also are all cold sauces and dressings used not only in the Garde-Manger but in the kitchen or dining room services as well.

This sub-department, therefore, must hold quite a considerable amount of stock-in-hand, and also have available a considerable and varied amount of mise-en-place if it is to operate effectively. It follows, also, that there must be adequate provision for storage and working space.

Ordering

The first consideration should be the ordering of supplies, both from the stores and from the provision merchants. This is usually done in consultation with the Chef Garde-Manger who has overall responsibility for the sub-department.

Naturally the menus, the list of functions and the estimated amount of *à la carte* trade will be taken into account and the ordering will be done at least 24 hours in advance to enable the head chef to 'vet' the order, and to include any supplies required from outside in his kitchen orders. In most establishments the stores are issued only once, or possibly twice, per day. Therefore, care must be taken to ensure that no items are forgotten on the requisition list. Broadly speaking, a selection of Hors d'Œuvre will consist of:

(1) *Vegetable Salads:* e.g. tomato, potato, cucumber, beetroot, mixed vegetables, celery, celeriac, cabbage, French beans, sweet peppers, etc.

(2) *Cooked Vegetable, Pickles, Grecques, Portugaise:* e.g. cauliflower, celery, artichokes, button onions, mushrooms, etc.

(3) *Pickled, Brined or Marinaded or Smoked Fish:* e.g. soused herring, Bismark herring, mackerel portugaise, soft roes in marinade, etc.

(4) *Canned or Bottled Specialities:* e.g. sardine, anchovy, smoked herring fillets, tunny fish, pimento, olives, gherkins, sweetcorn, etc.

(5) *Salads or Mayonnaises:* prepared from cooked fish, meat, poultry and game.

(6) *Salads or Mayonnaises:* prepared from eggs, rice, haricot or butter beans etc.; garnishing and decoration will require lettuce, onions, parsley, watercress, mustard-and-cress, lemons, capers, etc.

The 'Single Dish' Hors d'Œuvre will also have to be taken into account and a stock will have to be kept up-to-date of such items as smoked salmon, trout, eel, etc., caviar, foie gras, salami, and any specialities of the establishment such as pâté, terrine, or any other fish, meat, poultry, game or vegetable preparation particular to the 'Maison'. Sea foods and fruit for cocktails must also be available, if such items are featured on the menu.

Salads in Season will have to be provided: lettuce, cos, chicory, endive, corn salad, etc., as well as spring onions, radishes, chive etc., when in season.

Finally, the spices and seasonings, olive oil, vinegars, wines, tinned and dried requirements, must be considered and, where cocktail parties are catered for, bread, butter, biscuits and other bases, as well as fillings, will be required. Here again, the necessary garnishing and finishing materials must be taken into account.

It will be seen from the foregoing that the sources of supply can be many and varied but on the whole they consist of: (1) The dry ration store or central store; (2) The outside provision suppliers – fishmonger, poulterer, butcher, greengrocer, (via the Chef Garde-Manger); (3) 'Leftovers' from the kitchen (again via the Chef Garde-Manger).

Preparing Hors d'Œuvre

As to the actual preparation and serving, this of course is where the skill and experience of the Hors d'Œuvrier is essential and they are best acquired in practical work in this field. A few points are mentioned here that will help the successful operation of this sub-department.

Quantity. It is essential to know how much to prepare if wastage is to be avoided. One must consider, therefore, the number of 'services' required for any given meal; the number of 'Raviers' or individual dishes of Hors d'Œuvre per service, and the approximate number of servings or portions in each Ravier. For single dish Hors d'Œuvre, or in the type of establishment where Hors d'Œuvre are set out on plates by the Hors d'Œuvrier, this calculation is very much easier.

Next, one should consider the 'content', taking into account the factor of popularity. Certain basic Hors d'Œuvre, being more popular than others, are almost always included in any variety or selection of Hors d'Œuvre.

Having reckoned these two factors, one can then set about preparing the necessary amount of each variety.

Quality, Texture, Flavour, Colour, Temperature, etc. Hors d'Œuvre are intended to be 'appetizers', as well as being the 'overture' to the meal, and their function must be to stimulate the appetite and set the tone for the ensuing courses. Both composition and colour are of utmost importance. The fresh natural colours of fresh vegetables, greens and reds, will blend tastefully with the whites of eggs, rice, Grecques, etc., and with the cream colour of mayonnaises, the browns of meat salads and smoked fish and the variegated colours of fish, pickles and salads.

The vegetables should be carefully cut and *never overcooked*. They must always be crisp and bright. This applies also to eggs, rice and potatoes. The texture of any sauces should be correct, not too puddingy or thick and, contrariwise, not too thin and watery.

The Grecques, Portugaises or other pickles should be just sufficient to cover the foodstuffs so that they may get the maximum flavour from it, and they should of course be served with the foodstuffs.

The Hors d'Œuvre should be served chilled but not frozen. The garnishing should be fresh and crisp and should be added at the last moment, before serving. No artificial colouring matter should be used: fresh, natural colours only. When 'dressing' them on a tray or trolley, they should be arranged harmoniously, alternating the colours and the types of food so as not to have colours and flavours clashing with each other. The basic Hors d'Œuvre, i.e. egg, tomato, potato, Russian salad, sardine, is supplemented with a variety of other preparations to provide an assortment and to allow scope for ringing the changes.

Practical experience and good management, good taste, an educated palate, an eye for colour and decor, insistence on absolute cleanliness, and considerable pride in one's work, are the minimum requirements to produce a good Hors d'Œuvrier.

Serving Hors d'Œuvre

Hors d'Œuvre can be served on plates or in square or oblong dishes made of earthenware or plastic called 'Plats Russes' or in crystal, glass or even plastic or wooden bowls, and dishes called Raviers. These, again, should be placed on polished silver flats or wooden trays, with a doily of appropriate size or even a decoratively broken serviette.

Hors d'Œuvre Variés are often served on large trays or trolleys, especially designed for this purpose. Here the guests can inspect and choose under the best rules of hygiene and presentation the various items of proffered delicacies. Figure 3 shows plated, tray and trolley service.

TYPES OF HORS D'ŒUVRE

Differentiation can be made between the following basic types of Hors d'Œuvre:

(1) Hors d'Œuvre variés: a selection of side-dishes.
(2) Hors d'Œuvre froid singulier: single side-dishes.

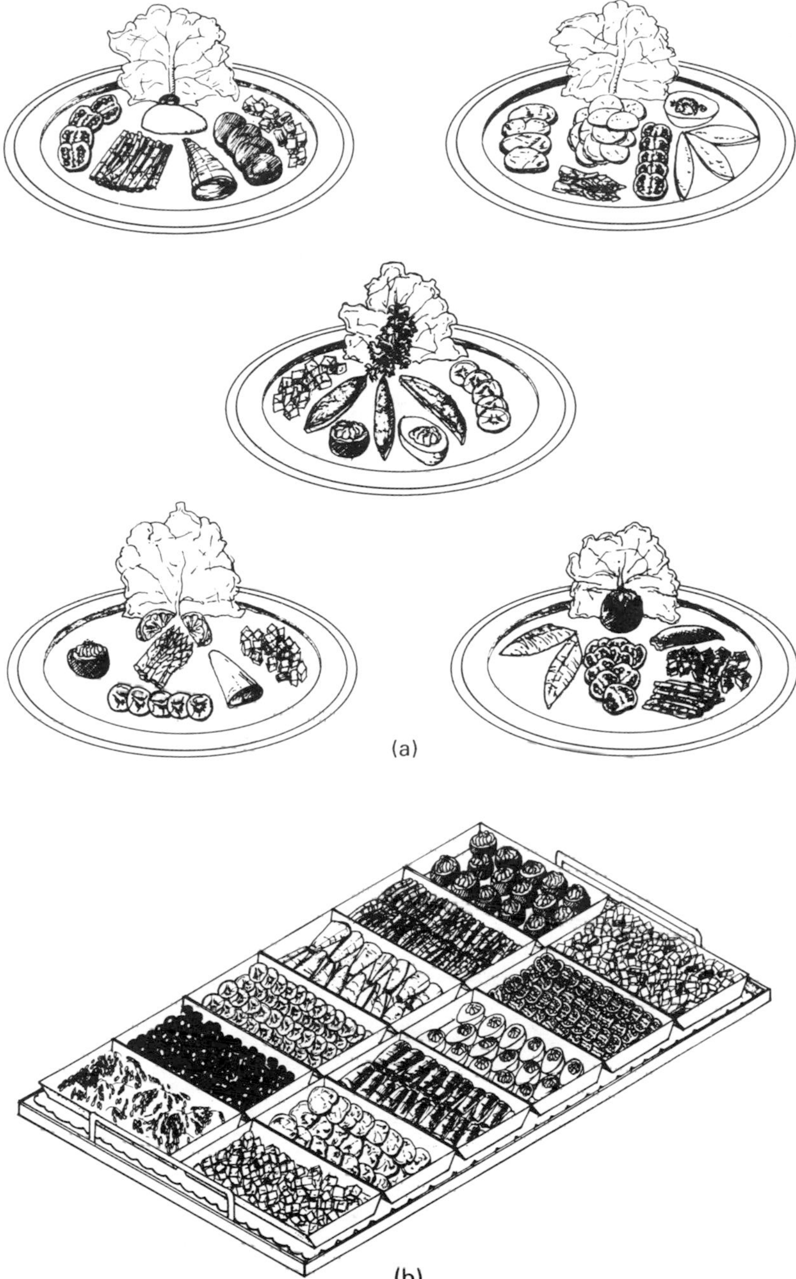

(a)

(b)

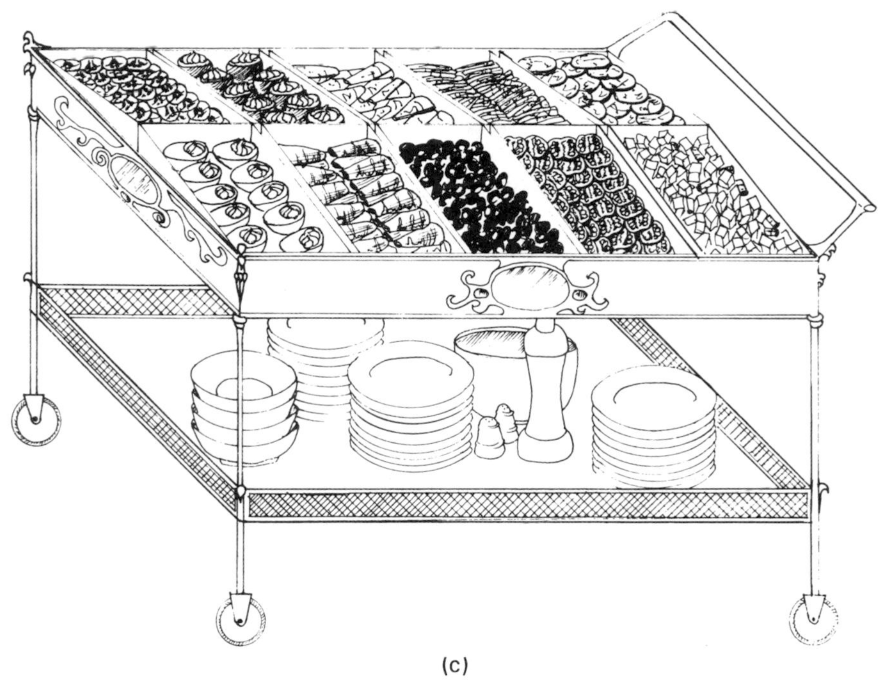

(c)

FIG. 3. (a) *Variations on plated Hors d'Œuvre variés* (b) *Hors d'Œuvre variés on tray to be presented to guests* (c) *Hors d'Œuvre variés on silver trolley*

(3) Hors d'Œuvre chaud: hot side-dishes.

These Hors d'Œuvre are served to the following rules: (a) Selection of side-dishes, usually for lunch and before soup; (b) Single side-dishes, usually for dinner and before soup; (c) Hot side-dishes, for lunch, dinner and suppers, always after soup; (d) A selection and a single side-dish are prepared and served from the larder. Hot side-dishes are prepared and served from the kitchen, e.g. *entremettier, rôtisseur, pâtissier, poissonnier*, etc.

Hors d'Œuvre Singuliers

As the word 'single' already implies, these side-dishes consist of one food only, in one piece or of one portion. Served only with certain dressings, sauces, garnishes and accompaniment. Below are given a list of the most common single side-dishes:

Avocado pears, Bismark herring, Boudins, Caviar, Cray-fish, Craw-fish, Crab, Carolines, Duchesse, Eel, Esprots Fumés, Stuffed Eggs, diverse Fruit-cocktails, Grapefruits, Galantines, Hareng Fumé, Hareng Marine, Hors d'Œuvre Russe, Lobster, Langouste, Melons, Mousses, Mussels, Mortadella, Oysters, Pâté de Foie Gras, Pâté de Foie, Pâté Maison, Potted Shrimps, Potted Ham, Potted Beef, Potted Salmon, Prawns, Parma Ham, Plovers' Egg, Smoked Salmon, Trout, Sardines, Sausages, Salami, Saucissons, Tunny, Tartare Beef, Zakouskis, etc.

In this section can be included: egg – fish – shellfish – meat – poultry – game – vegetable and certain fruit salads; and egg – fish – shellfish – meat – poultry – game – vegetables and certain fruit mayonnaise. Tomato and Fruit Juices may be included.

Apart from the importance of good decoration and presentation for the Hors d'Œuvre, ice can make the service and presentation of all cold Hors d'Œuvre most pleasing to the eye. For example:

Crushed Ice for oysters, shellfish, shellfish or fish cocktail, etc.

Ice pieces and cubes for Avocado pear, melons, grapefruit, all potted meat and fish etc.

Carved or sculptured blocks of Ice for caviar, pâté de foie gras, pâté maison, mousses and mousselines, etc.

Hors d'Œuvre Chauds

These, as already explained, are always served after the soup and are the concern of different departments in the kitchen. Hot side-dishes can be made of many things, such as eggs, fish, meat, poultry, game, vegetables and even certain pastries. Hot Hors d'Œuvre are also referred to as *Entrées Volantes* or *Petites Entrées*. Here are the most commonly known Hot Side Dishes:

Alumettes; Artichokes; Aubergines; Blinis; Bouchées; Ballotines; Brioches, Barquettes, Canapés chauds; Coquilles; Cromesquis; Crêpes; Crêpinettes; Croûtons; Croûtes; Croquettes of Meat – Game – Fish –

Shellfish and Vegetables; Dartois; Duchesses; Dariols; Fondants; Medallions; Moules; Quiche Lorraine; Ragoûts fins; Rissoles; Soufflées; Tartelettes; Timbales, etc.

It has already been said that the hot side-dishes do not concern the Larder and Hors d'Œuvrier in particular, except maybe for normal larder preparation. Otherwise, the Entremettier, Rôtisseur, Poissonnier and Pâtissier will cook and serve the hot Hors d'Œuvre.

Savouries

It is a custom in the British Isles to serve, after the Sweet, so called savouries. These are in many ways similar to the hot canapés, croûtons and croûtes mentioned above, e.g. Welsh Rarebit, Scotch Woodcock, Angels on Horseback, etc. This is a typical British custom, contrary to the Continental practice whereby these foods are usually served at the beginning of a meal.

HORS D'ŒUVRE VARIES

These can be made of a thousand and one things, viz. meat, poultry, game, fish, shell-fish, eggs, fruits and vegetables, as well as left-overs of such items.

The above-mentioned items used for Hors d'Œuvre Variés should always be small. Cut into dice, cubes, strips, or pieces, they can be seasoned, pickled, brine soused and marinaded, served with additions of different herbs, vinaigrette, dressings or mayonnaise to allow for different flavours and appearance.

Many side-dishes are also prepared *à la grecque* or *à la portugaise*, whether a simple item as an onion or cauliflower, or fish like a herring or mackerel, or the more expensive salmon, sole, etc. In all cases a simple and appropriate decor should not be forgotten.

There is hardly any limitation to their use and presentation. Expertly prepared and dressed, these little tit-bits (even when made of leftovers and trimmings) can be very pleasing to the eye and palate at the same time and, moreover, prove to be quite inexpensive.

HORS D'ŒUVRE MOSCOVITE

This is a special Hors d'Œuvre, very old and one of the classics of side-dishes. Although much of the normal items of the vast range of Hors d'Œuvre are used, it has nevertheless a distinct way of preparation and presentation.

It is usually served on special large silver or crystal flats which have been given a mirror of clear aspic. The centrepiece is always Russian Salad which has been set, or is like a Mousse, wholly surrounded with aspic.

Around the centrepiece of Russian Salad, a colourful display of petits Hors d'Œuvre is arranged; these should always be small, in neat portions, or pieces with much variation of colour and appetizing look, such as:

Œuf farci;
Tomato farci;
Barquette de Caviar, Crevettes Roses, Anguille fumée, Sardines, Anchois, etc.;
Tartelette de Viande, Volaille, Gibier ou fromage;
Cornet de Jambon et Saumon fumé;
Coquilles et Timbales;
Bouches filled with creamed meats, poultry, game and fish;
Cannelons, spiral shaped puffpaste, filled with various savoury fillings;
Carolines (Diverses), small choux-paste éclairs, filled with various mousses of fish, meat, poultry and game, covered with chaud-froid sauce and glazed with aspic – Carolines au Caviar (filled with caviar);
Duchesses (Diverses), small choux-paste profiterolles about the size of a walnut, filled with various mousses or farces of fish, meats, poultry and game, e.g. Duchesses à la Reine (Chicken purée), Duchesses au Saumon fumé (Smoked Salmon-purée), etc.; Duchesses, as Carolines above, can again be covered with a sauce chaud-froid, according to filling or just glazed with aspic.

SINGLE HORS D'ŒUVRE

CAVIAR

This is the roe of a fish of the sturgeon family which has been removed freshly caught and then sieved to clear it of all skin, veins and fat. This roe is then salted and packed in tins or tubs.

The main supply, and indeed the best quality, comes from the Black and Caspian Seas and the fish are caught when spawning during winter and spring when they swim up the rivers. The Port of Astrakhan exports the majority of the world's supply.

The best known types are: *Beluga*, a large grain and light colour; *Ship*, a medium size grain and light colour; *Sevruga*, a small grain and a little darker colour; *Oscetra*, a small grain and a little darker colour (Figure 4).

Generally the best quality roes are lightly salted and therefore do not keep well and, although it is generally true that the lighter coloured caviar is the best flavoured, the preparation and storage will ultimately determine the quality.

Caviar should be stored at approximately 1-2°C (32°F) and should be handled carefully, using a horn, wood or plastic spoon to transfer it to

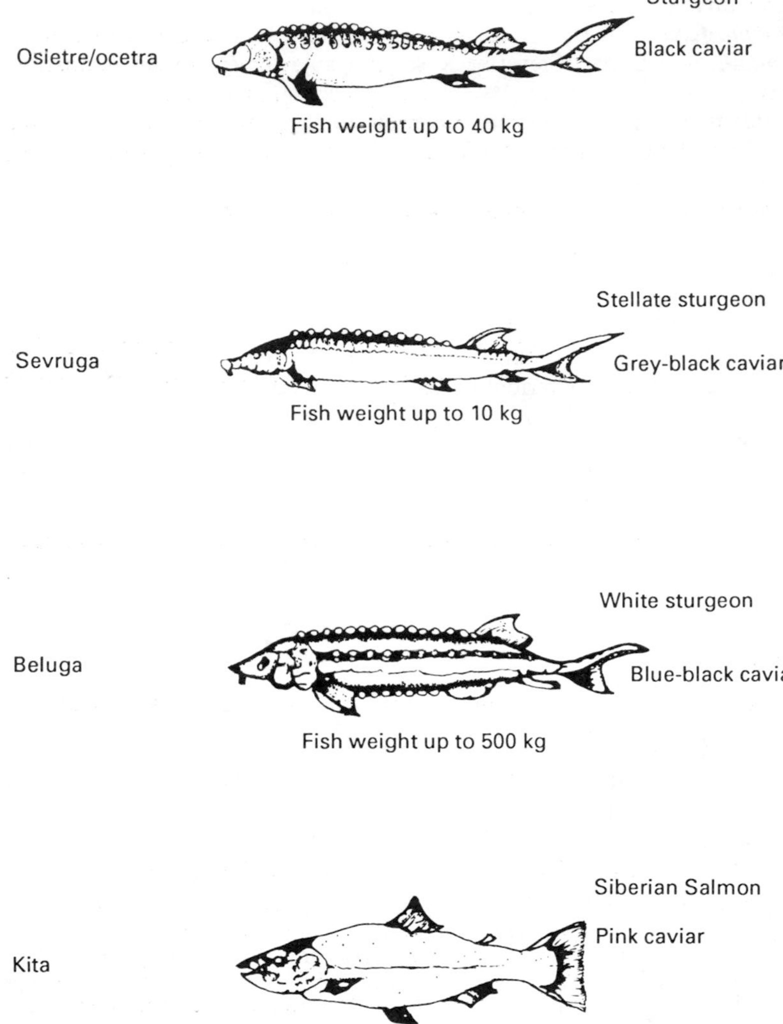

FIG. 4. *Types of sturgeon and the caviar produced*

smaller jars, for service. *Caviar should look bright, shiny and whole.* Some caviar is pasteurised and packed in airtight jars.

'Pressed' caviar is that which has been prepared by blanching and pressing between cloths and then packed. This type is of inferior quality. It is also packed in airtight jars.

Caviar is served very cold. The best quality is generally served direct from the tin or jar which has been on a socle of ice or surrounded by crushed ice. A portion is approximately 15 grammes or $\frac{1}{2}$ oz.

Hot thick toast, thinly sliced brown bread and butter, or blinis are served with caviar; lemon, sieved hard boiled egg and finely chopped onions are also served.

Caviar is also served in pastry barquettes and on toast.

Botarga – Boutargue

Red caviar is prepared from salmon, carp, pike, grey mullet and other fish. The grain is much larger than that of real caviar and is from pink to red in colour. It has not the flavour of real caviar.

Dark Caviar/Substitute

A type made from various fish roes, sold as a cheap caviar but very inferior in flavour.

Vesiga – Visigha

Vesiga is the dried marrow from the backbone of sturgeon. When soaked it resembles sago, cooked in water.

Blinis

250 *g* (8 *oz*) *buckwheat flour*	20 *g* (1 *oz*) *yeast*
250 *g* (8 *oz*) *medium flour*	2 *eggs*
$\frac{1}{2}$ *l.* (1 *pint*) *milk and* 2 cl ($\frac{1}{4}$ *gill*) *cream*	*Salt to taste*

Dissolve the yeast with $\frac{1}{2}$ pint warm milk; add 8 oz flour to make a thin paste. Place aside for one hour in a warm place to ferment. Add the remainder of the warm milk and flour, then add the salt and yolks of eggs. Place aside in a warm place for 30 min and then add the stiffly whisked white of egg. The blinis are cooked in small individual iron pans. Heat the pans, add a little clarified butter and then the mixture. Cook in a hot oven or at the side of a hot oven stove for 6–8 min, turning over when set.

OYSTERS – HUÎTRES

The oyster is enclosed in two shells, the top shell being flat. These shells are hinged together at a point and the oyster has a strong muscle attached to the centre of each shell by means of which it opens and closes them.

Care should be taken to ensure that the oysters are alive when purchased. If the shell is open, they should be discarded since their flesh deteriorates rapidly.

If the oysters contain a milky substance, this is known as white sickness. If the oysters are full of a greyish liquid, this is grey sickness and if heavily floating with tiny black specks, it is black sickness. This means that the oysters are breeding. Oysters under these conditions are *not* in prime condition and should be returned to the supplier.

It is imperative that oysters should be kept in wooden containers, deep shell downwards, covered by a wooden lid which must be weighted to keep the oysters from gaping. Store in a cool, damp room, preferably not in a refrigerator.

English oysters are in season from September to April and are not at their best during the other months when they are breeding. British oysters are called 'Natives'. The best known are: Royal Natives or Royal Whitstable, Colchester, Purfleet, Whitstable, Poole, Falmouth, Helford, Shannon.

The best known Continental oysters are: *French*, Marennes Vertes, Marennes Blanches, Belons, Cancale, Brittany; *Dutch*, Natives; *Belgian*, Victorias; *Portuguese*, Blue Points (Gryphas).

Oysters are graded by quality and price. The best are generally accepted as being Whitstable, Colchester, Belons and Marennes.

Preparation of Oysters

The oyster is opened by the use of a special knife, care being taken to ensure that the oyster is not damaged.

Method 1: Hold the oyster in a folded cloth in the palm of the hand with the hinged or pointed end nearest the fingers. Hold the oyster knife in the other hand with the handle in the palm and the point inserted at the point of the oyster. The knife is then pushed and given a slight twist to break the hinge (ligament). The first finger of the hand holding the oyster is placed to hold the shells apart, so allowing the oyster knife to be pushed along the top shell and thus cut the muscle of the oyster from this shell. The blade of the oyster knife is then used to cut the muscle of the oyster from the bottom shell. It is most important to keep the oyster knife close to the shell to avoid cutting or damaging the oyster. Care must also be taken to avoid splintering the shell.

Method 2: As before but opening the oyster from the round edge of the shell with the pointed end toward the palm of the hand.

Method 3: Use a bench with a small grooved hollow to hold the oyster and so avoid it slipping while being opened.
Method 4: Use a special machine.

Oysters are generally served in the deep shell on a bed of crushed ice but occasionally may be ordered served on the flat shell, when the customer does not like the liquor. If oysters are ordered 'bearded', a teaspoon is placed over the 'eye' of the oyster so that the 'beard' can be removed from its edge.

Oysters for service as Hors d'Œuvre should be opened at the last possible moment and served in their shells on crushed ice.

Lemon, thinly sliced brown bread and butter and, if required, finely chopped shallots and vinegar are served with them.

FISH HORS D'ŒUVRE

Anchovy Fillets – Fillets d'Anchois

The anchovy fillets are cut in lengths and neatly arranged trellis fashion on a Ravier, with a border of sieved hard boiled yolk and white of egg, and chopped parsley with a caper placed within the trellis work divisions. Sprinkle with a little olive oil. Anchovy fillets may also be presented paupiette fashion.

Dressed Crab

(1) Scrub well to remove scum.
(2) Remove legs and claws.
(3) Open the crab by gently removing under-shell (soft shell); start at the tail and lever up the shell with the point of a knife, taking care not to break the upper shell.
(4) Remove the sac and the gills from the shell and discard them.
(5) Remove the liver or soft dark part of the crab and place in a clean basin.
(6) Crack the claws, after removing pincers, remove flesh and place in clean basin.
(7) Split bony centre of soft shell and with a fork remove white and brown flesh, and place in respective basins.
(8) Shred the white meat with the tips of fingers and remove any splinter of shell or bones from it. Dress with seasoning and vinaigrette.
(9) Rub the dark meat through a wire sieve, add half its volume of white fresh breadcrumbs soaked in milk and pressed dry, dress with seasoning, vinaigrette and a few drops of Worcester sauce.
(10) Clean the inside of the shell, press around the edges to break it clean at the natural line, dry it well and brush with little oil to polish it.
(11) Fill the centre of the shell with the dark meat, smooth with a palette

knife. Fill both ends with shredded white meat, tuck well into the corners, but keep well separated from brown meat. Now separate the 3 sections with lines of finely chopped parsley, sieved white and yolk of hard boiled egg or lobster-coral if available. Finish the garnish with trimmed fillets of anchovies and stoned olives.

Potted Shrimps – Crevettes au Beurre

250 *g* (8 *oz*) *fresh shelled shrimps*
250 *g* (8 *oz*) *butter*
5 *cl* ($\frac{1}{2}$ *gill*) *white wine*
Salt, pepper, nutmeg to taste

(1) Melt butter and wine and seasonings.
(2) Bring to the boil.
(3) Add washed and peeled shrimps, reboil.
(4) Place into small moulds to set.
(5) Make sure that all portions have an even amount of butter.
(6) Place in refrigerator to set.
(7) For service, carefully remove the mould, place on lettuce leaves, garnish with parsley and lemon.

Potted Prawns – Crevettes Roses au Beurre

As above, using prawns instead of shrimps. Both can be purchased ready-made in little cartons.

Kilkis – Gaffelbitar

These are proprietary preparations of Norwegian or Swedish origin and are available under many brand names. They are usually made from herrings, or the smaller Baltic herring, and are found in flat, square or oval tins in different sauces, *viz*. Tomato, Mustard, Dill, Onion, Cream etc.

Sardines – Sardines à l'Huile

Remove carefully from tin, dress neatly in Ravier, add a little oil from tin. Garnish with picked parsley, thin slices lemon.

Smoked Salmon – Saumon Fumé

Smoked salmon is produced in Scotland, Denmark, Holland, Norway and other countries. Smoked Scotch Salmon is pre-eminently the finest.

The flesh side of the smoked salmon is carefully trimmed of the hard outer surface engendered by the smoking and brining process. All bones are carefully removed, the small ones with a pair of tweezers.

The flesh is sliced thinly, starting at the tail end and cutting at an angle, towards the tail. The first slices tend to be dry and should be put on one side for other uses.

The salmon is rubbed with oil and wrapped in an oiled paper, after it has been trimmed. It is then hung in a cool dry place. This is done because the salmon quickly absorbs any other flavours.

Serve with lemon and thin slices of brown bread and butter.

Smoked Cod's Roe

This is purchased whole or ready in jars, and is shaped by spoons into portions and dressed in lettuce leaves. Serve with thinly sliced brown bread and butter.

Smoked Trout – Truit Fumée

The skin is loosened, and the lateral and dorsal bones are removed. The skin can be re-formed to facilitate the service of the whole trout. A second method is to separate the two trout fillets and serve them without the skin.

In both cases present on crisp lettuce leaves, garnished with hard-boiled egg whites and yolk sieved separately. Fans of gherkins and a lemon quarter complete the presentation. Horseradish cream and brown bread and butter are served separately.

Buckling

Prepared and served as for smoked trout.

Smoked Eel – Anguille Fumée

Cut into tronçon; skin and remove the bone. Re-form. Store as for smoked salmon. Serve on lettuce leaves with a fan of gherkin. Horseradish sauce is served separately.

Smoking Herring Fillets – Filets de Harengs Fumés (Gendarme)

Fillets of smoked herrings are packed in oil. Serve in a Ravier garnished with onion rings.

Smoked Mackerel (Whole) – Maquereau Fumé

Carefully remove the skin from the mackerel with a pointed knife. Remove the backbone; try to keep the two fillets whole. Serve one large or two smaller fillets as a portion. Garnish and present as for smoked trout above.

Smoked Mackerel Fillets – Filets de Maquereau Fumé

Remove possible dry edges from fillets of mackerel. Cut into two or three diamond-shaped pieces according to size. Otherwise present as smoked trout above.

Peppered Mackerel Fillets – Filets de Maquereau Fumé au Poivre

The peppered mackerel fillets are prepared as above. Serve with brown bread and butter. Creamed horseradish is not normally served with either.

Smoked Sprats – Harenguets Fumés

These are supplied in bundles or in small flat boxes. Serve *au naturel*, accompanied by brown bread and butter and sections of lemon.

Tunny Fish – Le Thon

Remove carefully from tin, cut or shred, dress neatly in ravier, with a little oil on top. Garnish at will with picked parseley, tomato, hard boiled egg, cucumber.

FISH AND SHELLFISH COCKTAILS

Of the many fish cocktails available the prawn cocktail is the most popular, but there are others just as good which we should consider to give variety to this much-liked type of starter.

Prawn Cocktail – Cocktail de Crevettes Roses
(4 portions)

160-220 *g* (6-8 *oz*) *shelled prawns; if frozen they should be defrosted and washed, and then marinaded with a little oil, salt and lemon juice and left to stand for 10-30 minutes*
$\frac{1}{4}$ *heart of lettuce, cut into juliennes, not too long*
12.5 *cl* ($\frac{1}{4}$ *pint*) *cocktail sauce (see later in this chapter)*
4 *channelled lemon slices*
4 *unpeeled prawns*
4 *springs of dill, mint or parsley*

(1) Place lettuce in even amounts into cocktail glass.
(2) Divide prawns evenly on to lettuce.
(3) With a spoon, cover prawns evenly with sauce.
(4) Place a slice of lemon on the edge of the glass.
(5) Garnish with a sprig of herbs of your choice.
(6) Hang an unpeeled prawn by its tail on the rim of the glass.
(7) Serve with brown bread and butter.

Prawn and Palmhearts Cocktail – Cocktail Côte d'Azur

As for prawn cocktail, with the addition of one palmheart per cocktail.

Shrimp Cocktail – Cocktail de Crevettes

As for prawn cocktail, replacing prawns by the same amount of shrimps.

Mussel Cocktail – Cocktail de Moules

As for prawn cocktail, replacing prawns with equal amount of freshly cooked mussels.

Lobster Cocktail – Cocktail de Homard

Proceed as for prawn cocktail, replacing prawns with a 500 g (1-1¼ lb) cooked lobster cut into neat even pieces. Retain one good piece of claw and lobster coral (if any) to garnish the top of the cocktail.

Fish Cocktail – Cocktail de Poisson

As for prawn cocktail, replacing prawns with equal amount of poached white fish, such as turbot, halibut, sole or cod.

Seafood Cocktail – Cocktail Fruits de Mer

Replace prawns with about equal amounts of (a) poached flaked fish (b) prawns (c) mussel or slices of scallops, or any other fish or shellfish deemed to be fruit of the sea.

Mary's Cocktail – Cocktail de Marie
(4 portions: suitable for vegetarians)

50 *g* (2 *oz*) *cooked French beans, cut short*
50 *g* (2 *oz*) *celery or celeriac, cut into brunoise*
50 *g* (2 *oz*) *cooked kidney beans*
50 *g* (2 *oz*) *tomato concassé*
2 *tablespoons of vinaigrette*
⅛ *lettuce, cut into juliennes*
12.5 *cl* (¼ *pint*) *cocktail sauce*
4 *springs of dill, mint or parsley*

(1) Combine French beans, celery, kidney beans and concassé with vinaigrette; leave to stand for 10 to 30 minutes.
(2) Divide shredded lettuce evenly into glasses.
(3) Add vegetable mixture, and coat with cocktail sauce.
(4) Garnish with herbs of your choice.
(5) Serve with brown bread and butter.

FISH AND SHELLFISH SALADS

Fish Salad – Salade de Poisson

160-200 *g* (6-8 *oz*) *poached cooled fish, usually turbot, halibut, sole or cod*
4 *tablespoons of vinaigrette, without mustard*
50 *g* (2 *oz*) *of asparagus tips, or blanched red or green peppers, or avocado pieces*
8-12 *crisp lettuce leaves of your choice*
8-12 *capers*
1 *large or* 4 *small cherry tomatoes*
4 *springs of dill, mint or parsley*

(1) Combine flaked fish, asparagus or peppers or avocado, and vinaigrette; leave to stand for 10-30 minutes.
(2) Line plates or silver flat with lettuce leaves.
(3) Divide fish mixture evenly on to lettuce.
(4) Garnish with capers, tomatoes and herbs of your choice.
(5) Serve with brown bread and butter.

It is a nice thought to actually name the fish with which the salad is being made, for example:

Salad of Turbot – Salade de Turbot

Halibut Salad – Salade de Flétan

Fish salad can be made from other fish and shellfish, such as the following.

Shrimp Salad – Salade de Crevettes

As for fish salad, replacing fish with fresh shrimps.

Prawn Salad – Salade de Crevettes Roses

As for fish salad, replacing fish with fresh prawns.

Mussel Salad – Salade de Moules

As for fish salad, replacing fish with freshly cooked, cooled mussels.

Lobster Salad – Salade de Homard

As for fish salad, replacing the fish with a 500 g (1-1$\frac{1}{4}$ lb) lobster cut into even neat pieces. Here as extra garnish the asparagus is better suited than peppers or avocado.

Seafood Salad – Salade de Fruits de Mer

As for fish salad, replacing fish with a mixture of fish, prawns, mussel, scallops or any other fish or shellfish deemed to be fruits of the sea.

FISH AND SHELLFISH MAYONNAISE

Fish Mayonnaise – Mayonnaise de Poisson

160–200 *g* (6–8 *oz*) *poached, cool fish, usually turbot, halibut, sole or cod*
2 *tablespoons of vinaigrette, without mustard*
4 *anchovy fillets*
8–12 *capers*
8–12 *crisp lettuce leaves of your choice*
2 *hard-boiled eggs*
12.5 *cl* ($\frac{1}{4}$ *pint*) *mayonnaise*
1 *large or* 4 *small cherry tomatoes*
4 *sprigs of dill, mint or parsley*;

(1) Combine flaked fish and vinaigrette; leave to stand for 10 to 30 minutes.
(2) Line plates or silver flat with lettuce leaves of your choice.
(3) Divide fish equally on lettuce; coat with mayonnaise, which should be of pouring but covering consistency.
(4) Garnish with anchovy fillets, capers, slices or quarters of eggs, tomatoes and herbs of your choice.
(5) Serve with brown bread and butter.

Fish mayonnaise can be made with other fish or shellfish to add variation to a basic theme, for example:

Cod Mayonnaise – Mayonnaise de Cabillaud

Halibut Mayonnaise – Mayonnaise de Flétan

Prawn Mayonnaise – Mayonnaise de Crevettes Roses

Mussel Mayonnaise – Mayonnaise de Moules

Lobster Mayonnaise – Mayonnaise de Homard

Seafood Mayonnaise – Mayonnaise de Fruits de Mer

FISH AND VEGETABLE MOUSSES

Fish Mousse – Mousse de Poisson
(12–16 portions: white fish)

250 *g* (10–12 *oz*) *white poached, cooled fish, usually turbot, halibut, sole or cod*
25 *cl* (½ *pint*) *mayonnaise*
25 *g* (1 *oz*) *gelatine leaf, soaked*
6 *cl* (⅛ *pint*) *dry white wine*
25 *cl* (½ *pint*) *whipped cream; some or all may be replaced by yoghurt*
½ *lemon, zest and juice*
Salt and pepper to taste

(1) Dissolve soaked gelatine in heated white wine; cool.
(2) Place flaked fish, free of skin and bone, in food processor. Add mayonnaise, lemon zest and juice, and salt and pepper. Cut to fine purée and emulsion.
(3) Remove from processor to a bowl; fold in whipped cream.
(4) Correct seasoning.
(5) While still of pouring consistency, fill individual moulds such as darioles, sponge tins or soufflé dishes. Alternatively, for multiple portions pour into oiled, greaseproof paper lined, loaf-shaped mould container. Allow to set for 1–3 hours or overnight.
(6) Carefully remove from moulds by dipping the mould into hot water for a second. Serve individual portions as they are. Serve multiple loaf-shaped moulds by cutting into neat portions, using a sharp knife dipped into hot water.
(7) Present on crisp lettuce leaves on plates or silver flat.
(8) Garnish with tomatoes, cress, lemon, dill, mint or parsley.
(9) Serve with toast, Melba toast or brown bread and butter.

It is usual to name the fish which was the base of the mousse, for example:

Mousse of Halibut – Mousse de Flétan

Mousse of Sole – Mousse de Sole

Salmon Mousse – Mousse de Saumon
(12–16 portions: pink)

250 *g* (10–12 *oz*) *poached, cool salmon or two tins of salmon*
25 *cl* (½ *pint*) *mayonnaise*
6 *cl* (⅛ *pint*) *dry white wine*

25 g (1 oz) gelatine leaf, soaked
25 cl (½ pint) whipped cream, some or all of which can be replaced by yoghurt
½ lemon, zest and juice
Salt and pepper to taste

Proceed as for fish mousse above. However, slices of peeled cucumber are a must for the garnish.

Smoked Salmon Mousse – Mousse de Saumon Fumé

Follow ingredients and method for salmon mousse, replacing fresh or tinned salmon with smoked salmon or good smoked salmon trimmings. The flavour is very distinct and slightly stronger.

Asparagus Mousse – Mousse d'Asperge
(12–16 portions: suitable for vegetarians)

As for salmon mousse, replacing salmon with 250 g (10–12 oz) of fresh asparagus or two tins of asparagus tips. The type of asparagus used – white or green – will determine the final colour of the mousse.

Avocado Mousse – Mousse d'Avocat
(12–16 portions: green: suitable for vegetarians)

Ingredients as for salmon mousse, replacing salmon with two large, very ripe avocados. After removing the stones, scrape out the avocado pulp. Be sure to get the dark green pulp near the skin, which will ensure a good deep green colour for this mousse. Follow the method of preparation and presentation as for salmon mousse.

Combinations

The mousses described can of course be combined as two or more layers and flavours, being pleasing to both eye and palate at the same time. It is important, however, to let each layer set before the next is added. It is advisable therefore to leave some time between the making of the various mousses to be combined, as they will begin to set quite quickly once the gelatine has been added.

Examples of combinations are as follows:

Halibut and Salmon Mousse – Mousse de Flétan et Saumon
(white and pink)

Salmon and Avocado Mousse – Mousse de Saumon et Avocat
(pink and green)

Turbot, Salmon and Avocado Mousse – Mousse de Turbot, Saumon et Avocat (white, pink and green)

Presentation

To be absolutely correct, a mousse made in an individual portion mould should be called a *mousseline*. A mousse which is a portion from a multi-portioned loaf mould is called a *mousse*. Both should be presented on lettuce leaves of various types and garnished with cress, tomatoes, cucumber and herbs such as dill, mint or parsley (Figure 5). However, in the

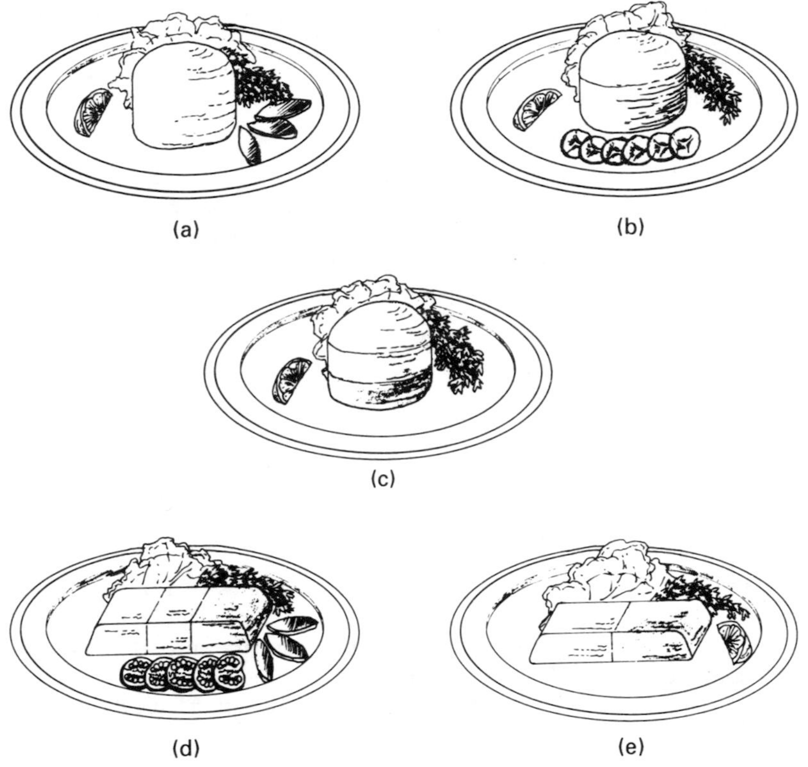

FIG. 5. *Various mousselines and mousses.* (a) *One colour/flavour mousseline, e.g. fish, poultry, or ham* (b) *Two colour/flavour mousseline, e.g. turbot and salmon, or avocado and ham* (c) *Three colour/flavour mousseline, e.g. turbot, salmon, and avocado* (d) *Three colour/flavour mousse portion, cut from larger mould* (e) *Two colour/flavour mousse portion*

modern *nouvelle cuisine* style of presentation this garnish may be omitted, and the mousse portion is set directly on a plate or flat which has been lined with a contrasting sauce, for example:

Sauce Verte (green) under a Salmon Mousse
Sauce Andalouse (red) under a Halibut Mousse
Sauce Mayonnaise (yellow) under an Avocado Mousse.

Where mayonnaise-based sauces are considered too rich, the same presentation and effect can be achieved by a lighter sauce such as a coulis, for example:

Tomato Coulis (red) under an Avocado Mousse
Cucumber Coulis (green) under a Salmon Mousse
Asparagus Coulis (green or white) under a Turbot Mousse.

These sauces and coulis are described later in this chapter.

FRUIT HORS D'ŒUVRE

Grapefruit

1. *Halves – Demi Pamplemousse*

(a) Cut crosswise and remove centre core and pips with sharp pointed knife or grapefruit knife; (b) Start at centre and carefully cut around each segment to loosen it from dividing skin; (c) Sprinkle with caster sugar and chill; (d) Serve in grapefruit holder, Maraschino cherry in centre.

2. *Grilled – Demi Pamplemousse Grillé.*

(a) Prepare as above; (b) Grill under salamander grill prior to serving; (c) Serve hot.

3. *Cocktail – Cocktail de Pamplemousse.*

(a) Cut top and bottom to expose flesh; (b) Carefully trim off skin and pith; (c) Cut each segment from dividing skin; (d) Extract remaining juice and add to segments; (e) Add caster sugar and chill; (f) Serve in wine glasses, Maraschino cherry in centre.

4. *Grapefruit and Orange Cocktail – Cocktail Florida.*

Use half grapefruit and half an orange and proceed as for grapefruit cocktail. Pineapple segments may be added.

5. *Orange Cocktail.* As for grapefruit cocktail, using oranges in lieu of grapefruit.

6. *Fruit cocktail – Cocktail de Fruits Frais.*

(a) A mixture of fresh fruits, such as pears, pineapples, grapes, cherries, oranges, etc.; (b) Wash, peel, cut into neat segments or dice, chill in syrup and lemon juice, serve in cocktail glasses.
The above are commonly flavoured with suitable liqueurs.

Ugli or Tamgelo

A large citrus fruit, the size of a grapefruit, with loose irregular skin. In colour and flavour a cross between orange and grapefruit, served in similar manner to grapefruit.

Ortanique

Citrus fruit, cross between orange and tangerine. Has fine delicate flavour. Prepared in same manner as grapefruit. Can be used for Hors d'Œuvre or dessert.

Avocado or Alligator Pear – Poire d'Avocat

The avocado pear has gained considerable popularity as a starter in the home as well as in most restaurants.

We differentiate between two types, one reddish and one green. The latter is considered the better, and it does not matter whether it has a dark-green smooth skin or a silver-green pitted skin.

Any avocado must be served ripe. To test for ripeness, gently press the ends; they should give.

Preparation
(1) Cut pear into even halves with a stainless steel knife (to avoid discolouring).
(2) Remove stone, without damaging the soft flesh.
(3) Brush avocado with a mixture of even amounts of oil and lemon juice. This is particularly important with larger numbers at functions for banquets, to prevent the pears becoming black after preparation.
(4) Place in fridge; serve chilled.

Presentation
Avocados can be served in many different ways. The most common is with an acid dressing, such as:

Avocado with French Dressing – Poire d'Avocat a la Française

Avocado with Lemon Dressing – Poire d'Avocat au Citron

Avocado with Fine Herbs Dressing – Poire d'Avocat Fines Herbes

Avocado with Blue Cheese Dressing – Poire d'Avocat Roquefort

Avocado with Russian Dressing – Poire d'Avocat à la Russe

Should a simple dressing not be suitable for a particular service, mayonnaise or a mayonnaise-based sauce can take the place of the dressing, such as:

Sauce Andalouse: tomato-flavoured mayonnaise
Sauce l'Anneth: mayonnaise, cream and finely chopped dill
Sauce Remoulade: mayonnaise with herbs, gherkins and chopped egg
Sauce Rose: cocktail sauce
Sauce Verte: mayonnaise with many fine chopped herbs.

Service
In the case of dressing and mayonnaise based sauce, these should be filled in the stone cavity of the avocado, as well as proffering dressing and sauce apart.

Fillings
Avocados can also be filled with particular foods such as:

Avocado with Shrimps – Poire d'Avocat ou Crevettes

Avocado with Prawns – Poire d'Avocat ou Crevettes Roses

Avocado with Crabmeat – Poire d'Avocat ou Crabe

Fill cavity with shellfish as appropriate. Garnish and serve.

Avocado with Tomato – Poire d'Avocat Provençale

Remove avocado meat from skin and cut into fine dice. Mix with an equal amount of fresh tomato concassé and flavour with garlic and a little French dressing. Return carefully to avocado skin, garnish and serve chilled.

Avocado with Mousses

A most tasty way of serving the avocado is to fill its cavity with suitable mousses, such as:

Poire d'Avocat ou Mousse d'Asperge (vegetarian)
Poire d'Avocat ou Mousse de Poisson
Poire d'Avocat ou Mousse de Jambon
Poire d'Avocat ou Mousse de Tomate (vegetarian)

See recipes for mousses given earlier in this chapter.

Avocado as a hot Hors d'Œuvre
Avocados as a hot starter have gained much favour, say at a dinner party on a cold winter's day. Examples of this are as follows:

Hot Avocado Florentine – Poire d'Avocat Florentine Chaud

Fill cavity of avocado with a purée of creamed spinach. Coat with sauce Mornay and sprinkle with cheese. Bake in medium-slow oven to a golden brown.

Hot Avocado with Crabmeat – Poire d'Avocat ou Crabe Chaud

Fill cavity of avocado with heated crabmeat. Cover with sauce Mornay and sprinkle with cheese. Bake in medium-slow oven to a golden brown.

Hot Avocado with Scallop – Poire d'Avocat St Jacques

Fill cavity of avocado with poached scallop, one or two according to size. Cover with sauce Mornay or vin blanc, and sprinkle with cheese. Bake in medium-slow oven to a golden brown.

Melon

Cantaloup. Considered the best. Round with top and bottom flattened; skin ribbed, mottled green and yellow in colour. Flesh inside pink.
Cavaillon. Oval shape, web-like pattern over the skin; flesh red.
Charentais. Size of large grapefruit; similar to cantaloup in appearance. Half melon represents portion – serve well-chilled.
Ogen. Size of a grapefruit. Similar to charentais, but smooth and more green in colour outside and with light green flesh inside. Half an ogen melon again represents a portion. It is often much cheaper than charentais, but of good quality and flavour. Serve well chilled.
Honeydew. Oval in shape, hard green or smooth yellow skin, flesh colourless.
Pastèque. Water melon, round, yellow or green skin, flesh bright red, rather tasteless.

Melon must be ripe before serving. Store in dry place to ripen. Test by gentle pressure on base, which will give slightly if ripe enough. Chill thoroughly.
Method of serving: (a) *Whole* (*Melon Frappé*), from top cut a plug $7\frac{1}{2}$ cm (3 in.) in diameter, with a silver spoon remove pips, add wines if desired (usually Port, Madeira, Marsala), chill for some three hours, dress in bowl of crushed ice or ice socle, serve caster sugar and ground ginger separately; (b) *In Portions*, wedge-shaped, pips removed, on crushed ice; (c) *Cocktail*, in dice, or cut with spoon cutter (Parisienne), serve well-chilled in Coupe glasses, Maraschino, Kirsch, brandy or white port added if desired. See Figure 6.

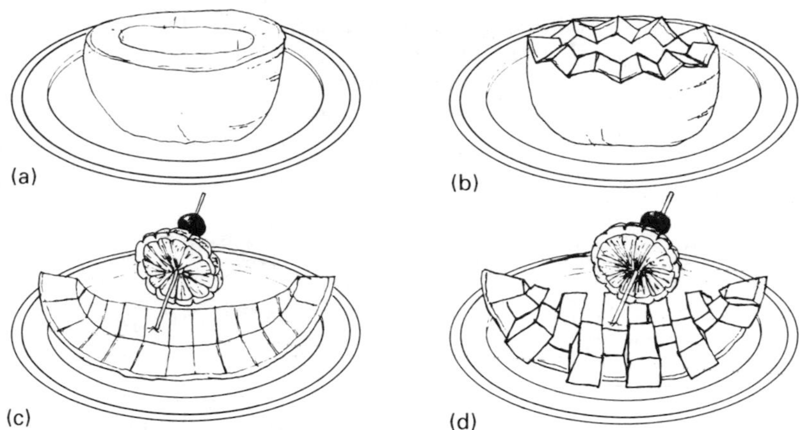

FIG. 6. *Melon presentation.* (a) *Small melon, plain cut* (b) *Small melon, crown cut* (c) *Large melon section, segment cut* (d) *Large melon section, with alternate segments moved*

MEAT HORS D'ŒUVRE

Parma Ham – Jambon de Parme

Prague Ham – Jambon de Prague

French Ham – Jambon de Bayonne

Westphalian Ham – Jambon de Westphalie

These types of hams are examples of smoked and raw hams. Each has a very distinct flavour. In the last few years raw hams from many other countries have become available, but the above are the oldest and best known. The Parma ham is without doubt the most famous.

These hams can be bought whole on the bone; whole off the bone; in easy-slice joints of varying quality; or ready sliced in round tins with ten to a dozen slices.

The most important aspect of the service of raw ham is that it should be very thinly and very freshly sliced. Serve on plates or flats, with a garnish of gherkin fans, tomatoes, or red and white radishes or lemon. Buttered rye or brown bread is the normal accompaniment (see pages 170-3).

Smoked Ham with Fruits – Jambon Fumé avec Fruits

A much liked Hors d'Œuvre is the combination of hams with fruits such as melon, avocado, dates, papaya, mango and kiwi fruit. Presentation varies from fruit to fruit; the following details and Figure 7 will be of help.

Ogen or charentais melon and smoked ham

These smaller types of melon are cut in half, using either a straight or a crown cut, and the pips are removed. Thin slices of ham are added to overlap the edge of the melon. A quarter of lemon completes the presentation.

Open melon with Parma ham

Parma ham with slices of melon

Parma ham with dates

Parma ham with kiwi

Honeydew melon with Parma ham

FIG. 7. *Smoked ham and fruits*

Cantaloup or honeydew melon and smoked ham

From this larger type of melon we cut four to eight portion wedges according to the size of the melon, and remove the pips. We can again lay the slices of ham across the melon wedge, or on the plate or the flat like a fan, with the melon alongside. A quarter of lemon completes the presentation.

Dates and smoked ham

Fresh or dried dates may be used, and four to six are normally sufficient for a portion. The dates are placed as a nest on one side of the plate or flat. The slices of ham are set in a fan on the plate, or possibly arranged in two or three cornets to vary the presentation. Again a quarter of lemon is included.

Papaya and smoked ham

A well-ripened papaya is carefully cut in half lengthwise, and the black pips are removed. The slices of ham are laid across the half fruit. Papayas available in the UK are usually quite small, and half a fruit is a good portion. In tropical countries the papaya may reach melon size; in that case it should be cut and presented like the large melon above. A quarter of lemon or lime completes the presentation.

Mango and smoked ham

Cut a ripe mango in half lengthwise, and carefully remove the flat stone. Then present as for ogen melon above.

Kiwi and smoked ham

One or possibly one and a half kiwi fruit are cut in a neat crown pattern and stood on their ends on the side of the plate or flat, on which the smoked ham is placed in a fan pattern. A lemon or lime quarter is a must.

Smoked Turkey – Dinde Fumée

Smoked breast of turkey is a more recent addition to our Hors d'Œuvre. It can be bought in whole smoked breast, or already sliced; two to three slices make a portion. The turkey should be placed on crisp lettuce leaves of your choice, and garnished with mustard and cress and tomatoes. Mill pepper and brown bread and butter are offered at the table.

Smoked Duck Breast – Aile de Canard Fumé

Smoked Reindeer – Renne Fumé

Smoked Venison – Chevreuil Fumé

Prepare and serve as for smoked turkey above.
Sauce Cumberland is an ideal accompaniment to the four meats above.

Charcuterie

Various cooked hams; salami sausages of Belgian, Danish, Dutch, German or Italian origin; other sausages such as beer sausage, garlic sausage, ham sausage, liver sausage, mortadella, tongue sausage; many types of pâtés, potted meats, brawns, and rillettes; various pies, en croutes and galantines; are all served as single Hors d'Œuvre all over the world.

In all cases the chosen charcuterie is placed in suitable portions on plates or flats and garnished with lettuce of various types, cress, mustard and cress, tomatoes, gherkins, pickled dill cucumbers, and sometimes onion rings, Toast, Melba toast, brown bread and butter, French bread, rye bread, vollkorn bread or pumpernickel should be offered according to custom or taste.

Beef Salad – Salade de Boeuf
(4 portions)

160–200 g (6–8 oz) *cooked beef cut into juliennes or neat dice*
50 g (2 oz) *blanched onions in juliennes or dice*
50 g (2 oz) *julienned or diced pickled cucumber*
4 *tablespoon of garlic-flavoured vinaigrette*
8–12 *crisp lettuce leaves*
1 *large or* 4 *small cherry tomatoes*
Little chopped parsley or chives

(1) Combine beef, onions, cucumber, parsley and vinaigrette. Leave to stand for 10–30 minutes.
(2) Dress plates or flats with lettuce, which may be green, Iceberg, chicory, raddichio or endive.
(3) Place salad in even portions on lettuce. Garnish with tomatoes and cress.
(4) Serve with brown bread and butter.

Ham Salad – Salade de Jambon

As for beef salad, replacing beef with the same amount of julienned or diced ham.

Garlic Sausage Salad – Salade de Saucisse à l'Ail

As for beef salad, replacing beef with the same amount of juliennes or dice of garlic sausage.

In all three salads above, onions or pickled cucumber may be replaced with juliennes or dice of blanched red or green peppers.

Chicken Salad – Salade de Volaille

160–200 g (6–8 oz) *juliennes or dice of boiled chicken*
100 g (4 oz) *juliennes or dice of fresh pineapple*
or equal amount of asparagus
50 g (2 oz) *blanched juliennes or dice of red or green peppers*
4 *tablespoons of lemon dressing (see later in this chapter)*
8–12 *crisp lettuce leaves of your choice*
4–8 *pieces of fresh pineapple or asparagus tips*
Little mustard and cress

(1) Combine chicken with pineapple or asparagus, peppers and dressing. Leave to stand for 10–30 minutes.
(2) Dress plates or flats with lettuce leaves; for contrast this can be raddichio or even endive leaves.

(3) Divide chicken into even portions on lettuce, and garnish with pieces of pineapple or asparagus tips and cress.
(4) Serve with hot toast.

Chicken Mayonnaise – Mayonnaise de Volaille

The ingredients are the same as for chicken salad, plus 12 cl ($\frac{1}{4}$ pint) of mayonnaise, which may be thinned with a little pineapple juice. Proceed as for chicken salad. After the chicken is placed on the lettuce, coat each portion with the mayonnaise, and garnish with pineapple or asparagus tips and cress. Hot toast is again the best accompaniment.

MEAT MOUSSES

Ham Mousse – Mousse de Jambon
(12–15 portions)

250 *g* (10–12 *oz*) *cooked ham; larger amounts may be minced first*
25 *cl* ($\frac{1}{2}$ *pint*) *mayonnaise*
6 *cl* ($\frac{1}{8}$ *pint*) *dry white wine or sherry*
25 *g* (1 *oz*) *gelatine, soaked*
25 *cl* ($\frac{1}{2}$ *pint*) *whipped cream, some or all of which can be replaced by yoghurt*
1 *tablespoon Worcestershire sauce*
4 *tablespoons port or Madeira*
Salt and pepper to taste

(1) Place ham, mayonnaise and Worcestershire sauce in food processor; cut to a fine purée.
(2) Add gelatine dissolved in wine or sherry; mix again.
(3) Remove from processor to a bowl; add whipped cream or yoghurt.
(4) Add port or Madeira, correct seasoning.
(5) While still of pouring consistency, place into individual or large mould (see fish and vegetable mousses earlier). Leave to set for 1–3 hours or overnight.
(6) Carefully remove from individual moulds, or cut large mould into neat portions with a knife dipped into boiling water.
(7) Place on lettuce leaves on plate or flat; garnish with tomatoes, cress or dill cucumbers.
(8) Serve with toast, Melba toast or brown bread and butter.

Chicken Mousse – Mousse de Volaille
(12–15 portions)

250 *g* (10–12 *oz*) *cooked white diced chicken; larger amounts may be minced first*
25 *cl* (½ *pint*) *mayonnaise*
6 *cl* (⅛ *pint*) *dry white wine*
25 *g* (1 *oz*) *gelatine, soaked*
25 *cl* (½ *pint*) *whipped cream, part or all of which can be replaced by yoghurt*
4 *tablespoons of dry sherry*
½ *lemon juice and zest*
Cayenne, salt, pepper to taste

Follow method of preparation and presentation for ham mousse.

Game Mousse – Mousse de Gibier

The game may be named, as for pheasant mousse below.

Pheasant Mousse – Mousse de Faisan
(12–15 portions)

250 *g* (10–12 *oz*) (2–3 *breasts*) *raw, boned and skinless breast of pheasant*
100 *g* (4 *oz*) *large button mushrooms, cut into juliennes*
12.5 *cl* (¼ *pint*) *Madeira*
25 *cl* (½ *pint*) *good demiglace or jus lie (flavoured with game bones/stock where possible)*
25 *g* (1 *oz*) *gelatine, soaked*
25 *cl* (½ *pint*) *whipped cream, some or all of which can be replaced with yoghurt*
½ *lemon juice*
Cayenne, salt and pepper to taste
Little brandy

(1) Sauté pheasant breast in small pieces in a little butter.
(2) Add ⅓ of Madeira and reduce. Set aside to cool.
(3) Cover juliennes of mushrooms with ⅓ of Madeira. Cook and cool.
(4) Place into a food processor the pheasant meat, the demiglace, and the gelatine dissolved in the final ⅓ of the Madeira. Cut to a fine purée.
(5) Place mixture into a bowl. Fold in gently the whipped cream and the cooked juliennes of mushrooms and brandy. Correct seasoning.
(6) Place into individual moulds, or an oiled and greaseproof paper lined loaf mould. Leave to set for one to three hours, or overnight.
(7) Present as for ham mousse.

Pheasant breast can be replaced by other game birds or even by tender venison in the same amounts. Follow the method above. Again it would be nice to actually name the game used, such as:

Partridge Mousse – Mousse de Perdrix

Snipe Mousse – Mousse de Bécassine

Grouse Mousse – Mousse de Grouse

Quail Mousse – Mousse de Caille

Roebuck Mousse – Mousse de Chevreuil

Combinations

Naturally mousses can again be combined into a mousse with two or three layers and flavours given earlier. See instructions for fish and vegetable mousses. Thus we could serve:

Ham and Chicken Mousse (pink and white)
Ham and Game Mousse (pink and light brown)
Ham, Chicken and Game Mousse (pink, white and light brown)
Chicken and Avocado Mousse (white and green)
Chicken and Asparagus Mousse (white and light green)
Ham and Avocado Mousse (pink and green)
Chicken, Ham and Avocado Mousse (white, pink and green)

If the normal presentation garnish of lettuce, tomatoes, cucumbers, radish etc. and herbs such as parsley, dill or mint is not desired, then coulis of mayonnaise-based sauces (as suggested for the fish mousses) are of course applicable to these meat based mousses.

EGG HORS D'ŒUVRE

Plovers' Eggs – Oeufs de Pluvier

Fresh eggs of the plover are available only in season from April until June. In recent years, however, plovers' eggs have become available cooked, peeled and preserved in brine in glass jars to be used all the year round.

Plovers' eggs are a little larger than pigeon eggs. They have a white/pastel-green colour base with black spots. They are slightly pear shaped, with one end more pointed than the other.

Fresh plovers' eggs are cooked by placing them in a pan with cold water, bringing them to the boil gradually, and allowing them to simmer gently for 6–8 minutes. Refresh them in cold water, then peel straight away and store in cold water.

Presentation
Two or three plovers' eggs represent a portion. They are placed on a plate or a flat on a bed of mustard and cress or of finely shredded lettuce, shaped like a nest. Some prefer to serve plovers' eggs fully shelled, some partially shelled and others unshelled. With unshelled service, it is a good idea to garnish the nest with two or three empty half-shells; this shows that fresh plover eggs have been used, and in addition the half-shells look most attractive as part of the presentation (see Figure 8).

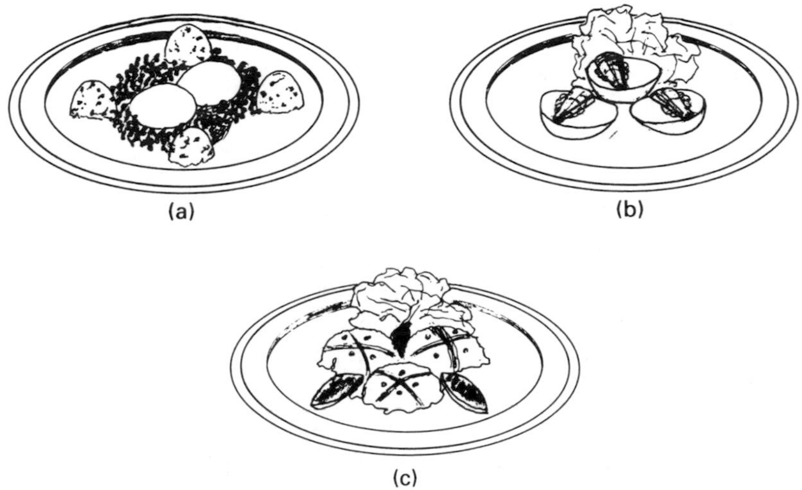

FIG. 8. *Egg presentations.* (a) *Plovers' eggs on mustard and cress bed, garnished with empty half-shells* (b) *Garnished eggs with sardines* (c) *Egg mayonnaise with capers and anchovy*

Accompaniment
(a) Mayonnaise, or mayonnaise to which some cream has been added.
(b) Mayonnaise slightly flavoured with French mustard.
(c) Sauce Andalouse (see cold sauces and dressings later in this chapter).
(d) Just salt and pepper.

As with most Hors d'Œuvre, brown bread and butter are served.

Quails' Eggs – Oeufs de Caille

These are about the same size as plovers' eggs. They are more beige than white in colour, and again have brown-black spots. They are available more widely than plovers' eggs, because most quail eggs are today supplied fresh from quail farms throughout the year.

Preparation and presentation for quails' eggs is the same as for plovers' eggs.

Egg Salad – Salade d'Oeufs
(4 portions)

6 *hard-boiled eggs*
8–12 *crisp lettuce leaves*
4 *anchovy fillets*
Cress, parsley, chives
4 *tablespoons of vinaigrette*
8–12 *capers*
1 *large or* 4 *small cherry tomatoes*

(1) Place lettuce leaves on plates or flats.
(2) Cut eggs with egg cutter into neat slices.
(3) Neatly place egg slices on lettuce, omitting the white end pieces.
(4) Sprinkle with chopped chives or other herb of your choice.
(5) With a tablespoon, neatly coat the egg slices with vinaigrette.
(6) Garnish with capers, cress, tomatoes and parsley.
(7) Serve with toast or brown bread and butter.

Egg Mayonnaise – Mayonnaise d'Oeufs
(4 portions)

6 *hard-boiled eggs*
12.5 *cl* ($\frac{1}{4}$ *pint*) *mayonnaise, of pouring but covering consistency*
8–12 *crisp lettuce leaves*
8–12 *capers*
4 *anchovy fillets*
1 *large or* 4 *small cherry tomatoes*
Cress, parsley, chives etc.

(1) Line plates or flats with lettuce leaves.
(2) Cut eggs in slices or in halves, lengthways or horizontal.
One and a half eggs are considered a portion.
(3) Place on lettuce leaves of your choice.
(4) Coat with mayonnaise, which may have to be thinned but must be of covering consistency.
(5) Garnish with anchovy fillets, capers, tomatoes and herbs of your choice.
(6) Serve with brown bread and butter (see Figure 8(c).

Stuffed Eggs – Oeufs Farcis
(4 portions)

6–8 hard-boiled eggs | *4 tablespoons of firm mayonnaise*
Little salt and pepper to taste

(1) Cut eggs neatly in half horizontally or diagonally, using a sharp knife dipped into boiling water.
(2) Carefully remove the yolks and place into a sieve.
(3) Place empty white of egg halves on pastry wire.
(4) Force egg yolks and any of the broken whites of eggs through the sieve into a small bowl. Add mayonnaise, salt and pepper to taste, mix well, and correct seasoning.
(5) Place egg yolk mixture into a piping bag with a rose tube. Neatly pipe it into the cavities of the egg white halves.
(6) Place into fridge for 10–30 minutes, then serve.

This is the basic preparation of stuffed eggs. We can add many variations by the following two methods.

Flavouring
The yolk filling may be flavoured with: curry powder, slightly cooked in a little oil prior to use; fresh tomato purée; garlic paste; finely chopped herbs; paprika powder, slightly cooked in oil before use; French or English mustard; and so on.

Garnishes
The egg halves may be garnished after they have been filled as described above. The garnishes may comprise: anchovy; caviar; ham cornets, slices or strips; stuffed or plain olives; prawns; salmon cornets, slices or strips; and so on.

Figure 9 shows a range of garnished eggs. Eggs 1–16 have been cut horizontally, eggs 17–22 vertically. The garnishes are as follows:

(1) Asparagus tips.
(2) Stuffed, garnished with olive slices.
(3) Turned cooked mushroom and peas.
(4) Piped filling garnished with stuffed olive slices.
(5) Garnished with shrimps.
(6) Garnished with slices of plovers' eggs.
(7) Garnished with Dublin Bay prawn and slices of radish.
(8) Garnished with anchovy fillets.
(9) Garnished with large prawn.
(10) Garnished with diamond of Bismarck herring.
(11) Garnished with cornet of ham or smoked salmon.
(12) Garnished with blanched estragon (tarragon) leaves and black olive.
(13) Garnished with crossed anchovy fillets and parsley.

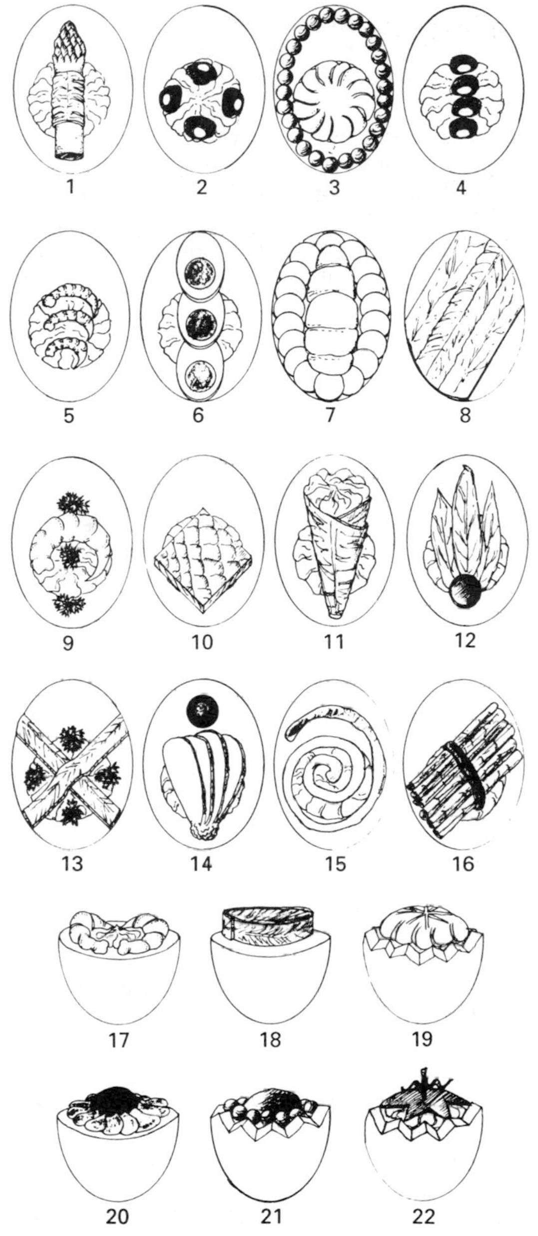

FIG. 9. *Stuffed egg garnishes: see text for key to numbering*

(14) Garnished with gherkin fan and olive.
(15) Garnished with piped Danish pink caviar.
(16) Garnished with bundle of cooked French beans held by strip of red pepper.
(17) Piped, filling garnished with two prawns.
(18) Piped, filling garnished with anchovy ring.
(19) Crown-cut egg half, filled garnished with cooked turned mushroom.
(20) Garnished with black olive and blanched watercress leaves.
(21) Garnished with blanched and peeled tomato top and peas.
(22) Filled with normal egg filling, topped with crown-cut tomato base inclusive of stalk.

LETTUCE AS GARNISH BASE

Throughout this presentation of Hors d'Œuvre, the use of lettuce has been advocated to display the dishes at their best and most appetizing. This applies both to a single portion on a plate and to multiple portions on silver flats.

It must be realized that for this purpose many different types of lettuce can be used, such as:

Lettuce
Cos lettuce
Chicory
Endive
Oakleaf lettuce
Raddichio
Watercress
Mustard and cress.

Indeed, some of these lettuce suit a particular presentation more than others, and this fact should be given some consideration when deciding which of the many lettuce types to use. The examples in Figure 10 may aid in the decision as to which salads to use as garnish (see also the section on salads later in this chapter).

MAYONNAISE AND DERIVATIVES

Sauce Mayonnaise

2 *yolks of eggs*	$\frac{1}{4}$ *teaspoon English mustard*
2 *teaspoons of vinegar*	*A pinch of salt and white ground pepper*
1 *teaspoon hot water*	$\frac{1}{4}$ *l.* ($\frac{1}{2}$ *pint*) *olive oil or groundnut oil*

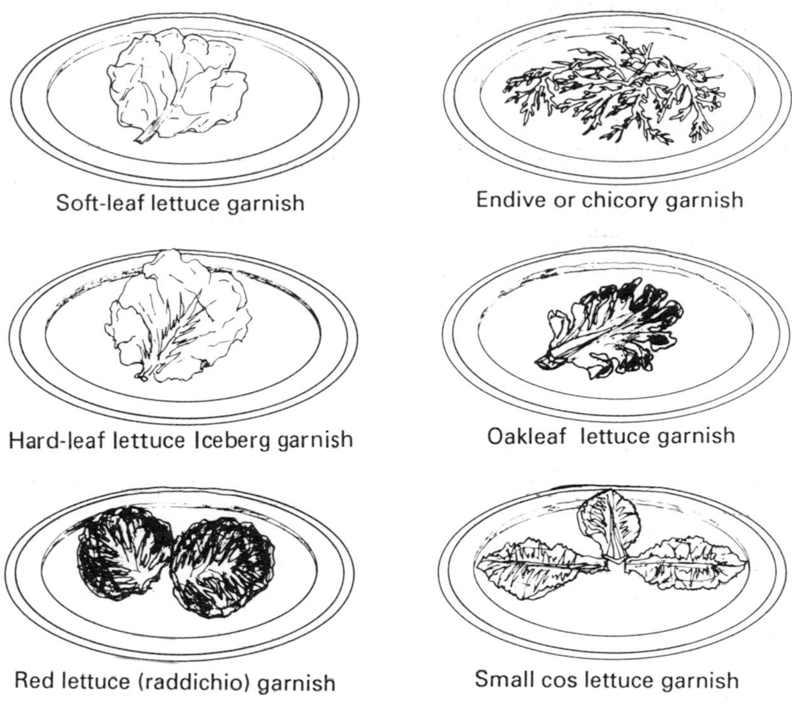

FIG. 10. *Lettuce garnishes*

(1) Place yolks, mustard, vinegar, and seasoning into a china bowl.
(2) Whisk well.
(3) Gradually pour in the oil, at first a drop at a time.
(4) When about half the oil is added, one can be a little more bold, whisking all the time.
(5) Finally, whisk in the water, and correct seasoning.

Note. If the sauce is too thick, thin out with a drop of vinegar, or water. Mayonnaise will curdle (a) If oil is too cold, (b) If oil is added too quickly, (c) If sauce is not whisked evenly and briskly enough, (d) If yolks are old and weak.

To reconstitute curdled mayonnaise, recommence with a fresh yolk of egg or a teaspoon of hot water in a new clean china bowl; whisk well and run in the curdled mayonnaise a little at a time.

Mock Mayonnaise (Salad Cream)

¼ l. (½ pint) béchamel
6 cl (½ gill) vinegar
6 cl (½ gill) aspic
1 teaspoon of made mustard
¼ l. (½ pint) cream
salt and pepper to taste

(1) Add vinegar, seasoning and made mustard to hot béchamel.
(2) Strain through a tamis-cloth into a clean bowl.
(3) Whisk until cool, then whisk in cool aspic and cream.
(4) Correct seasoning.

Mayonnaise Colée

2 parts of mayonnaise
1 part of aspic according to use

Whisk melted but cold aspic into mayonnaise. Used for coating of cold fish.

Sauce Tartare

¼ l. (½ pint) mayonnaise
50 g (2 oz) finely chopped gherkins
25 g (1 oz) chopped capers
15 g (½ oz) finely chopped parsley

Add all ingredients to mayonnaise, whisk well, correct seasoning. Serve with fried fish.

Sauce Rémoulade

3 cooked yolks of eggs
2 teaspoons of vinegar
1 teaspoon of hot-water
¼ teaspoon English mustard
¼ l. (½ pint) olive oil
pinch of salt and ground white pepper
50 g (2 oz) finely chopped gherkins
25 g (1 oz) of chopped capers
15 g (½ oz) finely chopped wet parsley
15 g (½ oz) of fresh anchovy – purée or
1 tablespoon of anchovy essence

(1) Force cooked yolks through a fine sieve.
(2) Place into a china bowl, add mustard, vinegar and seasoning.
(3) Gradually add oil, at first carefully, as for mayonnaise.
(4) Finally add garnish, and correct seasoning.

Note. Serve with fried fish, grills, and cold egg dishes. In the trade, it is the normal practice to add the anchovy purée or essence to a sauce tartare.

Sauce Andalouse

3 parts of mayonnaise
1 part of fresh tomato purée or ketchup
20 g (½ oz) Julienne of pimento

Mix all ingredients, correct seasoning. Serve with cold fish, meats and salads.

Sauce Verte

¼ l. (½ pint) mayonnaise
50 g (2 oz) of finely chopped spinach
tarragon, chervil, chives, and watercress

(1) Pick, wash and blanch the green leaves.
(2) Squeeze dry.
(3) Pass through a fine sieve, and mix into the mayonnaise, correct seasoning. Serve with cold salmon, salmon-trout, or other cold fish.

Sauce Gribiche

A sauce tartare, made with cooked yolks of egg, as Remoulade, with the addition of the finely chopped whites of eggs.

FISH AND SHELLFISH COCKTAIL SAUCES

Method 1

¼ l. (½ pint) mayonnaise
50 g (2 oz) tomato ketchup or juice
Salt, cayenne pepper, Worcester sauce
Combine all ingredients to taste

Method 2

2 dl (¼ pint) fresh cream, lightly beaten
50 g (2 oz) tomato juice or ketchup
Salt, pepper, Worcester sauce

Method 3

2 dl (¼ pint) mayonnaise
2 dl (¼ pint) fresh cream, lightly beaten
Salt, pepper, Worcester sauce
100 g (4 oz) tomato ketchup or juice

Note. To the 3 different cocktail sauces given above, one may add blanched, finely chopped shallot, finely grated fresh horseradish, or finely cut lemon peel and some sherry or brandy.

COULIS

Coulis are small sauces made from fruits or vegetables. They are served as a sauce or dressing with other foods, such as salads or mousses as well as cold meats and fish. They are very old preparations and were almost forgotten, but they have found renewed use and popularity with the modern *nouvelle cuisine* presentation (see the sections on fish and meat mousses earlier in this chapter).

Asparagus Coulis – Coulis d'Asperge

250 *g* (10 *oz*) *fresh or tinned asparagus, green or white*
75 *g* (3 *oz*) *shallots, diced*
2 *tablespoons of oil*
1 *small clove of garlic*
12.5 *cl* ($\frac{1}{4}$ *pint*) *white wine*
2 *tablespoons of double cream or yoghurt*
Little salt, pepper, lemon juice

(1) Cook shallots and garlic in oil, without colour.
(2) Add asparagus cut in small pieces, plus wine. Cook for 30 minutes.
(3) Place into food processor and cut to a fine purée. Pass through a fine sieve. Correct seasoning with salt, pepper, lemon juice.
(4) When cold, add cream or yoghurt (optional).

Cucumber Coulis – Coulis de Concombre

1 *small cucumber, peeled and free of pips*
75 *g* (3 *oz*) *shallots*
1 *tablespoon of oil*
1 *small clove of garlic*
12.5 *cl* ($\frac{1}{4}$ *pint*) *white wine*
2 *tablespoons of double cream or yoghurt*
Little salt, pepper, lemon juice

(1) Cook shallots in oil, without colour.
(2) Add peeled, seeded and diced cucumber and wine. Bring to boil and allow to simmer for 30 minutes.
(3) When cooked, place in food processor or liquidizer and cut to a fine purée. Pass through a fine sieve. Correct seasoning.
(4) When cold, add a little cream or yoghurt (optional).

Tomato Coulis – Coulis de Tomate

250 *g* (10 *oz*) *tomatoes cut into quarters*
75 *g* (3 *oz*) *shallots cut into dice*
2 *tablespoons of oil*
1 *small clove of garlic*
12.5 *cl* ($\frac{1}{4}$ *pint*) *white wine*
1 *heaped teaspoon of tomato purée*
Salt, pepper, sugar, vinegar to taste

(1) Cook shallots in oil without colour.
(2) Add tomato quarters, garlic, wine and seasoning. Bring to boil and simmer for 30 minutes.
(3) When cooked, place into food processor or liquidizer, add tomato purée and cut to a fine purée. Pass through sieve and correct seasoning.
(4) When cool, add cream or yoghurt (optional).

COLD SAUCES – SAUCES FROIDES

Mint Sauce – Sauce Menthe

50 g (2 oz) mint
25 g (1 oz) sugar
1 tablespoon water
12 cl (1 gill) vinegar

Pick mint leaves and wash well. Drain and chop finely, adding sugar. Blanch quickly in water. When quite cold, add vinegar. Serve with Roast Lamb.

Niçoise

¼ l. (½ pint) basic vinaigrette
½ teaspoon French mustard
15 g (½ oz) chopped capers
15 g (½ oz) chopped olives
15 g (½ oz) diced anchovy
15 g (½ oz) chopped parsley

Mix all ingredients together. Serve with Meat Salads and Cold Eggs.

Oxford Sauce

Similar to Cumberland, but with chopped blanched zest of orange and lemon, instead of Julienne of orange zest. Serve with Cold Ham, Meat Mousses and Smoked Meats.

Persillade

½ pint ravigote
1 sieved egg
½ clove crushed/chopped garlic
½ teaspoon French mustard

Mix all ingredients. Serve with Cold Meat and Cold Fish.

Ravigote à l'Huile

¼ l. (½ pint) basic vinaigrette
1 tablespoon chopped onions or shallot blanched, refreshed, squeezed dry
1 tablespoon chopped fine herbs
1 tablespoon chopped capers
15 g (½ oz) diced anchovy fillets (optional)
1 hard boiled egg pressed through sieve (optional)

If served with Calf's Head, add chopped Calf's Brain and 2 tablespoons of cooking liquor. Mix all ingredient into vinaigrette. Use for Calf's Head or Beef Salad.

Sour Cream Sauce – Crème Acidule

3 parts fresh cream
1 part lemon juice or white vinegar
Salt, pepper from mill to taste
Pinch cayenne pepper

Whisk together lightly. Serve with Cos Lettuce or Salads, containing fresh fruit.

Spanish Cream Sauce – Crème Espagnole (4 portions)

1 teaspoon English mustard
1 teaspoon castor sugar
juice of 1 lemon
¼ l. (½ pint) fresh cream
Salt, cayenne pepper

Dissolve mustard and sugar with lemon juice. Whisk in cream, lightly. Season to taste. Serve with Green Salads.

Cumberland Sauce

2 parts red currant jelly
1 part port wine
1 teaspoon English mustard
25 g (1 oz) chopped shallot
juice of 1 lemon
juice of 1 orange
Zest of orange in fine Julienne

(1) Warm and melt red currant jelly with port wine.
(2) Add blanched and refreshed shallot.
(3) Add mustard dissolved in fruit juice.
(4) Add blanched and refreshed zest of orange. Serve with Cold Ham.

French Mustard Sauce – Sauce Moutarde

As for Spanish Cream Sauce, using French mustard in lieu of English mustard and omitting sugar. Serve with Beetroot, Celery or Cold Egg Dishes.

Thermidor Sauce – Sauce Thermidor

1 teaspoon French mustard
1 teaspoon English mustard
juice of 1 lemon
¼ l. (½ pint) (lightly whisked) fresh cream
Salt, cayenne pepper to taste

(1) Mix mustard with lemon juice.
(2) Stir into the cream.
(3) Season with salt and cayenne.
Serve with Cold Fish or Shellfish for Hors d'Œuvre.

Horseradish Sauce (1)

40–50 g (1½ oz) horseradish
1 dl (1 gill) lightly whipped cream
Salt, pinch of cayenne

Combine ingredients. Season. Serve with Smoked Fish or Roast Beef.

Horseradish Sauce (2)

Equal quantities: grated horseradish, white crumbs soaked in milk
1 gill cream, half whipped
Salt, white vinegar
Cayenne pepper to taste

As above.

Swedish Sauce – Sauce Suédoise

Juice of half a lemon
250 g (8 oz) apples, peeled & quartered
50–100 g (2–4 oz) freshly grated horseradish
1 dl (1 gill) white wine or wine vinegar
2 tablespoons mayonnaise

(1) Bring apples with wine and lemon and pinch of sugar to boil.
(2) When cooked, force through a sieve; cool.
(3) Add freshly grated horseradish.
(4) Finish with Mayonnaise, correct seasoning.
Serve with Cold Meats

COMPOUND BUTTERS – BEURRES COMPOSÉS

In first-class kitchens a very large number of compound butters are used, usually served with grilled fish or meats. They can also be used in certain cases for the finishing and liaison of sauces and soups, as well as for Hors d'Œuvre accompaniments.

Most of these compound butters are savoury but there are also a number which are sweet and used in the pastry for the garnishing and serving of sweets. One should make certain with what they are going to be served as there are a number which can be served either with savoury or sweet dishes, and they should be made accordingly, e.g. Lemon-butter savoury with fish, Lemon-butter sweet with pancakes.

Here is a list of the best known and most commonly used savoury butters.

Parsley Butter – Beurre Maître d'Hôtel

250 g (8 oz) of butter
30 g (1½ oz) finely chopped wet parsley
A few drops of lemon juice
Salt, pepper and cayenne pepper to taste

(1) Soften the butter in a china bowl with a wooden spatula.
(2) Add all other ingredients and seasoning for taste.
(3) Mix well.
(4) Roll in a wet sheet of greaseproof paper for shaping and easy portion control.
Used for grilled fish and meats.

Anchovy Butter – Beurre d'Anchois

250 g (8 oz) butter
50 g (2 oz) anchovy fillets, or 25 g (1 oz) of anchovy essence
A few drops of lemon juice
Salt and pepper to taste

(1) Drain Anchovies.
(2) Pass through a sieve.
(3) Add this purée together with the rest of the ingredients to the soft butter.
(4) Mix well; correct seasoning.
(5) Roll in a wet sheet of greaseproof paper.

Mustard Butter
English (Beurre Moutarde à l'Anglaise)
French (Beurre Moutarde à la Française)

250 g (8 oz) butter
50 g (2 oz) English or French mustard
A few drops of lemon juice

(1) Soften butter in the normal way.
(2) Add mustard and lemon juice.
(3) Blend well, correct seasoning.
(4) Roll in a wet sheet of greaseproof paper, as above.

Garlic Butter – Beurre d'Ail

250 g (8 oz) butter
4–6 cloves of garlic
A few drops of lemon juice

(1) Peel and blanch garlic-cloves, drain and dry.
(2) Crush with a large knife, and purée with a little salt.
(3) Pass garlic paste through a fine sieve.
(4) Mix with softened butter and lemon juice.
(5) Roll in a wet sheet of greaseproof paper, as above.
Used for grilled steaks.

Horseradish Butter – Beurre de Raifort

250 *g* (8 *oz*) *of butter*
50 *g* (2 *oz*) *finely grated fresh horseradish*
A few drops of lemon juice

(1) Grate horseradish very fine, force through a fine sieve.
(2) Add with lemon juice to softened butter.
(3) Roll in wet greaseproof paper, as above.
Used for grilled fish and steaks.

Colbert Butter – Beurre Colbert

As for Parsley Butter, with the addition of one tablespoon of finely chopped tarragon and one tablespoon of glace de viande. Used for Fish *à la Colbert*, roast fillet of beef.

Red Wine Butter – Beurre Vin Rouge

250 *g* (8 *oz*) *of butter*
75–100 *g* (3 *to* 4 *oz*) *of finely chopped shallots*
12 *cl* (1 *gill*) *of red wine*
Salt and pepper to taste

(1) Place shallots and red wine in a small sauteuse.
(2) Reduce until almost dry; cool.
(3) Add to the softened butter, mix well.
(4) Correct seasoning with salt and mill pepper.
Used for roast fillet of beef and steaks.

Wine Merchant Butter – Beurre Marchand de Vin

As above, with the addition of a tablespoon of chopped parsley and a tablespoon of glace de viande.

Butter with Caviar – Beurre de Caviar

250 *g* (9 *oz*) *of butter*
50 *g* (3 *oz*) *Russian caviar*
A few drops of lemon juice
Little pepper

(1) Soften butter with a wooden spatula in a china bowl.
(2) Carefully blend in the caviar.
(3) Correct seasoning with lemon juice and mill pepper.
(4) Roll in a wet sheet of greaseproof paper, as above.
Used for grilled fish (*Canape à la Russe*).

Lobster Butter – Beurre de Homard

250 *g* (8 *oz*) *of butter*
100 *g* (6 *oz*) *lobster coral, eggs and creamy flesh, cooked*
A few drops of lemon juice
Salt and pepper to taste

(1) Pound the lobster coral, eggs and soft flesh very finely.
(2) Force through a fine sieve, mix with lemon juice.
(3) Mix well into the softened butter, correct seasoning with salt and pepper.
(4) Roll in a sheet of wet greaseproof paper, as above.

Used for grilled fish, cold fish, Hors d'Œuvre and sauces.

Note. Beurre rouge is a red butter, a name given to lobster butter as above, or butter made with other red shellfish.

Storage. All butters above will keep well in a refrigerator, rolled in the greaseproof paper described.

Service. At best, the butters are served in $\frac{1}{2}$ cm ($\frac{1}{4}$ in.) slices, two to three per portion, in a small crystal bowl with crushed ice underneath separately, or, in some cases, like *à la Colbert*, directly on the fish or meats.

SALAD DRESSINGS – ASSAISONNEMENTS POUR LES SALADES

Vinaigrette

Vinaigrette is the basic dressing suitable for green, simple and compound salads. It is an emulsion of oil, vinegar, salt, mill pepper and a little castor sugar if desired. It should not contain any mustards; if it does it becomes one of the many variations on the basic theme, and should be called mustard dressing or French dressing.

Oils

In the original recipe olive oil would have been used to make a vinaigrette. However, as olive oil is rather strong for the average British palate, it has been replaced by other vegetable oils and various blends. Indeed, of late many other oils such as hazelnut oil and walnut oil have been used in the making of vinaigrettes; although somewhat expensive to buy, these oils give any salad (particular the light green salads) a distinct nutty flavour.

The type of oil used is often a personal choice or the policy of the establishment. However, we should remember that different oils can give variety to the flavour of dressings and consequently to the salad.

Vinegars

In the original recipe, wine vinegar was used; it did not matter whether this was the lighter white or the darker red type of vinegar. In some parts of the world this has been replaced by distilled white vinegar, or as in England by malt vinegar. To these we can add cider vinegars, as well as some of the flavoured vinegars such as dill and tarragon.

Which vinegar we use is a personal choice. However, again we should remember that different types of vinegar can add variation to the taste of the same salad.

(1) *Basic Recipe for Vinaigrette*
1 part of vinegar of your choice
3 parts of oil of your choice
Salt, mill pepper, a little castor sugar to taste

(a) Place vinegar, sugar, salt and pepper into a bowl; allow to dissolve.
(b) Beat in the oil gradually to form an emulsion.
(c) Pour into a clean bottle. Perforate bottle top for easy application.
(d) Oil and vinegar, like oil and water, will separate. Always shake bottle well before applying to salads.
(e) Several bottles of different types of vinaigrette can be made ready for quick and easy use.

(2) *Lemon Dressing*
As for vinaigrett, but using half the amount of fresh lemon juice in place of vinegar.
(3) *English Mustard Dressing*
Add a heaped teaspoon of English mustard to $\frac{1}{4}$ litre ($\frac{1}{2}$ pint) of vinaigrette.
(4) *French Mustard Dressing (French Dressing)*
Add a heaped teaspoon of French mustard to $\frac{1}{4}$ litre ($\frac{1}{2}$ pint) of vinaigrette
(5) *Fine Herbs Dressing*
Vinaigrette with the addition of one tablespoon of finely chopped herbs like parsley, chives, tarragon, chervil, etc.
(6) *Marsellaise Dressing*
Vinaigrette with the addition of a half clove of garlic per pint, finely chopped and made into a paste with salt; reduce salt in proportion.
(7) *Swiss Dressing*
Mix three parts of rendered fat bacon, cut into dice, with one part of heated vinegar, salt, sugar and pepper from the mill, to taste.
(8) *Tomato Dressing*
Add to $\frac{1}{2}$ l. (1 pint) of vinaigrette 2 dl ($\frac{1}{4}$ pint) of reduced fresh tomato purée.
(9) *Paprika Dressing*
Add to $\frac{1}{2}$ l. (1 pint) of vinaigrette 50 g (2 oz) of finely chopped onions and paprika to taste.
(10) *Gasconne Dressing*
Marseillaise dressing, with the addition of some baked garlic flavoured flutes.
(11) *Anchovy Dressing*
Add two to four fillets of anchovy, rubbed through a sieve, to $\frac{1}{2}$ l. (1 pint) of vinaigrette.
(12) *Placa Dressing*
Vinaigrette with the addition of English mustard, chilli sauce and chutney.

(13) *Chiffonnade Dressing*

Vinaigrette with the addition of chopped hard-boiled egg, chopped parsley and fine brunoise of beetroot.

(14) *Roquefort Dressing*

Vinaigrette with the addition of 50 g (2 oz) of roquefort cheese, rubbed through a sieve, to ½ l. (1 pint) of vinaigrette.

(15) *St. Regis Dressing*

Vinaigrette with the addition of Worcester sauce, English mustard and paprika, to taste.

(16) *Cream Dressing*

Mix 4 parts of fresh cream with 1 part of wine-vinegar. Salt and mill pepper, to taste.

(17) *Mustard Dressing*

Mix 4 parts of fresh cream with 2 parts of made mustard, English or French. Salt, sugar and mill pepper, to taste.

(18) *Escoffier Dressing*

Flavour mayonnaise with lemon-juice, Worcester sauce, chilli sauce, paprika and chopped chives, to taste.

(19) *Special Dressing*

Flavour mayonnaise chopped tarragon, tarragon-vinegar, chopped chives; add beaten fresh cream.

(20) *Thousand Island Dressing*

Add to ½ l. (1 pint) of mayonnaise, 50 g (2 oz) of fine diced red and green peppers; flavour with paprika and chilli sauce, as well as a little single cream or yoghurt.

(21) *Chatelaine Dressing*

Mix equal amounts of fresh cream and mayonnaise.

(22) *Russian Dressing*

Add to ½ l. (1 pint) mayonnaise, the following: 1 teaspoon finely chopped beetroot, 1 teaspoon finely diced red and green peppers, 1 teaspoon finely chopped parsley and chives, 1 teaspoon caviar.

Correct seasoning with paprika, chilli sauce, salt, pepper and sugar.

(23) *Sweet Lemon Dressing (Dutch/German)*

1 tablespoon of fresh lemon juice
5 tablespoons of oil of your choice
1 heaped tablespoon of castor sugar
1 heaped tablespoon of finely chopped dill
Pinch of salt

Combine all ingredients in a good emulsion. Pour over any green salad just before service. Toss well. Sufficient for 4–6 portions.

(24) *Sweet and Sour Dressing (Scandinavian)*

1 cup of vinegar of your choice
1 cup of castor sugar
2 tablespoons of finely chopped parsley
Pinch of salt

Combine all ingredients and leave to dissolve overnight. When dissolved, pour over salads such as:
Sliced raw cucumber
Sliced raw onions
Sliced raw mushrooms
Sliced blanched red and green peppers
Peeled slice of avocado
Blanched button onions
Cooked beetroot, sliced or diced
Cooked sweetcorn
Cooked haricot beans
Cooked celeriac.

SALADS – LES SALADES

In establishments where the volume of business requires it, the salad preparation is part of the larder work. In particular it is the responsibility of the Hors d'Œuvrier, as salads and starters are very closely related. In large hotels and restaurants with perhaps a house speciality of many salads, the work may be undertaken by specially trained staff (the women are known as Saladières).

In an average hotel or restaurant, the preparation of salads is the responsibility of the Larder Chef. It may be carried out by a commis or apprentice chef, who will spend some of his or her training period in this section of the larder.

There are three types of salad:

Green Salads – Salades Verts
Simple or Single Salads – Salades Simples ou Singuliers
Compound or Blended Salads – Salades Composées.

GREEN SALADS – SALADES VERTS

This category includes all salads that are green or of the lettuce type. Thus, for example, it contains raddichio, which is not necessarily green but is a lettuce nevertheless; and watercress or mustard and cress, which are not really lettuce but are still green salad plants.

In this group we therefore classify the following salads. For each is given a selection of suitable dressings, identified by the numbers used in the list in the previous section.

Batavian Lettuce Salad	1 3 4 5 6	Salade d'Escarole
Chicory Salad	1 2 3 4 16 21	Salade d'Endive Belge
Cos Lettuce Salad	1 2 3 4 5 6 15 16 18	Salade de Romain
Dandelion Salad	1 2 3 5 7 9 16	Salade de Pissenlit
Endive Salad	1 2 3 5 11 16 21	Salade Chicorée
Iceberg Salad (hard leaved)	1 2 3 4 7 9 11 16	
Lambs' Lettuce Salad	1 3 4 5 6 20	Salade de Mâche
Lettuce Salad (soft leaved)	1 2 3 4 16 21	Salade de Laitue
Mustard and Cress Salad	1 2 3 4 5 6 15 16 18	Salade de Cressonette
Oakleaf Lettuce Salad	1 2 3 5 7 9 16 20	Salade de Feuille de Chêne
Red Lettuce Salad	1 2 3 5 11 16 21	Salade de Raddichio
Watercress Salad	1 2 3 4 7 9 11 15 16	Salade Cresson de Fontaine

Mixed Green Salad – Salade Panachée Verte

Any four to six of the green salads listed, with the dressing of your choice.

Green Mimosa Salad – Salade Verte Mimosa

An arrangement of cos lettuce, on top of which is carefully placed one sieved hard-boiled yolk. The salad resembles the wild mimosa of Southern France.

Preparation

(1) Always wash in cold water. Hold by roots, plunging into water to force water to centre, thus removing dirt and grit. Repeat process several times, each time in clean water.
(2) Remove bad or discoloured parts. Trim roots and carefully inspect inside for slugs and insects. Remove coarse ribs from outer leaves with fingers. Place into iced water to get crisp.
(3) Drain thoroughly. Shake well in a salad basket or colander. Place on clean cloth; avoid bruising leaves. Keep in a cool place until required.
(4) Serve neatly in china, glass or wooden bowls. Garnish as required. Serve dressing apart. Always keep cool.
Note. Do not: wash salads under tap; allow salads to soak in lukewarm water; forget to inspect centre for slugs and insects; drain on dirty table or trays or bruise leaves; cut salads with steel knife (use fingers or stainless steel knife).

SIMPLE OR SINGLE SALADS – SALADES SIMPLES OU SINGULIERS

This category includes all fruit or root salads. Some can be eaten raw, others have to be cooked.

In this group we therefore classify the following vegetable salads. For each is given a selection of suitable dressings, identified by the numbers used in the list earlier.

Raw		
Celery Salad	1 2 3 4 5 6 10	Salade de Céleri
Cucumber Salad	1 2 3 4 5 6 10 14 15	Salade de Concombre
Coleslaw Salad	1 2 3 4 5 6 7 10 14 15	Salade Choux Blanc
Radish Salad	1 2 3 5 6 7 10 17 22	Salade de Radis
Tomato Salad	1 2 3 4 5 6 10 19 20	Salade de Tomate
Sweet Pepper Salad	1 2 3 4 5 6 7 10 14 15	Salade de Piment
Cooked		
Artichoke Salad	1 2 3 5 6 7 10 17 22	Salade d'Artichauts
Asparagus Salad	1 2 3 4 5 6 10 14 15	Salade d'Asperge
Beetroot Salad	1 2 3 4 5 6 7 8 9 10	Salade de Betterave
Celeriac Salad	1 2 3 4 5 6 7 8 18 19 21	Salade de Célerirave
French Bean Salad	1 2 3 4 6 9 14 16 21	Salade d'Haricots Verts
Potato Salad	1 2 3 4 5 6 9 10 11	Salade de Pommes de Terre

Mixed Salad – Salade Panachée

Any 4 to 6 of the simple or green salads, with the dressing of your choice.

French Salad – Salade Française

This is a selection of salads, typically soft-leaved lettuce, tomatoes, cucumbers, spring onions, watercress or mustard and cress, neatly arranged in a colourful display. Quarters or slices of one hard-boiled egg are included. The salad is always served with French dressing.

Preparation

Except to use only the best and freshest of leaf, fruit or root vegetables for salads, no other basic general rule can be given. Each salad needs a particular approach, as indicated in the individual recipes to follow.

Garnishes

For either the green or the simple salads, no elaborate garnishes are necessary; some finely chopped herbs such as parsley, chives and tarragon, may be used. The flavour of some salads, such as cucumber and tomato, will benefit from the addition of some finely chopped onions.

Artichoke Salad – Salade d'Artichauts

8 cooked artichoke bottoms
5 cl ($\frac{1}{2}$ gill) of vinaigrette
Salt, pepper, chopped parsley

(1) Quarter artichoke bottoms.
(2) Mix with vinaigrette and seasoning.
(3) Dress on a leaf of lettuce.
(4) Sprinkle with parsley.

Asparagus Salad – Salade d'Asperges

8 pieces cooked white asparagus
5 cl ($\frac{1}{2}$ gill) lemon dressing
$\frac{1}{2}$ teaspoon finely chopped herbs

(1) Marinade asparagus for a while in lemon dressing.
(2) Add chopped herbs.
(3) Dress in a ravier with points uppermost.

Asparagus Salad Green – Salade d'Asperges Vertes

As above but with the addition of some finely chopped chervil.

Beetroot Salad – Salade de Betterave

250 g (8 oz) beetroot cooked
15 g ($\frac{1}{2}$ oz) chopped chives or onions
5 cl ($\frac{1}{2}$ gill) vinaigrette
Pinch chopped parsley
Salt, pepper, to taste

(1) Wash beetroot well.
(2) Steam, or simmer, till tender.
(3) Test by skinning. Cool and peel.
(4) Cut into dice, bâtons julienne.
(5) Mix with onion/chive vinaigrette.
(6) Dress in ravier; sprinkle with parsley.

Cabbage Salad (Raw) – Salade de Choux Crus

250 g (8 oz) crisp white cabbage
5 cl ($\frac{1}{2}$ gill) vinaigrette
Salt and pepper

(1) Trim outside leaves.
(2) Remove stalk, wash.
(3) Finely shred.
(4) Dress in ravier.
(5) Serve vinaigrette separately.

Cole Slaw

As above, with the addition of a small carrot and onion finely shredded, bound with 5 cl ($\frac{1}{2}$ gill) of mayonnaise.

German Cabbage Salad – Salade de Choux Allemande

250 g (8 oz) crisp white cabbage
50 g (2 oz) salt
5 cl ($\frac{1}{2}$ gill) of vinaigrette
Salt and pepper

(1) Trim outside leaves.
(2) Remove stalk and wash.
(3) Cut finely into long shreds.
(4) Add salt and knead with your hand until limp.
(5) Wash cabbage thoroughly until all salt is removed.
(6) Add vinaigrette, seasoning; serve neatly in ravier.

Swiss Cabbage Salad – Salade de Choux Suisse

250 g (8 oz) crisp white cabbage
30 g (1 oz) fine diced bacon
5 cl ($\frac{1}{2}$ gill) vinegar
Salt and pepper

(1) Trim outside leaves.
(2) Remove stalks, wash.
(3) Prepare as for German style.
(4) Add sautéd bacon, dice and fat.
(5) Correct seasoning, salt, pepper, vinegar.
(6) Serve neatly in a ravier.

Cabbage Salad (Cooked) – Salade de Choux Cuits

400 g (12 oz) crisp white cabbage
5 cl ($\frac{1}{2}$ gill) acidulated cream or 5 cl ($\frac{1}{2}$ gill) of mayonnaise
Salt, pepper

(1) Trim outside leaves.
(2) Remove stalks, wash.
(3) Cut into fine long shreds.
(4) Quickly blanch in salted water.
(5) Strain, refresh, cool.
(6) Bind with cream or mayonnaise.
(7) Correct seasoning, serve in ravier.

Red Cabbage – Salade de Choux Rouges

250 g (8 oz) crisp firm red cabbage
5 cl ($\frac{1}{2}$ gill) vinaigrette
50 g (2 oz) grated sweet apples

(1) Remove outside leaves.
(2) Remove stalk, wash.

(3) Cut into long fine shreds.
(4) Blanch, drain, refresh.
(5) Marinade with Vinaigrette.
(6) Leave for 1 hour before service.
(7) Add shredded apples, just before service, in ravier.
Red Cabbage Salad can also be made with Swiss dressing (bacon). All cabbage salads can be varied by the use of different dressings and by adding e.g. grated apples, pineapples, and slightly beaten cream.

Celeriac Salad (Raw) – Salade de Céleri-rave Cru

250 g (8 oz) celeriac
5 cl ($\frac{1}{2}$ gill) mustard cream sauce
Salt and pepper to taste

(1) Wash and peel celeriac.
(2) Cut into fine Julienne.
(3) Combine all ingredients.
(4) Dress in ravier.

Celeriac Salad (Cooked) – Salade de Céleri-rave Cuit

250 g (8 oz) cooked celeriac
30 g (1 oz) finely chopped shallots
5 cl ($\frac{1}{2}$ gill) vinaigrette
Pinch of chopped parsley
Salt and pepper to taste

(1) Cook celeriac in skin.
(2) Peel and cool.
(3) Cut into dice, triangles or Julienne.
(4) Mix with vinaigrette and shallots.
(5) Serve in ravier, sprinkled with parsley.

Cucumber Salad – Salade de Concombres

1 medium size cucumber
5 cl ($\frac{1}{2}$ gill) vinaigrette
30 g (1 oz) finely chopped shallots
Pinch of finely chopped parsley
Salt and pepper to taste

(1) Peel and wash cucumber.
(2) Cut into fine even slices.
(3) Mix with shallots and vinaigrette.
(4) Serve neatly in ravier.
(5) Sprinkle with parsley.

Russian Cucumber Salad – Salade de Concombres à la Russe

As above with the addition of a little sour cream or créme fraiche.

French Bean Salad – Salade d'Haricots Verts

250 g (8 oz) French beans, cooked
3 cl ($\frac{1}{4}$ gill) vinaigrette
Salt and pepper

Combine ingredients; dress in ravier.

Flageolets Salad – Salade de Flageolets

250 g (8 oz) cooked flageolets
3 cl ($\frac{1}{4}$ gill) of vinaigrette
1 teaspoon of chopped herbs
5 cl ($\frac{1}{2}$ gill) mayonnaise

(1) Marinade flageolets in vinaigrette and herbs for a while.
(2) Add mayonnaise, mix.
(3) Dress on leaf of lettuce.

Haricot Bean Salad – Salade d'Haricots Blancs

250 g (8 oz) cooked haricot beans
15 g ($\frac{1}{2}$ oz) chopped onion/chive
3 cl ($\frac{1}{4}$ gill) vinaigrette
Salt and pepper, chopped parsley

Combine ingredients; dress in ravier.

Potato Salad (1) – Salade de Pommes de Terre

250 g (8 oz) boiled jacket potatoes
15 g ($\frac{1}{2}$ oz) chopped onions/chives
5 cl ($\frac{1}{2}$ gill) vinaigrette
Salt, pepper, chopped parsley

(1) Peel potatoes, cut into neat dice.
(2) Mix with onions/chives vinaigrette.
(3) Correct seasoning.
(4) Neatly dress on a leaf of lettuce.
(5) Sprinkle with parsley.

Potato Salad (2)

250 g (8 oz) boiled jacket potatoes
15 g ($\frac{1}{2}$ oz) chopped onions/chives
3 cl ($\frac{1}{4}$ gill) vinaigrette
5 cl ($\frac{1}{2}$ gill) mayonnaise
Salt, pepper, chopped parsley

(1) Cut potatoes in 1 cm ($\frac{1}{2}$ in.) dice.
(2) Pickle in vinaigrette with onion.
(3) Season, add mayonnaise.
(4) Dress in ravier.
(5) Sprinkle with parsley.

Hot Potato Salad – Salade de Pommes de Terre Chaudes

4-6 *small jacket boiled potatoes*	12 *cl* (1 *gill*) *white consommé*
15 *g* (½ *oz*) *chopped onions/chives*	*Salt, pepper, chopped parsley*
5 *cl* (½ *gill*) *vinaigrette*	

(1) Mix vinaigrette, onions/chives, seasoning and consommé
(2) Cut peeled potatoes in slices still hot into this marinade.
(3) Toss to mix; leave in warm place.
(4) Correct seasoning, serve warm in vegetable dish.

German Potato Salad – Salade de Pommes de Terre Allemande

As above, with the addition of 50 g (2 oz) finely sliced eating apples; can be served hot or cold.

Dutch Potato Salad – Salade de Pommes de Terre à la Hollandaise

As for German potato salad, with the addition of 25 g (1 oz) Julienne of sautéd bacon and 25 g (1 oz) of Julienne of smoked herring.

Potato Salad (Paris Style) – Salade de Pommes de Terre à la Parisienne

As for German potato salad, but potatoes are cut warm into white wine, to marinade; finish with little vinaigrette and finely chopped chervil and parsley.
Variation
The 4 foregoing types of potato salad can be varied by the use of different dressings and addition of herbs and spice e.g. watercress, mustard and cress, sorrel, chives, thyme and others.

Tomato Salad – Salade de Tomates

250 *g* (8 *oz*) *tomatoes*	20 *g* (½ *oz*) *thin onion rings or chopped chive*
3 *cl* (¼ *gill*) *vinaigrette*	¼ *lettuce*
Chopped parsley	

(1) Wash tomatoes; remove eyes, blanch, peel, slice thinly.
(2) Dress on lettuce leaves with onion, sprinkle with vinaigrette and parsley; garnish with onion rings.

COMPOUND SALADS – SALADES COMPOSÉES

The second group of salads is made from a combination of ingredients, such as vegetables, fruit, fish, meats, poultry and game. They are marinaded and bound again with vinaigrette or one of its variations, acidulated cream, or one of its variations, or mayonnaise, or one of its variations.

Garnishes and Borders
One, or several, of the following items may be used:
(1) Neat, blanched rings of onion.
(2) Slices, quarters as well as coarsely chopped eggs.
(3) Slices of beetroot, cut into diamonds, triangles, or half moon shaped.
(4) Slices of truffles, cut into diamonds, triangles, or half moon shaped.
(5) Julienne of truffles, whites of eggs, pimentos, mushrooms, ham, tongue.
(6) Quarters or hearts of lettuce, whole or sliced radishes, cucumber, tomatoes, spring onions.
(7) Bouquets of fresh watercress, mustard and cress or asparagus.
(8) Dice, Julienne, diamonds, triangles, etc. of the main ingredient of the salad.
(9) Base, surround or borders can also be made of crisp lettuce leaves or quartered hearts, cos lettuce or chicory.

Preparation of Compound Salads

The preparation of Compound Salads, as well as the ingredients used, varies considerably from one salad to another. Again, only the best materials should be used, well washed, clean and dry.

Individual preparation is given with each recipe of Compound Salad given.

Dressing and Service
All salads, Simple or Compound, are best served in individual or larger crystal, glass, china or wooden bowls, called saladiers. Whereas the Green and Simple Salads can be served in the deeper saladiers, the Compound Salads whenever possible should be served on the flatter type of saladier, which will allow more room for border and garnishes which often surround this type of salad.

Uses
To say where and when Compound Salads should be used is very difficult, if not impossible, because their number is very great and their uses varied and many.

The first and most obvious use is that of side-salad to be served with all hot and cold meats, poultry, game and fish.

Compound Salads should always be present on the first-class cold buffet in many varieties. Quite a number of them are most useful as part of a Hors d'Œuvre Variés since many Compound Salads represent a first-class Single Hors d'Œuvre in their own right. Here the salads are separated into 4 basic types or categories. In this way they are easily recognised and their individual use best understood.

The 4 basic types are (a) Compound Salads with a fruit base, (b) Compound Salads with a vegetable base, (c) Compound Salads with a meat, poultry, or game base, (d) Compound Salads with a fish or shellfish base.

The following list does not attempt to give all Compound Salads but only a sample of each type most commonly known and used, leaving out those which are very similar to others.

FRUIT BASED COMPOUND SALADS

Alice Salad – Salade Alice

6 medium sized sweet apples
50 g (2 oz) red currants
20 g ($\frac{1}{2}$ oz) split almonds
5 cl ($\frac{1}{2}$ gill) fresh cream
4 crisp lettuce leaves
Juice of a quarter lemon

(1) Peel and core apples, sprinkle with lemon juice.
(2) Place 4 apples on crisp lettuce leaves.
(5) Cut remaining apples in little balls or dice.
(4) Mix these apples with currants, cream and lemon juice.
(5) Neatly fill this salpicon of fruit into core of 4 apples.
(6) Serve chilled, sprinkling almonds on the top.

Apple Salad – Salade de Pommes

4 medium sweet apples
50 g (2 oz) blanched rings of onions
Juice of a quarter lemon
1 tablespoon mayonnaise
4 crisp lettuce leaves

(1) Peel and core apples; cut into thin slices.
(2) Mix with blanched onion rings.
(3) Add mayonnaise and lemon juice.
(4) Mix gently.
(5) Serve on lettuce leaves.
(6) Garnish with sprigs of parsley.

Creole Salad – Salade Créole

1 small melon
5 cl ($\frac{1}{2}$ gill) of fresh cream
25 g (1 oz) cooked rice
Little salt and ginger
Juice of a quarter lemon

(1) Cut melon in half, remove pips.
(2) Take out flesh cutting into balls or dice.
(3) Mix melon with rice, salt, ginger, cream and lemon juice.
(4) Replace neatly into one half of empty melon.
(5) Serve surrounded by crushed ice.

Columbia Salad – Salade Columbia

2 *medium apples*
2 *large bananas*
25 *g* (1 *oz*) *grapes*
1 *small heart of celery*
1 *tablespoon of mayonnaise*
6–8 *pistachio nuts*
4–6 *leaves of crisp lettuce*
Lemon juice

(1) Peel and core apples, cut into thin segments.
(2) Split bananas lengthwise; keep shell intact.
(3) Peel and stone grapes.
(4) Cut celery into thin slices.
(5) Mix sliced bananas, apples, celery, grapes with mayonnaise and lemon juice.
(6) Place into 4 half shells of bananas, garnish with lettuce.

Eva Salad – Salade Eve

6 *medium sweet apples*
1 *slice fresh pineapple*
1 *banana*
5 *cl* ($\frac{1}{2}$ *gill*) *of fresh cream*
Juice of a quarter lemon
4–6 *crisp lettuce leaves*

(1) Wash apples, do not peel, cut away a neat lid, save.
(2) Core without cutting right through the apples.
(3) Peel remaining two apples, cut into small dice.
(4) Mix with diced banana, pineapple, lemon juice and cream.
(5) Fill this salpicon of fruit into core of 4 apples.
(6) Replace lids; a stalk of Angelica can be added.
(7) Serve cool on lettuce leaves.

Femina Salad – Salade Femina

2 *oranges*
1 *grapefruit*
1 *dl* (1 *gill*) *mayonnaise*
1 *large cleaned washed lettuce*

(1) Peel oranges and grapefruit. Cut into neat segments.
(2) Mix fruit, some fruit juice with mayonnaise.
(3) Remove the heart of a lettuce.
(4) Place this salpicon of fruit into the middle of lettuce so it is surrounded by it like a basket.
(5) Serve chilled.

Florida Salad – Salade Florida

4 *to* 6 *oranges*
1 *large cleaned and washed lettuce*
Zest of 4 *oranges*

(1) Remove zest of oranges, cut into Julienne, blanch, refresh.
(2) Peel oranges, cut into segments.

(3) Remove heart of lettuce.
(4) Place segments of oranges into middle of lettuce.
(5) Sprinkle with Julienne of zest of oranges.
(6) Can also be served on quarter heart of lettuce.

Japonaise Salad – Salade Japonaise

500 g (1 lb) peeled tomatoes
250 g (8 oz) fresh pineapple, diced
juice of ½ a lemon
juice of ½ an orange
sugar, salt, pepper
2 lettuce hearts

(1) Cut tomatoes in half, remove pips.
(2) Cut into neat dice, marinade with lemon juice, salt, sugar, pepper.
(3) Marinade pineapple with lemon.
(4) Mix lightly.
(5) Dress, on lettuce hearts.

Javanaise Salad – Salade Javanaise

4 to 6 oranges
1 cleaned and washed lettuce
5 cl (½ gill) of fresh cream
20 g (½ oz) freshly grated horseradish
juice of quarter lemon

(1) Peel oranges, cut into neat segments.
(2) Mix with lemon juice, cream and horseradish.
(3) Remove the heart of lettuce.
(4) Fill salpicon of fruit into this middle.
(5) Sprinkle with Julienne of zest of oranges.

Mimosa Salad – Salade Mimosa

4 halves of hearts of lettuce
2 oranges
50 g (2 oz) grapes
1 banana
5 cl (½ gill) cream
Juice of quarter lemon

(1) Peel oranges, cut into segments.
(2) Peel and stone grapes, dice banana.
(3) Mix fruit with cream and lemon juice.
(4) Neatly place on *saladier*.
(5) Serve surrounded by halves or quarters of lettuce.

Orange Salad – Salade à l'Orange

As for Florida Salad.

Vigneronne Salad – Salade Vigneronne

4 *crisp hearts of lettuce, cleaned and washed*
100 *g* (4 *oz*) *grapes*
5 *cl* ($\frac{1}{2}$ *gill*) *sour cream*
Juice of quarter lemon

(1) Neatly place hearts of lettuce on *saladier*.
(2) Garnish with peeled and stoned grapes.
(3) Mix sour cream and lemon juice.
(4) Serve cream separately in sauce boat.

Waldorf Salad – Salade Waldorf

1 *small cooked celeriac*
2 *medium sized russet apples*
8 *halves of peeled walnuts*
5 *cl* ($\frac{1}{2}$ *gill*) *mayonnaise*
Juice of $\frac{1}{4}$ *lemon*
4-6 *lettuce leaves*

(1) Peel celeriac, cut into neat dice.
(2) Peel apples, core, cut into neat dice.
(3) Marinade in lemon juice.
(4) Mix with mayonnaise.
(5) Serve chilled on lettuce leaves.
(6) Garnish with halves of peeled walnuts.

VEGETABLE BASED COMPOUND SALADS

Aida Salad – Salade Aida

2 *curled chicory*
2 *peeled tomatoes*
2 *poached or fresh artichoke bottoms*
50 *g* (2 *oz*) *Julienne of green pimentos*
1 *hard boiled egg*
5 *cl* ($\frac{1}{2}$ *gill*) *mustard dressing*
4-6 *leaves of lettuce*

(1) Cut chicory into neat pieces, slice tomatoes.
(2) Cut artichokes in strips of quarters.
(3) Cut white of egg into Julienne.
(4) Mix chicory, tomatoes, artichokes, pimento, whites of eggs.
(5) Marinade with mustard flavoured vinaigrette.
(6) Dress on leaves of lettuce.
(7) Sprinkle with yolk of egg pressed through a sieve.
(8) Serve chilled.

American Salad – Salade Américaine

4 peeled tomatoes, sliced
4 boiled potatoes, sliced
50 g (2 oz) Julienne of celery
25 g (1 oz) blanched onion rings
1 hard boiled egg
5 cl ($\frac{1}{2}$ gill) vinaigrette
4 lettuce leaves

(1) Mix sliced tomatoes, potatoes, celery and onion rings.
(2) Blend gently with vinaigrette, leave to marinade.
(3) Dress on leaves of lettuce.
(4) Sprinkle with chopped or Julienne of egg.
(5) Serve chilled.

Andalouse Salad – Salade Andalouse

4 peeled tomatoes
1 large red pepper, cut into Julienne
60 g (2 oz) plain boiled rice
30 g (1 oz) blanched onion rings
15 g ($\frac{1}{2}$ oz) chopped parsley
5 cl ($\frac{1}{2}$ gill) garlic flavoured vinaigrette
4–6 leaves of lettuce

(1) Quarter tomatoes, add Julienne of red pimento.
(2) Mix with boiled rice, onion rings and parsley.
(3) Marinade all in garlic flavoured vinaigrette.
(4) Dress on leaves of lettuce.
(5) Serve chilled.

Bagatelle Salad – Salade Bagatelle

100 g (4 oz) young carrots cut Julienne
50 g (2 oz) large white mushrooms, cut Julienne
12–16 asparagus tips
5 cl ($\frac{1}{2}$ gill) vinaigrette
4–6 crisp leaves of lettuce
A little chopped herbs

(1) Mix Julienne of carrots and mushrooms.
(2) Marinade with vinaigrette.
(3) Arrange neatly on leaves of lettuce for service.
(4) Now arrange asparagus tips on salad.
(5) Sprinkle with finely chopped herbs.

Canaille Salad – Salade Canaille

4 peeled tomatoes
12 green tips of asparagus
1 banana cut in slices
50 g (2 oz) boiled Patna rice
30 g (1 oz) blanched Julienne of celery
5 cl ($\frac{1}{2}$ gill) sour cream or acidulated cream
4–6 leaves of lettuce

(1) Cut tomatoes in quarters.
(2) Gently mix with banana, rice and celery.

(3) Blend with most of the cream.
(4) Neatly arrange on lettuce leaves for service.
(5) Dip part of asparagus tips into remaining cream and parsley.
(6) Neatly arrange on the salad in a circle.

Cresonnière Salad – Salade Cresonnière

100–150 *g* (4–6 *oz*) *sliced cooked potatoes*
2 *bunches of watercress picked and washed*
1 *hard boiled egg pressed through a sieve*
A little chopped parsley and chervil
5 *cl* ($\frac{1}{2}$ *gill*) *of vinaigrette or Swiss dressing*

(1) Mix sliced potatoes and picked watercress.
(2) Sprinkle with either dressing.
(3) Arrange neatly into a pyramid.
(4) Sprinkle with egg and herbs before service.

Italian Salad – Salade Italienne

50 *g* (2 *oz*) $\frac{1}{2}$ *cm* ($\frac{1}{4}$ *in.*) *diced celeriac, cooked*
50 *g* (2 *oz*) 1$\frac{1}{2}$ *cm* ($\frac{3}{4}$ *in.*) *diced carrots, cooked*
25 *g* (1 *oz*) *cooked small peas*
25 *g* (1 *oz*) $\frac{1}{2}$ *cm* ($\frac{1}{4}$ *in.*) *diced salami*
5 *cl* ($\frac{1}{2}$ *gill*) *mayonnaise*
8–12 *thin slices salami*
4–6 *anchovy fillets*

(1) Mix celeriac, carrots, peas, diced salami.
(2) Add mayonnaise, gently blend.
(3) Place slices of salami around the edge of a *saladier*.
(4) Place above salad in the middle of this.
(5) Garnish with fillets of anchovy.
(6) Serve chilled.

Macaroni and Tomato Salad – Salade de Macaroni aux Tomates

200 *g* (6 *oz*) *cooked macaroni, 2 cm* (1 *in.*) *long*
50 *g* (2 *oz*) *tomate concassé cru*
3 *cl* ($\frac{1}{4}$ *gill*) *vinaigrette*
3 *cl* ($\frac{1}{4}$ *gill*) *mayonnaise*

(1) Mix macaroni, tomatoes, and vinaigrette, leave for a while.
(2) Add mayonnaise, mix.
(3) Serve on lettuce leaf in ravier.

Macaroni and Beetroot Salad – Salade de Macaroni aux Betteraves

As above, using Julienne of beetroot instead of tomatoes. Should be mixed in the last moment, as beetroot will colour salad, which should be avoided.

Mercedes Salad – Salade Mercédès

50 g (2 oz) celery cut into Julienne
50 g (2 oz) beetroot cut into Julienne
2 endives cut into Julienne
5 cl (½ gill) vinaigrette made with walnut oil
1 hard boiled egg pressed through sieve
A little chopped parsley
4–6 leaves of crisp lettuce
A little Julienne of truffles

(1) Mix Julienne of celery, beetroot and endives.
(2) Marinade with walnut oil and vinaigrette.
(3) Place in little bouquets on leaves of lettuce.
(4) Sprinkle with egg and parsley.
(5) Sprinkle each bouquet with Julienne of truffles.
(6) Serve chilled.

Oriental Salad – Salade Orientale

100 g (4 oz) cooked Patna rice, dry
30 g (1 oz) diced peeled tomatoes
30 g (1 oz) diced pimentos, red
30 g (1 oz) of diamonds of cooked French beans
5 cl (½ gill) flavoured vinaigrette
4–8 fillet of anchovies
4–6 crisp leaves of lettuce

(1) Mix rice, tomatoes, pimentos and beans.
(2) Marinade with garlic flavoured vinaigrette.
(3) For service place in pyramid in *saladier.*
(4) Surround with leaves of lettuce.
(5) Garnish with fillets of anchovy.
(6) Serve chilled.

Rice Salad – Salade de Riz

150 g (6 oz) cooked rice
150 g (6 oz) cooked tomatoes
50 g (2 oz) peas
5 cl (½ gill) vinaigrette, salt and pepper

(1) Wash, blanch, skin and remove seeds from tomatoes.
(2) Cut into ½ cm (¼ in.) dice.
(3) Cook peas in salt water and refresh.
(4) Mix all ingredients.
(5) Add vinaigrette, mix well, correct seasoning, dress in ravier.

Rice Salad (Spanish Style) – Salade de Riz Espagnole

150 g (6 oz) cooked rice
50 g (2 oz) tomato concassé raw
50 g (2 oz) red peppers
25 g (1 oz) chopped olives
5 cl (½ gill) vinaigrette
Salt, cayenne, chopped parsley

(1) Mix all ingredients well.
(2) Leave 10 to 20 min. before serving.
(3) Serve on a lettuce leaf in a ravier.

St Jean Salad – Salade Saint Jean

50 *g* (2 *oz*) *cooked French beans*
4 *artichoke bottoms cut into quarters*
¼ *cucumber, peeled, cut into slices*
25 *g* (1 *oz*) *cooked peas*
8–12 *asparagus tips*
5 *cl* (½ *gill*) *mayonnaise*
2 *hard boiled eggs, sliced*
6 *gherkins, cut into fans*
6–8 *blanched tarragon leaves*

(1) Mix beans, artichokes, cucumber, asparagus, and peas.
(2) Blend with mayonnaise.
(3) Arrange into pyramid on flat *saladier*.
(4) Make a border of sliced egg and gherkins.
(5) Garnish with tarragon leaves.
(6) Serve chilled.

Spanish Salad – Salade Espagnole

75 *g* (2–3 *oz*) *cooked French beans*
4 *peeled tomatoes in quarters*
2 *red peppers (pimentos)*
50 *g* (2 *oz*) *sliced onions or onion rings*
25 *g* (1 *oz*) *sliced white mushrooms*
5 *cl* (½ *gill*) *vinaigrette*
4–6 *leaves of lettuce*

(1) Mix beans, quarters of tomatoes.
(2) Add blanched Julienne of pimentos and onions.
(3) Blend carefully with vinaigrette.
(4) Place for service on lettuce leaves.
(5) Garnish with a border of thinly sliced marinaded mushrooms.
(6) Serve chilled.

Yam Yam Salad – Salade Yam Yam

50 *g* (2 *oz*) *cooked French beans*
100 *g* (4 *oz*) *sliced pickled cucumber*
50 *g* (2 *oz*) *Julienne of celeriac*
4 *quarters of lettuce*
5 *cl* (½ *gill*) *vinaigrette*

(1) Mix beans, cucumber, celeriac.
(2) Marinade with little of vinaigrette.
(3) Place quarter of lettuce on *saladier*, as border.
(4) Place above salad in the middle.
(5) Serve rest of vinaigrette separately.
(6) Serve chilled.

MEAT BASED COMPOUND SALADS

Bagration Salad – Salade Bagration

200 g (6 oz) Julienne of white cooked chicken
50 g (2 oz) Julienne of celery
2 artichoke bottoms, cut Julienne
50 g (2 oz) cooked macaroni about 2 cm (1 in.) long
2 peeled tomatoes cut into dice
2 hard boiled eggs, sliced
8–12 thin slices truffles
5 cl ($\frac{1}{2}$ gill) mayonnaise
A little chopped parsley

(1) Mix chicken, celery, artichokes, macaroni and tomatoes.
(2) Bind with mayonnaise.
(3) Place in a pyramid on a *saladier*.
(4) Garnish with a border of slices of egg.
(5) Garnish these with slices of truffles.
(6) Sprinkle with chopped parsley.
(7) Serve chilled.

Beatrice Salad – Salade Béatrice

200 g (6 oz) Julienne of white chicken cooked
150 g (4 oz) Julienne of cooked potatoes
25 g (1 oz) Julienne of truffles
8–12 asparagus tips
5 cl ($\frac{1}{2}$ gill) mustard flavoured mayonnaise

(1) Mix Julienne of chicken, potatoes, truffles.
(2) Bind with mustard flavoured mayonnaise.
(3) Place on a *saladier* in pyramid.
(4) Surround by lettuce leaves.
(5) Garnish with asparagus tips.

Carmen Salad – Salade Carmen

4 red peppers (pimentos) blanched, skinned and diced
125 g (4 oz) diced cooked white chicken
25 g (1 oz) cooked small peas
50 g (2 oz) dry cooked Patna rice
5 cl ($\frac{1}{2}$ gill) French mustard flavoured vinaigrette
A little finely chopped tarragon
4–6 leaves of lettuce

(1) Mix diced peppers, chicken, peas and rice.
(2) Marinade with mustard flavoured vinaigrette.
(3) Neatly place on *saladier*.
(4) Surround with leaves of lettuce.
(5) Sprinkle with chopped tarragon.
(6) Serve chilled.

Egyptian Salad – Salade Egyptienne

100 g (4 oz) *cooked dry Patna rice*
50 g (2 oz) *small sautéd chicken livers*
25 g (1 oz) *boiled diced ham*
25 g (1 oz) *cooked diced mushrooms*
25 g (1 oz) *diced artichoke bottoms*
25 g (1 oz) *small cooked peas*
2 *peeled, diced tomatoes*
25 g (1 oz) *diced blanched pimentos*
5 cl ($\frac{1}{2}$ *gill*) *vinaigrette*
4–6 *leaves of crisp lettuce*

(1) Mix all ingredients, except lettuce.
(2) Marinade well with vinaigrette.
(3) Arrange in a pyramid on *saladier*.
(4) Surround with leaves of lettuce.
(5) Serve chilled.

Fanchette Salad – Salade Fanchette

150 g (6 oz) *Julienne of cooked chicken*
100 g (4 oz) *Julienne of raw mushrooms*
2 *chicories cut Julienne*
25 g (1 oz) *Julienne of truffles*
5 cl ($\frac{1}{2}$ *gill*) *vinaigrette*
A little chopped chives

(1) Remove good loose leaves of chicory.
(2) Arrange as star on *saladier*.
(3) Mix Julienne of chicken, mushrooms, chicory.
(4) Marinade with vinaigrette.
(5) Place this salad in middle of star of chicory.
(6) Sprinkle with chopped chives.

Hungarian Salad – Salade Hongroise

100 g (4 oz) *blanched Julienne of bacon*
100 g (4 oz) *blanched Julienne of cabbage*
100 g (4 oz) *blanched Julienne of potatoes*
25 g (1 oz) *scraped fresh horse-radish*
5 cl ($\frac{1}{2}$ *gill*) *lemon dressing*
4–6 *crisp leaves of lettuce*
A little paprika pepper

(1) Mix bacon, cabbage, potatoes.
(2) Marinade with lemon dressing.
(3) Place neatly on *saladier*.
(4) Surround with lettuce leaves.
(5) Place on each lettuce leaf a roll of scraped horseradish.
(6) Sprinkle with a little paprika pepper.

Mascotte Salad – Salade Mascotte

50 g (2 oz) *Julienne of cooked ham*
8 *cocks' kidneys sautéd*
4 *plovers' eggs*
8–12 *asparagus tips*
4 *crayfish tails*
8 *slices of truffles*
5 *cl* ($\frac{1}{2}$ *gill*) *acidulated cream with mustard*
Some mustard and cress

(1) Mix ham, kidneys, asparagus tips.
(2) Bind with two-thirds of acidulated cream.
(3) Place neatly on a *saladier.*
(4) Surround with a border of mustard and cress.
(5) Place plovers' eggs on mustard and cress.
(6) Place crayfish tails in star shape on cress.
(7) Coat plovers' eggs with remainder of cream.
(8) Served chilled.

Mexican Salad – Salade Mexicaine

250 g (8 oz) *Julienne cooked chicken*
100 g (4 oz) *Julienne of blanched celeriac*
100 g (4 oz) *Julienne of blanched red peppers*
2 *hard boiled eggs*
50 g (2 oz) *chopped blanched onions*
A little chopped chives
5 *cl* ($\frac{1}{2}$ *gill*) *saffron flavoured vinaigrette*
1 *endive lettuce*

(1) Wash and prepare in normal way.
(2) Remove heart leaves.
(3) Place outside leaves like a basket on *saladier.*
(4) Mix chicken, celeriac, peppers and onions.
(5) Marinade with saffron flavoured vinaigrette.
(6) Place this salad in the empty space of endive.
(7) Garnish with quarter of eggs and heart of endive.
(8) Sprinkle with chopped chives.

Nonne Salad – Salade des Nonnes

150 g (6 oz) *Julienne of cooked chicken*
150 g (6 oz) *cooked dry Patna rice*
25 g (1 oz) *finely chopped truffles*
6–8 *lettuce leaves*
A little chopped parsley
5 *cl* ($\frac{1}{2}$ *gill*) *French mustard flavoured vinaigrette*

(1) Mix chicken and rice.
(2) Marinade with vinaigrette.
(3) Arrange neatly in a pyramid on *saladier.*

(4) Surround with a border of lettuce leaves.
(5) Sprinkle with chopped parsley and truffles.

Opera Salad – Salade à l'Opéra

150 g (6 oz) *chicken cut in Julienne*
50 g (2 oz) *Julienne of tongue*
25 g (1 oz) *Julienne of truffles*
50 g (2 oz) *Julienne of celery*
6–8 *asparagus tips*
6–8 *cocks' kidneys sautéd*
6–8 *gherkins*
5 cl ($\frac{1}{2}$ *gill*) *thin mayonnaise*
6–8 *crisp leaves of lettuce*

(1) Mix chicken, tongue, truffles and celery.
(2) Bind with mayonnaise.
(3) Arrange neatly on a flat *saladier*.
(4) Surround with a border of lettuce leaves.
(5) Arrange on lettuce alternatively asparagus and cocks' kidneys.
(6) Serve chilled.

Regency Salad – Salade Régence

150 g (6 oz) *Julienne of cooked chicken*
8–12 *sautéd cocks' kidneys*
25 g (1 oz) *raw truffles cut Julienne*
50 g (2 oz) *raw Julienne of celery*
8–12 *asparagus tips*
5 cl ($\frac{1}{2}$ *gill*) *lemon dressing*
6–8 *crisp lettuce leaves*
A little chopped chives

(1) Mix chicken, cocks' kidneys, celery and truffles.
(2) Marinade with lemon dressing.
(3) Arrange into a pyramid on *saladier*.
(4) Surround with lettuce leaves as a border.
(5) Place asparagus tips around pyramid.
(6) Sprinkle with chopped chives.
(7) Serve chilled.

FISH BASED COMPOUND SALADS

Dutch Salad – Salade Hollandaise

150 g (6 oz) $\frac{1}{2}$ *cm* ($\frac{1}{4}$ *in.*) *diced smoked salmon*
250 g (8 oz) $\frac{1}{2}$ *cm* ($\frac{1}{4}$ *in.*) *diced cooked potatoes*
50–75 g (2–3 oz) *Dutch or Danish caviar*
5 cl ($\frac{1}{2}$ *gill*) *lemon dressing*
50 g (2 oz) *chopped blanched onions*
A little chopped chives
6–8 *crisp lettuce leaves*

(1) Mix salmon, potatoes and onions.

(2) Marinade with lemon dressing.
(3) Arrange neatly on *saladier.*
(4) Surround with a border of lettuce leaves.
(5) Shape caviar in little balls or domes.
(6) Garnish salad with balls of caviar on border.
(7) Sprinkle with chopped chives.

Beauty of the Night Salad – Salade Belle de Nuit

8–10 *crayfish tails cut into slices*
4 *small truffles, cut into slices*
5 *cl* ($\frac{1}{2}$ *gill*) *wine-vinaigrette*
2 *firm hearts of crisp lettuce*
1 *white of egg, finely chopped*
Mill pepper

(1) Mix crayfish and truffle slices.
(2) Marinade with wine-vinaigrette.
(3) Arrange neatly on *saladier.*
(4) Surround with a border of hearts of lettuce, cut into eight.
(5) Sprinkle with chopped white of egg.
(6) Give a few turns of pepper mill just before serving.
(7) Serve chilled.

Favourite Salad – Salade Favorite

8–10 *crayfish tails cut into slices*
2 *white truffles cut into slices*
8–10 *asparagus tips*
50 *g* (2 *oz*) *Julienne of celery*
A little chopped parsley
5 *cl* ($\frac{1}{2}$ *gill*) *lemon dressing*
6–8 *crisp leaves of lettuce*

(1) Mix crayfish, truffles and celery.
(2) Marinade with lemon dressing, place on *saladier.*
(3) Surround with a border of lettuce leaves.
(4) Garnish with asparagus tips.
(5) Sprinkle with chopped parsley.
(6) Serve chilled.

Francillon Salad – Salade Francillon

250 *g* (8 *oz*) *cooked and bearded mussels*
250 *g* (8 *oz*) *raw diced potatoes cooked in white wine*
50 *g* (2 *oz*) *chopped blanched shallots*
25 *g* (1 *oz*) *fine Julienne of truffles*
5 *cl* ($\frac{1}{2}$ *gill*) *vinaigrette*
A little chopped parsley
6–8 *leaves of lettuce*

(1) Mix mussels and cooked potatoes and shallots.
(2) Marinade with vinaigrette.
(3) Place on a *saladier* in pyramid.

(4) Surround with a border of lettuce leaves.
(5) Sprinkle with chopped parsley.
(6) Serve chilled.

German Salad – Salade Allemande

150 g (6 oz) ½ cm (¼ in.) *diced cooked potatoes*
150 g (6 oz) ½ cm (¼ in.) *diced eating apples*
100 g (4 oz) ½ cm (¼ in.) *diced pickled cucumber*
2–3 ½ cm (¼ in.) *diced soaked salt herring fillets*
100 g (4 oz) ½ cm. (¼ in.) *diced beetroot, cooked*
1 *small beetroot, whole*
2 *hard boiled eggs*
5 cl (½ gill) *mayonnaise*
6–8 *crisp leaves of lettuce*

(1) Mix potatoes, apples, cucumber, herring and beetroot.
(2) Bind with mayonnaise.
(3) Arrange in a pyramid on flat *saladier.*
(4) Surround with border of lettuce leaves.
(5) Garnish with slices of beetroot root and hard boiled egg.
(6) Serve chilled.

Mignon Salad – Salade Mignon

200 g (8 oz) *peeled shrimps or prawns*
4 *artichoke bottoms cut into strips*
50 g (2 oz) *chopped blanched shallots*
8 *slices truffles*
6–8 *crisp quarters of lettuce hearts*
5 cl (½ gill) *mayonnaise flavoured with cream and cayenne*

(1) Mix shrimps, artichokes, shallots.
(2) Bind and marinade with mayonnaise and cream.
(3) Season with little cayenne pepper.
(4) Place on *saladier.*
(5) Surround with a border of quarters of lettuce hearts and slices of truffles.
(6) Serve chilled.

Monte Cristo Salad – Salade Monte Cristo

1 *medium lobster, meat cut into 1 cm (½ in.) dice*
150 g (6 oz) *cooked potatoes*
1 *medium truffle and hard boiled egg cut into dice*
2 *hearts of lettuce cut into quarters*
5 cl (½ gill) *mustard flavoured mayonnaise*

(1) Mix lobster, potatoes, truffle and egg.
(2) Bind and marinade with mayonnaise.

(3) Arrange lettuce quarters in middle.
(4) Arrange salad as border around lettuce.
(5) Serve chilled.

Moscovite Salad – Salade Moscovite

$\frac{1}{2}$ *l.* (1 *pint*) *Russian salad* (*see recipe*)
5 *cl* ($\frac{1}{2}$ *gill*) *firm aspic*
8-12 *small tartlets*
50 *g* (2 *oz*) *caviar*
50 *g* (2 *oz*) *purée of eel with beaten cream*
8-12 *small crisp lettuce leaves*

(1) Add melted aspic to Russian salad.
(2) Place in charlotte or parfait mould to set.
(3) Carefully remove from mould.
(4) Place in middle of *saladier*.
(5) Surround with a border of lettuce leaves.
(6) Place tartlets on lettuce filled half with caviar half with purée of eel.

Russian Salad – Salade Russe

100 *g* (4 *oz*) *diced cooked carrots*
100 *g* (4 *oz*) *diced cooked turnips or celeriac*
30 *g* (1 *oz*) *diamonds of cooked French beans*
30 *g* (1 *oz*) *small cooked peas*
50 *g* (2 *oz*) *diced cooked mushrooms*
30 *g* (1 *oz*) *diced gherkins*
30 *g* (1 *oz*) *diced ham*
30 *g* (1 *oz*) *diced tongue*
30 *g* (1 *oz*) *diced lobster*
4 *fillets anchovy, diced*
A few capers
1 *small beetroot*
2 *hard boiled eggs*
25 *g* (1 *oz*) *caviar*
1 *dl* (1 *gill*) *of thick mayonnaise*

(1) Mix carrots, turnips, beans, peas, mushrooms, gherkins.
(2) Add dice of ham, tongue and anchovy.
(3) Bind all with two thirds of the mayonnaise.
(4) Place on *saladier* or silver flat in pyramid.
(5) Neatly cover with remainder of mayonnaise.
(6) Garnish with balls of caviar and capers.
(7) Give a border of slices of beetroot and eggs.

Scotch Salad – Salade Écossaise

150 *g* (6 *oz*) *flaked boiled salmon*
150 *g* (6 *oz*) *diced cooked potatoes*
2 *hard boiled eggs, diced*
1 *small diced truffle*
1 *small lettuce cut into Julienne*
5 *cl* ($\frac{1}{2}$ *gill*) *curry flavoured mayonnaise*
A little curry powder
3 *cl* ($\frac{1}{4}$ *gill*) *of lemon dressing*

(1) Mix salmon, potatoes, egg and truffle.
(2) Marinade with lemon dressing.
(3) Arrange in dome shape on *saladier*.
(4) Neatly cover with curry flavoured mayonnaise.
(5) Surround with a border of Julienne of lettuce.
(6) Sprinkle with a little curry powder.
(7) Serve chilled.

3. *Fishmongery and Shellfish*

Most fishes are edible and the world of fish represents an enormous source of good food. The most nourishing fishes come from the river: the eels and the lamprey family; then come salmon, salmon-trout, trout, char (charr), mackerel, fresh herrings, turbot and the conger-eel family. Among the less nourishing are sole, lemon-sole and bream, etc., but they are nevertheless well liked for their good taste and easy adaptation to the many different methods of preparation and cooking.

All fishes consist of nearly 75% of water and also the albuminoids (egg-whites) consistency varies little from fish to fish (about 18%). In consistency of fat the variation is much wider; about 26% for the conger-eel family, 12% for salmon and salmon-trout, 9% for trout, 8.2% for shad and 6% for herring.

From this it can clearly be seen that fish flesh does not vary much from that of land animals. Proportions of fat, minerals, and albuminoids are very much the same. Where the fish has the advantage is in the contents of phosphorated compounds and in the fact that fish, especially the leaner fishes, are much more easily digestible and so represent an excellent food for the sedentary worker and the sick.

From the practical point of view it is interesting to note that the quantity of waste in preparing fish is very high, about 35% to 50%, according to the kind and size of fish and the methods employed in preparation and cooking.

In general terms for recognition purposes, fish can be divided into two groups or types; the Flat Fishes which are to be found near the bottom of the sea; and the Round Fishes which are commonly found swimming near the surface. There are also, of course, Shellfish (crustaceans and molluscs). All of these are further sub-divided, first into Sea or Fresh Water Fish, White Fish, Oily Fish, etc.; and then into distinct families or groups.

With the exception of Shellfish, all fish have a number of fins. In some cases these can be used as a means of distinguishing one fish from another. The fins are to be found either in pairs or singly. The paired fins are the *pectoral*, found on the sides of the fish just behind the Gills, and the *pelvic* which are found on the underside or belly of the fish. The single or unpaired fins are the *dorsal*, which runs along the back, the *caudal* or tail, and the *anal* which is found on the underside of the fish near the tail.

(1) *White Fishes.* (a) *Round*, cod, hake, haddock, whiting; (b) *Flat*, halibut, lemon-sole, plaice, sole, turbot.
(2) *Oily Fishes.* (a) *Round*, eel, herring, mackerel, salmon, trout; (b) *Flat*, none.
(3) *Shellfish.* (a) *Crustacea*, crab, craw-fish, cray-fish, lobster, prawns, and shrimps; (b) *Mollusca*, cockles, mussels, oysters, and scallops.

Quality

Absolute freshness is essential if the best is to be obtained from any fish dish, both in flavour and nourishment. Stale fish are not only unappetizing but can also be the cause of digestive disorders or even poisoning. In these days of quick-freeze, of course, the bulk of the fish reaches the markets frozen and, if the fish was frozen whilst fresh and it is used immediately after defrosting, it will to all intents and purposes be equal to fresh fish, although some of the flavour will have been lost in refrigeration. The following are some tests which can be applied to determine the freshness or otherwise of fish:
(1) The eyes should be bright and 'full', not 'sunken';
(2) The gills should be bright pinkish red in colour;
(3) The flesh must be firm and springy, or elastic;
(4) Scales, if any, should be plentiful, firm and should not come off when fish is handled;
(5) The fish should have a pleasant, salty smell.

Sure signs and indications of staleness are (a) an unpleasant ammoniac odour which increases with its staleness, (b) limp flesh retaining the imprint of one's fingers, (c) sunken eyes, (d) gills dull and discoloured.

The quality is determined by the condition of the skin, which should be shining and of good colour. The flesh of white fish should be really white, not yellowish. The fish should feel heavy in relation to its size, the flesh plump and springy.

Storage

As already stated, freshness in fish is of the utmost importance. The period of storage, therefore, should be reduced to a minimum. If it has to be stored at all, fish must be cleaned, washed and dried with a clean cloth, then placed on a clean dry tray or rack, and stored in a suitable refrigerator.

Quick frozen fish can, of course, be stored in a deep freeze compartment until required but once it has thawed out, even if only partly thawed, it must *not in any circumstances be re-frozen.*

TYPES, RECOGNITION, AND PREPARATION

FLAT FISH

The Halibut – Le Flétan

Large fish. Dusky brown/olive colour, on dark side. White and smooth on opposite side. Both eyes on 'right' side. Even teeth in both jaws.

The Long Rough Dab – Le Carrelet

Resembles halibut but much smaller. Rough to the touch. Lighter in colour than halibut.

The Plaice – La Plie

Dark brown, with orange spots. Small mouth but broad. Blunt teeth, larger on lower side. Lateral line nearly straight.

The Dab, Flounder or Fluke – Le Carrelet

Resembles plaice but rougher to touch. Spiny scales. Lateral line curves sharply over pectoral fin. The flounder is dark in colour with bright white underside. No orange spots.

Lemon Dab or Sole – La Limande

Yellowish colour, mottled with dark and light spots. Small head and mouth.

Witch or Pale Dab – La Limande

Resembles Lemon sole. Pale brown on upper side. Yellowish white on lower side.

The Turbot – Le Turbot

No scales. Dark olive/brown colour with 'wart-like' tubercles or spines. Yellowish on underside.

The Brill – La Barbue

Smooth skin. Darker colour than turbot. More elongated shape.

Dover Sole – La Sole (de Douvres)

Eyes on right side. Teeth on lower jaw only. Brown with dark markings. White underside.

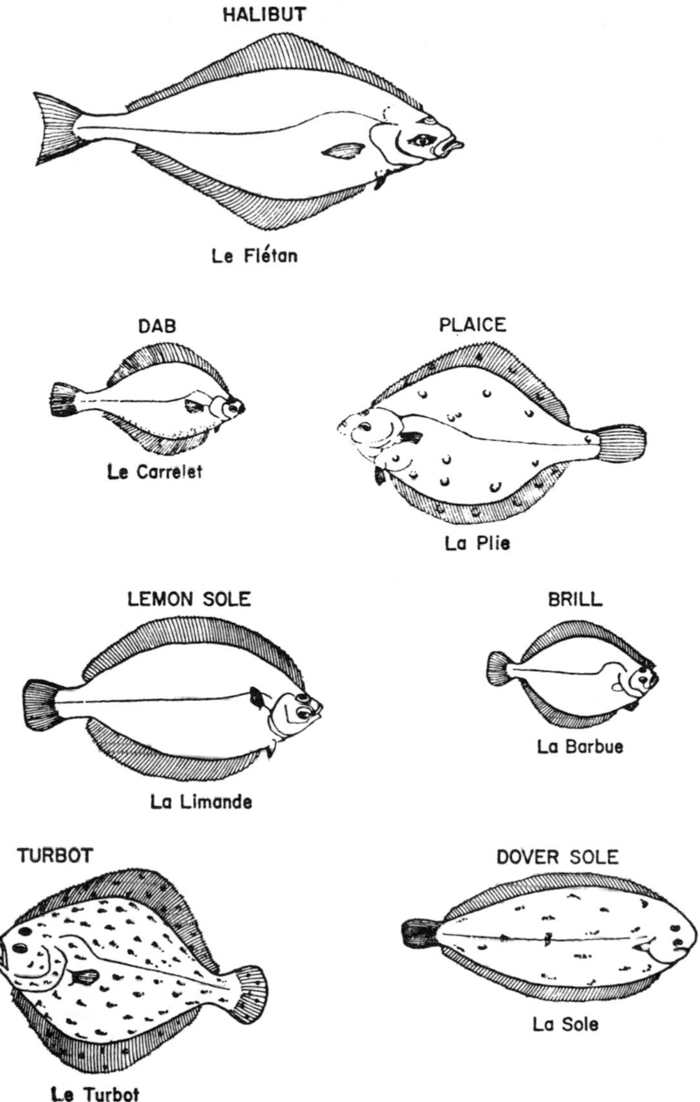

FIG. 11. *Flat fish*

Some of the flat fish are illustrated in Figure 11.

THE COD FAMILY

Group 1 (3 dorsal fins)

The Cod – Le Cabillaud

Brownish/olive colour with yellowish or brown spots. White lateral line. Single barbel on chin. Near human expression.

The Haddock – L'Aiglefin or L'Aigrefin

Large black patch either side of body immediately behind gills. Black lateral line.

(Smoked) – *(Fumé)*

Bronze/grey colour with white underside.

The Whiting – Le Merlan

Greenish colour, white underside. Small black spot at root of pectoral fins. Lateral line rather indistinct.

Coal Fish (Saithe) – Le Colin

Blue/black colour, whitish underside. White lateral line. Small barbel in adult fish.

Pollock, Lythe – Le Lieu-Jaune

Olive green colour. Curved and well marked lateral line. Protruding lower jaw.

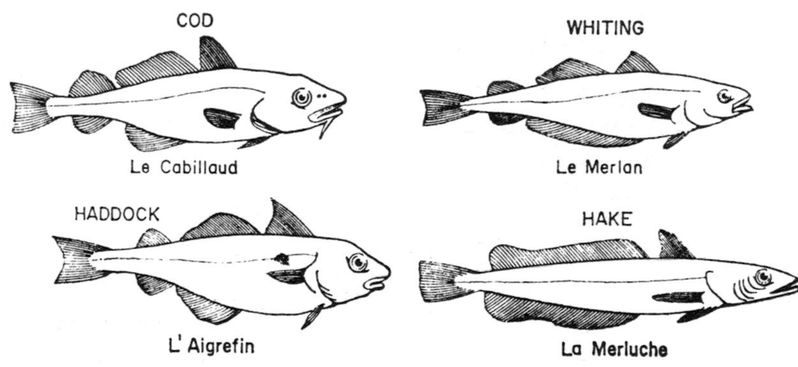

FIG. 12. *The cod family*

Group 2 (2 dorsal fins)

The Hake – La Merluche

Somewhat similar to eel in shape. Rather 'pleased' expression. Dark grey colour shading to dull silvery grey on underside. Long jaws, two rows sharp teeth. Inside of mouth, dark.

The Ling – La Lingue

Similar to conger, but with dorsal fin broken near tail. Smooth skin. Dull grey colour.

Some of the cod family are illustrated in Figure 12.

THE SALMON FAMILY

The Salmon – Le Saumon

Length approx. 1 m (3 ft). Weight up to 13.5 kg (30 lb). Plump and clear looking with bright silvery scales. Steel blue on back and head. Lighter on sides and belly. Teeth in upper and lower jaws. Edges of tongue notched. Young salmon are known as 'parr' for two years after hatching. When ready to swim down river to the sea they are known as 'smolts'. After a year at sea, they return up river as 'grilse' (weight 2 kg, 3-5 lb). After spawning, the grilse return to sea and come back after a few months as adult salmon (weight 4 kg, 8-10 lb). After spawning, the salmon return to the sea as spent fish or 'kelts' and are in poor condition and unseasonable.

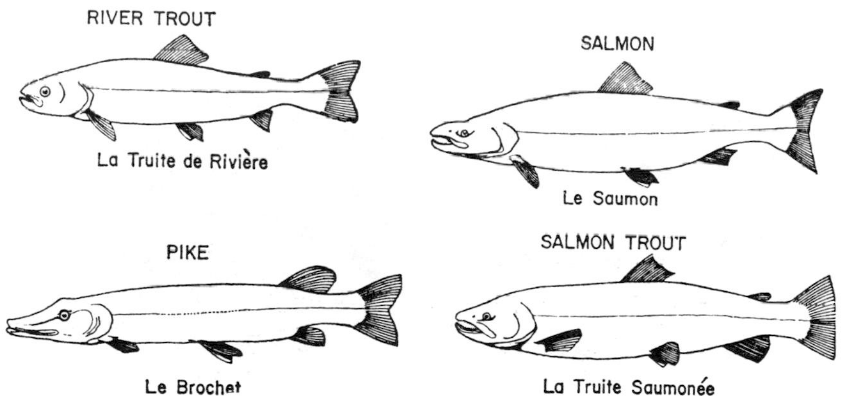

FIG. 13. *The salmon family*

River Trout – La Truite de Rivière

Differs from the salmon in minor structural characteristics, such as fewer rays to the dorsal fins and more rows of scales on tail.

Lake Trout – La Truite de Lac

Much smaller than salmon and live in fresh water.

Salmon-Trout, Sea-Trout – La Truite Saumonée

Trout that have been to sea. Paler in colour than salmon. When young, the flesh is finer but they can attain a weight of up to 13.5 kg (50 lb).

Smelt or Sparling – L'Éperlan

Light shade of olive green. Silvery sides and belly, 15-20 cm (6-8 in.) in length. Odour, when fresh, resembles cucumber.

Some of the salmon family are illustrated in Figure 13.

THE HERRING FAMILY

(Silvery colour, no lateral line).

The Herring – Le Hareng

Dorsal fin commences half way from tip of nose to commencement of tail.

The Sprat – Le Sprat

Seldom exceeds 15 cm (6 in.) in length. Resembles young herring of same size but edge of belly is serrated, dorsal fin is nearer tail and has larger scales.

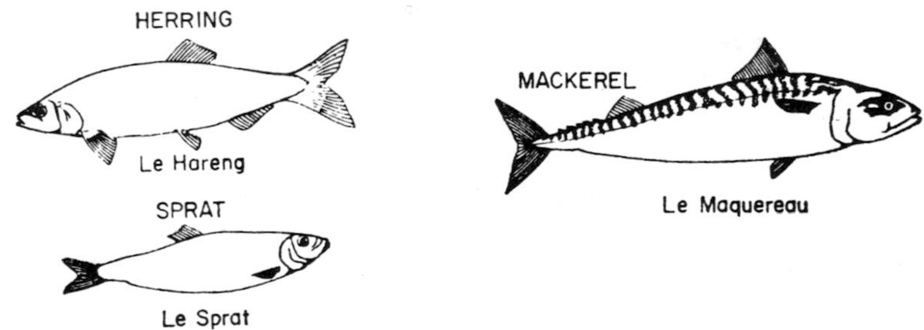

FIG. 14. *The herring family*

The Pilchard – Le Pilchard, Le Pelamide

Similar to herring but larger scales, more rounded body. Deeper green colour.

Whitebait – Les Blanchailles

Young herrings and sprats. Bright silvery colour and small in size.

The Anchovy – L'Anchois

A small fish with projecting snout. Green colour with broad silver band on sides. Deep forked tail.

Some of the herring family are illustrated in Figure 14.

CLEANING

(1) Wash and dry the fish with a clean cloth.
(2) Cut off all fins and trim the tail.
(3) Remove the eyes and trim the mouth if the fish is to be served whole. Remove the scales, if any, scraping with a knife, held at an angle of 45°, from tail to head.
(4) Remove gills and entrails from the gill slits, also the roes, if any.
(5) To do this, first make a small opening, some 5 cm (2 in.) in length, from the vent to the belly; in the case of round fishes, loosen the gut with the tip of a small knife.
(6) In the case of flat fishes, make the opening immediately behind the head of the fish where the gut is situated.
(7) Now open the gill slit, on one side of the back of the head, with the fish on its side on the board or slate. Hold the gills firmly with the fingers of the left hand and with a small knife or the fish scissors cut the gill loose from both the 'left' side, where it is attached to the throat, and the 'right' side where it is attached to the back of the gill slit.
(8) Repeat this operation on the other side of the fish until the gills are quite free.
(9) Now with the tip of the knife and the thumb making a pincer, draw out the entrail and the gills gently, taking care not to damage the flesh of the fish.
(10) In the case of large fish, use the prongs of a fork or the hook of a small ladle to get a purchase on the gills.
(11) Take care not to break the ligament that joins the body to the head of the fish.
(12) Now wash the interior of the fish thoroughly under the cold water tap and scrape the backbone with a finger nail or, in the case of large fish,

with the hook of a small ladle to remove all traces of blood or liver from the backbone. Re-wash and dry the fish with a clean cloth.
(13) Any roes removed from the fish should be placed *at once* into cold water and put under the cold water tap until the water is quite clear.
(14) Keep in a cool place until required.

SKINNING AND FILLETING

To Skin Dover Sole (Figure 15)

(1) Cut through the skin across the middle of the tail and, with the tip of the filleting knife, scrape across the tail to loosen a few inches of skin.
(2) Now raise the skin from the flesh, placing the thumb of the right hand between the flesh and the skin.
(3) Hold the tail in the left hand. Pull gently with the right hand, taking care not to tear the flesh.
(4) Follow along the fish with the thumb of the left hand, loosening the skin from the fins on either side of the fish.
(5) The use of a little salt on the fingers or, better still, a clean cloth, will ensure a firmer grip on the fish whilst skinning it.

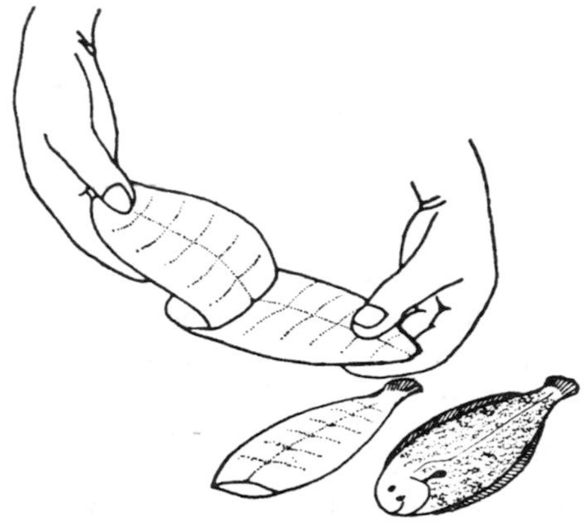

FIG. 15. *Skinning of Dover sole*

To Skin Whiting

(1) With the tip of a small knife slipped under the skin, cut along the skin that covers the whole fillet.

(2) Begin at the head and follow the dorsal fins to the tail, then along the belly of the fish, back to the gills.
(3) Thus the whiting skin is divided into two equal parts.
(4) Now loosen the skin along the length of the cut; then, starting at the head, pull the skin towards the tail in one stroke to remove the whole half skin neatly.
(5) Repeat on the other side.

To Skin Skate (Figure 16)

(1) Detach the skin from the thick part of the piece with a sharp knife.
(2) Ease the skin from the flesh until there is sufficient free to hold with a cloth.
(3) Pull in one stroke towards the edge of the fish, detaching with the point of a knife any flesh that may adhere to the skin, to avoid tearing the flesh.
(4) *All other fish are cooked with the skin on and skinned after cooking, if required.*
(5) In the case of 'fillets', the fillet is placed on the board or slate, skin downwards.
(6) Hold the tail firmly with one finger of the left hand.

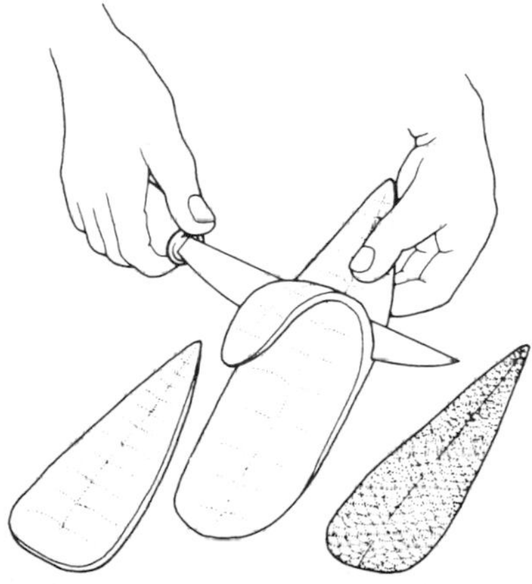

FIG. 16. *Skinning of round or flat fillets of fish*

(7) With the blade of the filleting knife held slantwise, start at the tail, close to the finger.
(8) Detach the flesh from the skin by placing the blade between skin and flesh and, with a scraping motion, push the flesh forward and roll it over to disclose the skin. Detach the flesh, neatly.

To Prepare Trout

The preparation of trout is shown in Figure 17.

Refer also to Figure 18(*a*) for the preparation of salmon for cooking whole, and (*b*) the skinning of eel.

FIG. 17. *Preparation of trout*

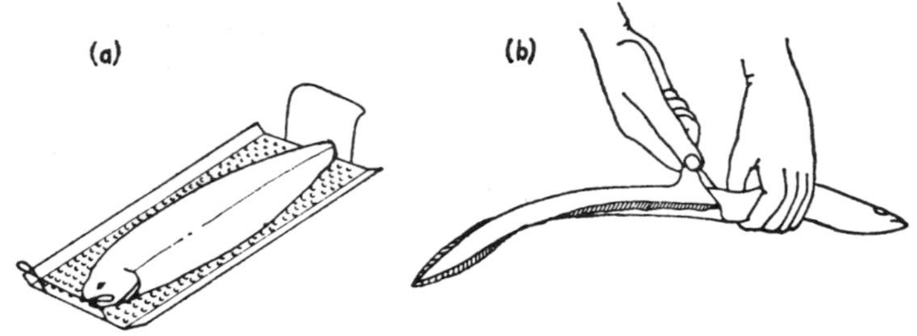

FIG. 18. (a) *Preparation of salmon for cooking whole* (b) *Skinning of eel*

To Fillet Flat Fish (Yielding Four Fillets) (Figure 19(*a*))

(1) Make an incision down the centre of the backbone from head to tail, with the fish flat on the board or slate. In the case of Dover sole, both skins will have been removed first.
(2) With the tips of the fingers of the left hand, feel along the bones and roll the flesh away from the ridge of the backbone.
(3) Next, separate the top of the left fillet, near the head, with the tip of the filleting knife.
(4) Now, with the blade of the knife flat on the bones of the fish, cut outward towards the fins, from head to tail.
(5) At the same time, roll the fillet to the left of the bones with the fingers

of the left hand, so as to follow the bones closely, and remove the fillet without damage to the flesh.
(6) Now turn the fish round, so that the head of the fish is nearest to the body and repeat the operation, this time cutting outwards from tail to head.
(7) Turn the fish over and repeat on the reverse side.
(8) Next, skin the fillets, trim the edges, wash dry with a clean cloth and place on a clean tray.

To Fillet Round Fish (Yielding Two Fillets) (Figure 19(*b*))

(1) Place the fish on its side on the board or slate, after cleaning, naturally.
(2) Make an incision along the backbone – close to one side of the dorsal fins, about 1 cm ($\frac{1}{2}$ in.) in depth from head to tail.
(3) Run the fingers of the left hand along the cut to feel the bones and separate the flesh from them by pushing the flesh to the left of the backbone.
(4) Now, with the tip of the knife, scrape over the ribs of the fish from head to tail, folding the flesh back with the fingers of the left hand, so as to follow the bones without cutting into the flesh.
(5) When near the tail, insert the blade of the knife between the fillet and the bones, by placing the fillet over it.
(6) Cut off the fillet neatly, by drawing the knife edge from head to tail.
(7) Skin the fillet, pull out any small bones you can feel with your fingers, trim, wash, dry and place on to a clean tray.

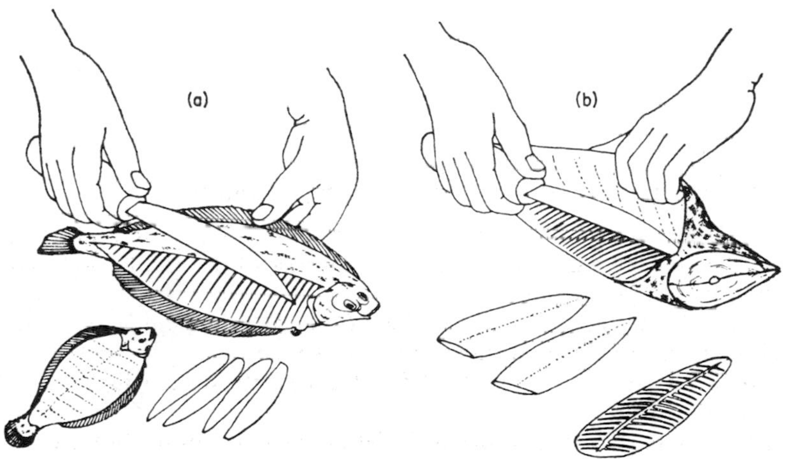

FIG. 19. *Filleting* (a) *flat fish* (b) *round fish*

Portions and Cuts

As a guide, a portion of fish *on the bone* should weigh 125 g (6 oz). A portion of fish *off the bone* should weigh about 100 g (4 oz). The exception here may be in the case of *à la carte* portions.

In case of fish cakes and croquettes 125 g (6 oz) are given.

BASIC CUTS

Refer to Figure 20.

La Darne

A slice or steak of round fish on the bone e.g. *Darne de Saumon, Darne de Cabillaud.*

Le Tronçon

A slice or steak of flat fish on the bone e.g. *Tronçon de Turbot, Tronçon de Barbue.*

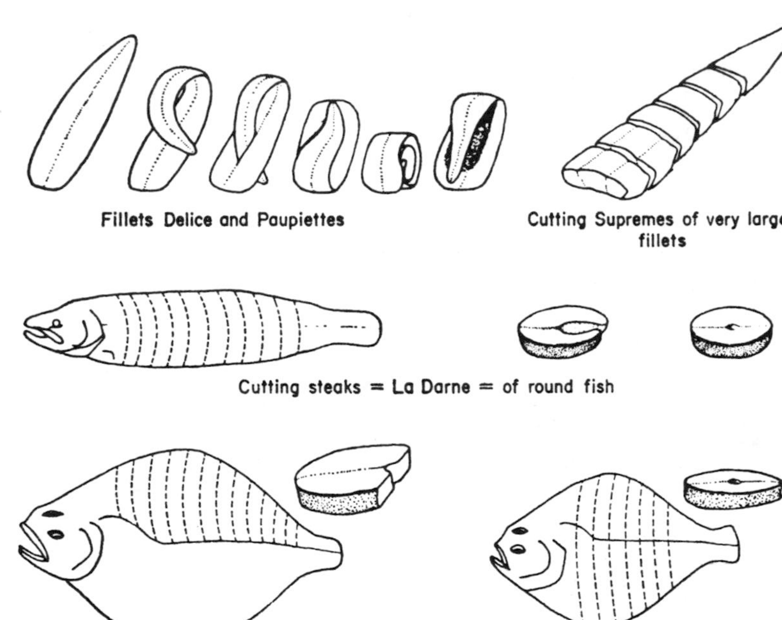

FIG. 20. *Basic cuts*

Le Filet

A fillet of fish, usually from a small fish without bones e.g. *Filet de Sole, Filet de Plie.*

Le Suprême

Applied to large fillets of fish, cut into portion on the slant e.g. *Suprême de Flètan, Suprême de Aigrefin.*

Le Délice

Applied to neatly folded fillets of fish e.g. *Délice de Sole, Délice de Merlan.*

Le Goujon

Applied to fillets of fish cut into strips approximately 6 cm × $\frac{1}{2}$ cm (3 in. × $\frac{1}{4}$ in.) usually floured, egg-washed and breadcrumbed e.g. *Goujon de Plie, Goujon de Sole.*

La Paupiette

This term is applied to fillets of smaller fish, usually sole, which are stuffed with farce, fish or vegetables, or a mixture of both, neatly rolled into a barrel shape, tied or pinned.

PREPARATION

Sole 'Colbert' (*flat*) (Figure 21)
(1) Clean and prepare sole in the normal way.
(2) Skin, as described.
(3) Make an incision along the backbone on one side, as if to fillet, within an inch or so from sides and ends of sole.
(4) Neatly fold back fillets.
(5) Break backbone in two to four places, for easier removal after cooking.
(6) Wash, dry, season, flour, eggwash and crumb.
(7) This preparation is used for smaller flat fish, usually sole, Lemon sole, etc.

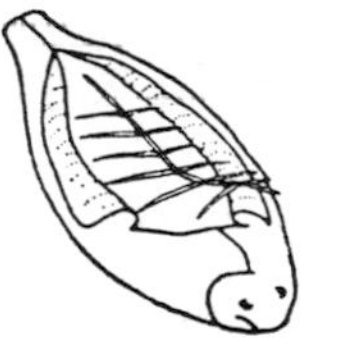

FIG. 21. *Preparation of sole for Colbert*

Whiting 'Colbert' (*round*)
(1) Skin whiting, as described (optional).
(2) Remove gill and eyes.
(3) Wash and dry the fish.
(4) Carefully remove backbone 2 cm (1 in.) away from head and tail, leaving both fillets attached to head and tail.
(5) Season, flour, eggwash and crumb.
(6) Flatten fillet gently into one still attached to head and tail, which stand in an upright position.
(7) This preparation can be used for other small fish, whiting, trout, charr etc.

'Curled' Whiting (Figure 22)
(1) Skin whiting, as described.
(2) Remove gill and eyes, force a knife through eye socket.
(3) Wash and dry, season.
(4) Flour, eggwash, breadcrumb.
(5) Push tail through eye-socket.
(6) Secure, if necessary, with cocktail stick.

Whiting – 'Colère' (Figure 22)
(1) Prepare whiting, as above.
(2) Place tail between needle sharp teeth of whiting.
(3) Other small fish, such as trout, tormy etc., may be prepared in the same manner.

'En Lorgnette' Whiting (Figure 22)
(1) Clean and skin whiting, as described.
(2) Remove backbone, leaving fillets attached to head.
(3) Season, flour, eggwash and crumb fillets.
(4) Now roll each fillet towards head – the two fillets representing the glasses of a pince-nez, the head, the handle.
(5) Other small fishes may be prepared in the same way.
(6) At times the skin may be left attached to fillets for easier rolling and preparation.

'En Tresse' Fillet of Sole (Figure 22)
(1) Fillet sole in the normal way.
(2) Cut each fillet into three strips, leaving them attached on one end.
(3) Now plait the three strips into a neat plait.
(4) Season, flour, eggwash, breadcrumb.
(5) Other small fish fillets may be prepared in the same way.
(6) Occasionally the plaits may not be crumbed but left in a natural state for poaching.

Grilling
Usually, small fish, cuts and fillets are cleaned in the normal way. If small fish, the head is removed, or at least the eyes removed from eye sockets. In the case of flat fish, the white skin does not have to be removed. Thus

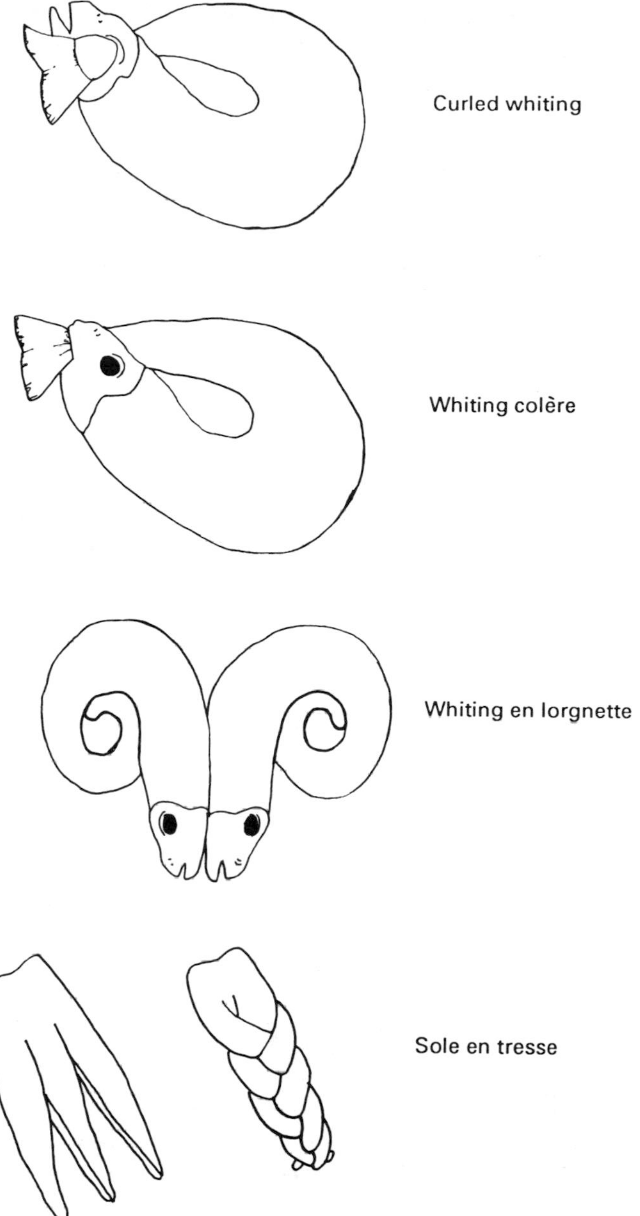

FIG. 22. *Fish preparation styles*

prepared, the small fish, cut or fillet is seasoned, floured and brushed with oil. To avoid the bending of small fish, i.e. trout and herring, two to three cuts may be made into the skin.

'St. Germain'

Usually, small skinned fish, cuts and fillets. These are seasoned, floured, dipped in melted butter and breadcrumbs, placed on a tray for cooking under salamander. Fishes prepared *St. Germain* can be marinaded before preparation.

Deep Frying

Á la Française. Usually fillets and cuts of fish, but also small whole fish, in particular whitebait. (1) Season fish well, leave for a while. (2) Pass through flour, milk and flour again. (3) This is usually done in the kitchen just before frying *à la française*, as any fish thus prepared will very quickly get wet and sticky.

Á l'Orly. Usually cuts and fillets of fish free of skin and bones. This means cooking in a batter which is prepared in the kitchen. As far as larder preparation goes, the fish is marinaded some time before cooking.

Á l'Anglaise. Uusually cuts and fillets of fish free from skin and bones. These are washed and dried, well seasoned, eggwashed and breadcrumbed with white breadcrumbs.

FISH MARINADE

(Sufficient 10-12 Portions.)

$\frac{1}{8}$ l. ($\frac{1}{4}$ pint) oil
$\frac{1}{8}$ l. ($\frac{1}{4}$ pint) white wine, dry
2 bay leaves
1 sprig each of parsley and thyme
Juice of half a lemon
Pinch of salt
Pinch of white pepper

Mix all ingredients; pour over fish to marinade for from 30 to 60 minutes before cooking.

FISH FRYING BATTER

(1) Yeast Batter

250 g (8 oz) flour
$\frac{1}{4}$ l. ($\frac{1}{2}$ pint) of milk or water, or both
15 g ($\frac{1}{2}$ oz) yeast
Pinch of salt

(1) Sift flour, place in basin with salt. (2) Dissolve the yeast in liquid. (3) Gradually add to flour, mixing into a smooth paste. (4) Leave in warm place to yeast for at least one hour before use.

(2) Egg Batter

250 *g* (8 *oz*) *flour*	2 *whites of eggs*
$\frac{1}{4}$ *l.* ($\frac{1}{2}$ *pint*) *of milk or water, or both*	1 *teaspoon of oil*
1 *yolk of egg*	*Pinch of salt*

(1) Mix sifted flour and liquid to a smooth paste. (2) Add yolk, oil and salt, mix well. (3) Beat the two egg whites until mixture is very stiff. (4) Gently fold under mixture. (5) This batter can be used straight away.

(3) Beer Batter

250 *g* (8 *oz*) *flour*	1 *egg*
$\frac{1}{4}$ *l.* ($\frac{1}{2}$ *pint*) *light ale or lager*	*Pinch of salt*

(1) Mix sifted flour and salt. (2) Gradually mix to a smooth paste. (3) Add whole egg, mix well in. (4) Leave in a warm place for from 30 to 60 minutes before use.

SHELLFISH – CRUSTACEA

Shrimps – Les Crevettes

Greyish-green with brown spots, found in shallow water around Britain's coast; to be cooked 3 to 5 minutes in salted water; pinky-brown in colour when cooked (Figure 23).

Prawns – Les Crevettes Roses

Pinkish in colour, 5–10 cm (2–4 in.) long with a toothed snout projecting over the front of the body. Found around the northern coast of Britain and imported in fairly large quantities from the Scandinavian countries. To be cooked in salted water 8–10 min; when cooked bright pink to red in colour, therefore called *rose* in French (Figure 23).

Dublin Bay Prawns – Les Langoustines

These prawns are also known as *scampi* (Italian), 'Mediterranean' or 'Norway Lobster', which gives at the same time some indication where they are found in Europe. They are approximately 8–15 cm (4–6 in.) long (similar to a small lobster). Its claws, however, are empty and only the tail-flesh is eaten. They should be cooked in a court bouillon 8–10 min with the addition of wine to taste (Figure 23).

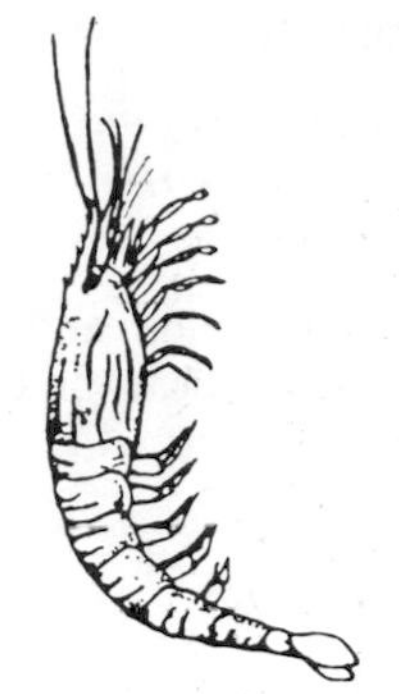

FIG. 23. *The prawn family*

Crayfish – Les Écrevisses

This is a long-tailed fresh-water crustacea, allied to lobster, found in certain rivers and inland lakes, but water pollution has done much damage and they are very scarce. Up to 12-15 cm (6 in.) long, they are at best eaten cooked in a court bouillon with wine about 8 to 10 min (Figure 24).

Lobsters – Les Homards

Black, with grey-green spots, long-tailed 10-legged sea shellfish with two fully fleshed claws of different size. Cook in a court bouillon 15 min $\frac{1}{2}$ kg (per lb). At best eaten fresh as salad or mayonnaise (Figure 25).

FIG. 24. *Crayfish* FIG. 26. *The crab* FIG. 27. *Dressed crab*

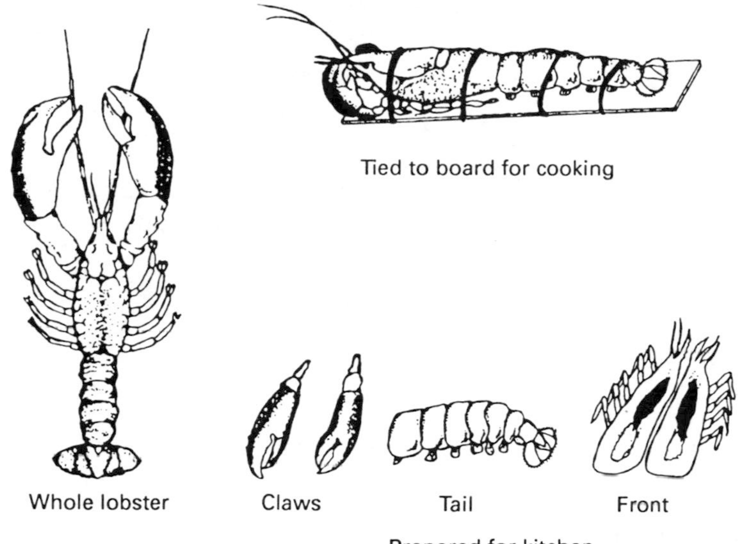

FIG. 25. *Lobster preparation*

Crawfish – Les Langoustes

Black-green to grey in colour, this shellfish has no claws, a very spiny body, cooked in a court bouillon 15 min $\frac{1}{2}$ kg (per lb). Most recipes given for lobster are suitable also for langouste (Figure 110).

Crab – Les Crabes

Light brown in colour, 10-legged and tail tucked under body. First 2 limbs represent 2 small claws; cooked in a court bouillon 15 min $\frac{1}{2}$ kg (per lb). Used for dressed crab, crab salad and mayonnaise (Figures 26 and 27).

Oysters – Les Huîtres

Best eaten raw, fresh from the sea; can be poached in own juice with little lemon juice 8–10 min (Figure 28). There are various types of oysters, at best from September to May, and differentiation is made between the wild and the cultivated oysters. The best known sold in England are Whitstable, Colchester and Helford.

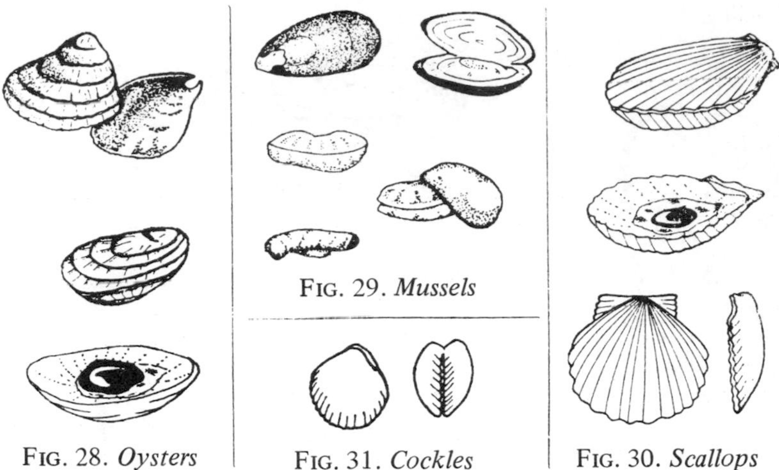
FIG. 28. *Oysters* FIG. 29. *Mussels* FIG. 31. *Cockles* FIG. 30. *Scallops*

Mussels – Les Moules

Found in both salt and fresh water, of bluish-black colour, an oblong shape about the size of a penny; must be cleaned very well with a hard brush before steaming or cooking in their own liquor with some aromates and lemon juice. Eaten as Hors d'Œuvres, used for salads and soups, and found in several fish-garnishes (Figure 29).

Scallops – Les Coquilles St. Jacques

A shell, light brown in colour, nearly twice as large as the oyster (Figure 30). Remove shell by putting scallop on hot stove; this will relax the muscle and the shell is easy to open. Blanch for 8–10 min in salted water, together with some lemon juice. Often the shell is used to serve the scallop, hot or cold.

FIG. 32. *Edible snail* FIG. 33. *Winkles*

Cockles – Les Clovisses

Black to brown in colour, found at most places around the coast of Britain in shallow sandy waters. Boiled in salt water 8–10 min (Figure 31).

Snails – Les Escargots

Edible land-snail of the gastropod family; usually found where vines grow; at present cultivated in special farms (Figure 32). When large enough, the snail is starved for a few days, then fed on flour to clear its intestines. Then the snail is scraped of its chalky substance and soaked in cold water with kitchen-salt, vinegar and flour; washed in plenty of water, blanched in water, drained and cooled under running water to remove its slime, and removed from its shell. The end of the tail, called cloaca, is removed and now the snail is ready for normal use; to be poached in a wine *Court Bouillon*, or canned and with its clean shell packed and sold for further use. When bought like this, the tin is opened, the snails with their liquid are heated, put into the shells and closed with a snail butter.

Snail Butter (for one dozen snails):

100 g (4 oz) butter
25 g (1 oz) finely chopped shallots
15 g ($\frac{1}{2}$ oz) finely chopped parsley
1 garlic clove, crushed
Salt and pepper to taste

Mix all ingredients to a smooth paste. Leave to rest for 30 min. Then close the snail shell with their butter.

Place snails on a snail-plate or on a silver flat with a layer of salt, so that the snail will stand. Cook in a hot oven or under the salamander.

There are, of course, many more ways of cooking and preparing snails but the above is the most commonly used, and the basic method of preparing snail is the same for all other recipes.

Frog (Legs) – Les Grenouilles

The green or common frog which is found in France is used for this delicacy; only the legs are used, which are removed from the body and skinned. Remove the feet and immerse the frog-legs in cold running water to whiten and swell the flesh. When the flesh is nice and white, dry the legs and they are now ready for use, *à l'anglaise* and *meunière* and many other ways. In England, frog-legs are usually bought frozen or canned.

Clams – Les Palourdes

A name applied to several edible bivalve molluscs known in some parts of France as *clovisses*. Fresh clams are eaten in the same raw state as oysters but other recipes given for oysters can also be applied to the clam.

The North American peoples are very fond of this mollusc. They are cultivated in France, where Auray and Roscoff are the main centres for clams.

Winkles – Les Bigorneaux

These are also known as periwinkle; found off the northern coast of England and Ireland (Figure 33). Dark to light brown in colour, they are cooked for 8-10 min in salted water and often eaten and used very much like mussels.

FROZEN FISH

Because of different and further afield fishing-grounds, as well as new fishing regulations, we sadly have to accept more and more of all kinds of fish frozen These come to us usually in two types:

(1) *Block Frozen Fish.* As the term implies, these are blocks of fish such as Cod, Haddock, Plaice, Lemon Sole etc., which are filleted but not always skinned and are frozen at sea in factory ships in blocks approximately 7 lb (3 kg) 14 lb (7.5 kg), 28 lb (15 kg) 56 lb (25 kg), the disadvantage of these block frozen fish is that the whole block must be defrosted to get at individual fillets or portions and then used within one or two days to ensure their freshness. Naturally such types of frozen fish are, therefore, only suitable for large establishments which can use large amounts of fish in a short space of time.

(2) *Free Flow Frozen Fish.* These, as the term implies, are fillets and portions of fish which have been frozen individually in a free flow freezer, and which, thereafter, are packed individually in plastic bags and carton boxes. Available again are fishes such as Cod, Haddock, Plaice, Lemon Sole etc. in fillets, portion or steaks, as well as certain shellfish such as Shrimps, Prawns, Mussells Scallops, always without shells. The advantage of this type of free flow fish is that one is able to provide individual portions or amounts for estimated daily consumption keeping the rest frozen for further use when required.

All frozen fish should be defrosted slowly, preferably in a fridge overnight, and never placed in water as this will even further impair the flavour of the fish, already lessened by the freezing process. When the fish is defrosted preferably on a colander to allow water to drain away onto a tray. The fish portions should then be dried on a clean kitchen-cloth or kitchen-paper to eliminate excess water.

The flavour and appearance of fish which is intended for grilling, deep or shallow frying can be much improved by allowing portions to soak in fish marinade (see page 104). Even prawns intended for prawn cocktail will benefit by this treatment. Free flow fish and shellfish are available in approximately 1 lb (500 g) 2 lb (1000 g) 7 lb (3 kg) 14 lb (7.5 kg) packs.

4. Poultry and Game

Present breeds of fowl originate from wild or jungle birds and there is evidence that the prevalence of cock fighting in the past contributed to the various breeds and their general distribution.

Breeders invariably take into account the qualities best suited to their requirements or market. Although there are many dual purpose breeds, in the main they seek either egg production or meat bearing types. Modern methods of poultry rearing have revolutionized the market and, all too often, weight and tender flesh are sought at the expense of flavour.

Some of the better known breeds of table birds are:

Chicken: Sussex, Old English Game, Indian Game, Dorking, Bresse, Courtes Pattes, Creve Coeur, La Fleche, etc.

Turkeys: Norfolk, Cambridgeshire, Devon, Scotland and Ireland, and America.

Ducks: Aylesbury, Peking, White Campbell, Stanbridge White, Rouen, Nantes, Huttegem, Blue Swedish, Merchtem, etc.

Geese: Emden, Toulouse, Roman, Chinese-White, Strasbourg.

POULTRY

AGE

A pliable breast-bone is probably the best indication when choosing young birds. Other indications are: pliable beak, smooth feet with slender claws, light comb, flight muscles undeveloped.

Old birds will have a hard, brittle breast-bone and beak, feet and legs scaly with strong claws and long spurs and well developed flight muscles. The flesh too will be much darker and the legs hairy.

QUALITY

The following points are the best indication:

(1) Flesh firm but pliable, with a fine texture.

(2) Not too much fat, especially in abdominal cavity.

(3) White or yellow skin, according to breed.

(4) No cuts, scores, rubbed portions on skin or blood patches.

(5) The breast should be straight, broad and well fleshed.

(6) Wings compact, small head, with neat comb and wattles.
(7) The bones fine, legs short and well fleshed.

MARKET TYPES

The term 'Poultry' (*Volaille*) applies in general to all domesticated birds, whether bred for table purposes, or for their eggs. Under this heading, the accompanying Table gives a useful list.

Market Types of Poultry

	English	*French*	*Average weight*	*Average age*
1.	Poussin	Le Poussin	250–300 g (8–10 oz)	4–6 weeks
2.	Cockerel	Le Jeune Coq	350–600 g (10–18 oz)	6–8 weeks
3.	Young Chicken	Le Poulet de Grain	1–1¼ kg (2–2½ lb)	8–12 weeks
4.	Chicken	Le Poulet Reine	1–2 kg (3–4 lb)	4–6 months
5.	Boiling Fowl	La Poule	2–3 kg (4–6 lb)	12 months
6.	Young Fat Chicken	La Poulardine	1–1½ kg (2–3 lb)	4–6 months
7.	Capon*	Le Chapon	2–4 kg (5–8 lb)	5–8 months
8.	Fat Chicken*	La Poularde	2–4 kg (4–8 lb)	5–6 months
9.	Turkey Cock	Le Dindon	6–12 kg (12–24 lb)	6–10 months
10.	Turkey Hen	La Dinde	4–7 kg (8–14 lb)	6–10 months
11.	Young Turkey	Le Dindonneau	3–4 kg (6–8 lb)	5–6 months
12.	Guinea Fowl	La Pintade	¾–1½ kg (1½–2½ lb)	4–6 months
13.	Duck	Le Canard	2–3 kg (4–6 lb)	3–4 months
14.	Duckling	Le Caneton	1½–2 kg (3–4 lb)	2–3 months
15.	Goose	L'Oie	4–7 kg (8–14 lb)	6–9 months
16.	Gosling	L'Oison	2–3 kg (4–6 lb)	4–6 months
17.	Pigeon	Le Pigeon	300–500 g (12–16 oz)	6–10 weeks

*The Capon and the Fat Chicken (Chapon, Poularde) are desexed birds (castrated cocks and ovariotomized hens).

It will be appreciated that the weights and ages given above are optimum for *fresh, farm* bred and reared poultry and are not necessarily related to the broiler or frozen poultry which is becoming increasingly popular on the market.

PREPARATION, DRESSING, AND CUTS

Killing

Usually carried out by dislocation of the neck. In some cases the jugular vein can be severed from inside the mouth; this method is known as 'sticking', special pliers being used for the purpose. Kosher killing is carried out by cutting the throat from the outside. With the exception of Kosher, the birds are commonly stunned electrically prior to killing.

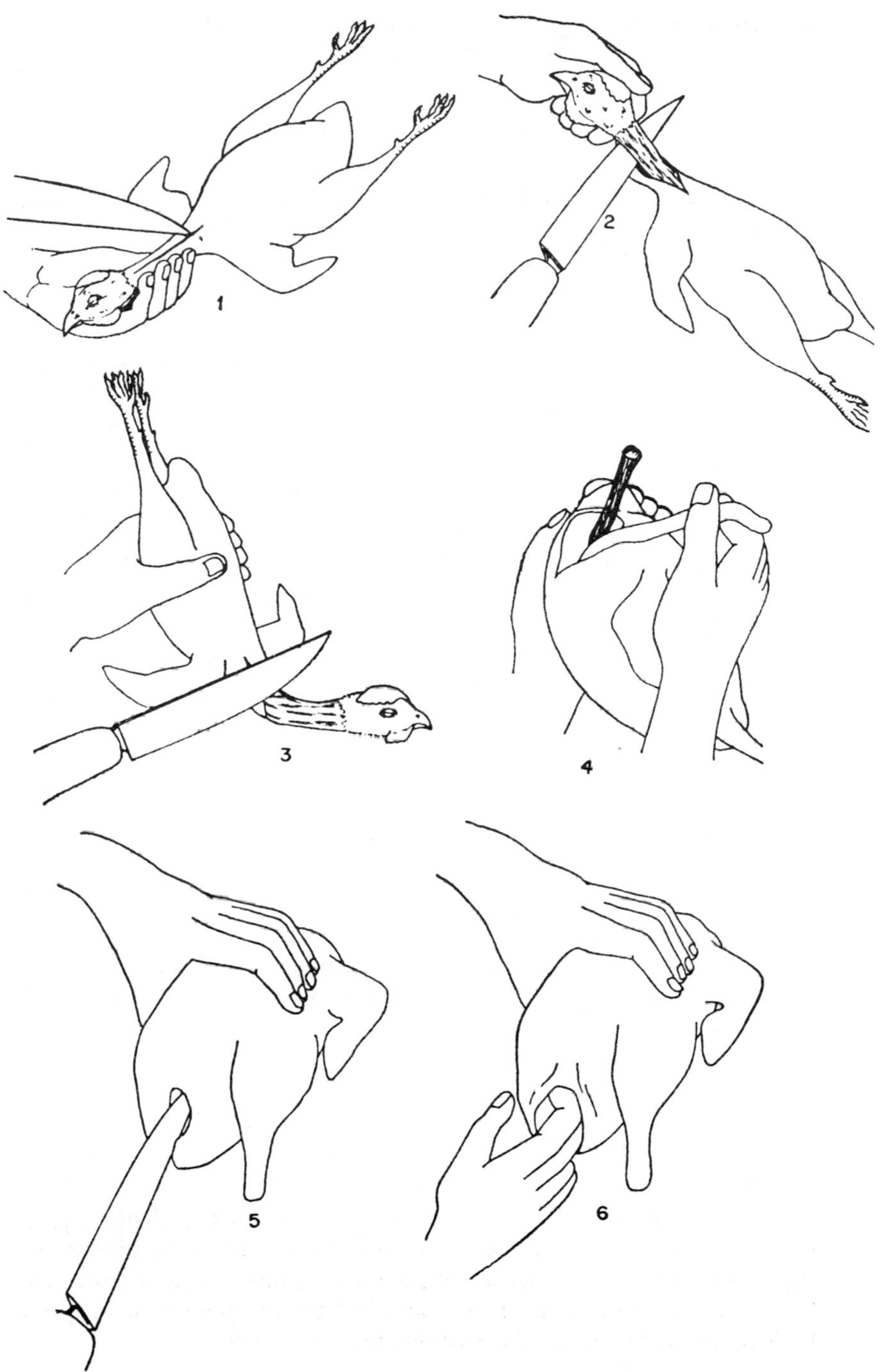
1
2
3
4
5
6

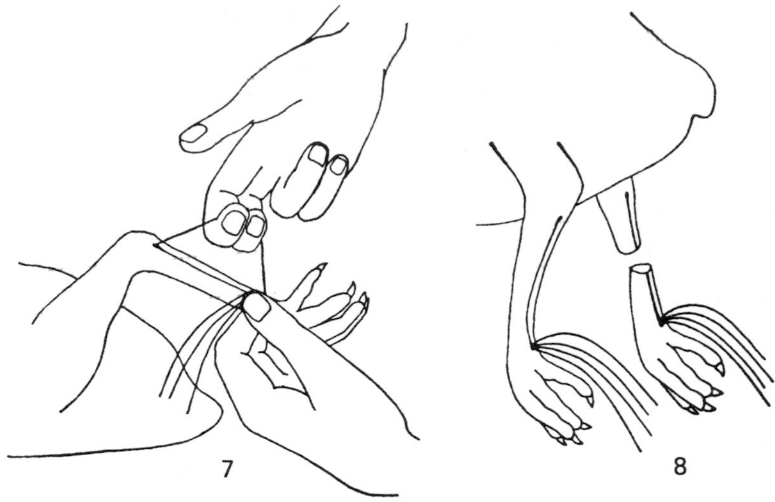

FIG. 34. *Removal of sinews from poultry and game legs*

Plucking

Plucking is normally done immediately after killing. The legs are held firmly and the wings are spread back between the knees. A firm motion, in the direction opposite to which the feathers grow, is used and the breast of the bird plucked first, followed by the back, wings and legs. Care must be taken not to damage the skin. Stub feathers must be removed, using the tip of a small knife for the purpose.

Scald or semi-scald methods can be employed, plunging the bird for periods into water varying in temperature between 60°C to 100°C for up to 18-20 sec or 5 to 6 sec, according to the water temperature.

In this day and age plucking is usually done by machine, either wet or dry, and is very seldom carried out in catering establishments, with the exception perhaps of the occasional pheasant or grouse sent in by one of the guests.

Hanging

The muscles or flesh of poultry will stiffen and toughen as soon as rigor mortis sets in, usually 3 to 4 hours after killing. Following this, tenderizing takes place rather quickly up to 24 hours and this should be the maximum time required to hang any poultry for the purpose of tenderizing.

If the bird is cooked during the onset of the process of stiffening, it results in tough and rubbery flesh.

It is important that fresh killed poultry be cooled as quickly as possible if the birds are to be stored. If left at normal atmospheric temperature for 2 days or more, 'off' flavours will develop very quickly and greening will appear at the vent and in the region of the kidneys. Seepage from the gall bladder will likewise spoil the liver. Stored at between 3 to 5°C, poultry should keep in good condition if undrawn. At 0–1°C it will keep for a week or so.

Singeing

Hold the bird by the head and feet, stretch it well and pass it over a gas jet quickly. Turn it around, so that every part is properly singed, including the underparts of the wings. Take care not to scorch the skin. Scorch the feet over the flame to enable the scales to be wiped off with a cloth. Shorten the toes and cut off any spurs.

Cleaning (Figures 34 and 35)

Place the bird on its side, hold the neck firmly in left hand, keeping the skin tight (1). Make a cut along the back of the neck, towards the body (2). Leave plenty of skin to cover exposed neck and cut off the head (3). Remove the neck close to the body. Hold the skin of the neck in the fingers of the left hand (4) and strip out the gullet, crop and windpipe with the right hand (5). Insert the second or third finger of the right hand into the chest cavity and with a rotary movement gently break all attachments and free organs from ribs, particularly lungs (6). Place the bird on its back, pinch the skin just above the vent between thumb and forefinger of left

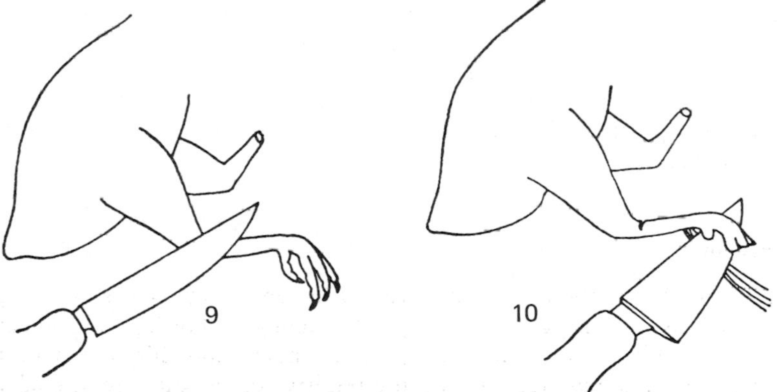

FIG. 35. *Preparation and cleaning of poultry.*

hand and cut out the vent, taking care not to puncture intestines or to cut off the parson's nose. Now insert two fingers into the body cavity and first remove any fat from around the vent opening, taking care to avoid enlarging the opening. Then, with one hand on either side of the bird, close the legs and press firmly to force the gizzard and entrail from the vent opening. Grip the gizzard with the fingers of the right hand and with firm pressure, withdraw all entrails, including heart, liver, lungs etc., in one operation (Figure 36). Now feel to ensure that nothing has been left in the front or back parts of the body and remove any fat or gut which may be adhering to the parson's nose. Finally, wipe out with a clean cloth. Set all edible offal on a clean tray, carefully pinch out the gall bladder (a green sac) from the liver without breaking it, remove fat from around the gizzard, cut through the curved edge, split the gizzard and remove the inner bag. Dispose of all inedible entrail and clean down the board or bench.

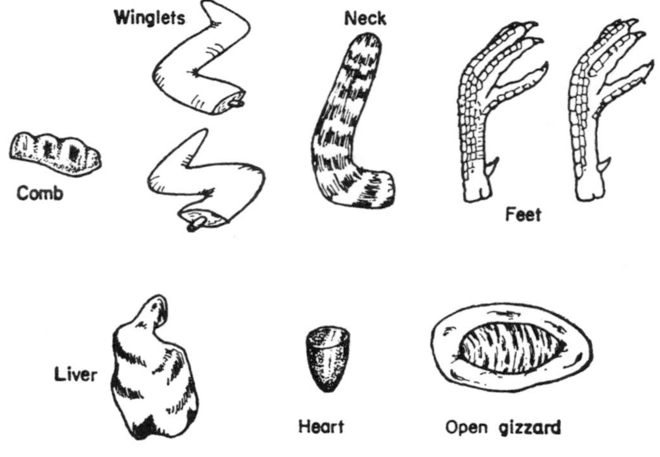

FIG. 36. *Entrails*

Trussing (Figure 37)

Remove wishbone; this greatly assists the carving of the bird, particularly if it is stuffed. To do this, scrape the bone lightly with the tip of a small knife, then slip the point of the knife under the bone on one side, push the knife down and cut the sinew, which holds it to the carcass. Repeat on the other side. Now hold both ends with the fingers and turn the bone over to release it from the middle of the breast, without breaking the bone. Use the point of the small knife to free it from the breast, without damaging the flesh.

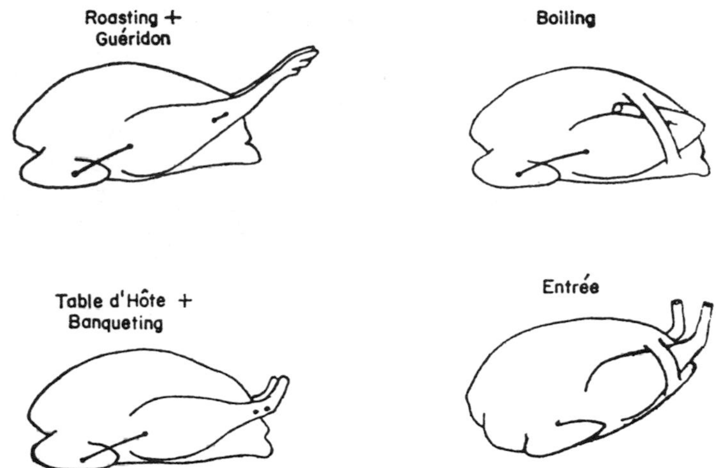

FIG. 37. *Trussed poultry*

To Truss for Roasting
Cut off tips of wings and trim bony spur from the sides. Cut off toes, except middle one which should be shortened. Cut off spurs. From abdominal cavity loosen skin covering the legs. Break the backbone in the region of the wings, with a smart tap with the back of a knife so that the bird will lie flat on the board or dish. Now place the bird on its back, raise the legs and press them down towards the front. Hold them in position with thumb and middle fingers of the left hand. Use a 16–20 cm (8–10 in.) trussing needle threaded with string, and push the needle immediately behind the legs at the hinge between drumstick and thigh, through the body and out the other side in the same position. Turn the bird on its side and pass the needle through the middle portion of the wing, draw the skin of the neck over the back to close the aperture, pass the needle through the skin and the middle of the backbone, then through the middle portion of the opposite aileron. Thus, the string has passed through the body, behind the legs, through the wings and under the back. The two ends of string can now be tied firmly together, bringing the wings close to the back and snugly into the sides.

Next pass the needle with a second string through the natural cavity in the thigh bone, through the carcass from one side to the other, then over the folded leg between the skin, through the end of the body without touching the breast, then through the skin of the opposite leg. Tie the ends firmly just below the hock. The parson's nose can now be pressed into the body cavity and the aperture closed with loose skin from the tip of the breast.

To Truss for Entree or Boiling

Cut off all claws and spurs, and remove wishbone. Hold up one leg with the left hand and cut into the hock on the underside of the leg about 1 in. above the joint with the leg. Cut down as far as the bone to ensure all sinews have been severed. Cut the sinews at the hinge, between leg and hock (drumstick). Now pass the forefinger through the vent opening until it reaches the thigh; pass in between skin and flesh until it emerges from the cut at the hock. Bend the finger and pull the skin down. Now, holding the feet of the bird with the left hand, push the leg forward and bring it back folded, inside the cut which is held open with the finger of the right hand. Cover the leg with the loose skin. Repeat with the other leg and then truss the bird, as for roasting. The wings may either be folded or the ailerons cut off at the first joint and used for other purposes.

For Grilling (Figure 38)

Prepare the chicken as for entree. Do not truss. Split the bird down the back along the backbone with a large poultry knife, passing the knife through the body with the bird on its back on a chopping board from neck to parson's nose. Flatten well with a cutlet bat, remove ribs, trim the backbone and place neatly on a clean tray. The bird can be marinaded in an instantaneous marinade (salt, pepper from mill, oil, lemon juice, thyme, bay leaf, parsley stalks) prior to grilling.

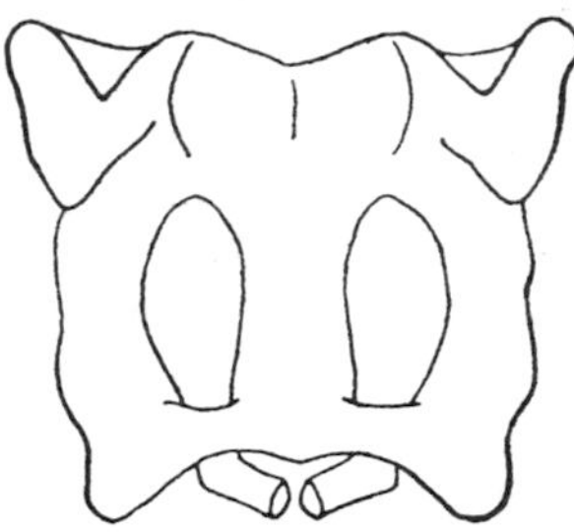

FIG. 38. *Prepared for grilling*

For Sauté (Figure 39)

Clean and singe the bird, and remove the wishbone, as above. Remove the legs from the carcass. With the blade of a large poultry knife, cut through the skin between thigh and body till the joint socket is reached. Pull the leg outwards and with the point of the knife cut through the connecting sinew along the fleshy part between sockets and parson's nose. Remove the whole leg and trim. Cut the feet off just below the joint with the hock and separate drumstick and thigh at the natural joint. Cut off the ailerons at the first joint of the wing and trim.

Remove the wings, cutting through the joint close to the body and along the breast. Remove the breast from the carcass and trim, then cut crosswise into two equal parts. Trim the carcass and cut into 3 parts, one with the blade bones of the bird, one with the oysters (two bone cavities at back of bird), and one with the parson's nose. You should now have: 2 wings, 2 pieces of breast, 2 ailerons, 2 drumsticks, 2 thighs and three sections of carcass.

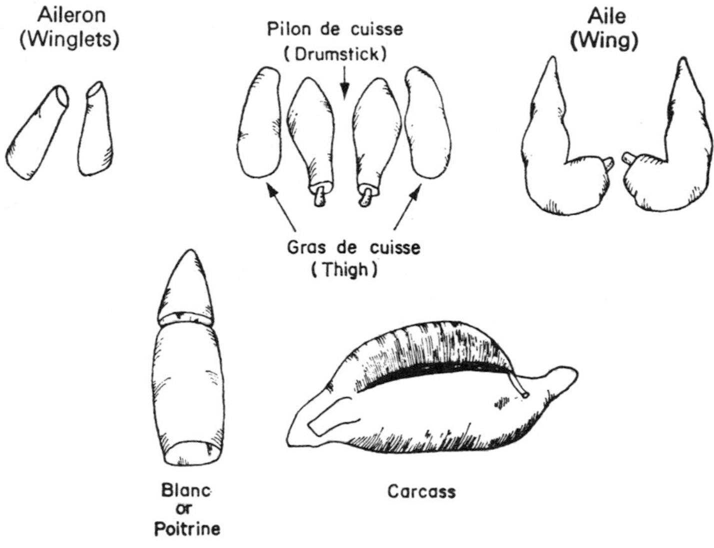

FIG. 39. *Cutting chicken for sauté*

Boning Out for Galantines etc.

For this purpose it is necessary to remove the skeleton of the bird completely. Although it can be accomplished without cutting the skin, it is more commonly carried out as follows:

Singe and draw the bird as usual, keeping the opening of the vent as small as possible. Cut off the winglets (ailerons) and feet just below the hock joint. Make a cut along the centre of the back of the bird from neck to tail. Carefully remove the flesh over the back, lifting it off the bones with the thumb and forefinger of the left hand and using the tip of a small knife to scrape the flesh off the bone where necessary.

On reaching the wings and thighs, find the joints and cut through the ligaments to detach them from the carcass. Continue towards the breast, carefully trimming away the fillets from the breast-bone. *Remember, the skin over the ridge of the breast-bone is very thin and there is no flesh under it*. Use the fingertips or the handle of a small spoon to raise the skin without tearing or perforating it. The thighs and drumsticks can now be boned out, leaving the knuckle of the hock attached to the skin to contain the stuffing. Bone out the wing, channelling the bone from the winglet; stuff the bird as required; sew up the back, shape and truss.

Suprême (Breast and Wing, Fillet of Chicken) (Figure 40)

Remove legs as for sauté. Leave them whole and set aside for other uses. Skin the breast and remove wishbone. With a filleting knife, make an incision along the breast-bone from end to end, either side of the ridge. Detach the flesh from the bone, carefully starting at the pointed end, and following the breast-bone closely, until the wing joint is reached. Cut through the joint and remove the wing/breast with the wingbone attached. Place the Suprême with the inside uppermost on a board. Lift off the under fillet and scrape off the sinew running through it with the tip of a knife. Make an incision lengthwise along the thick part of the wing to form a pocket. Place in the under fillet, close the pocket, bat out lightly with a wet cutlet bat to fuse the two together. Trim any skin or sinew from the Suprême, cut the winglet off at the joint with the aileron and clear the bone by pushing the flesh back towards the breast. Shape and use as required.

FIG. 40. *Cutting chicken suprêmes*

Ballotine (Figure 41)

These are small galantines made from the legs of chicken. After removing the leg from the carcass, remove the skin from the leg carefully to avoid tearing the skin. Leave the knuckle and approximately 2 cm (1 in.) of hock bone attached to the skin. With the flesh of the leg make a forcemeat. Refill the skin with the forcemeat, sew up the opening and shape like a small ham. These can now be poached or braised, for serving hot or cold.

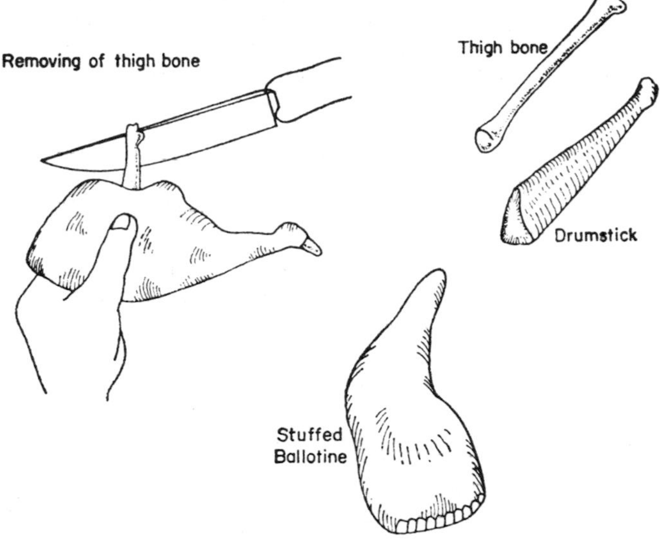

FIG. 41. *Ballotine*

Turkey Preparation

These are usually delivered with some feathers on the neck and wings. Pluck carefully and remove fine feathers as for chicken. Singe and draw the sinews from the legs. This operation is essential as the sinews will spoil the flesh of the legs and make it impossible to carve them. Cut the skin all round, just above the feet, break the bone, twist the foot, place it in a sinew hook and pull steadily on the leg, pulling all sinews out, attached to the foot (Figure 35). Trim tips of wings and clean and dress the same way as chicken.

Note that for larger birds a hook attached to the wall may be used.

Ducks and Ducklings

Ducklings should reach the market at between 8 and 9 weeks old and before developing any adult feathers. Fatness can be tested by pinching the flesh along the side of the breast, just behind the legs. In young birds the breast will be pliable, the feet soft and small and the underside of the wings downy. Soft flexible quills with a decided point are also a good indicator. The older the bird, the more rounded the tips. Cleaning and dressing etc. is carried out as for chicken.

Geese

To test the age of geese, press the windpipe where it enters the body. In young birds it should be yielding and pliable. In older birds, well developed wing muscles and a strong beak are evident. Treat as for chicken.

Guinea Fowl and Pigeon

These are judged and treated much the same as all other poultry.

GAME – LE GIBIER

The French word *gibier* applies to all animals being hunted and eaten. It is derived from the verb *gibercer* which means 'to hunt'.

In the old days on the great estates a day of hunting was a day of joy and feasting. As the evening drew to a close the beaters and hunters carried the game home on their backs – the small feathered game in strings around their necks, the heavier furred game over their shoulders with the two fore and hind legs firmly held in each hand. This made them appear like hunchbacks, relating to the Latin word *gibbosus* ('hunchback') from which the French perhaps derived their word for hunting.

The gourmet considers game an excellent food – warming and healthy and fit for the most delicate palates. In the hands of an experienced chef, game properly hung and prepared will give dishes of the highest quality and allows variations in one's daily menus.

There are two basic types of Game: (a) *le gibier à poil* (furred game); (b) *le gibier à plumage* (feathered game).

FURRED GAME: PREPARATION, DRESSING, AND CUTS

Although varied in kind and large in numbers, these are the most common of furred game of Central Europe:
la chevrette (deer or doe), *le cerf* (Young deer or stag), *le chevreuil* (roebuck), *la biche* (hind), *le chamois* (chamois or mountain goat), *le renne* (reindeer), *le sanglier* (wild boar), *le marcassin* (young wild boar), *le levraut* (young hare), *le lièvre* (hare), *le lapin* (rabbit), *le lapin de garenne* (wild rabbit)

Hoofed game is at its best at the age of 4 to 5 years; the fat should be bright and clear and the cleft of the hoof smooth and closed. The larger furred game like stag and roebuck are usually supplied skinned but, for those who receive their game directly from the hunter, the illustration (Figure 42) shows how to remove the skin reasonably easily.

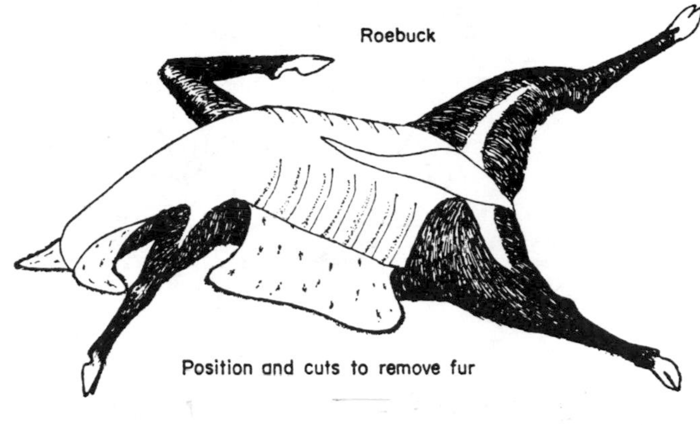

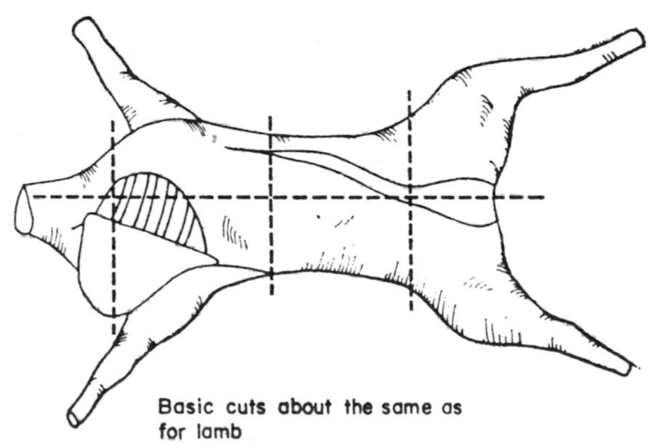

FIG. 42. *Preparation of larger furred game*

Once the skin is removed, the game should be rubbed with a mixture of salt, flour and crushed black pepper. Hang up to dry in a cool, well ventilated room, where it should be allowed to tenderize and to develop a good gamey flavour, for up to 3 weeks. As game is mostly in season in the cold winter months, this should present no great difficulties.

All furred game should, after hanging, be marinaded, usually from between 12 to 24 hours according to the type of game and size of joint. Marinading will much improve and bring out the characteristic flavour of the game. Game too is invariably a very lean meat and it is advisable to lard or even barder the joints for roasting or braising (Figure 43).

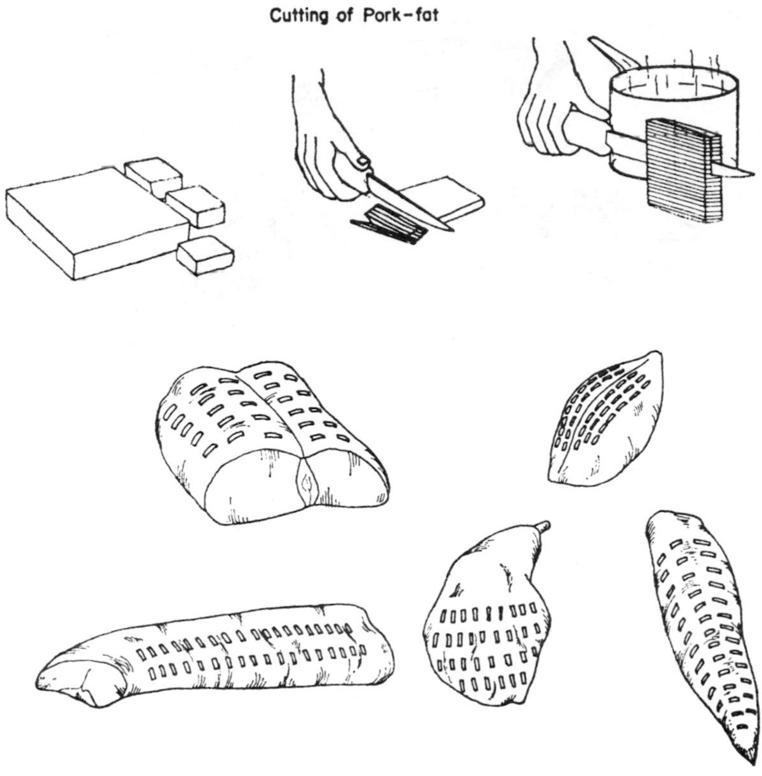

FIG. 43. *Larding of different joints of furred game and game birds*

Venison

This name is applied to all horned furred game, e.g. roebuck, stag, deer. Venison is dissected very much like a carcass of lamb except that no best end is cut but one retains what is called a 'long saddle'.

A carcass of venison, therefore, falls into the following basic cuts (Figure 44): Long Saddle (*la selle de chevreuil*), Legs (Haunch) (*le gigot de chevreuil*), Shoulders (*l'épaule de chevreuil*). Neck, breast as well as trimmings are usually removed from the bone and used in the making of game stews (ragoûts). Game farces, patés and terrines are other good uses for these secondary cuts.

Wild Boar

To be dissected very much like a carcass of pork. Instructions given for pork can be followed.

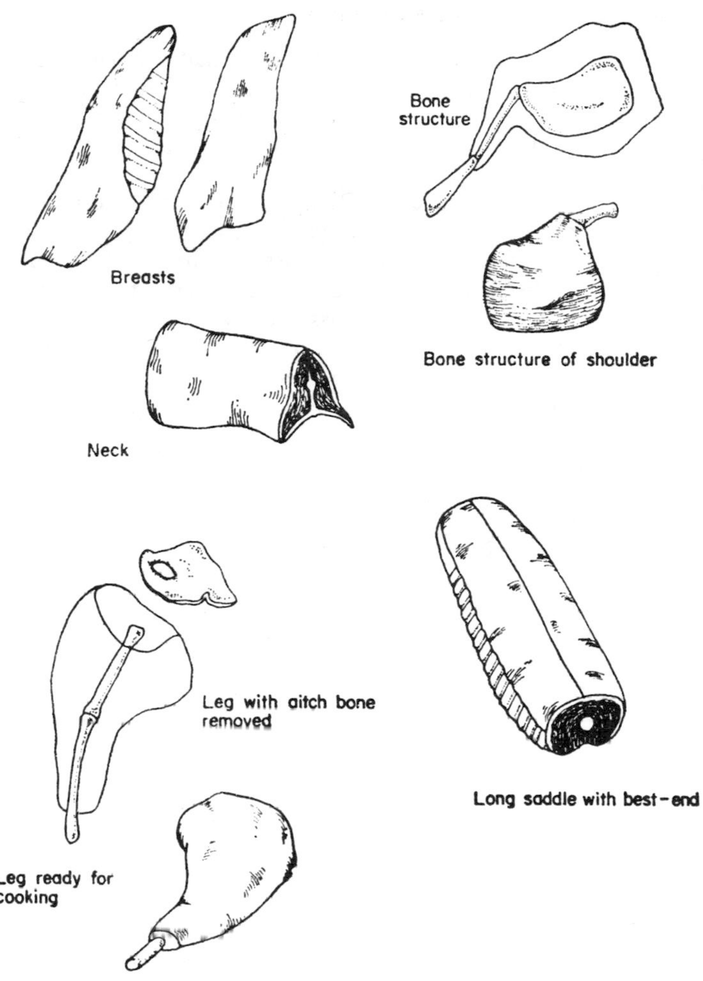

FIG. 44. *Basic cuts of venison*

Hares (August to March)

These have very tender ears, tear easily, have short, easily broken claws; harelip only faintly defined; best at the age of 7 to 8 months and weighing then about $2\frac{1}{2}$–3 kg (5 to 6 lb). Hang by its foreleg for about a week to collect the blood, which is used in the making of sauces and of course jugged hare. Young hares are best used for roasting, frying sauté, and poêlé as well as for the making of pies and casseroles. Older hares are best used for jugged hare, pies, terrines, mousse and soups.

Wild Rabbits (August to March)

These are best at 3 to 4 months old. They are smaller than hare and tame rabbit; under-jaw tender and very easily broken; very short neck and large joints; paws well developed in proportion to size. Hang by its forelegs for 1 week. Rabbit's flesh is often flavoured by wild thyme on which it feeds.

(1) Hang hare or rabbit from two hooks, one through each leg sinew and spreading legs apart (Figure 45). Make an incision upwards on the inside of one of the legs, cut around the paws and draw each leg out of the skin. Cut through the tail and draw the skin downwards, towards the head, using the tip of the knife to cut the tissue between skin and flesh. At the forelegs, loosen skin around the shoulder blades, cut around the front paws and continue to draw the skin over the head. Cut through the ears and take care to trim the skin off the head, making use of the tip of the knife.

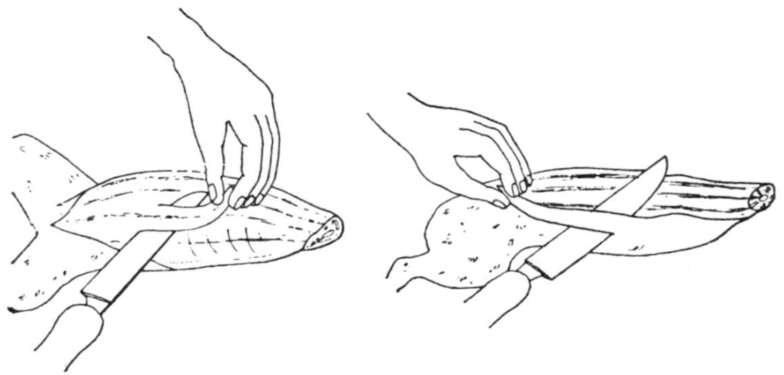

FIG. 45. *Trimming the back sinew of hares and rabbits*

(2) Make an incision from vent to ribs along the middle of the belly, inserting middle and index finger into the cut and cutting between them, so as not to perforate the intestines. Split the pelvic bone and remove intestines which are disposed of. Next, break through the skin of diaphragm, separating belly from the organs, lift out the lungs, liver and heart and place in a bowl together with the blood which will run from the cavity. A few drops of vinegar will keep the blood fluid till required.

(3) Hare and rabbits are jointed into: (a) Legs (*Cuisses*), (b) Saddle (the whole back, excluding scrag end – *Râble*). The shoulders, middle neck, and neck are fit for stewing only and are used for Jugged Hare (*Civet de Lièvre*), as are also the legs if not required for sauté or casserole. The head, breast and any trimmings or bones are used for game stocks, or soups.

FEATHERED GAME: PREPARATION, DRESSING, AND CUTS

The seasons listed below are when the game birds are at their best or allowed to be shot; with modern deep freezing they are often available all the year round.

English	*French*	*Season*
Pheasant	*le faisan*	Oct-Dec
Partridge	*la perdrix*	Sept-Oct
Young partridge	*le perdreau*	Sept-Dec
Rock partridge	*la bartavelle*	September
Woodcock	*la bècasse*	Sept-Apl
Snipe	*la bècassine*	Sept-Dec
Hazel hen	*la gelinotte*	Sept-Dec
Mountain cock	*le coq de bruyère*	Sept-Dec
Ptarmigan	*la poule de neige*	December
Grouse	*la grouse*	12 Aug to Dec
Wild duck	*le canard sauvage*	Sept-Dec
Teal	*la sarcelle*	Dec-Jan
Plover	*le pluvier*	Sept-Dec
Lapwing	*le vanneau*	Sept-Dec
Quail	*la caille*	July-Sept
Corncrake	*le râle*	July-Sept
Fieldfare	*la grive*	Sept-Dec
Ortolan	*l'ortolan*	Sept-Dec
Lark	*l'alouette*	Sept-Dec
Guinea fowl	*la pintade*	

Note that guinea fowl originally was a wild bird and it is nowadays bred on special farms. Because of this it is often classified under the Poultry Section.

With all feathered game the flavour will improve by hanging for a few days in a cool, well ventilated place. Care should be taken with waterbirds not to get them too 'high' (a certain smell from hanging). After plucking, game birds are prepared very much like poultry only that, in the case of

FIG. 46. *Snipe trussed with its own beak*

game, larding and barding is more common. Long beaked birds, e.g. Snipe, should not be completely drawn; only the gizzard, the intestines and gall-bladder are removed, from a small opening under the leg. The thighs are pressed close to the body and the long beak is pushed through the leg, serving very much the purpose of a trussing needle and string (Figure 46).

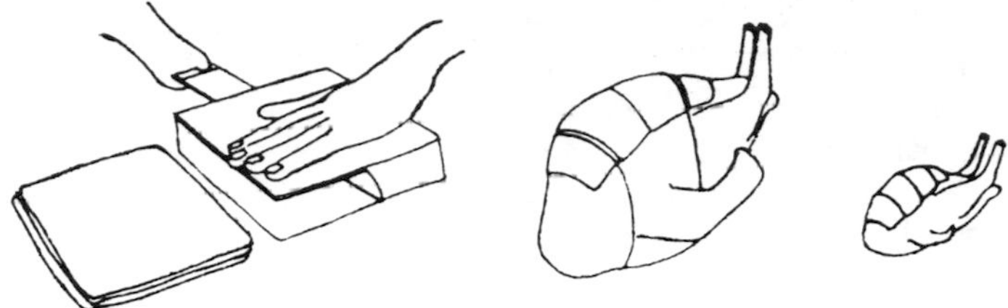

FIG. 47. *Barding of feathered game*

To barder, thin slices of fat pork are used to cover the tender breast of the game, to protect it from over browning, and getting dry in cooking (Figure 47). At times, certain herbs or vine leaves and put between pork fat and breast to give a distinctive flavour. Slices of fat bacon should only

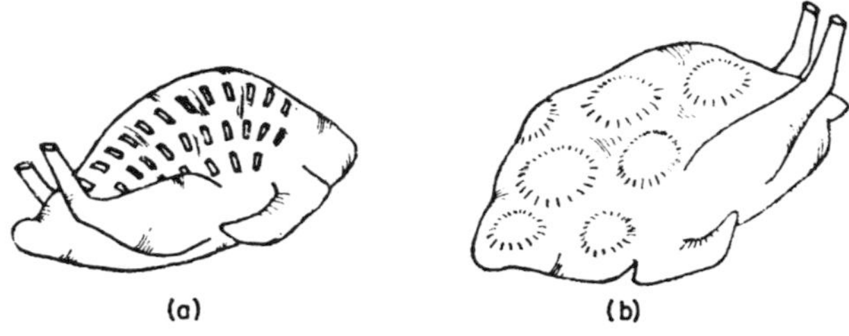

FIG. 48. (a) *Larding game birds* (b) *Slices of truffle placed under the skin*

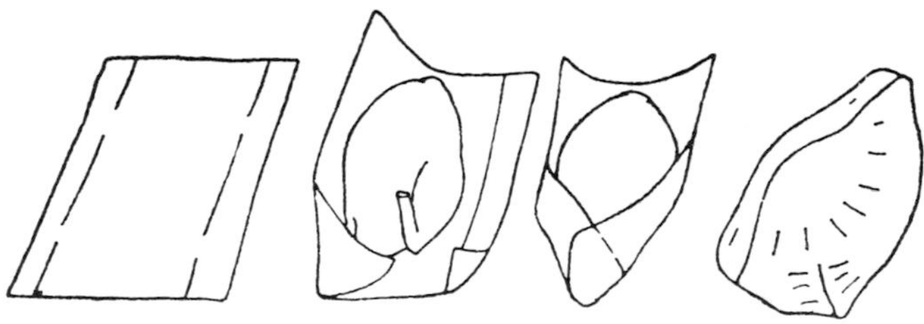

FIG. 49. *Preparation* en papillote

be used if no fat pork is available, as the smoky flavour of bacon can easily impair the characteristic flavour of game.

For larding, thin strips of fat pork are inserted neatly into the tender breast of feathered game (Figure 48(*a*)).

For truffling, thin strips of truffle are inserted into the breast, as with pork fat above, or thin slices of truffles are pushed with the finger under the skin of the bird (Figure 48(*b*)).

The preparation for small game birds *en papillote* is shown in Figure 49.

5. *Butchery*

BUTCHERY SUB-DEPARTMENT

The function of the Butcher in the Garde-Manger (Cold Larder) of a catering establishment is the preparation of all raw meat for the kitchens. This involves the breaking down of wholesale cuts of meat, or carcasses, into joints, steaks and small cuts for entrées, such as stews, pies, minces, escalopes etc., as required for the menus of the day or for banquets.

All preparations requiring raw meat, such as sausages, hamburg steaks, minced shin of beef for clarification etc., are naturally the province of the Butcher. Offal likewise comes into this class.

Unlike the shop butcher who is concerned with selling his meat to his best advantage and, therefore, cannot trim his prime cuts too closely, the Butcher in the catering trade has to prepare and trim each cut carefully so that it should be ready for cooking without further trimming of any kind.

This involves removing all excess fat, all gristle and sinew, and any bones which might interfere with easy carving of the meat when cooked. These by-products should of course be carefully sorted and made use of to their best advantage for stocks, dripping etc., and wastage must be kept to its lowest possible level. Careful storage, and the maintenance of all tools in an efficient condition will contribute to the elimination of waste in this very expensive product.

It follows from the above that the Butcher should be familiar with the various meats, should be able to distinguish quality, should have some knowledge of the bone formation of the carcasses to enable him to dissect efficiently, should know the various cuts of meat or joints and their best utilization, the number of portions obtainable from each and the cost per portion. He must also be familiar with the French names of each cut of meat, joint, entrée or grill.

'Fresh Meat' includes all meat not salted or cooked. It may be fresh, killed, chilled or frozen. No fresh killed meat is imported from the Continent for fear of spreading foot and mouth disease.

Only chilled meat is imported. It is produced chiefly in Argentine and Uruguay. After slaughter the beef is cooled, graded, quartered and sheeted and it is hung during transit in a non-freezing temperature in a sterile refrigeration chamber. It must be sold and used quickly after arrival in port. Storage temperature is $-1°$-$2°$C ($28°$-$30°$F).

Frozen beef is imported from New Zealand, Australia, Argentine, Uruguay, Brazil.

Lamb and mutton come mainly from New Zealand and Australia. After slaughter the carcasses are inspected, graded, stamped and sheeted, frozen solid, packed in layers in store refrigerators and in refrigerated ships at –29°C (–20°F). This enables all the space to be filled and therefore makes for cheaper rates of transport than chilled beef. On arrival at British ports it is kept frozen in cold stores and distributed by insulated rail, road, or barge containers to various parts of the country.

BUTCHERY

Best home-killed beef comes from Scotland, Norfolk and Devon and it is classified as (1) Steer or, (2) Heifer, (3) Cow, (4) Bull. Steer beef is considered best but in some districts heifers are preferred as these are smaller and the bones are lighter. The texture, too, is finer. Cow or bull beef is usually sold to the manufacturing industry.

The above classifications can easily be distinguished by reference to the hindquarters of the carcasses:

(1) Steer will have a curved pubic bone and a relatively narrow pelvic cavity. The cod fat will be heavy.

(2) Heifer will have a flat pubic bone and a relatively wider pelvic cavity. The udder fat will be firm.

(3) Cow pubic bone is flat and light with a wide pelvic cavity.

(4) The bull pubic bone will be large, the pelvic cavity narrow and cod fat almost non-existent.

Carcass quality is judged under three main headings:

(1) *Conformation*. One looks for the best proportion of good joints in relation to bone; rather more important in beef than other animals.

(2) *Finish*. An outer covering of fat, which should be smooth, evenly distributed over the carcass and creamy white in colour.

(3) *Quality*. The texture of the meat which depends on size and development of muscle and amount of connective tissue; marbling and juices or sap should be taken into account.

In principle, the above points apply to all carcass meat, irrespective of which animal they are applied to. With lamb or pork, however, more joints are prepared for cooking on the bone and additional points, such as well-fleshed legs and shoulders as well as loins and ribs, should be sought. Short, thick necks, fine bones, no excess fat and carcasses free from bruises or cuts can also indicate quality.

Quality of beef can be judged by these points:

(1) The meat should be firm and bright red.

(2) It should have a good showing of dots or flecks of white fat, i.e. marbled.

(3) The fat should be firm and brittle in texture, and creamy white in colour.

(4) Yellowish fat is always a sign that the animal is older or of a dairy breed.

(5) Beef should be fresh, or only chilled: frozen beef is never quite as good.

SKELETAL FORMATION

Cattle, sheep and pigs are similar in structure. The body consists of head, neck, trunk and tail, and is divided into the front part 'Forequarters' and the rear part 'Hindquarter'. The diaphragm forms a division between the chest or thorax and the abdomen or belly. The following bones are to be found in a side of beef (Figure 50):

(*a*) *Cervical Vertebrae*
Seven segments of bones in the neck region.

(*b*) *Dorsal Vertebrae*
Thirteen segments of bone in the chest region.

(*c*) *Lumbar Vertebrae*
Six segments of bone in the back region.

(*d*) *Sacral Vertebrae*
Five segments of bones fused into one at the end of back region.

(*e*) *Caudal Vertebrae*
The tail segments vary in number in different animals.

Ribs
Thirteen pairs, sometimes 12 or 14 of these are 8 pairs true ribs and 5 pairs false ribs.
Note: some breeds of pigs have 14 or even 15 segments of dorsal vertebrae and, as each segment has a pair of ribs attached, it follows that they will have 14 or 15 pairs of ribs too. The numbers of segments of bones in the sacral region and in the sternum breast-bone are also different, e.g. 4 segments of sacral vertebrae, 6 segments of sternum.

Sternum or Breast Bones
One Bone, 7 segments of bones, fused.

Pelvic or Haunch Bones
Consisting of Ilium (hipbone), Ishium and Os Pubis (aitchbone).

Hind Limb
Consisting of Femur (thigh bone), Patella (knee cap), Tibia Fibula (leg bones).

Fore Limb
Consisting of Scapula (blade bone), Humerus (shoulder bone), Radius and Ulna (foreleg bone).

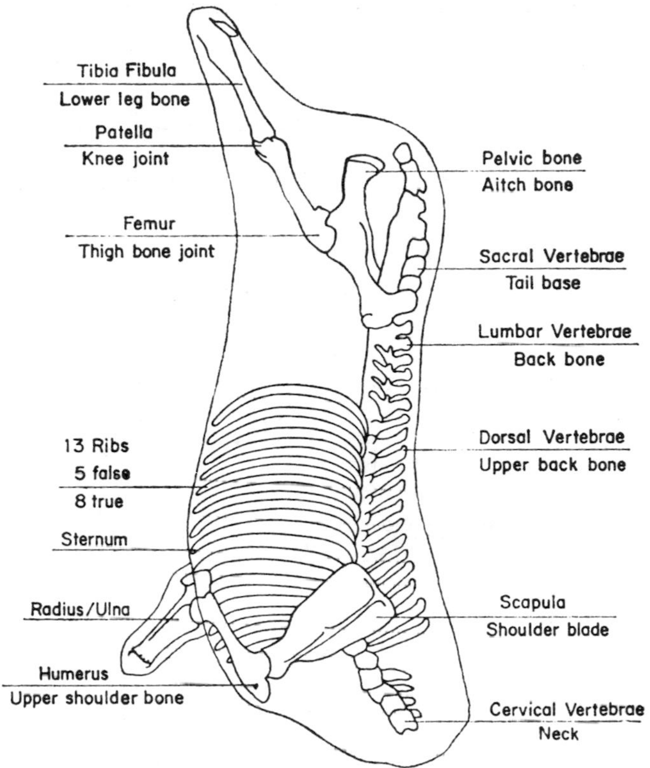

FIG. 50. *Bovine skeleton*

CLASSIFICATION OF CATTLE

Male

(*a*) *Entire*, (1) Bull calf up to 1 year, (2) Yearling bull in first year, (3) Bull, adult;
(*b*) *Castrated*, (1) Steer calf (castrated young), (2) Steer ox (castrated adult).

Female

(1) Heifer calf, (2) Heifer (not calved), (3) Cow-heifer (young female after calving), (4) Cow (after calving).

Ordering Wholesale Cuts

Hindquarter Beef ($H\frac{1}{4}$)
$H\frac{1}{4}$X = $H\frac{1}{4}$ – Thin Flank, $H\frac{1}{4}$XX = $H\frac{1}{4}$ – Thin Flank and Kidney Knob.
Top Piece (Tpce) = Shank, Thick Flank, Topside, Silverside, Aitchbone, Cod Fat.
Top Piece and Flank (Tpce. and Flk.) = Top Piece with Flank attached.
Rump and Loin (Rp. and Ln.) = Rump, Loin, Wing End, Kidney Knob, Fillet.
Rp. and Ln.X = Rp. and Ln. – Kidney Knob.
Round of Beef = Thick Flank, Topside, Silverside, Aitchbone, Buttock Bone.
Buttock = the above – Thick Flank.
Forequarter Beef ($F\frac{1}{4}$):
$F\frac{1}{4}$X = $F\frac{1}{4}$ – Plate, $F\frac{1}{4}$XX = $F\frac{1}{4}$ – Brisket and Plate.
$F\frac{1}{4}$XXX = $F\frac{1}{4}$ – Brisket, Plate, Shin = 'Australian Crop'.
Crop = Fore Rib, Middle Rib, Steak Meat.
Short Crop = Fore Rib, Middle Rib.
Pony = Steak Meat, Middle Rib.
Bottom Piece (Btm. Pce). = Clod, Sticking, Steak Meat and Shin.
Coast = Plate and Brisket.
Roasting Top Piece = Loin and Fore Rib.
Short = $F\frac{1}{4}$ – Fore Rib and Plate.

Definitions

Slink Veal
Unborn or stillborn calf carcass.
Calf
Young cattle from birth to six months.
Stirk
Weaned calves of both sexes.
Baby Beef
Beef between 12 and 18 months.

CLASSIFICATION OF SHEEP

Male

(*a*) *Entire*, (1) Ram, lamb or hogget (after wearning to shearing), (2) Ram (after shearing).
(*b*) *Castrated*, (1) Wether (from weaning to shearing), (2) Shearing wether (after shearing).

Female

Ewe lamb (from birth to weaning), (2) Ewe tegs (from weaning to shearing), (3) (after lambing).

CLASSIFICATION OF PIGS

(1) *Boar*. Entire male.
(2) *Hog*. Castrated young.
(3) *Stores*. Young, weaned pigs.
(4) *Suckling pigs*. Unweaned pig about 6 to 8 weeks old.

JOINTING OR DISSECTION

BEEF – LE BOEUF

The method of jointing described here is based on the skeleton of the animal. No one would take the trouble to chop through a bone, if a joint could be found which with very little effort one could cut through. Even in these days of mechanical saws, use is still made of the skeletal structure to facilitate jointing.

For convenience a side of beef quartered between the tenth and eleventh ribs and cut straight across is described. This provides a 10 rib Forequarter and a 3 rib Hindquarter. All imported chilled beef is quartered in this manner.

The large illustrations (Figures 51 and 52) show a whole side of beef and its cuts. The two smaller drawings (Figure 53) give the forquarter and hindquarter. Both the latter are related in size and cuts to the drawing of the whole animal. As a whole side of beef is very seldom supplied, the diagrams of the fore and hindquarters make more explicit the dissection of the respective pieces. The average weight of a side of beef is about 175-180 kg (350 to 380 lb) but it could, in certain cases, be even heavier or lighter. For this reason, the weights given for the different cuts are only approximately correct.

An analysis of the component parts of a hindquarter of beef will be found in the accompanying table. It will be found useful when buying or costing in respect of weight loss in bones and trimmings.

A whole side of beef, it has been said, is very seldom supplied to hotels and restaurants. If this should occur, it should be divided between the 10th and 11th rib in a straight line between wing rib of the hind and fore rib of the forequarter (see illustration).

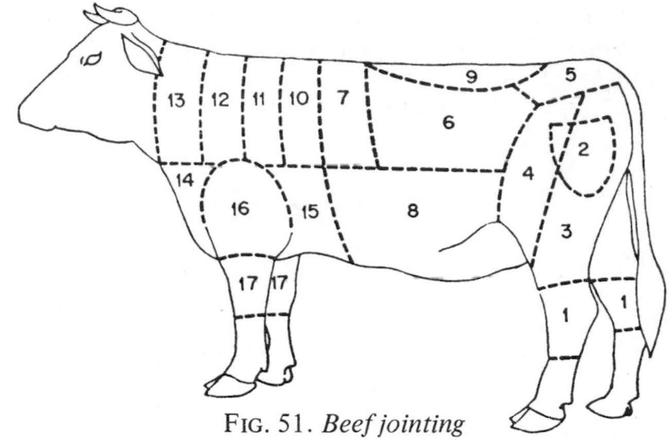

FIG. 51. *Beef jointing*

BEEF JOINTING
(Figure 51)

for A Side of Beef Weighing Approx 180 kg (360 lb)

Cuts	*Uses*	*Approx. Weight*
HINDQUARTER		
(1) Shank	Clarification, beef tea, stews	7–8 kg (14–16 lb)
(2) Topside	Braising, stewing, second-class roast	9–10 kg (18–20 lb)
(3) Silverside	Boiling, stewing, picked (boiled beef)	12–13 kg (24–26 lb)
(4) Thick Flank	Braising, stewing	11–12 kg (22–24 lb)
(5) Rump	Grilling, frying (rumpsteaks)	9–10 kg (18–20 lb)
(6) Sirloin	Roasting, grilling, frying (Entrecôtes)	10–11 kg (20–22 lb)
(7) Wing Rib	First-class roast, grilling, frying	4–5 kg (8–10 lb)
(8) Thin Flank	Stewing, boiling, mincing, sausages	9–10 kg (18–20 lb)
(9) Fillet	Roasting, grilling, frying	3–4 kg (6–8 lb)
FOREQUARTER		
(10) Fore Rib	Good roast, grilling, frying	7–8 kg (14–16 lb)
(11) Middle Rib	Roasting and braising	9–10 kg (18–20 lb)
(12) Chuck Rib	Stewing, braising, mincing	13–15 kg (27–30 lb)
(13) Sticking Piece	Stewing, mincing, sausages	8–19 kg (16–18 lb)
(14) Brisket	Boiling, brined and boiled pressed beef	17–18 kg (34–36 lb)
(15) Plate	Stewing, boiling, mincing, sausages	9–10 kg (18–20 lb)
(16) Leg of Mutton	Braising whole and steaks, stewing	10–11 kg (20–22 lb)
(17) Shin	Clarification, beef tea, second-class mince	6–7 kg (12–14 lb)
Kidney	Stews and pies	
Fat	First-class dripping	
Marrow	Sauces and soups	
Bones	White and brown stocks	

The methods of cutting vary considerably in certain parts of the world, even in Great Britain. There is, however, a broad correlation between the various systems based on the skeleton of the animal. The method given here is known as the 'London and Home Counties'.

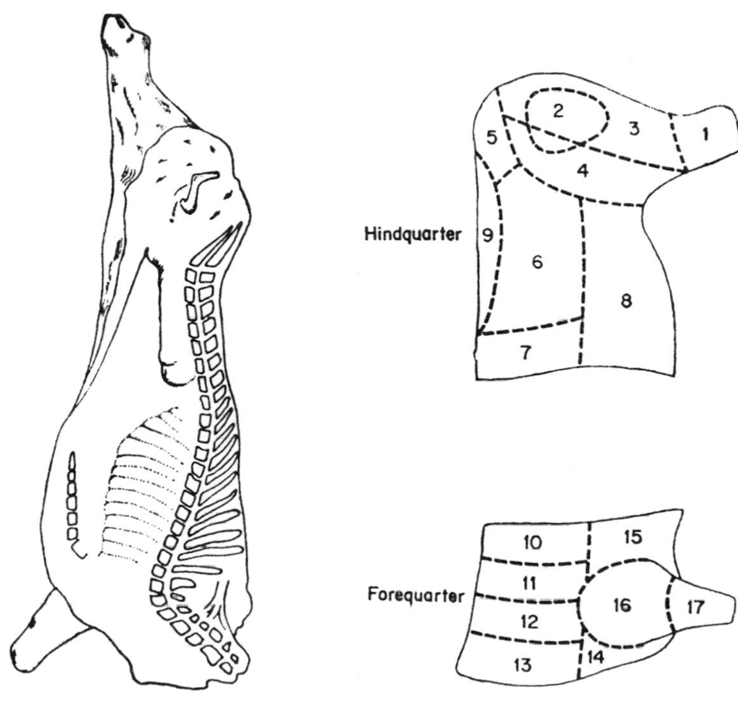

FIG. 52. *Whole side of beef*

FIG. 53. *Cuts of beef*

Hindquarter of Beef

(1) Place the Quarter on the block with the inside uppermost and remove the kidney knob and rump suet carefully, taking care not to cut into the Fillet which lies under the kidney suet.

(2) Remove the cod or udder fat and the goose skirt which is part of the inner muscle of the bellywall and is situated below the cod fat. Make a light incision where it joins the rump, then make a clean cut, removing the cod fat at its natural seam with the rump and flank.

(3) Remove the thin flank, estimating a point twice the length of the eye muscle from the chine at the wing end to just below the small external muscle, found below the cod fat. Use the knife as far as the ribs and complete the division by sawing through the 3 rib bones.

Analysis of Component Parts of a Hindquarter of Beef. Weight 68 kg.

Name of Cut or Joint	*Quality value**	*Weights un-trimmed joints*	*Percen-tage of hind-quarter†*	*Weight with-out bones*	*Weight of bones*	*Percen-tage of bones†*	*Weight of trimmed joint ready for use*	*Weight of trim-mings*	*Percentage of trim-mings per joint†*
		kg	%	*kg*	*kg*	%	*kg*	*kg*	%
1 Shank	*12*	5·250	8	2·750	2·500	49	2·250	0·500	12
2 Topside	*5*	9·500	14	8·250	1·250	13	7·250	1·000	11
3 Silverside	*7*	9·750	14	8·350	1·400	15	6·850	1·500	17
4 Thick Flank	*6*	6·750	10	5·500	1·250	22	4·000	1·400	20
5 Rump	*2*	9·650	14	7·500	2·150	29	4·750	2·550	26
6 Sirloin	*3*	6·500	9	4·600	1·900	30	3·450	1·150	19
7 Wing Rib	*4*	4·600	7	3·750	0·850	19	3·350	0·400	5
8 Thin Flank	*9*	6·400	9	5·500	0·900	13	4·400	1·100	18
9 Fillet	*1*	2·100	3	2·100	0	0	1·850	0·250	38
10 Large Trimmings (Stew)	*10*	1·125	2	1·125	0	0	1·125	0	0
11 Small Trimmings (Mince)	*11*	1·175	2	1·175	0	0	1·175	0	0
12 Ox Kidney	*8*	0·500	1	0·500	0	0	0·500	0	0
13 Suet	*13*	2·125	3	2·125	0	0	2·125	0	0
14 Fat	*14*	1·175	2	1·175	0	0	1·175	0	0
15 Bones	*15*	0	0	0	0	0	12·200	0	0
16 Sinews	*0*	0·750	1	0·750	0	0	0·950	0	0
17 Cutting Loss	*0*	0·650	1	0·650	0	0	0·750	0	0
	Total	68·000	82% of Meat	55·800	12·200	18% of bones	58·150	9·850	14½% of Trimmings
				68·000 kg			68·000 kg		

* In numerical order, ranging from 1 to 15. † Percentages rounded off.

(4) The hindquarter is now divided into Rump and Loin and Top Piece, taking a line 3 fingers' width below the round part of the aitchbone (approx. 5 cm (2 in.)) and the same height above the end of the rump bone. Cut through the fillet, if not previously removed, saw across the bone and complete the division by making a clean straight cut with the steak knife. This cut must be absolutely square, as sloping towards the Top Piece will mean cutting into a bone, whilst sloping towards the loin will result in a loss of Rump Steak.

(5) Remove the fillet, or undercut, carefully, if it is intended for steaks. Use a boning knife and commencing at the chine, follow the bones of the lumbar vertebrae closely, avoiding any cuts into the fillet muscle.

(6) Separate the rump from the loin at the cartilage between the sacral and lumbar vertebrae. Using this as a guide, locate the cartilage on the end of the rump bone (ilium) with the point of a knife. Make a cut just through the cartilage and sloping the knife towards the rump, to the point between the vertebrae, complete the separation by sawing through the bone. If not previously removed, remove the fillet head carefully from the rump with the skirt attached.

(7) Remove the wing end from the loin by cutting between the dorsal and lumbar vertebrae and in a straight line across the loin keeping the loin square. This will necessitate sawing through the tops of two of the ribs and the chine, to complete the division. Use the saw on the bones only and cut through the muscle with a clean stroke of a sharp steak knife.

(8) Remove the aitchbone from the Top Piece. Starting from the outside, lay back the thin layer of muscle and fat from the surface, baring the bone completely. Pass the point of the knife along the underside of the bone to loosen the muscle, follow the line of the hole with the tip of the knife and cut down the back of the surface, cutting the tendon in the ball to socket joint and remove the bone cleanly.

(9) To remove the thick flank, find the leg end of the Patella with the point of the knife and make a straight cut down on to the thigh bone (femur). Insert the point of the knife under the skin covering the bone and draw back the thick flank from the bone. Here will be found the seam of the silverside. Cut open the seam till the silverside muscle is reached, then cut through the skin with a clean cut to remove the thick flank.

(10) Remove the shank/hindshin by cutting through the cartilage and tendon at the joint, between the tibia-fibula and femur.

(11) The Topside is now separated from the Silverside at the seam. Start from the bone side of the buttock by cutting round the bone until the seam is located, following it until the external fat is reached, then cutting through the fat to remove the topside, leaving the bone clean and attached to the Silverside.

Forequarter of Beef

(1) Remove the shin at the elbow joint with a boning knife. Push the shin forward and downwards whilst loosening the joint with the knife. With frozen beef it is advisable to saw through the tip of the elbow to facilitate 'breaking' the joint.

(2) Remove the plate and brisket taking a line some 5 cm (2 in.) from the end of the skirt to the first bone of the sternum. Saw through the rib-bone, followed by cutting, taking care, when removing the brisket end, to find the seam between it and the leg of the mutton cut. The plate and brisket are divided by cutting between the 6th and 7th rib bones.

(3) Remove the sticking piece by finding the joint of the clod (humerus) and the blade bone (scapula). To find the cup-bone of the blade, cut between the cervical and dorsal vertebrae. Saw across and remove the clod and sticking, in one piece. The clod is separated from the sticking at the natural seam between the muscles, leaving the fat on the clod.

(4) Remove the fore-rib by cutting between the 6th and 7th ribs with a steak knife drawn between the ribs towards the chine. Finish by sawing through the chine. Keep the joint absolutely rectangular.

(5) The remaining portion is known as the 'pony' and from this remove the middle rib. This is done by cutting between the 3rd and 4th ribs, drawing the knife towards the chine till the bladebone is reached, cutting the muscle over the bone, then sawing through the bladebone. The cut between the ribs is then completed and the chine bone is sawn through.

(6) The remaining portion consists of chuck, bladebone and leg of mutton cut. With the joint on its back, saw through the 3 ribs and follow with a knife cut, just missing the bladebone to separate the leg of mutton cut from the chuck and bladebone. Divide these at the seam, leaving the fat on the chuck.

In most catering establishments the top part of the fore-ribs and middle-ribs are cut off to give a strip of rib tops, known as the flat-ribs. For this a line is drawn from the base of the 1st rib close to the cervical vertebrae to the end of the fore-rib, keeping the rib joints absolutely rectangular. Saw across the rib bones and finish with a clean stroke of a sharp knife. Naturally, this has the effect of giving a short cut fore-rib, which is not always convenient, particularly if it is put on display in a restaurant.

Preparation, Boning and Use of Cuts

Shank – La Jambe le Jarret

On the inner side of the shank the leg bone is clearly visible; if one follows this clearly visible seam around the bone with a sharp boning-knife, the shank is easily boned out. Thereafter, one only has to remove the very tough sinews and some excessive fat, and the meat of the shank is ready for use. Cut into large cubes; it can be coarsely minced for clarification or beef-tea. The upper, more tender part, of the shank can also be used for stews, especially Goulash. This meat can be cooked for a very long time to get it nice and tender, but it will never fall apart as some of the other stewing meats do.

Topside – La Tranche Tendre

The topside represents one of the leanest pieces of meat of the whole beef; reasonably tender, the topside has many excellent uses. Cut into dice, it will make a fine stew; cut into steaks, it gives some of the finest braising steaks. If the meat is of a very good quality, the topside will make an excellent roast but not always a first-class one. One of the best uses for the topside is for the making of *paupiettes de boeuf* or *roulades* as they are also called.

For *paupiettes* the meat is cut into large thin slices, slightly flattened with a bat, and seasoned; they can be filled with a large number of different fillings like stuffings, force-meats and duxelles; to vary flavours, herbs, English or French Mustard, onions, garlic, or gherkins may be added. Neatly rolled and tied with a string, or secured with a cherry stick, the paupiettes may even be barded or larded, which will add much to their flavour and appearance.

Silverside – Le Plat de Cuisse

This piece of meat is very coarse and needs a long cooking time; it is usually brined and boiled (Boiled Beef and Carrots) but it can also be cut into dice and used for a good stew, or minced to give a very good mince. The silverside consists really of two pieces of meat, which are separated by a seam; one is of a wide oblong shape, the other long and round, very much like a large sausage. This latter piece is often brined and boiled, and then served cold for cold meats, salads, sandwiches, etc.

Thick Flank – La Gite à La Noix

Again, a nice lean and tender piece of meat which, because of its tenderness, is not very good for braised steaks and stews, as it will easily disintegrate if cooked in this way. It is very suitable for braising in a large piece and could, for this method of cooking, even be larded with fat bacon and even marinaded in a red wine marinade (*Pièce de Boeuf Braisé*).

Rump – La Culotte

The rump (Figure 54) is carefully boned out of the hip-bone, and trimmed of excess fat and sinews. Very seldom is this piece used as a roast; most commonly one cuts large slices across the grain (rumpsteaks). If these slices are too big, they can be divided again into even steaks of the weight to be given, The rump is really two pieces, and in some cases they are divided; the heavier lower piece is still called and sold as rump, the upper lighter and pointed piece is sold as point steaks.

Sirloin – L'Aloyau

The true sirloin consists of sirloin and fillet (Figure 55). This should be

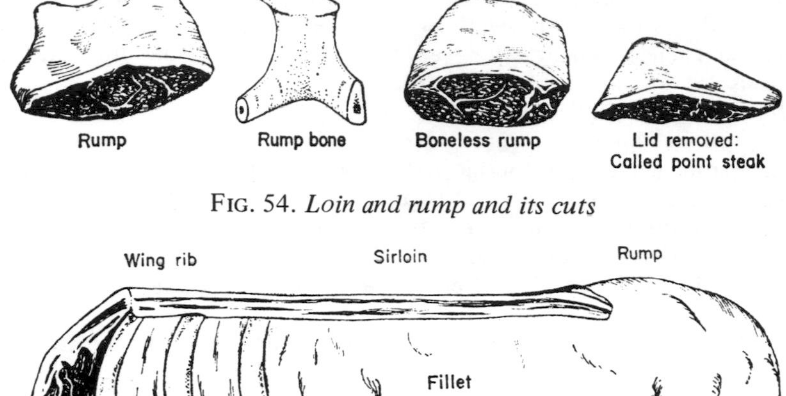

FIG. 54. *Loin and rump and its cuts*

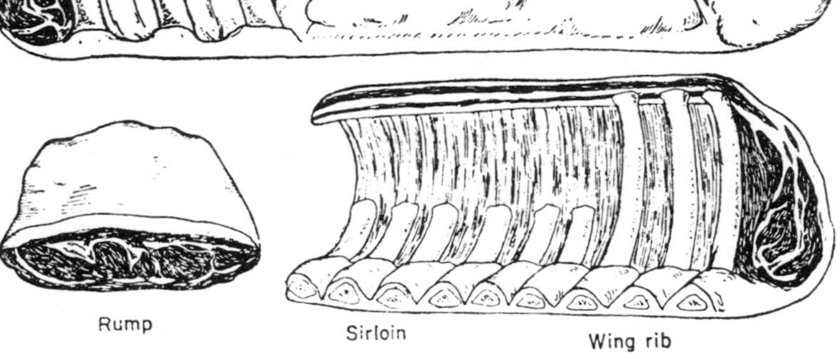

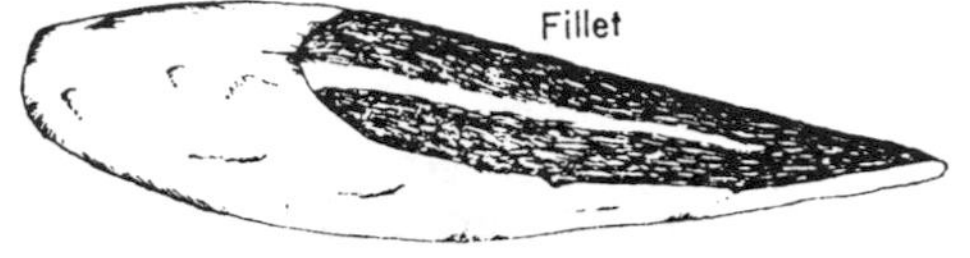

FIG 55. *Rump*

carefully removed with a sharp knife, as close to the bone as possible, without cutting into the fillet. After the fillet is removed, there are two ways of preparing the actual sirloin:

(*a*) *For roasting on the bone*. First saw through the chine-bone 3 or 4 times. Lift the covering fat nearest to the chine-bone about $7\frac{1}{2}$–10 cm (3–4 in.), which will allow one to take away the very tough sinew, which must always be removed. After the sinew is removed, the covering fat is replaced and, if necessary, tied with a string to keep it in position for roasting.

(*b*) *For roasting off the Bone and Entrecôtes. Contre-Filet* (Figure 56). To neatly bone the sirloin, one should always cut around the rib-bones with a very sharp knife, loosening the meat between the ribs. When this is done, the left hand draws away the upper, narrower part from the bone, as the righ hand cuts with a sharp knife between the bone and meat. Always keep away from the tender contre-filet and hold the knife towards the bones. Once the contre-filet is removed, it is trimmed of excess fat and sinews. It can then be roasted as it is, or it can also be rolled for this purpose. From this contre-filet are cut those famous steaks, like *Entrecôte Minute, Entrecôte*, and *Entrecôte Double.*

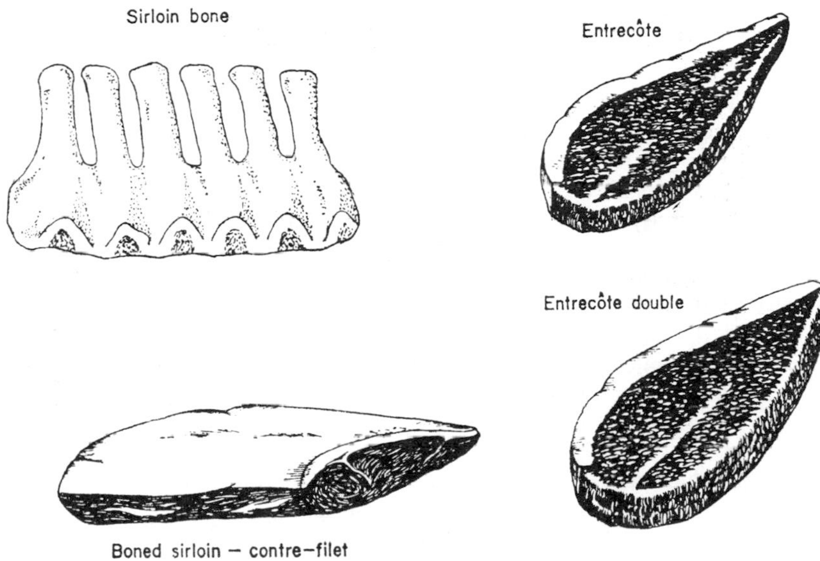

FIG. 56. *Boned sirloin and sirloin steaks*

Wing Rib – Les Côtes d'Aloyau

This joint consists, usually, of the last 3 rib-bones which, because of its excellent quality and its natural trivet, makes a first-class roasting joint for hot or cold, especially if it is going to be carved in front of the customer, or displayed on a cold buffet. To prepare for roasting, cut about three-quarters through the chine-bone, lift back covering fat and remove sinew and nerve. Saw through the rib from the underside, about 4-8 cm (2-4 in.) from the end. Trim off excess fat, replace fat and tie with a string to keep in position. The wing rib can also be boned like a sirloin and some excellent steak can be cut from it (Figure 57).

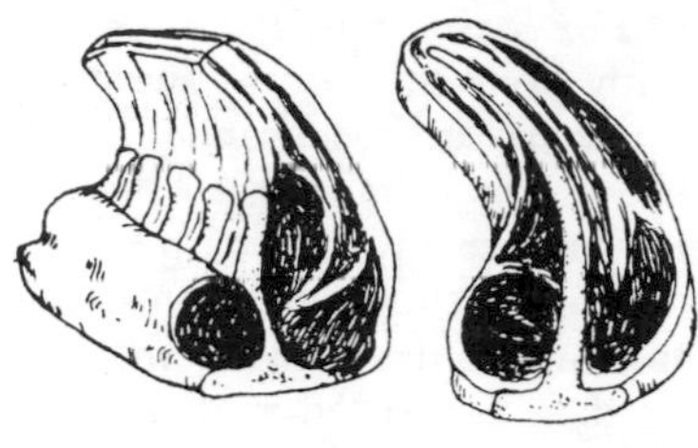

FIG. 57. *Cuts from wing rib*

Thin Flank – La Bavette d'Aloyau

This joint consists of about equal quantities of coarse meat and fat and is not a good cut; at best, it is used for the following: (a) Boiling; remove excess fat, bat out, trim and roll neatly, tie with a string; (b) Stewing; remove excess fat, cut into neat dice for stewing; (c) Mincing; remove most fat and put through the mincing machine for sausages, hamburgers etc.

Fillet – Le Filet

The fillet is without doubt the finest joint in the whole beef and many famous dishes are prepared from this cut. As the fillet is removed from the sirloin it cannot be used straight away and should be prepared in the following way:

All surrounding fat is carefully taken away.

Cut away the so-called fillet-string, which runs parallel to the fillet.

The fillet, thus prepared, is now freed from a very thin silvery skin. This is best done with a very sharp filleting-knife, taking about an inch at a time and removing it from the tail towards the head. It is really more of a drawing away, with the help of a knife, than an actual cutting.

As can be seen from Figures 58 and 59, the fillet falls into 3 parts:

FIG. 58. *Fillets*

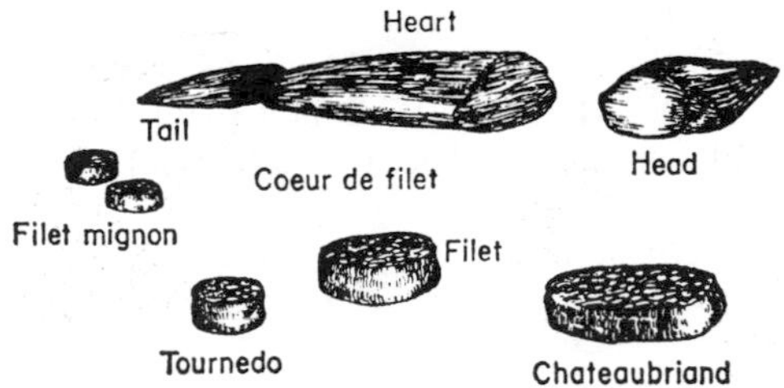

FIG. 59. *Parts of fillet*

(1) *Fillet Head* (*Tête de Filet*). This is the top and wider part of the fillet, which according to size is best used to cut Châteaubriands (a large fillet-steak for 2 to 3 persons slightly flattened with a bat to the shape of a roasting joint). If smaller in size, fillet steaks can also be cut from this part.
(2) *Middle or Heart* (*Coeur de Filet*). In French, called *Coeur de Filet*; this is the piece where fillet steaks and tournedos are cut, but it can also be roasted whole: in this way, there are many famous dishes like *Coeur de filet Wellington* or *Coeur de filet Matignon*, etc.
(3) *The Tail* (*Filet Mignon*). Known also as *filet Mignon* it can be – if large enough, cut into small fillet steaks, giving 2 per person, but more commonly it is cut into bâton for *Boeuf Sauté* or cut into very small dice when it is used for *sauce Bolognese.*

Fore-Rib – Les Côtes Premières

This perhaps the only good cut for roasting from the forquarter, consisting of usually 4 ribs. Again the chine-bone is cut in 2 or 4 places and excess fat and sinews removed. Before roasting, the back flat chine-bone should be broken with the back of a chopper. This will make it easier when the joint is cooked to take the bones away and allow for easier carving. The cut can also be boned, similar to the sirloin, and can be roasted without the bone, or cut into steaks for Kosher cooking.

Middle-Rib – Les Côtes Découvertes

Bone out, remove heavy sinews, cut into joints of 2.5 kg (5-6 lb) and tie firmly with string. Use for roasting or braising.

Chuck-Rib – Les Côtes Du Collier

The chuck-rib is usually boned out and its meat used for braising *en pièce* or braising steaks; cut into dice, it makes an excellent stew.

Sticking Piece – Le Collier-Cou

This is the neck of the beef, a mass of good lean beef around the neck-bone. Difficult to bone; one should keep as close to the bone as possible. Cut into dice, the meat makes a good stew; or minced it is very good for any dishes where minced beef is used.

Brisket – La Poitrine
A popular cut from the forequarter, which is usually brined and boiled and served as pressed beef (Figure 60). Boned in both cases, it can also be rolled and boiled fresh as boiled beef (French style).

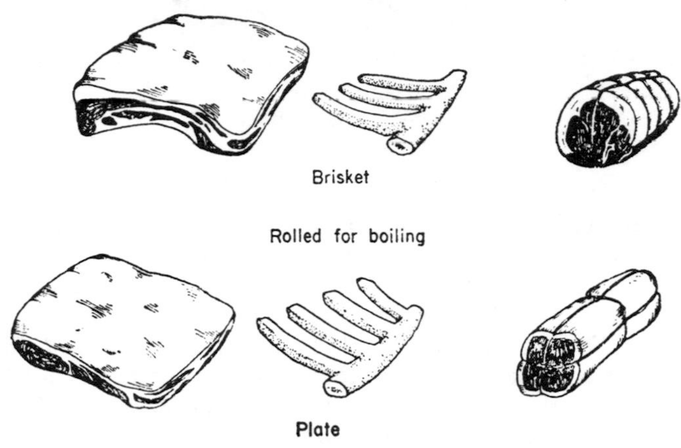

FIG. 60. *Brisket*

Plate – Le Plate de Côtes
Boned and cut into dice, it is quite useful for stews and even minced beef, but only in rare cases can it be used for boiled beef, when it should be of exceptionally good quality.
Leg of Mutton Cut – L'Epaule Macreuse
A good lean piece of meat which is very useful for braising *en pièce* as well as braising steaks. It may also be diced for stews or minced.
Shin – Le Jarret de Devant
Like the shank, the shin is carefully boned around the leg-bone. Excess fat and all sinews must be removed and it will find good use for clarification, beef-tea, and second class mince.
Fat – La Graisse
Except for suet and cod fat, all fat is coarsely minced and rendered down for first-class dripping.
Bones – Les Os
Upper leg-bone as well as shank and shin-bone should be carefully sawn and split to remove the bone-marrow. The marrow is then placed into cold water to soak out excess blood. All bones are then chopped and used for white and brown stocks.

VEAL – LE VEAU

Veal, illustrated in Figure 61, is the flesh of the calf. Its meat is at its best when the calf is about $2\frac{1}{2}$ to 3 months old. Solely fed on milk, its meat should be white with a slight tinge to green. If there is any sign of red coloration, it usually indicates the calf has been fed with solids, or grazing.

The meat is very lean; signs of light white fat are detected only around the kidneys, with a pleasant smell of milk. If the calf is killed too young, its meat is very loose and gelatinous and, as such, is very low in nutritional value.

Veal can be sold in a full carcass, like lamb, but more often it is split into two halves, like beef. The side of veal has 9 basic cuts, as illustrated.

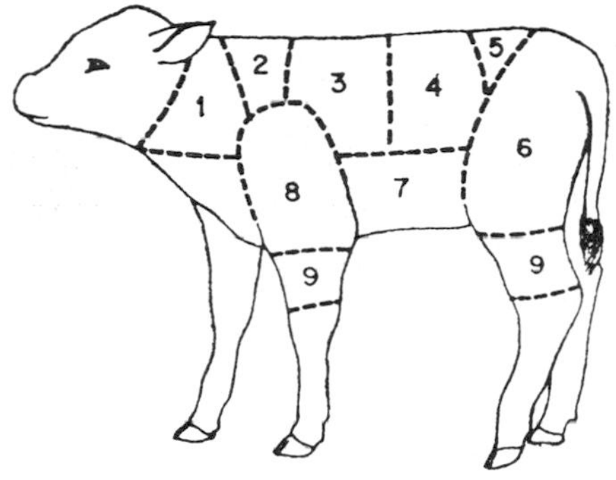

FIG. 61. *Veal*

Cuts or Joints	*French Term*	*Uses*	*Approx.* 48 kg *Weight* (96 lb)
(1) Scrag	*le cou*	Stewing, Stocks	2–3 kg (4–6 lb)
(2) Neck end	*les basses côtes*	Braising, Stewing, Stocks	3 kg (6 lb)
(3) Best end	*le carré*	Pot Roasting, Roasting, Braising, Frying	3–4 kg (6–8 lb)
(4) Loin	*la longe*	Pot Roasting, Roasting, Braising, Frying	3–4 kg (6–8 lb)
(5) Chump or Rump	*le quasi*	Braising, Roasting, Grilling	3 kg (6 lb)
(6) Leg	*le cuissot*	Pot Roasting, Roasting, Braising, Frying	20 kg (40 lb)
(7) Breast	*la poitrine*	Stewing, Roasting (Stuffed)	3 kg (6 lb)
(8) Shoulder	*l'épaule*	Roasting, Braising, Stewing	6 kg (12 lb)
(9) Knuckle	*le jarret*	Stock, Minced, Stew Osso Bucco	4 kg (8 lb)

Its cuts, uses, and French terms are given in the chart accompanying the drawing.

Quality points for home killed veal calves are as follows:

Conformation and Finish

Carcass compact, plump and well fleshed; loins well fleshed, legs rounded and well developed; knuckles, short; neck, short and thick; shoulders deeply fleshed. Finish: thin layer of fat over rump, back, shoulders and kidneys well covered; inside of ribs should show indications of fat; fat, white in colour; flesh, firm with distinctive pale pinkish colour, described as white.

Dissection

Small calves, known as bobby calves, are dissected in the same way as mutton carcasses. With veal calves, the leg is cut above the aitchbone, leaving the whole of the chump on the loin. The leg, minus the knuckle, is known as the 'fillet' and the shoulder, minus the knuckle, is known as the 'oyster'. The rest of the portions have the same names as those in mutton. The calf is chopped down into sides, then quartered between the 12th and 13th ribs, leaving 1 rib on the hindquarter.

(1) Remove the leg, by cutting straight across, just above the aitchbone.
(2) Separate the knuckle from the fillet by jointing just above the patella.
(3) Bone out the fillet in the same way as the Round of beef. This will produce 3 distinctive cuts; The Cushion (Top Side), the Undercushion (Silverside), and the Thick Flank.
(4) Separate the loin from the chump between the lumbar and sacral vertebrae.
(5) Remove the shoulder in the same way as mutton shoulder and joint the fore knuckle from the oyster.
(6) Remove the breast in the same manner. The portion of the breast corresponding to the 'plate' on beef is known as the tendons.
(7) Separate the best end from the middle neck between the 6th and 7th ribs.
(8) Divide neck-end from scrag, leaving about 5 to 6 bones on the neck end.

Uses for Cuts and Joints

Refer to Figure 62 in the following discussion.

Scrag – Le Cou

The neck of veal is not a very exciting cut. It is usually cut and chopped with the bones into 2–4 cm (1–2 in.) pieces and used for *Veal Blanquettes*. It can also be boned and then cut into dice of about 2 cm (1 in.) for other white and brown veal stews, or minced. Quite often scrag can be put to very good use in the preparation of first-class white or brown veal stocks.

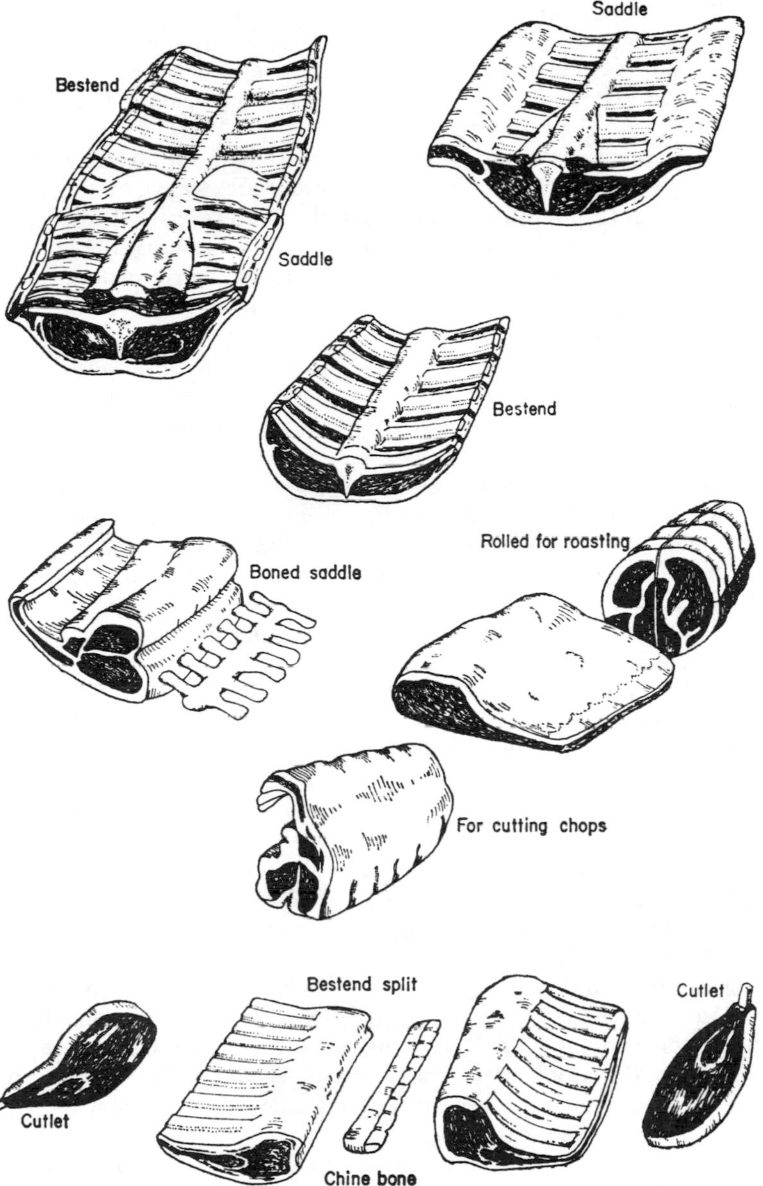

FIG. 62. *Cuts of veal*

Neck End – Les Basses Côtes de Veau
A slightly better cut than the scrag but still quite bony. Usually cut into secondary cutlets for braising, or cut with the bones into 2-4 cm (1-2 in.) pieces and used for *Blanquette*. Boned it can be used again for other white and brown veal stews, or minced and used in the preparation for *Pojarskis.*
Best End – Le Carrè de Veau
The first prime cut so far, which can be roasted or pot-roasted whole. For this purpose, one removes the chine bone and back sinew, cutting approximately 4 cm (2 in.) of meat away from the narrower part of the Best-End, cleaning meat and sinews between the bones and scraping the bone absolutely clean. After the above procedure, each of the rib bones is cut to a point on a slight angle, to allow cutlet frills to be fitted.
Veal Cutlets – Côtelettes de Veau
Cut from the Best-End given in the foregoing. The Best-End is prepared very much as for roasting. For cutlets, however, it is cut in between the bones into neat cutlets, which are slightly batted and trimmed, if necessary.
Loin of Veal – La Longe de Veau
This is the second Prime Cut and has many excellent uses. Usually roasted or pot-roasted whole, it can also be cut into chops. These are not suited very much for grilling or frying because of the leanness of the meat; they are therefore braised. For roasting or pot roasting, neatly loosen the bones from the loin; do not actually remove, but leave in its place as a trivet; remove back sinew, trim and roll to a neat roll, tie with a string in 2 or 3 places and it is ready for use.
Stuffed Loin of Veal – La Longe de Veau Farcie
Prepared very much for roasting or pot-roasting, the bones are removed in this case. After removing back-sinew, the boneless loin is batted slightly and trimmed, then filled with a stuffing which in England is usually a lemon, thyme, suet and bread mixture, but could also be a meat and duxelles stuffing, or even a combination of both. Now the loin is neatly rolled and tied with string. The bones which have been removed are chopped fine and used with the loin as a bed for roasting, and the making of gravy or sauces. The veal kidney is, in this case, rolled into the stuffed loin.
Saddle of Veal – La Selle de Veau
This can of course only be cut from a whole carcass of veal and not a side as described here (see notes on Lamb). Once the saddle is jointed, excess kidney fat and the kidneys are removed and, in certain cases, the tender loin. Now the saddle flaps are cut short, according to their length, by 2-4 cm (1-2 in.), and folded under the saddle, which is tied with string in 3 or 4 places, to keep the shape.

There are a great number of classical recipes for the use of whole saddle of veal. In the main it is used chiefly for banquets and dinners, the most favoured recipes being *La Selle de Veau Orloff, La Selle de Veau Soubise,*

La Selle de Veau Metternich.

Veal Chops – Chop de Veau

Cut from the loin of veal, the preparation of veal chops is very much the same as for lamb. The uses, however, are different in so far as Veal is seldom suitable for grilling and veal chops are usually braised or shallow fried. For frying, they are passed through flour, eggwash and breadcrumbs, or cooked naturally with just flour.

Chump or Rump of Veal – Le Quasi de Veau

Not really a joint in its own right; according to requirements, it is often left on the loin to gain a larger loin, or on the leg to use when cutting escalopes or grenadins. When jointed, however, the rump of veal cuts into excellent steaks or chops for braising or, when boned, its tender lean meat is most useful for *Sauté de Veau*, with its many recipes.

Leg of Veal – Le Cuissot de Veau

Representing the best and leanest cut of the whole veal; the leg has many uses and some of the most famous veal dishes come from this joint (Figure 63(*a*)). If not too big, the leg of veal may be roasted or pot roasted whole. For this purpose the aitchbone is carefully removed and the lower knuckle cleared, tied 2 or 3 times with string, where the aitchbone was removed. The leg is then ready for use. As veal is very lean and tends to get dry in roasting or pot roasting, it is advisable to larder or barder the leg of veal for better results.

More commonly, the leg of veal is, of course, boned; as the illustration Figure 63(*b*) shows. It falls into 4 distinct cuts: (a) Cushion (*Noix*), (b) Under cushion (*Sous Noix*), (c) Thick Flank (*Noix Pâtissière*), (d) Hind-Knuckle (*Jarret*).

Cushion – La Noix

This is the prime cut of the leg and is most tender; it forms the basis of a great number of varying Escalopes, of which the *Escalope Viennoise* or *Wiener Schnitzel*, are the most famous. For this, the cushion is cut into neat slices across the grain, trimmed and, if necessary, slightly batted. An ideal use for the cushion is also *Paupiettes de Veau*; for this the slices are cut slightly thinner and may be filled with a number of stuffings, rolled and secured with a cocktail stick or strung for cooking. *Grenadins de Veau* are also cut from the cushion; the slices are cut across the grain, slightly thicker, then sliced in half to a triangular shape, thus obtaining two Grenadins from each slice.

Under Cushion – Sous Noix

The largest cut in the leg, it is not quite as tender as the cushion and is slightly coarser grained. It represents a good joint for roasting or pot roasting, for which it should be barded or larded. The under cushion is also useful when diced for such dishes as Goulash, Fricassé or Sauté of Veal dishes, e.g. *Sauté de Veau Marengo.*

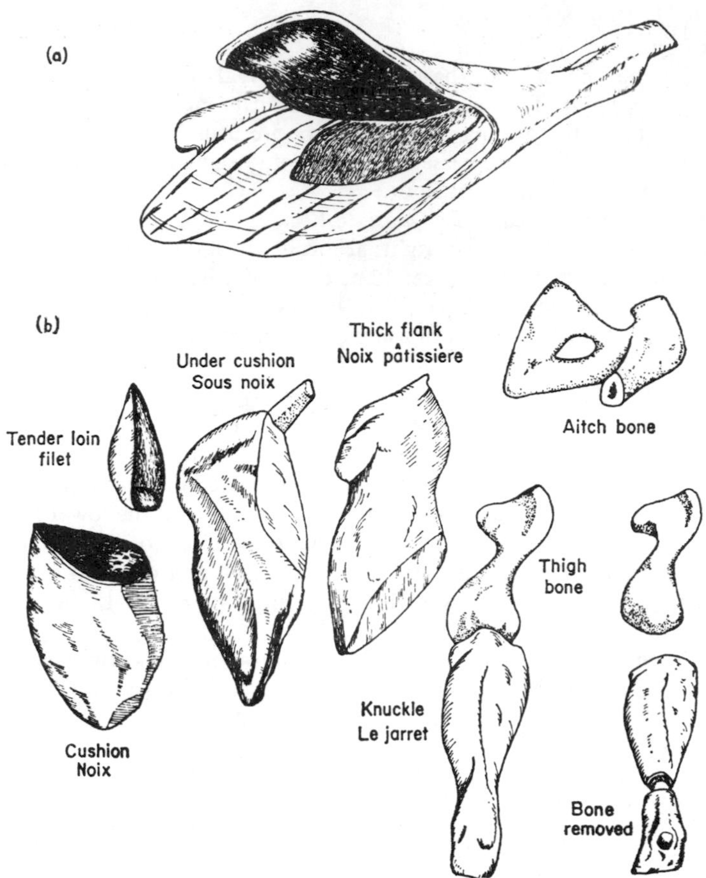

FIG. 63. (a) *Leg of veal partly boned with cushion lifted* (b) *Cuts of leg of veal*

Thick Flank – Noix Pâtissière

A nice, tender joint, but much smaller than the other two; only by cutting thick slices and batting them out will one be able to use this cut for Escalopes. It is, however, ideal for the cutting of Grenadins and Veal Steaks; or, cut into dice, it is most suitable for *Sautè de Veau* or Goulash.

Breast of Veal – La Poitrine de Veau

The breast of the medium to larger calf is ideal for stuffed breast of veal (Figure 64). For this purpose, the breast should be carefully denuded of all bones and gristle, without cutting through the thin skin or flesh. The breast thus prepared can be opened like a pocket; this must be done very carefully in order to avoid tearing the skin. The pocket is then filled with a force-meat, made mainly of minced veal but with the addition of some pork, or pork fat. Fillings of a duxelles, rice, or bread base, are also often used. The stuffed veal breast should, whenever possible, be pot roasted and barded to avoid drying out while roasting.

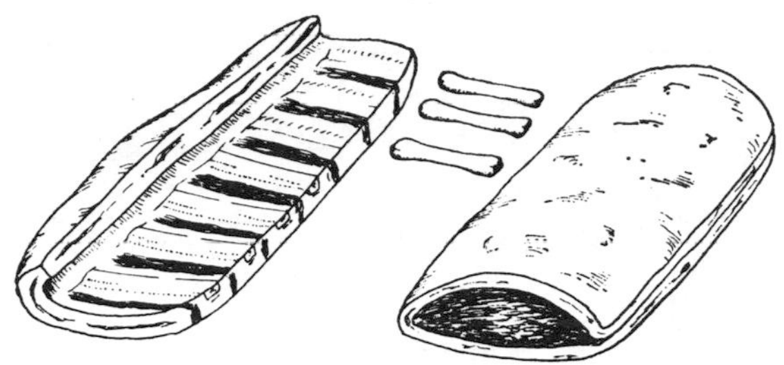

FIG. 64. *Breast of veal boned and stuffed for roasting*

Tendons of Veal – Tendrons de Veau
The part of the breast with no actual bone is called 'the tendons', or *tendrons* in French. Cut into 2 cm wide by 8 cm long (1 in. wide by 4 in. long) strips, they are usually braised, similar to Osso Bucco, representing a famous tasty dish.

Shoulder of Veal – L'Épaule de Veau
Most suitable for roast or pot roast and for this the shoulder must of course be boned. The shoulder is now batted slightly and filled usually with a lemon and thyme stuffing. Stuffings based on forcemeats, duxelles, rice or a combination of these, will give the chef scope for variation in preparing this dish. The shoulder, boned entirely, may be used for such dishes as Fricassé of Veal, Goulash of Veal, Hongroise and Sautéd Veal.

Knuckles of Veal – Les Jarrets de Veau
The most common use for the knuckles of veal of both fore and hind legs, is for a dish which is called 'Osso Bucco'. For this preparation, the knuckles are sawn into slices 2-4 cm (1-2 in.), with the bone in the middle. Freed of sinews and excess bones in relation to meat, this is a famous Italian dish which is liked all over the world. On the Continent, especially in Germany, Switzerland and Sweden, the hind knuckle of veal is featured often on the menus of hotels and restaurants. Here it is known as *Le Jarret de Veau roti*, being a popular à la carte dish of plump knuckles of veal, roasted to order and served with a little Jus Lié and salads. Other uses for the knuckles are in the making of stocks, broths and aspics, for which because of their gelatinous binding they are especially suited.

Veal bones – Les Os de Veau
Veal bones are excellent for the making of stocks, white and brown, and

because of their neutral flavour can be used with almost any meats, e.g. they are eminently suitable for the making of jus roti, jus lié, etc.

Veal Offal – Abats de Veau

Information regarding the above will be found under the general heading 'Offal'. *See also* Figure 65 for calf's head.

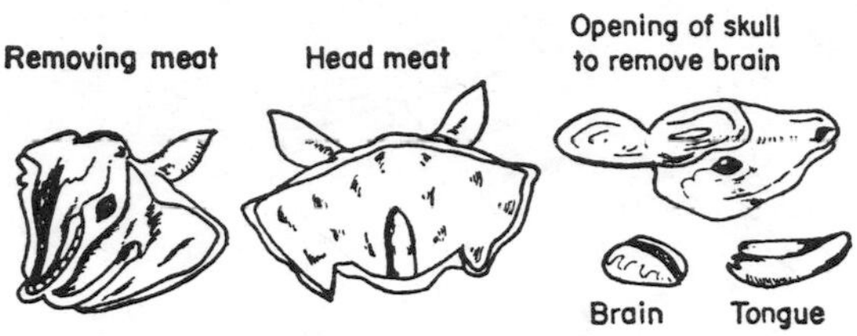

FIG. 65. *Calf's head*

Barding and Larding

As veal is usually very lean and tends to dry easily when roasted or pot roasted, it should whenever possible be barded or larded. Examples of barding and larding are given under 'Poultry and Game', and may be usefully employed here.

LAMB AND MUTTON – L'AGNEAU ET LE MOUTON

The illustration (Figure 66) shows a carcass of lamb, or mutton, with its 8 basic cuts or joints. The accompanying table give the English and French terms, together with best uses and approximate weights.

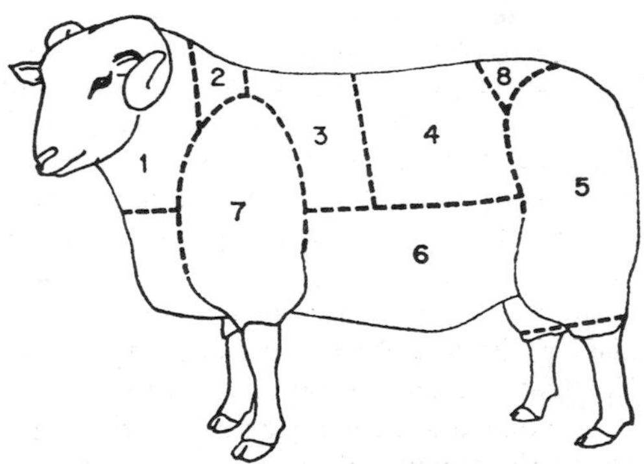

FIG. 66. *Cuts of lamb or mutton*

Cuts of Lamb and Mutton

			Approx. *Lamb* 16 kg (32 lb)	*Weight* *Mutton* 25 kg (50 lb)
Cuts or Joints	*French Term*	*Uses*	*Weight*	*Weight*
(1) Scrag end	*le cou*	Stewing broth	½ kg (1 lb)	1 kg (2 lb)
(2) Middle neck	*les basses côtes*	Stewing	2 kg (4 lb)	3 kg (6 lb)
(3) Best end	*le carré*	Roasting, grilling, frying	2 kg (4 lb)	3 kg (6 lb)
(4) Saddle	*la selle*	Roasting, grilling, frying	3½ kg (7 lb)	5 kg (11 lb)
(5) Legs (2)	*le gigot*	Roasting (M-boiled)	3½ kg (7 lb)	5 kg (11 lb)
(6) Breast (2)	*la poitrine*	Roasting, stewing	1½ kg (3 lb)	2½ kg (5 lb)
(7) Shoulders (2)	*l'épaule*	Roasting	3 kg (6 lb)	4½ kg (9 lb)
(8) Chump chops				

Bones are used for stocks and sauces.
Fat, rendered down – 2nd class dripping.

Points of Quality

(1) Compact and evenly fleshed.
(2) Firm lean meat.
(3) A pleasing dull red colour, fine texture and grain.
(4) Even distribution of *white*, fat.
(5) Bones in a young animal should be pink and porous.
(6) If old, bones become hard, white and splinter easily.

Dissection

1. (a) Remove the shoulder by incising at a point where the shoulder bulges at the neck and along the back to a point between the 6th and 7th ribs, where the cartilage of the top of the bladebone can be easily cut through; (b) The shape of the shoulder can vary from round to almost square; (c) Continue the incision along the line of the rib bone to a point parallel with the elbow; (d) Then curve the incision some 4–6 cm (2–3 in.) below the elbow and join it to the starting point; (e) Now, starting at the neck, find the natural seam between the shoulder and neck muscle with the point of the boning knife and strip off the shoulder without damaging the underlying neck muscle.

2. (a) Remove the legs, by first dividing the aitchbone, then by cutting through the cartilage in the case of lamb, or chopping or sawing in the case of mutton; (b) Now cut a small portion of the flap or flank on to the leg and saw through the bone at a slight angle towards the legs; (c) The actual point will depend on the amount of chump one requires to leave on the saddle but a point varying from the base of the tail to some 5 cm (2 in.) above the base of the tail should be a fair guide.

3. Remove the breasts, taking a line from 2 cm (1 in.) below the neck bone on the 1st rib to a point taking equal parts of fat and lean at the chump end (a fold in the flank will act as a good guide); join the two points in a straight line, saw across the ribs and finish by cutting along the line with a clean stroke of a sharp knife.

4. Remove the saddle at the cartilage pad between the 12th and 13th vertebrae, cut through the cartilage, and saw through the bone, keeping both joints rectangular.

5. Remove the pair of Best-Ends by cutting between the 6th and 7th dorsal vertebrae, cut through the cartilage and saw through the bone.

6. The middle neck and scrag or neck are now separated, cutting between the cervical vertebrae and the 1st dorsal vertebrae (Figure 67). Keep the middle neck joint rectangular.

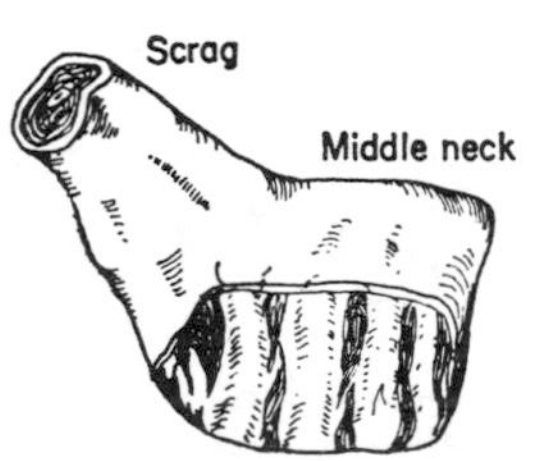

FIG. 67. *Scrag and middle neck with secondary cutlets*

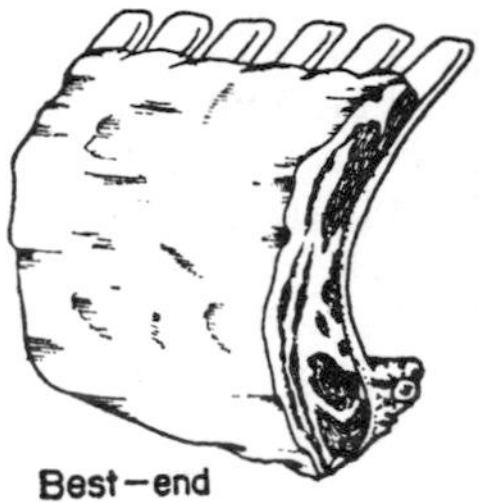

FIG. 68. *Best end of lamb for roasting whole or cutting cutlets*

Ordering Wholesale Cuts

Haunches	Pair of legs with chumps attached.
Saddle or Chine	Pair of loins.
Chines & Ends	Chines with pair of Best-Ends.
Hinds and Ends	Pair of legs, loins and Best-Ends.
Hinds	Pair of legs and loins.
Fores	Pair of forequarters and Best-Ends.
Short Fores	Forequarters.
Jacket	Carcass, legs and shoulders.
Trunk	Carcass, legs.
Necks	Pair of forequarters, shoulders.
Sets, Targets	Scrag, middle neck, breasts (part of Best-Ends, in some instances).

Preparation of Joints and Cuts

Scrag End

Usually used for stewing or stocks. (1) Leave whole or cut down the centre; (2) Remove excess bones, fat and gristle; (3) Cut into 5 cm (2 in.) pieces for stew; (4) Sometimes it is boned out for stew.

Middle Neck – Basses Côtes

Stews (*Navarin*): (1) Remove excess fat and sinew, (2) Cut between the bone into small cutlets, (3) Cut again if necessary and trim. If correctly butchered, this joint can give good uncovered second-class cutlets, called in French *côte seconde* or *côte découverte.*

Best-End – Le Carré

For roasting (Figure 68): (1) Cut on either side of the backbone, from the outside through fat and meat; (3) Then cut from the inside, with a chopping knife or light chopper through the bones, thus removing the complete chine bone (back); (3) Now skin the two Best-Ends from head towards tail and from breast to back; (4) Cut approx 4 cm (2 in.) of fat away from the narrower part of the Best-End, clean sinew between the bones, and cut each of the 6 bones to a point on a slight angle; now cut away back sinew and excess fat, score fat with the point of the knife to an attractive pattern.

Lamb Cutlets – Côtelette d'Agneau

(1) Prepare Best-End as above. (2) Cut into even cutlets between each bone, trim, bat if necessary. *See* Figure 69.

Double Cutlet – Côtelette d'Agneau Double

(1) As before, only cutting a cutlet with 2 bones. (2) Trim and slightly flatten, with bat.

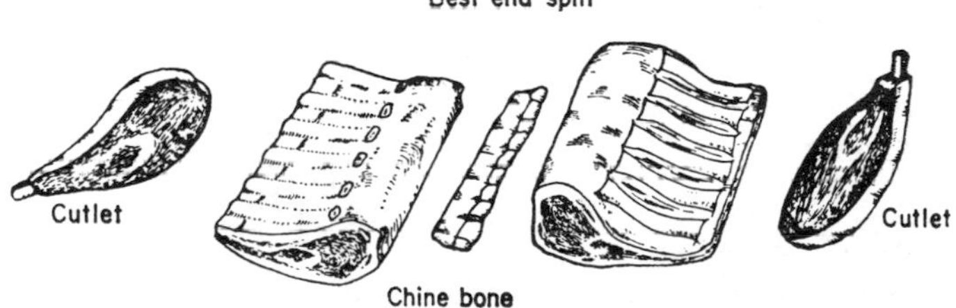

FIG. 69. *Lamb cutlets*

The Saddle – La Selle d'Agneau

A full saddle really consists of saddle and chump; as such it is mainly used for cold buffets and for banquets (*see* Figure 70). For Full Saddle: (1) Cut away about 1 in. of the thin flap, (2) Skin from flap to back and towards tail, (3) Remove kidney and excess fat, score the saddle, (4) Fold flaps under the saddle and tie neatly with string, (5) Bend fail upwards and, for roasting, cover with foil.

For Short Saddle, (1) Cut away chump, remove kidneys and excess fat, (2) Cut away about 2-4 cm (1-2 in.) of flap, skin from flap to back. (3) Fold flaps under, score and neatly tie with string.

The Loin – La Longe d'Agneau

Refer to Figure 71.

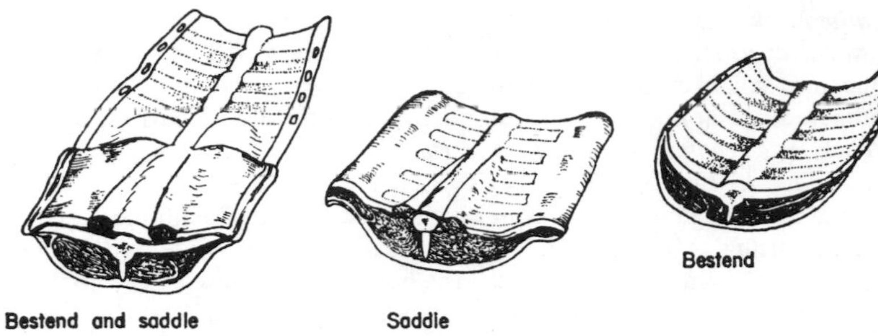

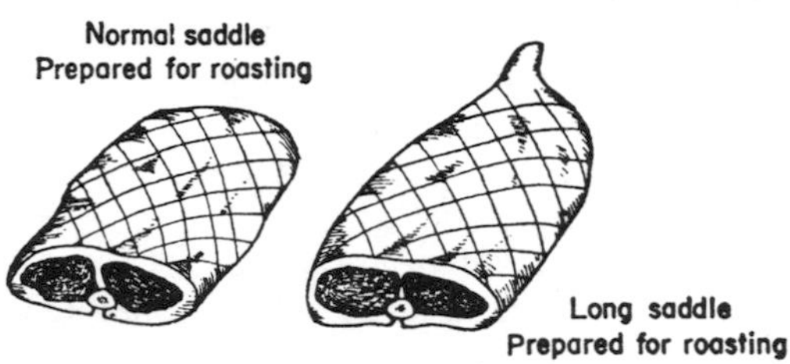

FIG. 70. *Best end and saddle of lamb*

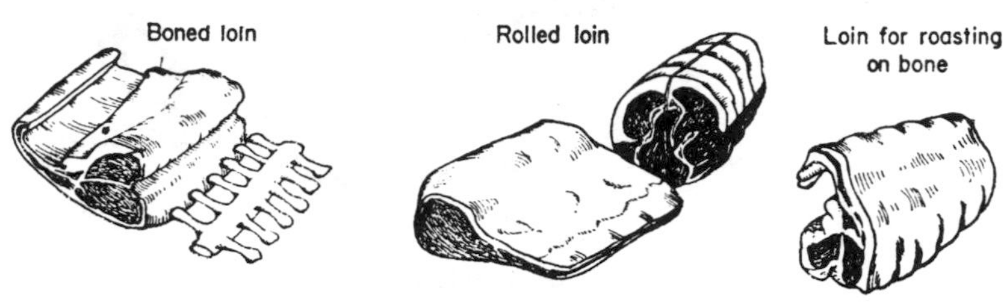

FIG. 71. *Loin of lamb*

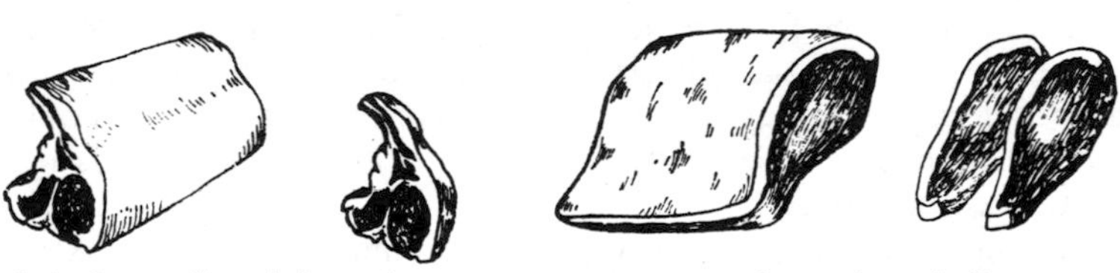

FIG. 72. *Lamb chop*

FIG. 73. *Noisette of lamb*

(1) Chop down neatly the centre of backbone (skewer), (2) Shorten the flap by 2 to 4 cm (1-2 in.), skin from flap to back and tail, (3) Loosen backbone, but leave in its place, score, tie with string.

Stuffed Loin – La Longe d'Agneau Farcie

(1) Prepare as above, but take out bone altogether, (2) Place boneless loin on a board, fill with stuffing, (3) Neatly roll, score and tie with string, (4) Chop bone very small, use with loin, for roasting and gravy (bed of bones).

Lamp Chop – Chop d'Agneau

(1) Trim, skin, and remove some of the inner bone of loin, (2) Fold over flap, stand loin on backbone, cut into chops, 4 to 6, according to weight required (Figure 72).

Noisette of Lamb – Noisette d'Agneau

This is illustrated in Figure 73.

(1) Prepare loin as above, do not roll, (2) Cut on a slight angle into 5 or 6 noisettes of triangular shape, (3) Bat slightly and trim.

Rosette of Lamb – Rosette d'Agneau

(1) Rosettes of Lamb are cut from a boned saddle (Figure 74); cut right across the saddle (it represents two boned chops), (2) The above are rolled towards one another, and secured to shape with a skewer. All recipes and garnishes given for lamb chops apply to Lamb Rosettes.

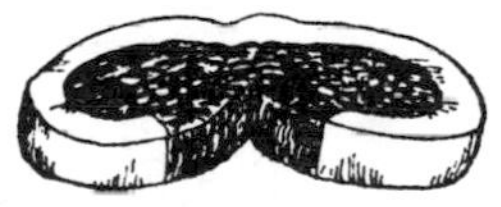

FIG. 74. *Rosette of lamb cut from boned saddle*

Leg of Lamb – Gigot d'Agneau

(1) Shorten, and trim leg bone to leave 4 cm (2 in.) of clean bone (Figure 75), (2) Carefully remove aitchbone, tie neatly the upper leg, (3) Chop knuckle and aitchbone, use as bed for roasting.

Stuffed Leg of Lamb – Gigot d'Agneau Farci

(1) Shorten and trim as above, remove aitchbone, (2) Now carefully loosen meat around leg bone and thigh bone; force steel along the bone, help if needed with knife, remove thus loosened leg bone, stuff and tie; again chop bones and use as bed for roasting.

Breast – La Poitrine

For roasting, (1) Remove skin, excess fat and hard edge, (2) Bone, stuff and roll, tie with string. *See* Figure 76.

For Stews, (1) Cut across into strips, 2 bones at a time, (2) Cut across strip to give a piece 4 cm × 4 cm (2 in. × 2 in.) approx., (3) Skin, excess fat (edge has of course been removed beforehand, as above).

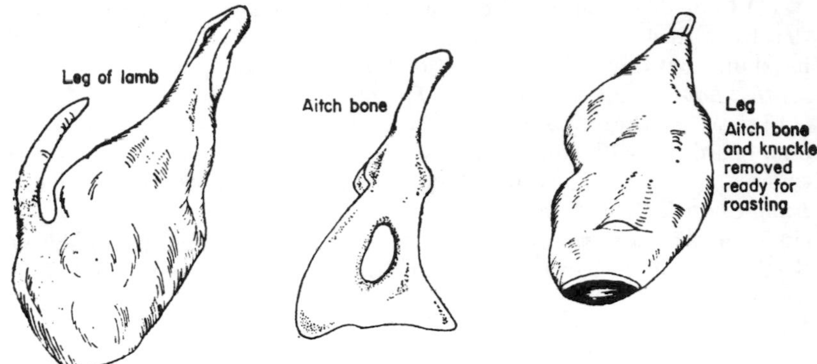

FIG. 75. *Leg of lamb*

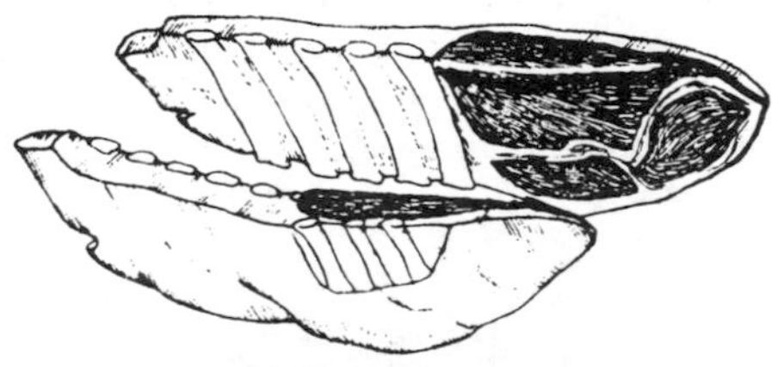

FIG. 76. *Breast of lamb (side views)*

Shoulder – L'Épaule

For Roasting, (1) Clean and trim knuckle bone, leave about 2–4 cm (1 in. to 2 in.) of cleaned bone (*see* Figure 77), (2) Remove blade bone by cutting through the ball-joint between blade and upper-arm bone, (3) With a sharp boning knife, cut under the bone, loosen all sinew and meat, then draw away with the help of a cloth, (4) Now remove upper armbone, by cutting around it with a pointed knife (sometimes a steel will help), (5) Roll, and tie with string.

For Stews, bone as above, cut into 25–50 g (1–2 oz) pieces.

Stuffed Shoulder of Lamb – L'Épaule d'Agneau Farcie (Figure 77)

(1) Prepare shoulder for roasting as described, (2) Remove all but the knuckle bone, (3) Remove excess fat and sinews, (4) Slightly bat opened shoulder, (5) Fill with a stuffing of bread and suet, forcemeat, Duxelles, or a combination of these, (6) Neatly roll and tie with string, (7) A bed of finely chopped bone can be utilized for the roasting.

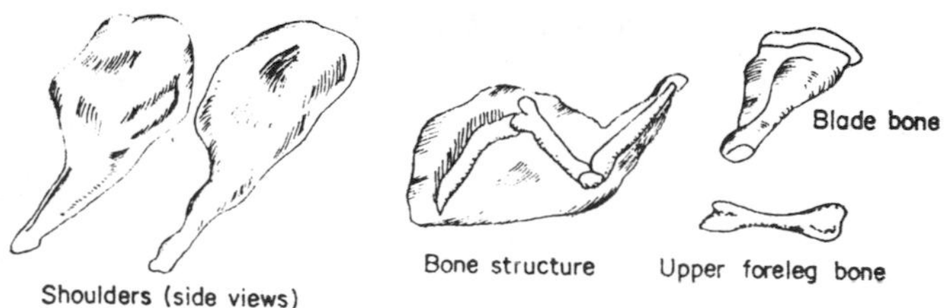

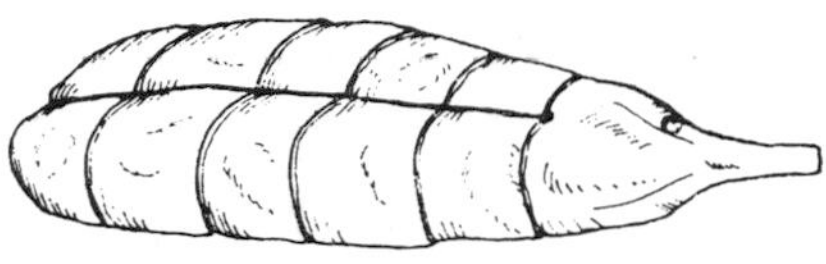

FIG. 77. *Shoulder of lamb*

Special Lamb Preparations

Baron d'Agneau
Consisting of both legs and saddle in one piece and roasted and served this way.
Agneau de Pauillac
Specially young milk lamb, fed in a special way and roasted whole. Usually served at Easter.
Lamb on a Spit – Agneau à la Broche
Here a young lamb is roasted whole on a spit with the aid of coke, charcoal, or gas.
Quarter of Lamb – Quartier d'Agneau
Applies for special parties where a quarter of lamb, that is to say, loin and leg (haunch) is prepared for roasting in one piece. In the case of Lamb Pauillac (a small milk-fed young lamb) both fore and hindquarters can be prepared for roasting as a joint. Sufficient for between 3 to 5 guests.

Lamb Stuffing (English)

50 *g* (2 *oz*) *chopped suet*	*Powdered thyme*
50 *g* (2 *oz*) *chopped onions, cooked*	*Chopped parsley*
1 *small egg*	*Salt and pepper*
100 *g* (4 *oz*) *white breadcrumbs*	

Method: Combine all to taste.

PORK – LE PORC

Dissection

The accompanying table gives general information about the cuts and uses of pork.

Cuts of Pork

Cuts or joints	French Term	Uses	Approx. Weight 30 kg (60 lb)
(1) Head	la téte	Brawn, whole, decorated for buffets*	3–4 kg* (8lb)
(2) Spare rib	l'échine	Roasting, pies	2 kg (3 lb)
(3) Loin	la longe	Roasting, frying, grilling	6 kg (12 lb)
(4) Leg	le cuissot	Roasting and boiling, ham	5 kg (10 lb)
(5) Shoulder, hand-spring	l'épaule/plat de côtes	Roasting, sausages and pies	3 kg (6 lb)
(6) Belly	la poitrine	Boiling, braising	2 kg (4 lb)
(7) Trotter	le pied	Grilling, boiling, brawn	2 kg (4 lb)

*Uses and weights are for a side of pork, except for the head, where the weight is given for the whole head.

With a whole pork carcass (Figures 78 and 79), start by splitting the first few vertebrae from the tail end by pulling down steadily with a knife. Find the line of the spinal processes by finger pressure and make a light cut through the skin, along the spine, from the original cut to the nape of the

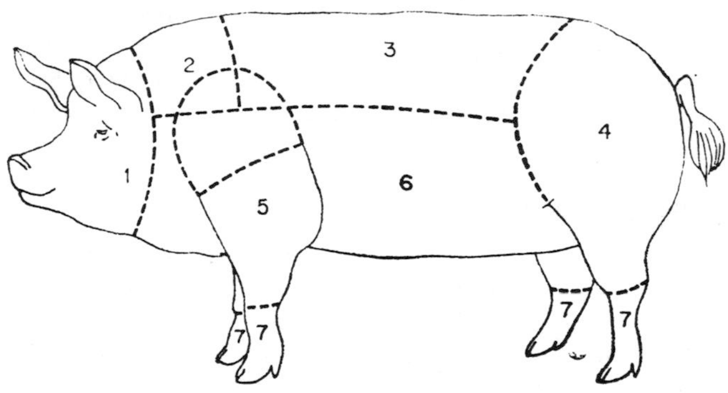

FIG. 78. *The pig*

neck. Hold the ear of the pig and make a clean incision across the back of the neck in line with the first cervical vertebrae. Continue the cut round the side of the joint, following the line of the jawbone, to remove the head.

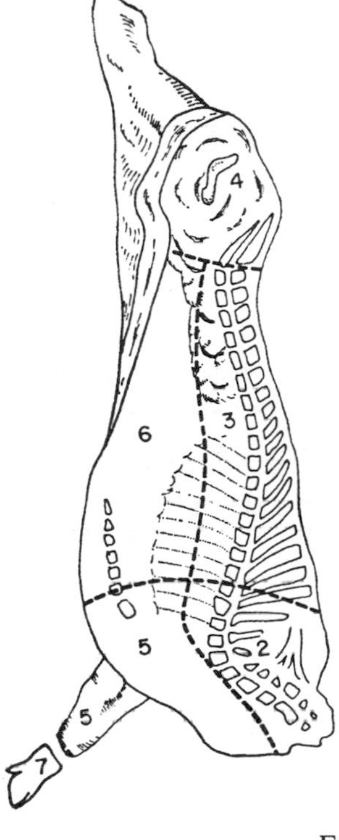

Chop down the line of the spine with a light chopper to separate the carcass into 2 sides.

(1) Lay the side on the cutting block and break the trotter by cutting across the back and pressing the trotter forward sharply. Remove the leg by marking across the joint 1 cm ($\frac{1}{2}$ in.) below the round part of the aitchbone, to a point slightly diagonally some 4 cm (2 in.) above the base of the tail. Saw through the bone and follow with a clean cut with the knife. This gives a square cut leg leaving the tail on the leg. The line can be varied according to the amount of chump end required on the loin.

(2) Separate the hand, spring and belly from the long loin by finding the joint between the bladebone and humerus and, from this point, mark down over the ribs and cut through the belly wall down to the chump end. Saw through the ribs and finish with a sharp knife. Avoid sawing through the meat. Complete by loosening the humerus from the bladebone and making one clean cut.

FIG. 79. *Pork dissection*

(3) Separate hand and spring from the belly by pulling the shin bone forward and cutting between the 1st and 2nd ribs.

(4) Separate the loin from the long loin by cutting between the 4th and 5th ribs. This will leave a small amount of cartilage of the bladebone in the loin. The loin can be divided between the 12th and 13th ribs, to produce 'fore loin' (Best-End) and 'hind loin' with chump End.

(5) The bladebone can be separated from the spare rib by cutting round the line of the bladebone, pressing on top with the left hand to tilt the bone from the spare rib. Then make a clean cut.

(6) A round cut leg, leaving the tail on the loin, can be obtained by cutting a semi-circular line from below the base of the tail, to a point 1–2 cm ($\frac{1}{2}$ in.) below the rounded part of the aitchbone, then straight across to the belly.

Ordering Wholesale Cuts

Loin, Long Loin	Loin, including neck end.
Short Loin	Loin, neck end.
Hog Meat	Loin, rind and some back fat.
Hand and Belly	Hand, spring, belly.
Fore-End	Neck end, hand, spring.
Hand	Hand and spring.
Jacket	Side, leg.
Pig X	Carcass, head.
Neck end	Spare rib and bladebone.
Middles	Short loins and bellies.

Uses for Cuts and Joints

Head – La Tête de Porc
The head of pork is used for the making of pig's or boar's head for cold buffets or for brawn itself. If the pig's head is to be used for boar's head, it should be cut a little longer, using part of the neck.
Spare Rib – L'Échine de Porc
A second-class roast, a little on the fat side (Figure 80); it should be freed of excess fat, the rind scored and tied in 2 to 3 places with string. The spare rib can be put to good use in the making of pork pies, patés, and sausages, for which it is better suited than for roasting. The spare rib may also be grilled and is especially useful for barbecues, when it should be boned and freed of rind and excess fat.

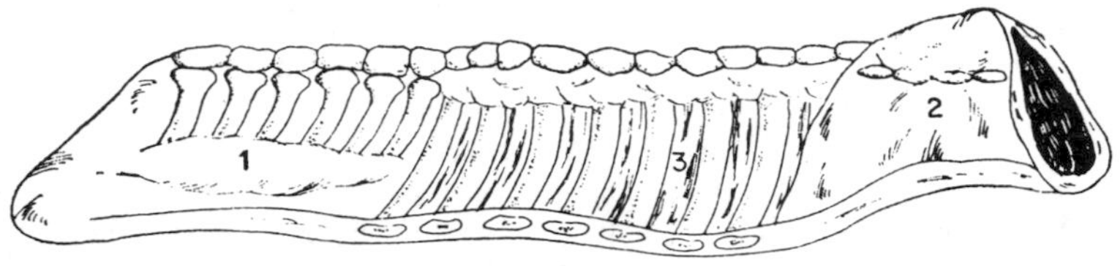

FIG. 80. *Long loin of pork:* (1) *loin,* (2) *spare rib and* (3) *cutlet piece*

Long Loin – La Longe de Porc
The long loin (Figure 81) is usually cut into 2 joints, representing as for lamb, a Best End or cutlets piece (fore loin); 'C' loin or chop piece (back loin). The fore loin can be roasted whole but it is more often used for the cutting of pork cutlets. For this purpose, remove the chine-bone and rind. It is a doubtful practice to leave the rind on pork cutlets and chops as some butchers do. The rind is very good if any joint of pork is going to be roasted but, in the case of cutlets and chops which are going to be fried or grilled, the rind should be removed. Once the fore loin is prepared, as described

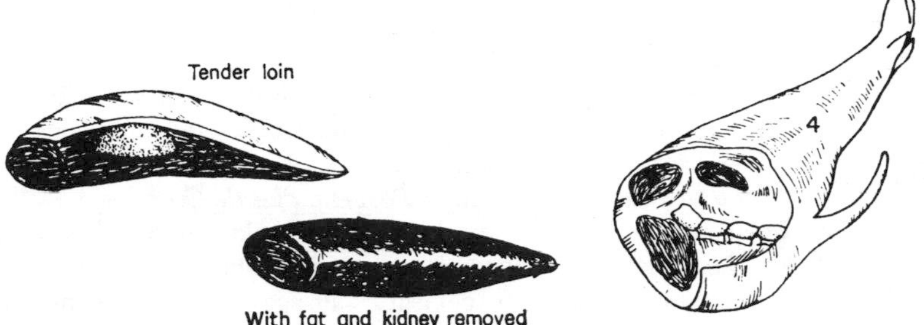

FIG. 81. *Loin of pork*

FIG. 82. *Leg and trotter*

above, cut it between each bone into neat cutlets which, if necessary, are slightly batted and trimmed.

Loin of Pork – La Longe de Porc

The actual loin is an excellent piece for roasting; it should be carefully boned but the bones are left in place. After removing the back sinew and scoring the rind, the loin has only to be tied in 2 or 3 places to be ready for roasting.

Stuffed Loin of Pork – La Longe de Porc Farcie

Stuffing the loin is prepared much as the loin for roasting as given above but in this instance the bones are actually removed. The loin is then batted slightly and filled with a stuffing of bread, forcemeat or duxelles, or a combination of these three. Neatly and evenly rolled, the rind should be scored and the loin tied in 2 or 3 places. The bones from the loin are finely chopped and used as a bed for roasting the loin. As in the case of veal and lamb, the kidney can be rolled with the stuffing used for the loin.

Pork Chop – Chop de Porc

The pork chops are cut from the loin; to cut neat chops, one should trim the backbone, remove back sinew and rind. Folding over the flap and standing on backbone, the bone is thus easily cut into neat chops which again can be slightly batted and trimmed if necessary.

Leg of Pork – Le Cuissot de Porc

The leg represents a most excellent roast (Figure 82); after removing the aitchbone and trotters, the rind is scored into a neat pattern with the point of a sharp knife. The aitchbone is chopped and used with the leg as a bed for roasting.

Boning a Leg of Pork

A leg of pork is boned in very much the same way as a leg of veal, the cuts being similar. Because of more fat on the leg of pork the dividing seams are not so easily found and the boning should be carried out with care. The instructions given for boning a leg of veal can otherwise be followed for pork. The joints can, as for veal, be roasted whole or cut into pork escalopes or steaks.

Leg of Pork as Ham

If the leg of pork is required for ham, it must of course be brined. For this purpose one usually removes the aitchbone and trotter and immerses the leg in a brine (see section on 'Brines').

Shoulder or Hand of Pork – L'Épaule de Porc/Le Plat de Côtes

Carefully boned and tied into a neat joint, the shoulder or hand is often acceptable as a 2nd-class roast. More often, however, the shoulder is boned and used in the making of pork forcemeats, sausages and pies. It can also be neatly diced and used in pork stews, especially Goulash.

Belly of Pork – La Poitrine de Porc

The best and most popular use for belly of pork (Figure 83) is in the making of pork sausages, as well as other German or French sausages. Boned and freed of its rind, it is also useful for the making of forcemeats – not necessarily of pork only, but of forcemeat of other meats where some fat pork is required. As a joint, it really has only one use, i.e. to be brined and to be boiled and served with various vegetables, or pease puddings, and even Sauerkraut, which should always be cooked with a piece of fat, brined pork or bacon.

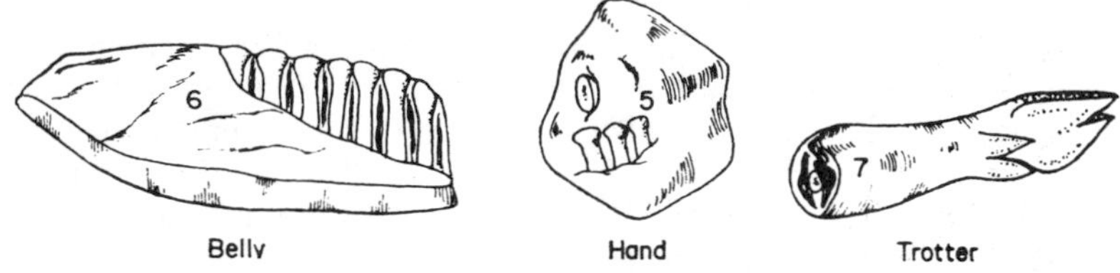

FIG. 83. *Belly, hand and trotter*

Pig Trotters – Pieds de Porc

After cleaning the pig trotters thoroughly, they are boiled usually in a seasoned blanc to gain a good white colour. Cooled in the stock in which they were boiled, pig trotters can be used for several tasty dishes.

Grilled Pigs Trotters – Pieds de Porc Grillés

Boiled as above, and cooled, the gelatinous meat of the trotters is removed from the bones in one piece. Seasoned, brushed with mustard and oil they are then grilled to a golden brown.

Pigs Trotters' Salad – Salade de Pieds de Porc

Cook in a blanc and cool; remove the meat from the trotters, cut into fine Julienne, mix with onions and herbs and flavour with a vinaigrette.

Pigs Trotters used for Brawn

Because of their gelatinous texture and binding, pig trotters can be put to various uses in the making of brawns. For this purpose the trotters should be boiled, not in a blanc but clear salted water with some seasoning and *Mirepoix* to get a clear stock (see 'Chef du Froid').

BACON, GAMMON, AND HAMS

BACON

The old French word *bacon* has passed into the English language like so many others. It meant pork generally and was used especially when talking about the pig's salted back-fat, which was used extensively for all sorts of larding and barding as well as for the making of soups and certain sauces.

In England, bacon means a side of pork partly boned, salted and cured and smoked. It is also found only salted or cured, and as such it is called 'green bacon' which is used very much the same as the smoked type.

Smoked or green bacon has a very high protein value, and one can make many a tasty dish from it, either by frying, grilling or boiling. The main cuts of bacon are illustrated in Figure 84. *Note:* These weights are approximately to a side of bacon weighing 30 kg (60 lb). A whole gammon would weigh 6-8 kg (13 to 85 lb).

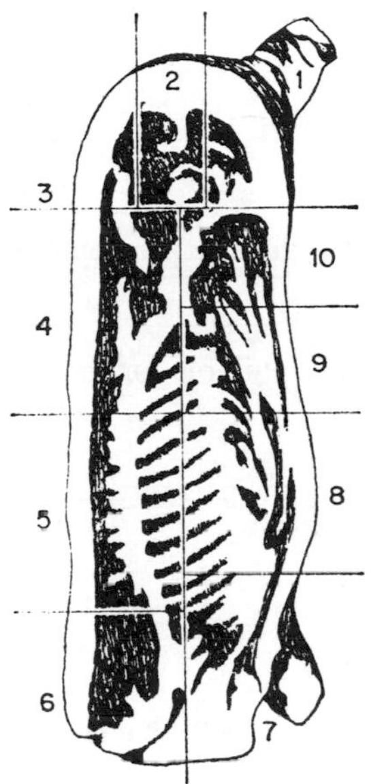

FIG. 84. *Cuts of bacon*

Cuts and Joints

(1) Hock of gammon	2 kg (3–4 lb)	Boiling
(2) Middle of gammon	3 kg (6–7 lb)	Grilling and frying
(3) Corner of gammon	2 kg (4–5 lb)	Grilling and frying
(4) Back-bacon	4 kg (7–8 lb)	Grilling and frying
(5) Thick end of back	3 kg (4–6 lb)	Frying and boiling
(6) Collar	4 kg (7–8 lb)	Boiling
(7) Fore-hock	4 kg (8–10 lb)	Boiling (shoulder ham)
(8) Best streaky	4 kg (7–8 lb)	Grilling and frying
(9) Thin streaky	2 kg (3–4 lb)	Grilling and frying lardons
(10) Flank	$1\frac{1}{2}$ kg (3–4 lb)	Boiling and frying

Preparation of a Side of Bacon

After removing the gammon from the side of bacon, the whole side of bacon (less gammon) is split lengthwise, in half. This is usually done by marking a line of the long cut to be made, with the point of a sharp knife. Follow this line with the knife to cut a straight line right through the side as far as the rib-bones will allow. A flat saw is now used to saw through the bones, continuing with a clean cut by a knife. At all times, one should avoid sawing through the actual meat. Once the side of bacon is split lengthwise, the two narrow parts, 'back' and 'streaky', are then jointed as indicated in the illustration.

Uses for Cuts and Joints

Hock of Gammon
Really the knuckle of bacon, good use can be made of it in the making of sauces, soups, stews etc.
Middle of Gammon
Ideal joint for gammon steaks. For this purpose, the thigh bone should be carefully removed, before cutting into slices.
Corner Gammon
Slightly trimmed of excess fat, the corner cut is most suitable for the cutting of gammon steaks.
Back Bacon
The joint with the leanest back-bacon: after removing the part of the small chine-bone, and sliced, it is ideal for grilling (breakfast).
Thick End of Bacon
This joint is still good back-bacon although slightly more fatty and broad. When sliced, it can also be used for braising in one piece.
Collar
Boned and rolled, it is usually boiled or braised. Boiled, it is (as ham) often used for the making of sandwiches (shoulder ham).
Fore Hock
Boned and rolled, it can be used for boiling or braising, as above. The fore-knuckle is removed for this purpose and used as guide-knuckle No. 1.
Best Streaky
After boning this joint with a piece of string, or wire, and removing the bacon rind, it is cut into thin slices for grilling, or used as a supplement to back-bacon. Many people prefer streaky bacon to the leaner back because of its good flavour. Best Streaky can also be used for *Lardons, Cromesquis, patés*, and potted preparations.
Thin Streaky
Although much narrower than the Best Streaky, it use is much the same.
Flank
Flabby and quite fat, the flank of bacon finds its best use in pies, patés and other potted preparations where fat pork or bacon is required.

GAMMON

A gammon is always the hind leg of a side bacon, whether it is green or smoked. Gammons are suitable for boiling, braising and baking and may be served hot or cold. The best known gammon types are *Danish* (green and smoked), *Wiltshire* (green and smoked).

Preparation of Joints and Cuts

Boiling. Soak the gammon in cold water for at least 24 hours, then scrub with a hard brush, especially around the aitchbone and knuckle. For boiling, place the gammon into a Jambonnière or similar type of pan. Cover with fresh cold water and bring to the boil. Skim and draw to the side of the stove. Allow the gammon to gently simmer 20 to 25 min per $\frac{1}{2}$ kg (lb). Leave to cool in its own cooking liquor.

Cold Gammon Service

Prepare and cook the gammon as above. When cooked, remove all rind and excess fat and clean knuckled bone to a handle for carving. Brush the gammon with made-up English mustard and sprinkle with freshly fried breadcrumbs. Surround with a ham-frill and the gammon is ready for carving.

A second method may be employed, which is more commonly used on the Continent: brush the prepared gammon, as above, with English or French mustard, then sprinkle with caster or brown sugar and place in a hot oven to achieve a good even brown glaze. Allow the gammon to cool, surround with ham-frill and the gammon is ready for carving.

Preparation for Gammon Chaud-Froid

See Chef du Froid section.

Braising

For braising, the gammon is prepared as for boiling. The cooking time should be cut down to only about 15 min per $\frac{1}{2}$ kg (lb) of gammon. Slightly cool, then removed rind and excess fat. Place the gammon whole, or boned and cut into neat joints, on a bed of root vegetables in a Jambonnière and neatly stud with a pattern of cloves. Now cover the gammon with *demi-glace*, or *espagnole*, plus some of its cooking liquor (about half way) and place in the oven to braise until cooked.

Baking

Prepare and boil the gammon, as above, for 15 to 20 min per $\frac{1}{2}$ kg (lb) of gammon. Remove rind and excess fat and leave gammon to cool on the outside. Now fold gammon into a large sheet of short or puff paste, the paste meeting underneath the gammon. Garnish with a design, using the pastry trimmings. Eggwash well; bake in a medium to hot over to set the pastry for about 20 to 30 min, then turn oven low and continue to bake in low oven, heat for another 40 to 60 min. This type of gammon is invariably served on cold buffets but it can also be served hot.

HAMS

Ham is always the hind leg of a side of pork and, as such, removed beforehand The ham is in most cases cut rather long into the loin to give a banjo shape. Dry cured by the rubbing in of salt, or wet cured in a brine, most hams are smoked and hung to dry. Differentiate between 3 basic types:
(a) Those which are usually cured in a brine, slightly smoked or dried and invariably cooked and served hot or cold, e.g. *Jambon Glacè, Hamburger Schinken.*
(b) These dry or wet cured hams, always smoked (often very deep), hung to dry over a period of months or years, always served raw or slightly sautéd, e.g. *Jambon de Bayonne, Toulouse, Westphalian.*
(c) Dry or wet cured hams but not smoked, hung to dry and to mature for a month and then cooked and served hot or cold, e.g. *York Ham, Gothaer Schinken*, or (dried and hung to mature for a long time) e.g. *Jambon de Parme*, served raw.

American Hams – Jambon d'Amérique

American hams are invariably of the green type and cured in a brine (wet cure) with the addition of molasses which makes them rather sweet. Often very large, they are suitable for boiling, braising and baking and can be served hot or cold.

British Hams – Jambon d'Angleterre

This type of ham is wet cured, with the addition of black treacle; this, together with smoking, gives the ham its very dark colour. Braden ham is slightly sweet in flavour, suitable to be served hot, or cold.
York Ham
The best known of the British hams, it is of long cut and distinct banjo shape. Cured, it is hung up to dry in cool cellars for up to 3 to 4 months. During this period a green mould grows on the ham, especially around the aitchbone and knuckle. This mould growth adds to the flavour and is easily washed off before cooking. York ham is considered to be one of the finest hams and is well known and appreciated as a delicacy on the Continent and elsewhere.

Czechoslovakian Hams – Jambon de Bohème

Of the Czechoslovakian hams, the *Jambon de Prague* is the most famous. Cured, smoked and dried, it is usually eaten raw but can be sautéd and served with egg dishes. Its appearance and flavour are similar to the raw German hams.

Danish Hams – Jambon Danois

With the Danish hams, the curing starts already while pigs are still alive. That is to say, they are fed on a special diet. Wet cured in a special brine, the Danish hams are hung to dry and are available smoked or green. The Danish ham has a very fine meat grain and is most suitable for boiling, braising, and baking and can be served hot or cold.

French Hams – Jambon Français

Jambon de Campagne
A ham, slightly sweeter in cure than most French hams, it is well smoked and invariably served raw. It can be sautéd and served with egg dishes and forms part of garnishes for several sauces and stews. It should not be boiled.

Jambon de Bayonne
This is a dried-cured ham, smoked and hung to dry and mature. Usually served raw in very thin slices, it is not suitable for boiling but it may be used as garnishes with certain sauces and stews, or slightly sautéd with egg-dishes.

Jambon de Toulouse
This ham is cured and dried, at times even smoked; it is usually eaten raw. It can be used in cooking but, again, must not be boiled.

Jambon Blanc, Jambon Demi-Sel, Jambon de Paris
These 3 hams are of the same type and usually green, but in certain cases they can be found slightly smoked, sweet in flavour. They are suitable for boiling and to be served cold but, more often than not, they are braised or baked and served hot. It is for this reason that these 3 hams are known as *jambon glacé*.

German Hams – Jambon d'Allemagne

Gothaer Schinken, Hamburger Schinken, Stuttgarter Schinken, Mainzer Schinken, Westphalian Schinken, Schwarzwälder Schinken. All six famous German hams can be eaten raw but the first 3 are often boiled, braised, or baked and served hot or cold. The last 3 are always eaten raw. Of delicate sweet cure and deep smoked, with selected woods, they are cut into paper thin slices and eaten as Hors d'Œuvre. The Germans will eat these hams at any time of day together with rye bread and a glass of lager. Lightly fried, they are delicious with all kinds of egg dishes.

Hungarian Hams – Jambon de Hongrie

Like the German hams, the Hungarian are also served raw; they are also similar in appearance and flavour. Some Hungarian hams are red or pink in colour; this is because they are rubbed with paprika before and after smoking, then hung to dry for several months. Here the *Jambon de Gynlai* and *Jambon Esterhazy* are the best known.

Italian Hams – Jambon d'Italie

There are a great number of Italian hams, of which the *Jambon de Parme* is the most famous of all. The Parma ham is cured and hung to dry for several months and served, invariably, raw. Lightly fried in butter, is is also served with a number of egg and pasta dishes. In Britain it can be bought in round flat tins, ready sliced, with a sheet of greaseproof paper between each slice to allow an easy service. Other Italian hams are suited for boiling, braising and baking and can be served hot or cold.

Spanish Hams – Jambon d'Espagne

The Spanish hams are usually mild in cure, with a delicate flavour and invariably smoked and dried. All Spanish hams are suitable for boiling, braising and baking and may be served hot or cold. The best known is the *Jambon de Asturias.*

Note. The description of curing and smoking of these different hams is necessarily cursory since the methods used, employing selected woods and special drying techniques, are closely guarded secrets of the respective countries and manufacturers; quite often these recipes are known only to a handful of people.

Preparations

Boiling, braising, baking – see instructions for gammon.

Ham 'Chaud-Froid'

See under Section 'Chef du Froid'.

Carving

After placing gammon or ham on a ham holder, it is cut with a long carving knife, starting from the knuckle upwards (*see* Figure 85). The carving is continued with neat cuts of a sawing motion. When the aitchbone part is reached, the ham is turned around and cut in the same way. Many bone the ham or gammon in advance to allow for easier cutting without a bone,

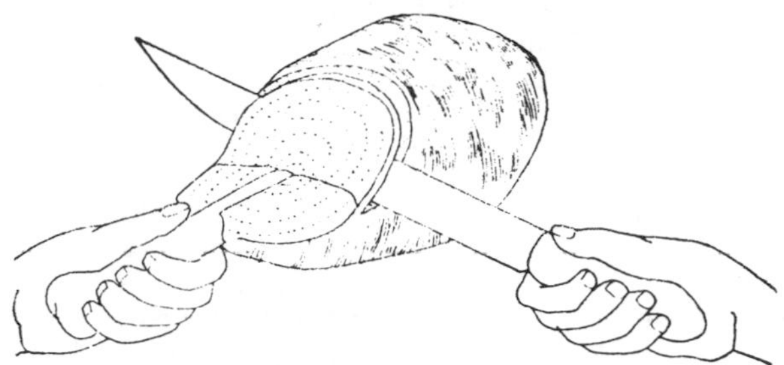

FIG. 85. *Carving boiled gammons and hams*

but there is no doubt that a ham cooked and carved on the bone has a much better flavour.

Carving Raw Ham

Raw ham is always surrounded by its rind. For carving, the rind should be carefully removed. For smaller establishments it is advisable only to remove as much rind as the ham required for a particular order, after which the ham is hung again in a cool place. For larger establishments, where large

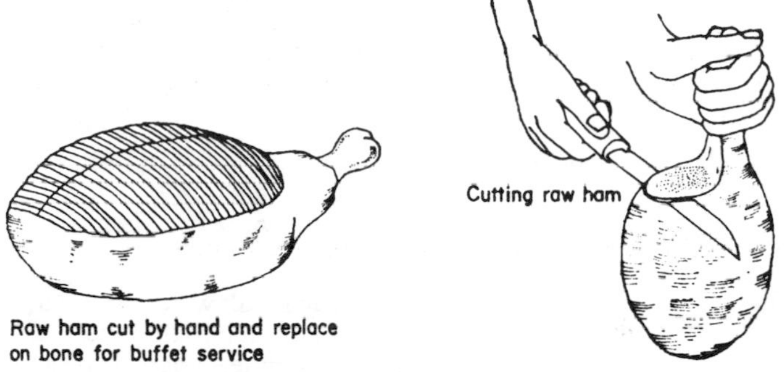

FIG. 86. *Carving raw ham*

quantities of raw hams are served each day, the whole ham may be freed of its rind and cut. With modern slicing machines, the raw ham may be boned and the rind removed beforehand, then sliced on the machine. The trimmings are then used for garnishes in sauces and stews. *See* Figure 86.

OFFAL

(1) Beef/Ox – Abats de Bœuf

English	*French*	*Preparation*
Brains	*cervelle*	Soak well in cold water. Clean and remove membranes which cover brain. Re-soak to whiten. Place in boiling strained *court bouillon.* *Cook 20–30 min. Cool in liquor. *Poach. *Uses: ravioli filling, hot and cold brain sauces.*
Heart	*coeur de bœuf*	Open the heart without separating halves. Trim off excess fat and tubes. Remove clots of blood. Sprinkle with olive oil and lemon juice. Marinade for 30 min. Season with salt and pepper. Stuff, if required, with pork forcemeat or savoury stuffing. Wrap in larding bacon cut paper-thin, or pig's caul. Tie with string.
Kidney	*rognon*	Trim off all fat and tubes. Remove membranes and skin. Cut into slices or dice, as required. *Uses: kidney pies, steak and kidney pies, kidney soup.*
Liver	*foie de bœuf*	Trim off tubes and sinew. Skin. Cut into thin slices. *Uses: braised ox liver.*
Muzzle	*museau*	Soak in salt water for 6–8 hours. Boil. Cool. Cut into thin slices, season with vinaigrette, chopped fine herbs, chopped onion. *Uses: Hors d'Œuvre.*
Palate	*palais*	Soak in cold water for 6 to 8 hours. Blanch, refresh, drain. Remove skin. Cook in *blanc.* *Uses: Palate Salad.*

Tail	*queue de bœuf*	(1) Trim skinned tail of excess fat. Cut into chunks through cartilage between segments of bone. *Uses: Oxtail soup or stew.* (2) Soak unskinned tail whole, in cold water. Bone without damaging skin. Season, salt and pepper, spices. Stuff, reshape, sew up. Wrap in cloth and tie with string. *Uses: stuffed oxtail.*
Tongue	*langue*	Can be used fresh or pickled. (1) Fresh: Soak in salt water for 24 hours; trim. (2) Pickled: Trim, soak in cold water for a few hours. Prick all over, rub with salt and saltpetre. Steep in brine 6–8 days. Soak in cold water, to remove excess salt. Boil 2–3 hours.
Tripe	*gras-double, tripe*	Usually bought clean, washed and blanched. Cut into square pieces or cooked in salt *court bouillon* and cut into squares or strips, as required.

(2) Pig's Offal – Abats de Porc

English	*French*	*Preparation*
Bladder	*vessie*	Washed, blown up, dried, used as casing for large sausages or wrapping lard. Can be used for wrapping poultry prepared *en chemise*.
Brains	*cervelles*	As for ox brains.
Smoked cheek 'Bath chap'	*joue de porc fumée*	Treated like ham. Boiled in water and usually served cold.
Pig's ears	*oreilles de porc*	Singe, clean insides, boil in salt water with carrot, studded onion and bouquet garni for 45–50 min. *Uses: salad for Hors d'Œuvre.*

Trotters	*pieds*	Prepare as for lamb trotters. When cooked, drain, straighten, press between 2 boards and cool. *Uses: salads, grilled.*
Kidney	*rognon*	Prepare as for lamb's kidney. Can be diced or sliced for pies, puddings, sauté, etc.
Pig's lights	*mou de porc*	Prepare and use as for lamb's pluck.
Liver	*foie*	As for ox liver.
Snout	*groin de porc*	Prepare as for ears or trotters.
Tail	*queue de porc*	Prepare as for ears or trotters. Cool under press. Can be grilled.
Tongue	*langue*	Prepare as for ox tongue. Can be pickled in same way and used as ingredient in potted head and brawn.

(3) Lamb/Mutton Offal – Abats d'Agneau/Mouton

English	*French*	*Preparation*
Brains	*cervelles*	As for ox brains.
Kidney	*rognon*	(1) Slit on bulging side and open without separating the two halves. Remove the skin, trim tubes, skewer to keep kidney open. (2) Divide into 2 halves lengthways, skin and trim. *Uses: grilled lamb's kidneys.*
Liver	*foie*	As for ox liver; can be skewered.
Lamb Pluck	*fressure d'agneau*	(Liver, heart, spleen, lungs). Blanch spleen and lungs in salt water for 10 min. Slice all thinly. Fry in clarified butter. *Uses: hash, sauté, stews.*
Sweetbreads	*ris d'agneau*	Soak in cold water. Blanch, trim, cook in white stock, butter and lemon juice. Simmer for 25 min. Cool, used as garnish in vol-au-vents, pies, etc.

Tongue	*langue*	Soak in cold water, scald, skin and trim.
Trotters	*pieds*	Blanched, boned, singed. Hair in cleavage of hoof removed, also hoof. Cook in *blanc*.
Heart	*coeur*	As for ox heart.

(4) Veal Offal – Abats de Veau

English	*French*	*Preparation*
Spinal marrow	*amourette*	Prepared and used as for brains.
Brains	*cervelles*	Prepare as for ox brains.
Ears	*oreilles de veau*	Prepare as for pig's ears.
Calf's feet	*pieds de veau*	Soak in cold water, bone out, blanch, cook in *blanc*. Treat as for sheep's foot.
Calf's head (Figure 59)	*tête de veau*	Bone out, soak in acidulated water for a few hours. Blanch, refresh, rub all over with cut lemon; trim, particularly insides of mouth, eyes, nostrils and neck. Cut into squares (portions) or leave whole. Cook in white *court bouillon* (*blanc*).
Heart	*coeur*	Prepare as for ox or sheep's heart.
Kidney	*rognon*	Skin, trim off tubes, and excess fat. Cut into slices or escalopes or leave whole.
Liver	*foie de veau*	Prepare as for ox or sheep's liver. *Uses: fried, sauté, braised.*
Lungs	*mou de veau*	Beat vigorously to expel air. Cut into uniform pieces. Blanch. *Uses: hash, stews.*
Sweetbreads	*ris de veau*	Two glands taken from calves. The long ones near the throat and the round ones near the heart. Soak in

		cold water to whiten. Blanch, refresh, drain. Press between 2 boards after carefully trimming off tubes and sinews with larding needle, stud with truffle, ham or tongue as required. Braise white or brown. Can be cut into escalopes and eggwashed and crumbed.

(5) Poultry Offal – Abatis

English	*French*	*Preparation*
Chickens' livers	*foie de volaille*	Pinch out gall bladder carefully, so as not to burst it. Trim the livers into 2 or 3 pieces. Season, seal quickly in sizzling butter. Arrange on skewers alternating with blanched bacon and thick slices of mushroom, tossed in butter. Can be used sauté without skewers or as ingredient for *farce au gratin* or *pâté maison.*
Duck livers	*foie de caneton*	Prepare and use as above.
Giblets	*abatis*	Head, neck, heart, winglets, feet, liver, cocks combs, kidney. These are found on all poultry and the giblets of large birds are used for ragoûts or for improving taste of stocks or soups. They should be thoroughly washed and trimmed, the neck, head and winglets singed, the feet scalded and scaled, the spurs trimmed. The gizzard is split on the curved side, opened and the inner bag removed. The gall bladder pinched out and the upper part of the heart trimmed. The cocks comb scalded and rubbed with salt to remove the outer skin.

6. *Forcemeats, Garnishes, and Seasonings*

FORCEMEATS – LES FARCES

In the making of forcemeats it is very important that only the best of meats and other materials are used. All forcemeats should have a good binding but at the same time should be light and not too dry. To get a good binding, breadcrumbs are used for the simpler forcemeats, and so-called Panades for the finer ones. To make them smooth, light and white, water, milk, or cream is used according to the forcemeat made.

There are numerous forcemeats, from the simple sausage-meat to the finer forcemeats used for the making of hot mousses and soufflés. They are usually made from the white meats, like veal and pork as well as from poultry, game, fish and certain vegetables and bread. To call the latter forcemeats would, in English, not be quite correct; those made of vegetables and bread are usually called stuffing, whereas, in French, all of these are known as farces.

Although they differ in method within one section, there are 3 basic types: (1) Forcemeats made of raw meats, (2) Forcemeats made of cooked meats, (3) Farces or stuffings made of vegetables or bread.

Bindings, or panades, are very important to make a good forcemeat. First in use are breadcrumbs soaked in water, milk or cream, which are used in the making of sausage-meats, veal-loaf or pojarski. Secondly come the panades, of which five in everyday use are given here. If some recipes name mashed potatoes, béchamel or veloutés for the binding of certain forcemeat, although these are widely in use they are in fact only a simplification of the panades used in first-class cooking.

Bread Panada – Panade au Pain

100 g (4 oz) white breadcrumbs
¼ l. (½ pint) milk
25 g (1 oz) butter
Salt, pepper and grated nutmet

(1) Soak breadcrumbs for 15 mins. in milk.
(2) Place into a sauteuse, bring to boil.
(3) Gently simmer on the side, stirring with spatula until almost dry.
(4) Add seasoning and butter, continue to stir until firm.
(5) Place on a buttered tray and cover with butter-paper, cool.
Used for fish forcemeats (e.g. quenelles), veal forcemeats.

Potato Panada – Panade à la Pomme de Terre

250 g (8 oz) cooked sieved potatoes
$\frac{1}{4}$ l. ($\frac{1}{2}$ pint) milk
25 g (1 oz) butter
Salt, pepper and nutmeg

(1) Moisten potatoes with milk in a sauteuse.
(2) Place on the stove, gradually bring to the boil.
(3) Add butter and seasoning.
(4) Take to the side, stirring all the time with a spatula until almost dry.
(5) Place on a buttered tray and cool.
Used for large white-meat quenelles and fricadelles.

Rice Panada – Panade au Riz

2 cups of Caroline rice
6 cups good veal or chicken stock
1 studded onion
25 g (1 oz) butter
Salt, pepper and grated nutmeg

(1) Bring the stock to the boil.
(2) Add the washed rice, stir until stock reboils.
(3) Gently boil on the side of the stove until rice dissolves.
(4) Pass through a fine sieve.
(5) Return to stove in a clean sauteuse, add butter and seasonings.
(6) Gently simmer on side of stove, stirring all the time with a spatula.
(7) Place on a buttered tray, cover with buttered paper and cool.
Use for large meat and fish quenelles.

Flour Panada – Panade pour Farce à la Farine

$\frac{1}{4}$ l. ($\frac{1}{2}$ pint) water
50 g (2 oz) butter
100 g (4 oz) flour
Salt, pepper and nutmeg

(1) Bring water, butter and seasoning to boil, take aside.
(2) Add the sieved flour, stirring with a spatula all the time (choux paste).
(3) Continue to stir until mixture loosens from the bottom of the pan.
(4) Place on a buttered tray, cover with a buttered cartouche.
(5) Cool.
Used for meat forcemeats and quenelles.

Frangipane Panada – Panade à la Frangipane

$\frac{1}{4}$ l. ($\frac{1}{2}$ pint) milk
75 g (3 oz) butter
100 g (4 oz) of flour
4 yolks of eggs
Salt, pepper and grated nutmeg

(1) Heat milk, butter and seasoning.
(2) Mix yolks and flour in a china bowl to a smooth paste.

(3) Pour hot milk on to yolk and flour paste in the bowl, stirring all the time.
(4) Put mixture into a sauteuse, gently cook on the side of the stove until it loosens from the bottom of the pan.
(5) Place on a buttered tray, cover with a buttered cartouche and cool.
Used for all finer forcemeats of fish, chicken or game (farce fine). *All panadas must be very cold before adding to meats.*

SIMPLE RAW FORCEMEATS

Pork Sausagemeat – La Farce de Porc (Saucisses) Anglaise

250 g (8 oz) *lean pork, diced*
100 g (4 oz) *pork fat, diced*
100 g (4 oz) *white breadcrumbs*
12 cl (¼ *pint*) *of iced water*
15 g (½ oz) *spice salt or other sausage seasonings*

(1) Moisten crumbs with water.
(2) Mix pork fat, meat and seasoning.
(3) Mince through a fine mincer-blade.
(4) Mix all ingredients, correct seasoning and consistency.

Beef Sausagemeat – La Farce de Boeuf (Saucisses) Anglaise

250 g (8 oz) *lean diced beef*
100 g (4 oz) *pork or bacon fat, diced*
100 g (4 oz) *white breadcrumbs*
2 dl (2 *gills*) *iced water*
15 g (½ oz) *spice salt or other sausage seasonings*

As for pork sausagemeat.

Veal Forcemeat – La Farce de Veau

250 g (8 oz) *diced lean veal*
100 g (4 oz) *diced fat pork*
75 g (2 *to* 4 oz) *white breadcrumbs*
1 dl (1 *gill*) *of cream or milk*
15 g (½ oz) *of spice salt*

(1) Soak breadcrumbs in cream or milk.
(2) Mix diced veal, fat pork and seasoning.
(3) Mince through a fine mincer blade.
(4) Mix minced meat, crumbs and eggs to a smooth mixture.
(5) Correct seasoning and consistency.
Used for stuffing of veal, veal loaves, etc.

Bitok à la Russe

350 g (12 oz) finely minced beef
100 g (4 oz) finely minced pork
150 g (6 oz) white breadcrumbs
100 g (4 oz) finely chopped onions
15 g (½ oz) chopped parsley
12 cl (¼ pint) milk
15 g (½ oz) salt approx.
10 g (¼ oz) ground white pepper
Pinch of nutmeg
1 raw egg

(1) Cook onions in a little dripping; cool.
(2) Soak bread in milk.
(3) Place minced beef, pork and crumbs in a bowl.
(4) Add onions, egg and seasonings.
(5) Mix to a smooth paste.
(6) Divide into 6 to 8 even parts (approx. 125 g (5 oz)).
(7) Shape in wet hand, like a tournedo.
(8) Flour, sauté in clarified butter.

German Beef Steaks – Hamburgers

350 g (12 oz) minced beef
100 g (4 oz) minced fat pork
100 g (4 oz) white breadcrumbs
100 g (4 oz) chopped cooked onions
15 g (½ oz) salt approx.
10 g (¼ oz) black mill pepper
1 pinch of allspice
1 raw egg

(1) Cook onions in a little dripping, cool.
(2) Place crumbs in bowl, soak with 2 cl (¼ pint) water.
(3) Place minced pork, beef, crumbs, egg and seasoning in a china bowl.
(4) Mix well, to a smooth paste.
(5) Divide into 4 to 6 even parts (approx 125 g (5 oz)).
(6) Shape in wet hands to the size of a fillet steak.
(7) Flour, shallow fry in clarified butter.
(8) Usually served with fried onions and fried egg.

The name 'Hamburger' is unknown in Germany: it is an American term, given to a minced steak similar to the German beefsteak.

Veal Pojarskis – Les Côtelettes de Veau Farcies

350 g (12 oz) finely minced veal
100 g (4 oz) finely minced pork
150 g (6 oz) white breadcrumbs
1 dl (1 gill) cream
50 g (2 oz) butter
15 g (½ oz) salt
Pinch of white pepper
Pinch of nutmeg
1 egg
15 g (½ oz) chopped parsley

(1) Melt butter and mix with crumbs; add cream to soak.
(2) Place the minced meats in a china bowl.
(3) Add egg, parsley, seasoning and soaked crumbs.

(4) Mix to a smooth paste.
(5) Divide into 5 or 6 even parts (approx 125 g (5 oz) each).
(6) Shape with wet hands and palette knife into cutlets.
(7) Eggwash and breadcrumb.
(8) Shallow fry in clarified butter.

It is usual to force into these cutlets a Best-End bone, scraped and neatly trimmed, or a piece of macaroni to imitate the bone. The macaroni should be blanched; only then will the breadcrumbs stick well when frying.

Chicken Pojarskis – Les Côtelettes de Volaille Farcies

As for Veal Pojarskis, using 350 g (12 oz) of finely minced chicken, free of bones, skin and sinews; all other ingredients and method are the same.

Keftédés

As for *Bitok à la russe*, using lamb, pork or veal, instead of beef, e.g. Keftédés d'agneau, Keftédés de porc, Keftédés de Veau. Keftédés of any meat are usually shaped into small tournedos of approx 50 g (2 oz) each, 2 of these comprising a portion.

Swedish Meat Balls – Köttbullar

250 *g* (8 *oz*) *finely minced beef*
250 *g* (8 *oz*) *finely minced pork*
100 *g* (4 *oz*) *stewed onions*
100 *g* (4 *oz*) *white breadcrumbs*
15 *g* (½ *oz*) *salt*
Pinch of black pepper
Pinch of allspice
15 *g* (½ *oz*) *chopped parsley*
1 *raw egg*

(1) Soak breadcrumbs in approx 2 dl (¼ pint) of cold water.
(2) Place minced meat in a china bowl.
(3) Add egg, seasonings, parsley, onions and soaked crumbs.
(4) Mix to a smooth paste.
(5) Roll meat paste into very small balls, not larger than 2 cm (1 in.) in diameter.
(6) Place the little balls, as they are rolled, on an oiled plate.
(7) Heat a pan with good dripping, about 1-2 cm (½ in.) deep.
(8) Slide meat balls into hot fat.
(9) Quickly fry gold brown, tossing pan.
(10) Place meat balls in colander to drain fat.
(11) Repeat procedure as often as necessary.

The Swedish Meat Balls are part of a Swedish Hors d'Œuvre, served hot or cold. They can, however, be made slightly larger, about 4 to 5 per person and portion and re-heated in a little jus lié or demi glace and as such served as an Entrée or Main Course. Boiled potatoes and conserved cranberries usually accompany these meat balls.

SIMPLE COOKED FORCEMEATS

Cromesquis

350 g (12 oz) minced cooked meat (invariably chicken)
2 dl ($\frac{1}{4}$ pint) chicken velouté or flour panada
2 yolks of egg
Pigs caul
Salt and pepper to taste

(1) Place chicken into a sauteuse.
(2) Add velouté or panada and seasoning.
(3) Bring to the boil, reduce if necessary.
(4) Bind with yolk of eggs.
(5) Spread onto a buttered tray, cool.
(6) When really cool, cut into neat rectangular shapes.
(7) Wrap each in pig's caul.
(8) Dip in butter, deep fry golden brown.
Other meat than chicken may be used in a similar way.

Chicken Cutlets – Les Côtelettes de Volaille

500 g (1 lb) coarsely minced or diced cooked chicken
$\frac{1}{4}$ l. ($\frac{1}{2}$ pint) of chicken velouté or béchamel
1 yolk of egg
Salt, pepper, nutmeg to taste

(1) Place chicken into a sauteuse.
(2) Add velouté or béchamel, bring to boil.
(3) Add yolk of egg and seasoning, bind.
(4) Place mixture on a buttered tray; cool.
(5) When really cold, divide into 4 to 6 cutlets.
(6) Flour, eggwash, breadcrumb.
(7) Deep or shallow fry golden brown.

Chicken Croquettes – Croquettes de Volaille

Proceed as for chicken cutlets but cut into 8 to 10 fingers; flour, eggwash, breadcrumb and deep fry golden brown: serve 2 per portion.

Chicken and Ham Cutlets

As for the basic recipe; using 350 g (12 oz) of cooked chicken, with 125 g (5 oz) of cooked, diced ham.

Chicken and Mushroom Cutlets

As the basic recipe, using 350 g (12 oz) of cooked chicken, with 150 g (6 oz) diced sautéd mushrooms.

Fricandelles

350 g (12 oz) of minced cooked meat (usually beef)
150 g (6 oz) mashed potatoes or potato panada
100 g (4 oz) chopped onions stewed in butter
15 g (½ oz) chopped parsley
Salt and pepper
1 raw egg

(1) Mix all ingredients to a smooth paste
(2) Divide into 12 to 14 even parts.
(3) Shape to small cutlets.
(4) Fry in clarified butter.
(5) Serve 2–3 per portion.

Fish Cakes – Médaillions de Poisson

300 g (10 oz) cooked fish, free of skin and bone
1 raw egg
15 g (½ oz) chopped parsley
250 g (8 oz) mashed potatoes or potatoe panada
Salt and pepper

(1) Combine fish, potatoes, egg and seasoning.
(2) Divide into 4 or 6 even parts.
(3) Shape into tournedo type cakes.
(4) Flour, eggwash and breadcrumbs.
(5) Deep or shallow-fry, golden brown.

Meat and Potato Cakes

350 g (12 oz) cooked minced beef
250 g (8 oz) mashed potatoes or potato panada
50 g (2 oz) cooked diced onion
15 g (½ oz) chopped parsley
Salt and pepper to taste

(1) Mix all ingredients to a smooth paste.
(2) Divide into 4 to 6 even parts.
(3) Shape into tournedo-shaped cakes.
(4) Flour and shallow fry to golden brown.

Salmon Cutlets – Les Côtelettes de Saumon

350 g (12 oz) cooked salmon, free of skin and bones
¼ l. (½ pint) fish velouté or béchamel
2 egg yolks
Salt and pepper to taste
A little lemon juice

(1) Bring velouté or béchamel to boil in a sauteuse.
(2) Add flaked salmon, seasoning and juice.
(3) Add egg-yolks and bind.
(4) Place on a buttered tray, cool.
(5) When really cold, mould into 4 to 6 cutlets.
(6) Flour, eggwash and breadcrumb.
(7) Deep or shallow fry golden brown.

Salmon Croquettes – Les Croquettes de Saumon

As basic recipe above, but shape cooled mixture into 8 to 10 fingers. Floured, eggwashed and crumbed, they are cooked as above.

THE FINER FORCEMEATS – LES FARCES FINES

In this section of Forcemeats come the 'finer' ones, as they are called; in nearly all cases a panada and cream are used (Figure 87). The first is used as the binding, the second serving to give a good white colour and lightness to the different forcemeats. The one exception is the famous *Godiveau*, where the binding is achieved solely by the use of whites of eggs and ice.

In nearly all recipes of the older cookery books, a mortar and pestle is used. Not many hotels or restaurants have them nowadays. A very fine mincer blade, where the holes are not bigger than 3-5 mm ($\frac{1}{16}$th-$\frac{1}{26}$th in.) will work very well. It is advisable to mince the meats or fish at least twice or more times. All sinews, gristle, and skin should be carefully removed before mincing. Using only the best and freshest of meat will always ensure a good binding.

All finer forcemeats have basically the same uses, as follows: Small quentelles for garnishes or soups, Large quenelles as a separate dish, usually 2 per portion, Hot mousses, Soufflés, Hot mousselines.

To the basic use the name of meat or fish is always added, e.g. *Petites quenelles de veau, Quenelles de brochet, Mousse Chaude de Homard, Soufflès de volaille, Mousseline de perdrix, etc.*

Small quenelles are usually forced through a piping bag and poached in salted water or respective stock.

Large quenelles are usually forced with 2 dessert-spoons which have been dipped each time in water. The quenelles are then placed on a buttered plaque à rôtir, covered with a buttered cartouche and poached in respective stocks.

Mousse Hot is a fine forcemeat placed into a soufflé dish which has been buttered, covered with a cartouche and poached *au bain marie* in a medium hot oven.

Mousseline, as described only individual soufflé dishes are used.

Soufflé, a normal *farce fine* to which 2 or 3 beaten whites of egg have been added, then prepared and cooked as a Hot Mousse.

Veal and Kidney Fat Forcemeat – Godiveau

250 g (8 oz) *lean diced veal, free of skin and sinews (fillet or leg)*
250 g (8 oz) *good white beef suet, free of all skin, finely chopped*
50 g (2 oz) *of finely chopped shallots, cooked in butter*
2 *whole eggs* 15 g ($\frac{1}{2}$ oz) *spice salt*
150 g (6 oz) *finely crushed ice*

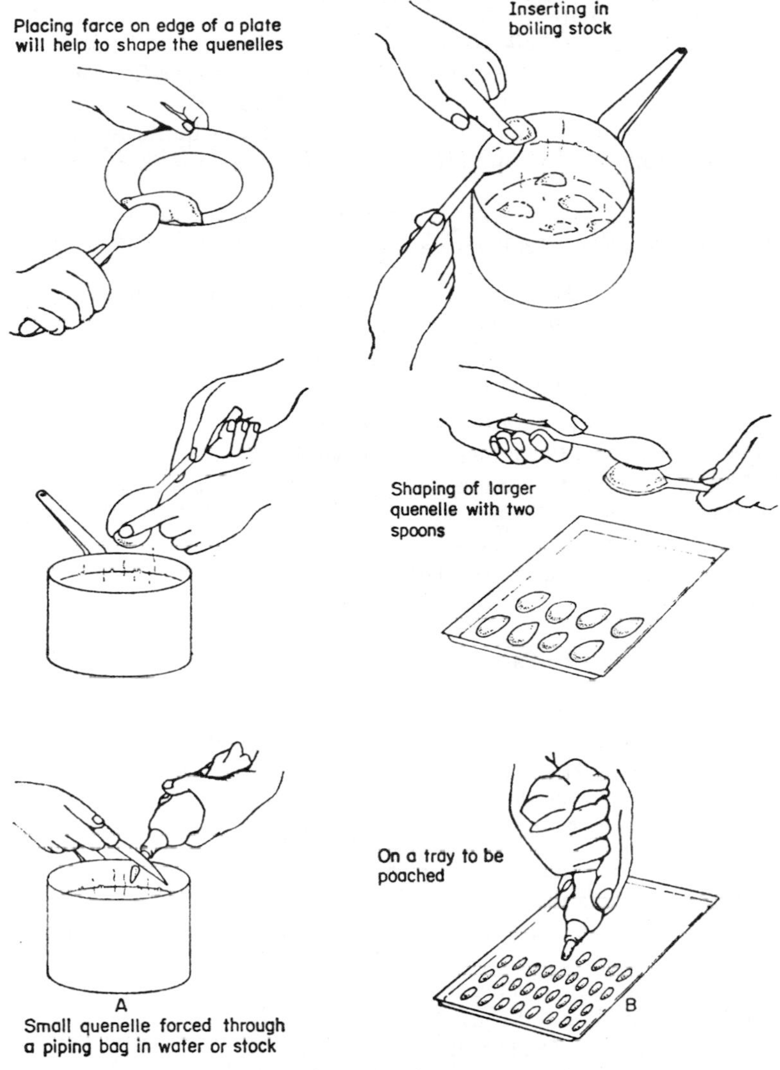

FIG. 87. *Forcemeats*

(1) Remove all skin and sinew from suet, chop roughly.
(2) Cut veal into small dice, mix with suet and spice salt.
(3) Mince in a very fine mincer blade 5 mm ($\frac{1}{20}$ in.) 2–3 times.
(4) Add the whites of egg and mix well, place on ice for at least 1 hour.
(5) Now place in a bowl cutter or mortar and pestle.

(6) Add cooked shallots and crushed ice.
(7) Mix in a bowl cutter or mortar vigorously.
(8) Gradually add the yolk of egg.
(9) When all the ice is melted and absorbed, pass through a fine sieve.
(10) Correct seasoning and consistency; test before use.
Used for Large meat quenelles. This forcemeat can be made with other meats especially poultry and game, e.g. *Godiveau de volaille, Godiveau de gibier.*

Chicken Forcemeat – La Farce de Volaille

175 g (6 oz) chicken, free of bones, sinews and skin
50 g (2 oz) lean diced veal
50 g (2 oz) diced pork fat
1 dl (1 gill) of frangipane panade
1 egg
1 dl (1 gill) of cream
15 g (½ oz) of spice salt

(1) Mix chicken, veal, pork fat and spice salt.
(2) Mince through a fine mincer once or twice.
(3) Mix minced meats, panade, and egg to a smooth paste, rest on ice for 30 mins.
(4) Gradually work in the cream.
(5) Correct seasoning and consistency.
Use for rough quenelles, terrines, stuffing for chickens.

Game Forcemeat – La Farce de Gibier

175 g (6 oz) of any game, free from skin, bones and sinews
50 g (2 oz) lean veal
50 g (2 oz) pork fat, diced
10 cl (1 gill) of cream
1 dl (1 gill) of panade (au riz or frangipane)
15 g (½ oz) spice salt
Pinch of thyme and marjoram
1 egg

(1) Mix game, pork fat, veal and spice salt and herbs.
(2) Mince through a fine mincer 2-3 times.
(3) Add the panade and egg and mix well with a wooden spatula, place on ice for 30 mins.
(4) Gradually add the fresh cream.
(5) Correct seasoning and consistency.
Used for game quenelles, terrines, etc.

Fish Forcemeat – La Farce de Poisson

300 g (10 oz) of pike, jacksalmon or whiting, free of skins and bones
1 white of egg
1 yolk of egg
1 dl (1 gill) of cream
Salt, pepper, few drops of lemon juice or spice salt
2 dl (2 gills) of panade (au pain or frangipane)

(1) Mince fish 2 or 3 times through a fine mincer.
(2) Place in a dish on ice, add seasoning, whites of egg and panade.
(3) Mix on ice, work in well.
(4) Gradually work in cream.
(5) Correct seasoning and consistency.
(6) Test before use.

Used for large fish quenelles. To all Forcemeats (mentioned above), a little Brandy or Madeira wine may be added. Poached Julienne of Truffles or Mushrooms may be added where a garnish is required.

Finer Forcemeats with Cream – Les Farces Fines à la Crème

In the 3rd section of raw forcemeats come the so-called *farces fines à la crème*. These again are made from meats, usually the white meats like veal, poultry and fish as well as game. With the finer forcemeats panades are seldom used but, if they are, it is only in exceptional cases. The binding here is achieved by a very old method. This is to work the forcemeats on crushed ice in two different sized *plats à sautèr*. The larger one is filled with crushed ice; the smaller one is placed on top of the ice, and contains the minced meat or fish to be made into a forcemeat (see Figure 88). First whites of egg and salt, and then the cream, are gradually worked into the mixture; the coolness of the ice ensures good emulsion and firm binding.

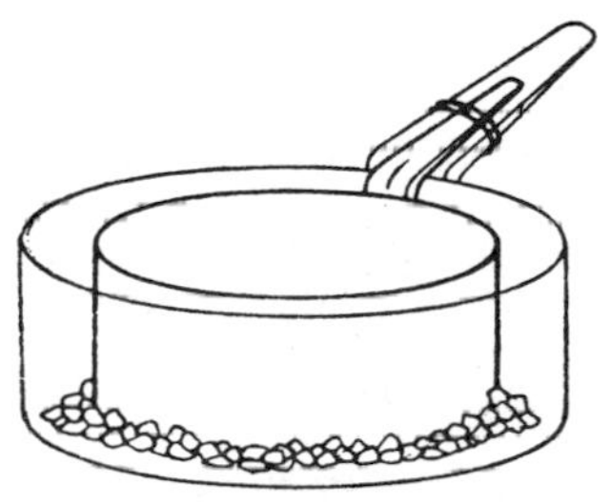

A method of making finer forcemeat on crushed ice

FIG. 88.

For more individual approaches, see the recipes to follow.

A more modern method is to make farce with the aid of a food processor, of which there are basically two types:

(1) A less expensive plastic construction. In most cases these have a raised opening which allows additions to be made, such as herbs, spices and cream, while the processor is running. This less expensive machine is suitable for the smaller, less demanding establishment (see Figure 89(*a*)).
(2) A more expensive stainless steel construction. This normally has no raised opening; the processor has to be switched off and the lid removed to

add further ingredients. The construction and safety features of this type of machine are more suited to heavy use, and the components (especially the blade) have a longer life. It is a very good investment for the larger and even the smaller first-class establishment, where the making of forcemeats, mousses, pâtés and terrines is an almost daily occurrence (see Figure 89(*b*)).

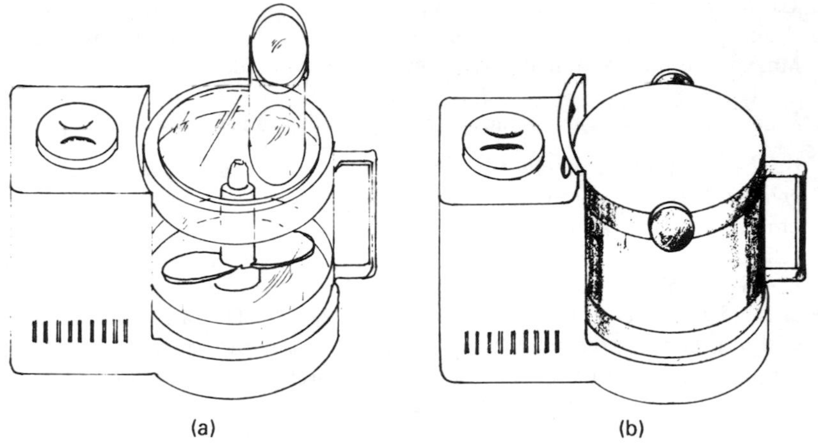

FIG. 89. *Food processors.* (a) *Plastic* (b) *Stainless steel*

When using a processor for the making of any type of forcemeats, follow the methods given in each recipe, replacing of course the double *plat à sauter*. However, it is advisable to mince the meat or fish two or three times before placing it into the processor; some blades in smaller machines will be unable to cope with large pieces of meat, resulting in a stringy rather than a smooth farce.

Always make sure that both the processor and the minced meat or fish are very cold before starting the procedure. They can both be placed into the fridge for a while. A little crushed ice (about 25 g or 1 oz per 500 g or 1 lb of meat or fish) can be added when first cutting the farce with a few fast turns of the blade, and before the cream is added.

There is no doubt that the *farce fines* are some of the oldest recipes in French cuisine of which the *Godiveau* is the best known. These are some of the most commonly used:

Godiveau with Cream – Godiveau à la Crème

Follow recipe given in the previous section, leaving out the ice and using $\frac{1}{2}$ pint of fresh cream instead. The method is very much the same, only that the cream is added gradually to the mixture and not all at once as happens with the ice. At all times the mixture must be absolutely ice cool. Again different meats can be used, e.g. *Godiveau à la crème* (veal), *Godiveau de volaille à la crème, Godiveau de gibier à la crème.*

Fine Veal Forcemeat – La Farce Fine de Veau à la Crème

250 g (8 oz) lean veal
2 whites of egg
1 yolk of egg
$\frac{1}{4}$ l. ($\frac{1}{2}$ pint) cream (approx)
10 g ($\frac{1}{4}$ oz) spice salt

(1) Mince veal 2 to 3 times through a very fine mincer 5 mm ($\frac{1}{20}$ in. plate).
(2) Place into a *plat à sauté* or *sauteuse*, with a larger one with crushed ice underneath.
(3) Gradually work in the whites of eggs and spice salt.
(4) A little at a time stir in about half of the cream.
(5) Slightly beat the remainder of cream and fold into the mixture.
(6) Add yolk of egg and correct seasoning.
(7) Test before use.

Fine Chicken Forcemeat – La Farce Fine de Volaille à la Crème

As above, using chicken instead of veal. The chicken should be free of bones and skin. Other poultry may be used, e.g. *Farce fine de caneton à la crème* (duck), *Farce fine de dindonneau à la crème* (turkey), and others.

Fine Game Forcemeat – La Farce Fine de Gibier à la Crème

As for veal forcemeat, using young game of any kind, free of bones, sinews and skin:

La farce fine de perdreau à la crème (Partridge)
La farce fine de faisan à la crème (Pheasant)
La farce fine de grouse à la crème (Grouse)
La farce fine de lièvre à la crème (Hare)
La farce fine de lapin à la crème (Rabbit)
etc.

Fine Fish Forcemeat – La Farce Fine de Poisson

350 g (12 oz) fish, free from skin and bones, preferably pike, jacksalmon, whiting (in that order)
2 whites of eggs
1 yolk of egg
$\frac{1}{4}$ l. ($\frac{1}{2}$ pint) cream (approx)
15 g ($\frac{1}{2}$ oz) spice salt

(1) Mince fish 2 to 3 times through a fine mincer.
(2) Place and work on ice (see drawings and veal forcemeat).
(3) Gradually work in the whites of egg and spice salt.
(4) When a good binding is achieved add about $\frac{1}{2}$ the cream, a little at a time.
(5) Slightly beat remainder of cream and gently fold into the mixture.
(6) Test before use.

Fine Forcemeat from Shellfish (Lobster) – La Farce Fine de Homard à la Crème

150 *g* (6 *oz*) *raw lobster meat*	1 *yolk of egg*
100 *g* (4 *oz*) *pike or whiting*	$\frac{1}{4}$ *l.* ($\frac{1}{2}$ *pint*) *cream* (*approx*)
50 *g* (2 *oz*) *lobster coral*	15 *g* ($\frac{1}{2}$ *oz*) *spice salt*
2 *whites of egg*	

(1) Mince lobster meat, pike and coral through a very fine mincer.
(2) Place and work on ice (see illustration for veal forcemeat).
(3) Gradually work in whites of egg and spice salt.
(4) When binding is achieved, gradually work in about half the cream.
(5) Slightly beat remainder of cream and gently fold into the mixture.
(6) Correct seasoning and test before use.

Sautéd Forcemeats (Liver) – La Farce à Gratin

The *farce à gratin* is the base for all dishes where liver of meats, poultry and game come to be used, e.g. pâtés, quenelles, potted preparations and others. Here the liver is slightly sautéd, or even cooked in butter or the fat of the liver used, e.g. chicken-liver pâté; the liver would be sautéd in chicken fat, etc. The following recipe given for calves' liver can be applied to all other liver forcemeats.

Calves' Liver Forcemeat – La Farce à Gratin de Foie de Veau

300 *g* (10 *oz*) *of calves' liver, free from skin and sinews*	100 *g* (4 *oz*) *butter*
150 *g* (6 *oz*) *pork fat, diced*	15 *g* ($\frac{1}{2}$ *oz*) *spice salt*
100 *g* (4 *oz*) *mushrooms or mushroom trimmings*	*A pinch of thyme and marjoram*
50 *g* (2 *oz*) *sautéd shallots*	1 *bayleaf*
	2 *tablespoons madeira or brandy*

(1) Brown the pork fat in the butter slightly, in a frying pan or a *plat à sauté*.
(2) Remove with perforated spoon so that fat stays in pan.
(3) Quickly sauté calves' liver in the same butter, and pan.
(4) Return pork fat to pan, add mushrooms, seasoning and shallots.
(5) Sauté all for a few moments on an open fire.
(6) Add Madeira or brandy, take aside to cool.
(7) When nearly cold mince through a very fine mincer plate, about 5 mm ($\frac{1}{20}$th in.).
(8) Mix well with a wooden spatula, if necessary pass through a fine wire sieve.
(9) Correct seasoning.
Used for liver pâté, potted preparations, terrines and borders.

La farce à gratin de foie de volaille
As above, using chicken-liver instead of calf.
La farce à gratin de foie d'oie
As for calves' liver forcemeat but using goose-liver instead.
La farce à gratin de gibier
As for calves' liver forcemeat, using game liver, instead of calf, e.g. *La farce à gratin de foie de perdrix, La farce à gratin de foie de faisan, La farce à gratin de foie de lapin*, etc.
La farce de croûton
This is a forcemeat made very much like the liver forcemeats. The difference is that some cold butter and cream is worked into the liver forcemeats to make them smooth and tasty. This paste is then spread on to heart-shaped croûtons and served with a number of different poultry and game dishes, or piped as borders around cold poultry and game dishes.

STUFFINGS

As already stated, the French culinary term *Farce* includes also what is known in the British Isles as 'Stuffings'. These are used mainly in the preparation of shoulders of veal, lamb, chicken and turkey, or as an accompaniment with such dishes. Here are some of the best known.

Suet Stuffing – La Farce à l'Anglaise

25 *g* (1 *oz*) *butter*
250 *g* (8 *oz*) *chopped onions*
350 *g* (12 *oz*) *white breadcrumbs*
250 *g* (8 *oz*) *chopped suet*
2 *eggs*
1 *teaspoon of powdered thyme*
1 *teaspoon chopped parsley*
The grated rind of a lemon
Salt and pepper to taste

(1) Sweat onions in butter without colour, cool.
(2) Add finely chopped suet, breadcrumbs, lemon, parsley, thyme, salt and pepper.
(3) Stir in the whole eggs.
(4) Correct seasoning.
Used for veal, turkey, chicken, stuffed loin of veal or lamb.

Suet and Bread Stuffing – (Beef Olives)

As above, with the addition of the trimmings of the batted beef-olives, or some finely minced beef.

Sage Stuffing – La Farce à la Sauge

100 g (4 oz) *good beef-dripping (or dripping of joint to be served)*
350 g (12 oz) *finely chopped onions*
300 g (10 oz) *white breadcrumbs*
1 *teaspoon powdered sage*
1 *teaspoon chopped parsley*
Salt and pepper

(1) Fry onions golden brown in part of the dripping.
(2) Fry breadcrumbs golden brown in other part of dripping; they must be crisp.
(3) Add all other ingredients, mix well.
(4) Correct seasoning.
Used for all fatty foods like pork, duck, goose, etc.

Mushroom Stuffing – Farce de Champignons

250 g (8 oz) *finely chopped mushrooms*
50 g (2 oz) *butter*
100-150 g (4-6 oz) *white breadcrumbs*
25 g (1 oz) *finely chopped parsley*
50 g (2 oz) *cooked finely chopped onions*
2 *yolks of eggs*
Salt, pepper and cayenne pepper
Juice of half a lemon

(1) Sauté finely chopped mushrooms in butter.
(2) Add cooked onions.
(3) Add parsley, crumbs and lemon juice.
(4) Correct seasoning with salt, pepper and cayenne pepper.
Used for the stuffing of veal, lamb or poultry, sometimes together with sausagemeat.

Ham and Mushroom Stuffing – Farce à l'Italienne

100 g (4 oz) *fine brunoise of ham*
100 g (4 oz) *finely chopped mushrooms*
50 g (2 oz) *butter*
Salt, pepper and cayenne papper
50 g (2 oz) *white breadcrumbs*
25 g (1 oz) *tomato ketchup or purée*
1 *whole egg*

(1) Sauté mushrooms in butter, cool.
(2) Add ham and tomato ketchup.
(3) Fry with breadcrumbs.
(4) Mix in whole egg.
(5) Correct consistency and seasoning.
Used for stuffings for veal and fillet of beef Wellington.

Chestnut Stuffing – Farce de Marrons

750 g ($1\frac{1}{2}$ *lb*) *of chestnuts*
$\frac{3}{4}$ *l.* ($1\frac{1}{2}$ *pints*) *stock*
50 g (2 oz) *butter*
1 *dl* (1 *gill*) *of cream*
Salt, pepper and a pinch of sugar

(1) Cut through the outer skin of chestnuts with a very sharp knife.
(2) Blanch roast or fry to remove outer skin.
(3) Remove outer and inner skins.
(4) Chop coarsely, place in pan, add stock and butter.
(5) Gently simmer on side of stove until they fall apart.
(6) Pass through a fine sieve, work in cream and correct seasoning.
Used for the filling of poultry and veal, often in conjunction with sausage-meat.

GARNISHES

During a week, with a daily changing menu, the different chefs de partie need numerous garnishes. The following garnishes, or fillings, as used in different departments of the kitchen, are a few examples in each case of this large subject. They will serve to emphasize their importance and the need for detailed study of this branch of Cold Larder work. Only by being familiar with most of these will the Chef Garde-Manger be able to order all items of food needed, thus promoting a smooth liaison between departments.

Potager

Small quenelles of meats
Small quenelles of poultry
Small quenelles of fish
Small quenelles of bone-marrow
Slices of bone-marrow
Slices, or dice, of chicken, ham and tongue
Brunoise of chicken, ham and tongue
Julienne of chicken, ham and tongue
Clarification for consommé
Giblets for consommé
Marrow croûtons

Poissonnier

Quenelles de brochet (fish or main course)
Small quenelles de poisson
Slice or dice of crawfish and lobster
Tails of crayfish and scampis
Stoned olives and grapes
Shrimps
Prawns
Soft roes, plain or pané
Slices or dice of truffles
Oysters and Mussels
Fish, croquettes, cutlets and cakes (fish or main course)

Saucier

Salpicons of varying compositions
Ragoûts and fillings for vol au vent
Sliced, diced, or chopped truffles
Chicken livers
Dice of pork fat
Lardons

Champignons
Stoned olives
Cockscombs
Cocks kidneys
Brunoise of meats, poultry and vegetables
Julienne of meats, poultry and vegetables
Slices of beef-bone marrow

Rôtisseur/Grilladin

Various compound butters
Various cold sauces
Various mayonnaise derivatives
Mirabeau, anchovy butter, anchovy, olives
Holstein garnish
Vienna garnish

Entremettier

Diced cooked ham (Omelettes)
Chicken livers (Croûtons – Savouries)
Oysters (Croûtons – Savouries)
Lamb kidneys (Egg dishes Meyerbeer)
Crayfish tails (Egg dishes Rothschild)
Chipolatas (Egg dishes Bercy)

Pâtissier

The Pâtissier need is not so much for garnishes as for fillings.

Sausage meat (Sausage rolls)
Diced meat (Cornish pasties
Salpiçon of different compositions (Dartois)
Anchovy (Dartois)
Sardines (Dartois)
Meat, poultry and game farces (Pies – Pâté en Croûte)
Pre/part cooked ham and gammons (Baked in Crust)
Chopped suet (Suet Pastry)
Ravioli filling (Ravioli)

CLASSICAL GARNISHES

(1) *Amèricaine* (Fish): Slices of lobster and truffles.

(2) *Dieppoise* (Fish): Shrimps, bearded mussels, mushrooms.

(3) *Financière:* Chicken quenelles, cockscombs, cocks' kidneys, truffles, stoned olives.

(4) *Marinière* (Fish): Shrimps or prawns, bearded mussels.

(5) *Milanaise:* Julienne of ham, mushrooms, tongue, truffles, tomato.

(6) *Mirabeau* (Grills): Anchovy butter, fillets of anchovy, stuffed olives.

(7) *Normande* (Fish): Bearded oysters and mussels, mushroom heads, crayfish tails, goujon of sole, slices of truffle, croûtons.

(8) *Règence* (a) Fish: Fish quenelles, crayfish tails, mushrooms, bearded oysters, soft roes, slices of truffles.
(b) Chicken Sweet-bread: Chicken quenelles, cockscombs, triangles of foie gras, mushroom heads.

(c) Game: Game quenelles, cockscombs, triangle of foie gras, mushroom heads, croûtons.

(9) *Réforme:* Julienne of ham, tongue, beetroot, whites of egg, gherkins.
(10) *Strasbourgeoise:* Lardons of boiled bacon, slices of foie gras, chipolatas.
(11) *Tortue:* Quenelles, mushroom heads, gherkins, round slices of tongue, calves brain, deep fried egg, crayfish tails, truffles, croûtons.
(12) *Toulousaine* (Chicken Sweet-Bread): Chicken quenelles, sweet-bread, cockscombs, mushrooms, slice or dice of truffles.
(13) *Viennoise* (Entrée): Slices of lemon, anchovy, sieved whites and yolks of egg, parsley.
(14) *Walewska* (Fish): Slices of lobster tails, slices of truffles.
(15) *Zingara:* Julienne of ham, mushrooms, tongue, truffles.

SEASONINGS

Seasonings play a most important part in the culinary arts and most dishes would be impossible to produce – with a taste to which we are accustomed – without these seasonings. They should always be used with discernment and in well-defined proportions. Thus, the finished food will not be dominated by the seasonings but may blend with its own flavour (whatever the food may be), and association of seasonings, to create a perfect harmony of taste.

Here are 5 basic types of seasoning: (1) Single seasoning or spices, (2) Mixed or compound seasoning or spices, (3) Herbs, (4) Acids, (5) Condiments.

Salt – Sel Fin

Table salt containing sodium phosphate, used in most cooking and baking.

Coarse Salt – Sel Gris

Known also as freezing salt, it is much coarser than table salt, used for culinary purposes and freezing.

Celery Salt – Sel de Céleri

A blend of celery root and table salt, usually purchased ready prepared; may be used wherever celery or celery-seed is used.

Garlic Salt – Sel d'Ail

A blend of garlic and normal table salt, usually purchased ready prepared, used for all dishes where garlic normally is used.

Monosodium Glutamate

Salt-like crystals known as 'M.S.G.'. It is marketed under various brand names and is produced by a special process from wheat, soya and sugar-beet. It can be used to enhance the flavours in the cooking of every dish, with the exception of sweets.

Saltpetre

A salt like powder but not really a salt, used in conjunction with salt in the case of pickling or brining meats to retain a good red colour.

SPICES – ÉPICES

Allspice – Quatre Épices

The fruit of the *Pimenta officinalis* is a grain, similar to black pepper in appearance, only twice as large. It combines the properties of pepper, cloves, nutmeg, and cinnamon. Used in pickling and sausage making; also found finely ground to a brownish powder.

Aniseed – Anis

The dried seed of the plant *Pimpinella anisum*. Has a slight licorice flavour, cultivated in most European countries. It is grey-green in colour and pear-shaped. It is used in bakery and in the manufacture of liqueurs.

Cardemom – Càrdomome

From the plant *Elettaria càrdamomum Maton* from Ceylon and Guatemala; it presents one of the ingredients of curry powder; used also in the manufacture of sausages and Danish pastries.

Caraway – Carvi

The fruit of the plant *Carum carvi*, cultivated mainly in Holland. It has stimulating and digestive properties, used in the making of cheeses, sprinkled on rolls and bread, cooked in Sauerkraut.

Cayenne Pepper – Cayenne

The ground pod and seed of hot chilli peppers, finely powdered, with a very hot, zesty flavour; it must be used very sparingly.

Chilli

Small red very hot peppers, with seed, from Mexico, West Africa, Louisiana, and California. Used in Mexican and South American cooking. It is the most pungent of all spices and must be used very carefully. Best known and used in Europe as part of a pickling spice.

Cinnamon – Canelle

The bark of an oriental tree *Cinnamomum zeylanicum* – the best coming from Ceylon, but also grown in China. Commercially sold as stick, ground and cinnamon sugar. Very useful in bakery, syrups, puddings and punches.

Celery Seed – Céleri

Grown in Europe, India and other countries, it is used in pickling and dishes where a celery flavour is desired.

Coriander Seeds – Coriandre

These seeds are the fruit of the plant *Coriandrum sativum*, cultivated in southern European countries, as well as Asia. A round seed, similar to white peppercorn. Strong aroma but mild flavour and used in the making of jellies, roast pork and certain cakes.

Cloves – Clous de Girofle

The nail shaped flower bud of East Indian tree *Eugenia caryophyllus*. The preparation of this spice begins before the buds of the tree are open. Dipped in hot water, they are partly smoked and dried. Used moderately in soups, stocks, sauce studding for onions and braised stews and pies. Found also ground to a fine powder and used in stews and with vegetables.

Cumin Seeds – Cumin

Resembling Caraway seed in appearance. It has quite a different flavour and is grown chiefly in India. It is one of the ingredients and spice of curry, much used in Mexican cookery and most tasteful with all rice dishes. Also available, ground.

Dill Seed – Aneth

A small seed, grey-green in colour and similar to Caraway, but round, and used mostly in mixed spices and for pickling. Often new potatoes are cooked with this spice, instead of mint.

Ginger – Gingembre

Ginger is the root of the plant *Zingiber officinale*, which grows wild in India. Found cultivated in West Indies, Jamaica and Malabar. In these countries it can be obtained fresh; in Europe, usually only preserved in a heavy syrup, as dried root or in powder form obtained from the dried root. It is used as an ingredient for curry powder in confectionery and pickling.

Juniper Berries – Baies de Genièvre

These are the fruit of the shrub *Juniperus communis* cultivated all over Europe. They are of a black-blue colour, twice as large as black pepper corns. Most famous as flavouring for gin, they are also used for pickling, brining and when cooking sauerkraut.

Mace – Macis

The outer shell of nutmeg *Myristica fragrans* grown in the Far East. It is of similar flavour to that of nutmeg, and orange-red in colour. Its delicate flavour is used for pickling, fish-dishes, and as a ground fine powder in the seasoning of various types of sausage.

Mustard Seed – Moutarde

Cultivated in Europe, California and the Orient. It is a seed used mainly in pickling and the making of chutney. When ground it is the base for English, French and German types of mustard commercially manufactured.

Nutmeg – Muscade

The seed of the *Myristica fragrans* resembling a brown root grown in the East and West Indies. Also found ground and is used in baking and cooking, especially with potatoes and vegetables.

White Pepper Corns – Poivre en Grains Blanc

A most universal spice from the East Indies, originated in Malabar. Obtained by soaking the black pepper grains in rye or sea water to remove the black skin. Used with most savoury foods where pepper that doesn't show may be preferred. Ground into a fine white powder for easy use.

Black Pepper Corns – Poivre en Grains Noir

The dried outer shell of white pepper corns (above) with about the same use, especially in the preparation of charcuterie.

Paprika – Paprika

Sweet Hungarian peppers, dried and powdered. As a member of the pepper family, this one is not strong and has a most sweet, agreeable flavour, and adds a bright red colour to foods.

Pimento – Piment-Poivron

Jamaican and Spanish type peppers. Slightly stronger than paprika but still mild. Used in the flavouring of sausages and manufacture of potted meat and fish preparation.

Pistachio – Pistaches

These nuts are the fruit of the shrub *Pistacia vera*, growing in Asia, India and Near East. The small nuts have a purple skin and bright green inside. The skin is usually removed. The nuts are used in confectionery, soups, potted meat preparations and galantines.

Poppy Seeds – Pavot

Grown in Europe, especially Holland. Used when fresh for bread rolls and biscuits, as the filling of Poppy Seed Strudle and tasty with buttered noodles of all types.

Sesame Seed

Transported from Turkey, India and the Orient, has a mild, nutty flavour. Sprinkled on bread, rolls, biscuits and vegetables.

Saffron – Safran

Stems from a flower called *crocus sativus*. Originated in Asia Minor. The flowers are picked when fully open, the stamens removed and dried at a low temperature. They are a light, strong, yellow colour. Used with fish and rice dishes, as well as for confectionery.

Turmeric – Curcuma

A root of the ginger family with a bright yellow colour and appetizing odour. Used in the making of curry powder, mustard sauces and pickling.

MIXED OR COMPOUND SPICES – ÉPICES COMPOSÉES

There are a great number of spices which are mixed and are combinations of different spices, salt and spices, or salt spices and herbs. Instead of adding off-hand a number of different spices to a food, the spices and seasonings are mixed in well-defined proportions beforehand, thus allowing for easy and correct use with different foods. These mixed spices and seasonings may be a simple mixture of salt and ground pepper only, which is extensively used with most savoury foods. Or they may be a complicated mixture of spices of up to a dozen or more, and herbs as, for example, curry-powder. Many of these compound spices are bought ready mixed and are often closely guarded secrets of the manufacturers. Others are mixed to one's own taste allowing for personal or regional flavours.

Curry Powders

A combination of up to a dozen different spices and herbs, some of which have been named above; their combination is a guarded secret of different manufacturers.

Mixed Spices

A combination of ginger, cloves, nutmeg, mace, and pepper, etc., bought ready made and used in baking for puddings, cakes and biscuits, usually bought ready-mixed, but can be composed to one's own taste.

Pickling Spice

A combination of coriander, mace, pepper, etc., bought ready-mixed for pickling.

Spice Salt (General)

500 *g* (1 *lb*) *salt*
50 *g* (2 *oz*) *ground white pepper*
50 *g* (2 *oz*) *ground black pepper*
50 *g* (2 *oz*) *ground nutmeg*
25 *g* (1 *oz*) *ground mace*
25 *g* (1 *oz*) *ground ginger*
15 *g* (½ *oz*) *ground allspice*

Use 15 *g* (½ *oz*) *per* 50 *g* (1 *lb*) *of meat.*

Pork Sausage Seasoning (Basic)

500 *g* (1 *lb*) *salt*
50 *g* (2 *oz*) *ground white pepper*
50 *g* (2 *oz*) *ground black pepper*
50 *g* (2 *oz*) *ground nutmeg*
25 *g* (1 *oz*) *ground mace*
25 *g* (1 *oz*) *ground ginger*
50 *g* (2 *oz*) *powdered sage*

Use 15 *g* (½ *oz*) *per* 500 *g* (*lb*) *of meat.*

Beef Sausage Seasoning (Basic)

500 *g* (1 *lb*) *salt*
50 *g* (2 *oz*) *ground white pepper*
50 *g* (2 *oz*) *ground black pepper*
50 *g* (2 *oz*) *ground nutmeg*
25 *g* (1 *oz*) *ground mace*
25 *g* (1 *oz*) *ground ginger*
25 *g* (1 *oz*) *powdered thyme*
15 *g* (½ *oz*) *ground coriander*

Use 15 *g* (½ *oz*) *per* 500 *g* (*lb*) *of meat.*

Pork Sausage Seasoning (Regional)

Cambridge:

750 g (1¾ lb) white pepper
50 g (2 oz) ground coriander
40 g (1½ oz) ground pimento
40 g (1½ oz) ground nutmeg
10 g (¼ oz) ground sage
10 g (¼ oz) ground cayenne
2 kg (4½ lb) fine salt

Use 15 g (½ oz) per 500 g (lb) of meat.

Oxford:

750 g (1¾ lb) white pepper
25 g (1 oz) ground mace
25 g (1 oz) ground nutmeg
15 g (½ oz) ground ginger
15 g (½ oz) cayenne
15 g (½ oz) ground coriander
15 g (½ oz) ground sage
2 kg (4 lb) fine salt

Use 15 g (½ oz) per 500 g (lb) of meat.

General:

750 g (1¾ lb) white pepper
40 g (1½ oz) ground mace
40 g (1½ oz) ground nutmeg
25 g (1 oz) ground ginger
15 g (½ oz) ground cayenne
10 g (¼ oz) ground sage
50 g (2 oz) ground coriander
2 kg (4 lb) fine salt

Use 15 g (½ oz) per 500 g (lb) of meat.

Beef

750 g (1½ lb) white pepper
150 g (6 oz) ground mace
50 g (2 oz) ground nutmeg
100 g (4 oz) ground coriander
25 g (1 oz) ground marjoram
2 kg (4 lb) fine salt

Use 15 g (½ oz) per 500 g (lb) of meat.

German Smoked Sausage Seasoning

2 kg (4 lb) white pepper
50 g (2 oz) ground mace
40 g (1½ oz) saltpetre
25 g (1 oz) ground ginger
4½ kg (9 lb) fine salt
50 g (2 oz) ground nutmeg
50 g (2 oz) sage

Use 15 g (½ oz) per 500 g (lb) of meat.

Tongue Sausage Seasoning

No. 1

1¾ kg (3½ lb) white pepper
50 g (2 oz) ground mace
25 g (1 oz) ground nutmeg
25 g (1 oz) ground ginger
40 g (1½ oz) ground cayenne
4 kg (8 lb) fine salt

No. 2

1 kg (2 lb) white pepper
25 g (1 oz) ground ginger
15 g (½ oz) ground cloves
15 g (½ oz) ground coriander
2 kg (4 lb) fine salt

Use 15 g (½ oz) per 500 g (lb) of meat for No. 1 and No. 2.

Ham Sausage Seasoning

1 kg (2 lb) ground white pepper
25 g (1 oz) ground mace
15 g (½ oz) ground ginger
15 g (½ oz) ground cayenne
25 g (1 oz) saltpetre
2 kg (4½ lb) fine salt

Use 15 g (½ oz) per 500 g (lb) of meat.

Liver Sausage Seasoning

No. 1
1 kg (2 lb) white pepper
50 g (2 oz) ground cayenne
100 g (4 oz) ground ginger
25 g (1 oz) ground pimento
2½ kg (5 lb) salt

No. 2
500 g (1 lb) white pepper
50 g (2 oz) ground allspice
25 g (1 oz) ground cayenne
50 g (2 oz) bruised garlic
1½ kg (2 lb 10 oz) fine salt

Use 15 g (½ oz) per 500 g (lb) of meat for Nos. 1 and 2.

Chipolata Sausage Seasoning

1¾ kg (3½ lb) white pepper
100 g (4 oz) ground coriander
75 g (3 oz) ground pimento
75 g (3 oz) ground nutmeg
15 g (½ oz) ground thyme
15 g (½ oz) ground cayenne
4 kg (8 lb) fine salt

Use 15 g (½ oz) per 500 g (lb) of meat.

Saveloy Sausage Seasoning

2 kg (4 lb) white pepper
100 g (4 oz) ground ginger
75 g (3 oz) ground sage
50 g (2 oz) ground cinnamon
4½ kg (9 lb) fine salt

Use 15 g (½ oz) per 500 g (lb) of meat.

Garlic Sausage Seasoning

No. 1
75 g (3 oz) white pepper
15 g (½ oz) bruised garlic
15 g (½ oz) ground coriander
15 g (½ oz) ground pimento
250 g (8 oz) fine salt

No. 2
500 g (1 lb) white pepper
25 g (1 oz) ground mace
50 g (2 oz) ground coriander
50 g (2 oz) ground pimento
75 g (3 oz) bruised garlic
1½ kg (3 lb) fine salt

Use 15 g (½ oz) per 500 g (lb) of meat for Nos. 1 and 2.

Italian Smoked Sausage Seasonings

1 kg (2 lb) white pepper
50 g (2 oz) ground mace
25 g (1 oz) ground cloves
25 g (1 oz) ground garlic

50 g (2 oz) ground nutmeg
2 kg (4¼ lb) fine salt
Use 15 g (½ oz) per 500 g (lb) of meat.

Mutton Sausage Seasoning

1 kg (2 lb) white pepper
50 g (2 oz) ground ginger
15 g (½ oz) ground marjoram
15 g (½ oz) ground savory
1 kg (4½ lb) fine salt
Use 15 g (½ oz) per 500 g (lb) of meat.

Brawn Seasonings

Oxford Brawn:
1 kg (2 lb) white pepper
40 g (1½ oz) pimento
40 g (1½ oz) cayenne
25 g (1 oz) ground mace
1 kg (4½ lb) fine salt
Use 15 g (½ oz) per 500 g (lb) of meat.

Lancashire Brawn:
1 kg (2 lb) ground white pepper
25 g (1 oz) ground cayenne
25 g (1 oz) ground cloves
25 g (1 oz) ground ginger
25 g (1 oz) ground mace
2 kg (4½ lb) fine salt
Use 15 g (½ oz) per 500 g (lb) of meat.

Faggot Seasoning:
500 g (1 lb) black pepper
50 g (2 oz) ground cloves
25 g (1 oz) fine sage (sieved)
25 g (1 oz) fine thyme (sieved)
1 kg (2½ lb) fine salt
Use 15 g (½ oz) per 500 g (lb) of meat.

Hand Raised Pie Seasonings (Regional)

Melton Mowbray:
1 kg (2 lb) ground white pepper
25 g (1 oz) ground cloves
40 g (1½ oz) ground nutmeg
25 g (1 oz) cayenne
2 kg (4½ lb) fine salt
Use 15 g (½ oz) per 500 g (lb) of meat.

Nottingham:
750 g (1½ lb) ground white pepper
40 g (1½ oz) ground cayenne
25 g (1 oz) ground nutmeg
25 g (1 oz) ground mace
1.65 kg (3½ lb) fine salt
Use 15 g (½ oz) per 500 g (lb) of meat.

Liverpool:
500 g (1 lb) ground white pepper
15 g (½ oz) ground cinnamon
25 g (1 oz) ground cayenne
1 kg (2 lb) of fine salt
Use 15 g (½ oz) per 500 g (lb) of meat.

Yorkshire:

750 g (1½ lb) ground white pepper
40 g (1½ oz) ground cayenne
25 g (1 oz) ground nutmeg
1½ kg (3 lb) fine salt

Use 15 g (½ oz) per 500 g (lb) of meat.

Manchester:

500 g (1 lb) ground white pepper
15 g (½ oz) ground cloves
15 g (½ oz) ground nutmeg
15 g (½ oz) ground coriander
15 g (½ oz) ground mace
1 kg (2 lb) fine salt

Use 15 g (½ oz) per 500 g (lb) of meat.

Lincolnshire:

1 kg (2 lb) ground white pepper
100 g (4 oz) ground Jamaica ginger
25 g (1 oz) ground fine sage
2 kg (4½ lb) fine salt

Use 15 g (½ oz) per 500 g (lb) of meat.

Potted Meat Seasoning, Potted Ham Seasoning

25 g (1 oz) ground white pepper
15 g (½ oz) ground mace
15 g (½ oz) ground cayenne
100 g (4 oz) fine salt

Use to 5 kg (12 lb) of paste.

Potted Ham and Tongue Seasoning

25 g (1 oz) white pepper
15 g (½ oz) ground mace
10 g (¼ oz) ground cayenne
100 g (4 oz) fine salt

Use to 5 kg (12 lb) of paste.

Potted Turkey Seasoning

50 g (2 oz) white pepper
10 g (¼ oz) ground cayenne
10 g (¼ oz) ground marjoram
100 g (¼ lb) fine salt

Use to every 5 kg (12 lb) of meat.

Potted Salmon and Shrimp Seasoning

75 g (3 oz) white pepper
15 g (½ oz) ground mace
10 g (¼ oz) ground cayenne
100 g (4 oz) fine salt

Use to 15 g (½ oz) per 500 g (lb) of fish.

Note: All mixed and compound spices and seasonings, above, should, after careful mixing, be placed in jars of approximate size with a tightly fitting top. This must always be tightly screwed on after using some of the spice.

HERBS – HERBES AROMATIQUES

Angelica – Angélique

Archangelica officinalis: the hollow stems of this plant are crystallized and used in pastry and confectionery work for flavouring and decoration. Its seed is used in the manufacture of gin.

Basil – Basilic

Ocimum basilicum, a herb of western Europe, very mild and sweet in flavour and used in the flavouring of green beans and pies, as well as green vegetables and pastas. One of the ingredients of turtle herb mixture.

Bay Leaves – Laurier

Lauras nobilis, grown in the eastern Mediterranean countries and used for flavouring in a bouquet garni, pastry and confectionery.

Borage – Bourrache

Borago officinalis, a cucumber-flavoured plant, the leaves of which are used in salads and fruit cups when fresh and also most decorative in shellfish cocktails.

Chervil – Cerfeuil

Scandix cerefolius, has a most delicate flavour and is used as an ingredient in several mixed herbs and as garnish for certain soups, salads and punch preparations.

Chives – Ciboulette

Allium schoenprasum: this plant of the onion family has a light, fresh, onion flavour and is used finely chopped on salads, certain sauces and other preparations.

Dill – Aneth

A plant growing to 1.2 m (4 ft) and similar to asparagus fern. It has a delicate mild flavour and is used in sauces with salads and its young, fresh sprigs are most decorative for all fish and shellfish cocktails and can be cooked with new potatoes instead of mint. Its crown or seed of the crown is used in pickling, especially cucumber. It is also dried (dill seed).

Fennel – Fenouil

Foeniculum vulgare: the fresh or dried leaves of this plant are used for flavouring in bakery, pickling and in the manufacture of liqueurs.

Garlic – Ail

Allium sativum: another of the family of onion plant. It is white and separates into small cloves. The reputation of French and Italian cookery rests, to a large extent, on the use of garlic. It is very pungent and must be used sparingly. It is best crushed and mixed with salt into a garlic paste.

Horseradish – Raifort

Cochlearia armoracia: the roots are used grated as an accompaniment mainly to roast beef and as sauces for various smoked fish. It can also be used for certain other meat dishes and hot and cold sauces. Best fresh, the roots are available from early autumn to early winter, and they can be kept reasonably fresh in a box with damp sand. Also available in jars ready grated under various brand names.

Mint – Menthe

Mentha spicata: this well known herb is mainly used for mint sauces, peas and new potatoes. Wild mint is also used for the making of teas and liqueurs (peppermint).

Marjoram – Marjolaine

Origanum vulgare, has a very strong flavour and is an ingredient in turtle herbs. It is also used in sausage manufacture, especially liver sausage, and the making of pâtés, where liver is used. Wild marjoram or origanum is used in the preparation of Italian pizza.

Mixed Herbs – Herbes Composées

A mixture of dried herbs, like turtle herbs, and others, usually available ready mixed under various brand names.

Oregano

Transported from Italy and Mexico and used with vegetables, meat farces and sauces. Important in Italian cookery, wheat dishes and pizza.

Parsley – Persil

Petroselinum sativum, the best known of all herbs; its stalks are found in bouquet garnis flavouring and nearly all basic cookery. Its sprigs are widely used as garnish or decoration with many foods, fresh or fried.

Rosemary – Romarin

Rosmarinum officinalis: the rather tough leaves of this shrub are used mostly with veal, and feature greatly in Italian cooking.

Sage – Sauge

Salvia officinalis, has a strong pungent flavour, and is used extensively in English cooking for stuffings and sausage manufacture.

Savory – Sarriette

Sateureia hortensis: this herb of the mint family comes from France and Spain and features in these countries' cooking. It is rather strong and rarely used in England.

Thyme – Thym

Thymus vulgaris, a well known herb used extensively in bouquets garnis and is an ingredient of several herb mixtures and should be used sparingly.

Tarragon – Estragon

Artemisia dracunculus, has a very pungent flavour and is an ingredient of mixed herbs. When fresh, it is used with salads and sauces, and also as cold larder decoration. It is also available in jars pickled in vinegar in whole leaves, or as flavouring to tarragon vinegar.

Wild Thyme – (Thym) Serpolet

Thymus Serpyllum: has the same uses as thyme above, but is even more pungent and must be used sparingly.

Those of us who are fortunate enough to have a varied herb garden will be able, at least during the summer and autumn months, to use fresh herbs and enjoy their beautiful flavours and smells. Even then, it is only for this time of the year. During winter and spring, use has to be made of dried herbs, but with modern methods of production and careful grading and packing most of these dried herbs are excellent and many manufacturing brands are available. Some firms will supply a selection of up to a hundred or more herbs and spices.

It is advisable *not* to buy herbs and spices in too big a quantity but to buy smaller quantities as required. Repeated opening of tins and jars, leaving them in warm places and not closing them properly, will greatly reduce the flavours and will not be very economical.

The composition of some of the mixed herbs and spices cannot be given in full since many of these recipes are closely guarded secrets of the manufacturers.

CONDIMENTS AND SAUCES – CONDIMENTS ET SAUCES

All these preparations are manufactured and available in jars, bottles and tins. They are with certain exceptions accompaniments rather than additions to foods and are available to the hotel or restaurant guest on request, to be eaten with ready cooked or cold foods.

Pickles, pickled mixtures, and sauces and seasonings do not really represent seasoning and spices as such although seasoning, spices and herbs are used in their manufacture. The best known are: Anchovy essence (Essence d'anchois), Gherkins (Cornichons), Harvey sauce, Ketchups, Mustards (Moutardes), Maggi seasoning, Mustard Sauces, Pickles (Achards), Pickled capers (Câpres), Pickled walnuts, Piccalilli, Soya sauce, Tabasco sauce, Worcestershire sauce, Chutneys.

Where the French translation is not given, the produce is known under its English, or same, name.

BRINES, MARINADES AND PICKLES

The Larder uses a number of marinades, pickles and brines, most of which have been known for hundreds of years. Whereas the marinades are always used to give a certain distinctive flavour and/or to tenderize in some cases, the pickles and brines were originally used to preserve food. In modern times of refrigeration and deep-freezing, pickling and brining may be thought to be unnecessary but this is not so.

Although pickling and brining does preserve, the foods treated in this way attain a certain colour in the case of brine and, what is more important, flavour in the case of pickles and marinades; people have become accustomed to this and would not care to miss it. This does not imply, however, that pickle and brine is not also used to preserve; under certain circumstances, this purpose still exists today.

BRINES

Raw Brine – La Saumure Crue

10 l. (2 gal) water
2½ kg (4 lb) salt
25 g (1 oz) saltpetre
100 g (4 oz) brown sugar

Dissolve saltpetre in a little water and place with all the other ingredients in a large tub of cement, glazed bricks, slate or earthenware (plastic of special make can also be used). Stir every so often and leave for 24 hours until all salt has dissolved. Add meats to be brined, rubbed in salt.
Test with salinometer at approx. 60° with an egg, which should float on

the surface of the brine; this method is not altogether safe because it only shows that there is enough salt, but not if there is too much.

Red Brine – La Saumure Liquide Rouge

10 *l.* (2 *gal*) *water*
2½ *kg* (4 *lb*) *salt*
50 *g* (2 *oz*) *saltpetre*
150 *g* (6 *oz*) *brown sugar*

For method and test, see above.

Spice Brine – La Saumure aux Aromates

10 *l.* (2 *gal*) *water*
2½ *kg* (4 *lb*) *salt*
15 *g* (½ *oz*) *saltpetre*
250 *g* (8 *oz*) *brown sugar*
20 *peppercorns*
20 *juniper-berries*
2 *sprigs thyme*
500 *g* (1 *lb*) *sliced carrots*
500 *g* (1 *lb*) *sliced onions*
4-6 *bay leaves*

As for Raw Brine.

Cooked Brine

Has salt and diluted saltpetre added to the brine after it has been boiled and strained. All brines listed here can be brought to the boil for about 2 20 mins. and must be really cold – at best, cooled overnight – before meats should be added. The spice-brine is usually strained. The cooked brines will, of course, keep much longer. Cuts of meat weighing up to 3 kg (6 lb), will brine in 4 to 6 days. Cuts of meat weighing from 3-6 kg (6 to 12 lb) will brine in 6 to 8 days. Cuts of meat weighing more than 6 kg (12 lb) should be left proportionately longer in the brine or should be treated with a pickling syringe, that is to say, cold brine is injected into the middle of the large piece. This technique can also be used if a piece of meat is required quickly.

MARINADES (UNCOOKED)

Uncooked White Wine Marinade – La Marinade Crue au Vin Blanc

100 *g* (4 *oz*) *sliced onions*
50 *g* (2 *oz*) *sliced carrots*
1 *crushed clove of garlic*
25 *g* (1 *oz*) *sliced celery or celeriac*
20 *g* (½ *oz*) *parsley stalks*
10 *g* (¼ *oz*) *spice salt*
8-12 *peppercorns*
1 *clove*
2 *sprigs thyme*
½ *l.* (1 *pint*) *white wine or wine-vinegar*
⅛ *l.* (¼ *pint*) *oil*

(1) Rub meat with spice salt.
(2) Place into a deep dish of china, earthenware, slate, glazed bricks or cement.
(3) Sprinkle herbs, vegetables, spices over the top.
(4) Moisten with wine and oil.
(5) Keep in a cool place 24 to 72 hours.
(6) Turn meat frequently, so that it absorbs the flavour from all sides.
Used for white meats and poultry.

Uncooked Red Wine Marinades – La Marinade Crue au Vin Rouge

As above, with red wine instead of white. Used for all red meats.

Uncooked Marinade for Game – La Marinade Crue au Vin Rouge pour Gibier

As for uncooked red wine marinade, with the addition of 6–8 coriander-seeds, 6–8 juniper berries.

Uncooked Marinade for Lamb or Mutton – La Marinade 'en Chevreuil'

As for uncooked white wine marinade with the addition of 6–8 juniper berries, a good pinch of rosemary. The term *en chevreuil* is purely a culinary term and not a translation.

Uncooked Marinade for Fish – La Marinade Crue pour Poisson

Juice of half a lemon
$\frac{1}{8}$ l. ($\frac{1}{4}$ pint) of olive oil
20 g ($\frac{1}{2}$ oz) parsley stalks
salt and ground white pepper to taste

Used for fried and grilled fish (Orly).

MARINADES (COOKED)

These marinades have the advantage of keeping for a very long time, provided they are kept in a very cool place and they are brought to the boil, according to the time of the year, every 2nd to 4th day. When reboiled a little wine or wine-vinegar should be added each time to improve the flavour. Ingredients are the same as for uncooked marinades. Method: (1) Place oil in a russe of appropriate size, (2) Add vegetables, herbs and spices, (3) Sweat and brown slightly, then add wine, or wine-vinegar, (4) Must be very cold before marinading meats (24 to 72 hours).

Cooked White Wine Marinade – La Marinade Cuite au Vin Blanc

As for uncooked marinade, using method for cooked.

Marinade Cuite au Vin Rouge

As for uncooked marinade, using method for cooked.

Marinade Cuite au Vin Rouge pour Gibier

As for uncooked marinade, using method for cooked.

Marinade 'en Chevreuil' Cuite

As for uncooked marinade, using method for cooked.

VINEGAR AND SALT PICKLES

Cooked Vinegar Pickle or Spice Vinegar

1 *l.* (1 *quart) malt vinegar*
$\frac{1}{4}$ *l.* ($\frac{1}{2}$ *pint) water*
25 *g* (1 *oz) pickling spice*
15 *g* ($\frac{1}{2}$ *oz) salt*
20 *g* ($\frac{1}{2}$ *oz) sugar*

Bring all ingredients to the boil; cool, if desired, strain, pour over food to be pickled. Leave at least 10 to 12 days. Used with cucumber, onions, red cabbage, etc.

Cucumber

Use young cucumbers, or so-called 'ridge-cucumber'. If these are not available, large cucumbers may be used, cut into about 4–6 cm (2–3 in.) pieces. After carefully scrubbing and washing the cucumbers, they are sprinkled with salt and left overnight. After washing and draining they are packed into jars, and covered with above cold spice vinegar for up to 3 months.

Onions

Select even, small onions not larger than 2 cm (1 in.) in diameter. Peel and wash, sprinkle with salt, leave overnight to brine. Wash and drain, pack into jars, and cover with above cold spice vinegar for up to 3 months.

Red Cabbage

Trim outer leaves, quarter, remove stalks, shred into long shreds very finely; sprinkle with salt; leave overnight, wash and drain, then pack into jars and cover with cold spice vinegar.

Cooked Salt-Pickles

1 *l.* (1 *quart) water*
180 *g* (6 *oz) salt, best is coarse kitchen salt*
100 *g* (2 *oz) fresh horseradish cut into fine slices*
20 *g* ($\frac{1}{2}$ *oz) dill seeds*
25 *g* (1 *oz) sugar*

Bring all the ingredients to the boil; pour piping-hot over the foods to be pickled in this way. Leave to pickle and ferment in a cool place for at least 6 to 8 weeks. Store very cold. Used with large and medium cucumber, gherkins, red, green, and yellow peppers, etc. Prepare vegetables according to previous instructions; peppers are cut in halves, the stem and inner-seed being removed.

SWEET-SOUR PICKLES

Cooked Sweet-Sour Pickle

1 *l.* (1 *quart*) *of wine-vinegar*
$\frac{1}{4}$ *l.* ($\frac{1}{2}$ *pint*) *water*
150 *g* (6 *oz*) *sugar*
25 *g* (1 *oz*) *pickling spice*
15 *g* ($\frac{1}{2}$ *oz*) *dill seed or* 2 *crowns of fresh dill*
15 *g* ($\frac{1}{2}$ *oz*) *spice salt*

Bring all ingredients to the boil, pour over the food to be pickled piping hot, cool, and keep for at least 4–6 weeks, or more. Used with cucumber, pearl onions, fennel, pumpkin, etc.

Cucumber

Scrub and wash cucumbers well; place into jar, add 2 to 3 extra crowns of dill, cover with hot pickle – as described above, cool, and store in fridge or cool place. In this case, cover jar with cellophane.

Onions (Pearl or Cocktail Onions)

Select even onions; peel and wash well, pack into jars and cover with hot pickle above; and store in a cool place.

Fennels or Celery

Cut fennels or celery short, to leave a root of about 7–10 cm (3–4 in.); wash in several waters very thoroughly and pack into jars, covering with the hot pickle mentioned above.

Pumpkin or Marrow

Peel marrow or pumpkin, cut in halves, remove pips, neatly cut into strip or dice not too small and pack into jars with a cinnamon stick; cover with sweet-sour pickle and store in a cool place.
With all of the hot sweet-sour pickles, a slight fermentation takes place; only when this has stopped should the pickled vegetable be served.

SWEET-RAW PICKLES

Sweet-Raw Pickle – Scandinavian origin

$\frac{1}{2}$ *l.* (1 *pint*) *white or wine-vinegar*	2 *sliced onions, red.*
$\frac{1}{2}$ *l.* (1 *pint*) *of castor sugar*	12 *peppercorns*
2 *bayleaves*	

Combine all ingredients until dissolved; pour over foods to be pickled.

Cauliflower

Cut small roses off the cauliflower; blanch for 30 secs, cool, place into jars and cover with the above pickle, omitting onions; leave 3–4 days.

Mushrooms

Select small to medium mushrooms which have not yet opened; remove part of the stalk. Wash well and blanch in lemon water for 30 secs, cool and place in jars. Cover with above pickle, leave for 3–4 days before use.

Onions (Pearl or Cocktail Onions)

Select even onions within type, peel and wash, blanch for 30 secs, cool and place into jars. Cover with pickle as described in the aforegoing page, but omitting onions, and leave 3–4 days before using.

Fennel/Celery

Prepeare fennel or celery as for sweet-sour pickle; blanch, place into jars, cover with sweet pickle, omitting onions, and leave 3–4 days before use.

Pumpkin and Marrow

Prepare pumpkins or marrows as for sweet-sour pickle, cut into neat strips or dice, not too small, place into jars and cover with sweet pickle: force a cinnamon stick into the jar and leave 3–4 days before use.

Herring

Fillet 8–10 salted herrings, free of all skin and bone, soak for 12 hours in cold, fresh water, changing water 2–3 times. Cut each herring fillet into 6–8 pieces, place into a deep tray; sprinkle with coarsely crushed pepper and/or allspice corn. Cover with onion rings, preferably of the red type, add 2–3 bay leaves and cover with vinegar in which sugar has been dissolved: use the following day.

HORS D'ŒUVRE À LA GRECQUE

Basic Liquor (Pickle):

3 cl ($\frac{1}{2}$ gill) olive oil
$\frac{1}{4}$ l. ($\frac{1}{2}$ pint) water
3 cl ($\frac{1}{2}$ gill) white wine
juice of 1 lemon
salt
1 sprig thyme
1 bayleaf
6 peppercorns
6 coriander seeds
fennel, celery

Simmer all ingredients together for 10 mins. Use to braise vegetables as required. Vegetables should be cooled in the liquor and served chilled with a little unstrained liquor.

Artichokes (Artichauts)

Peel, trim and rub with lemon. Cut leaves short, remove chokes; wash; blanch in acidulated water, wash again, simmer in liquor for 15-20 mins.

Button Onions (Petits Oignons)

Peel, wash, blanch, refresh. Simmer in liquor until tender.

Cauliflower (Chou-fleur)

Trim, wash, break into small springs (flowers). Blanch, refresh, simmer in liquor, keep firm.

Leeks (Poireaux)

Trim, wash, tie into bundle. Blanch, refresh, cut into 2 cm (1 in.) lengths, place in shallow pan, cover with liquor and simmer until tender.

Celeriac (Céleri-rave)

Wash and peel.

Mushrooms (Champignons)

Trim roots, wash well, peel if necessary, blanch.

HORS D'OEUVRE PORTUGAISE

Basic Liquor

3 cl ($\frac{1}{2}$ gill) olive oil
1 clove garlic
1 chopped onion
salt and pepper
white wine
3 cl ($\frac{1}{2}$ gill) water

500 g (1 lb) tomatoes
1 teaspoon tomato purée
20 g ($\frac{1}{2}$ oz) chopped parsley
1 bouquet garni

(1) Lightly stew onion in the oil.
(2) Skin and remove seeds from tomatoes.
(3) Chop and dice and add to the onion.
(4) Add garlic clove and other ingredients.
(5) Simmer for 5 min.
(6) Use as required.

Cool in Liquor and serve chilled.

All vegetables used for *Hors d'Œuvre à la Grecque* can be used and prepared in a similar manner using basic Portugaise liquor. Also suitable for fish and fish roes.

HERRINGS

Soused Herring – Hareng Dieppoise

25 g (1 oz) channelled carrots
25 g (1 oz) button onions
salt and pepper
$\frac{1}{2}$ bayleaf
1 sprig thyme
6 peppercorns
1 parsley stalk
3 cl ($\frac{1}{2}$ gill) vinegar
3 cl ($\frac{1}{2}$ gill) water

(1) Clean and scale fish and fillet herrings.
(2) Wash well and season with salt and pepper.
(3) Roll fillets with skin outside.
(4) Place in earthenware dish.
(5) Peel and wash carrots and onions, cut into thin rings and blanch for 2-3 min.
(6) Add to fish with rest of ingredients. Cover with oiled paper, and cook in moderate oven for 15 to 20 min.
(7) Allow to cool; serve on dish with the garnish, decorate with picked parsley.
Four portions = 2 fresh herrings (4 fillets).

Salt Herrings – Harengs Salés

500 g (1 lb) grey salt
2$\frac{1}{2}$-3 kg (5 lb) herrings

(1) Clean, cut and scale herrings.
(2) Pack in layers of salt in non-metal container.
(3) Cover with weighted lid.
(4) Keep in cool place at least 2 days before use.

Bismark Herrings – Hareng de Bismark

400 *g* (12 *oz*) *sliced onions*
10 *g* ($\frac{1}{4}$ *oz*) *mustard seed*
12 *bayleaves*
10 *g* ($\frac{1}{4}$ *oz*) *peppercorns*
12 *cloves*
12 *chillies*
250 *g* (8 *oz*) *sliced brined cucumber*
1 *l.* (2 *pints*) *wine vinegar*
1 *l.* (2 *pints*) *water*

(1) Use salt herrings; cut off heads, open and remove bones, and clean.
(2) Soak in cold water for 2 hours to remove salt.
(3) Place in china or glass container alternating with layers of the garnish.
(4) Cover with vinegar and water and pickle at least 3 days.
Pickle for $2\frac{1}{2}$-3 kg (5 lb) herrings.

Rollmops

Fillet herrings; prepare as for Bismark herrings but roll each fillet round a piece of brined cucumber. Pack in glass jars with the garnish and cover with the liquor. Pickle at least 3 days.

GRAVAD LAX

Gravad Lax or Gravlax (Swedish) or Grav Lachs or Gravlachs (Norwegian), that is cured raw salmon, is of Scandinavian origin, and is eaten as a starter or main course. It is quite easily made, and not surprisingly is found today on many restaurant menus and even in the home.

The ingredients for approximately 16-20 portions are as follows:

1 *small side* (2 *kg*, 4-5 *lb*) *of fresh salmon, trimmed of all bones but not skin*
100 *g* (4 *oz*) *sea salt*
75 *g* (3 *oz*) *castor sugar*
25 *g* (1 *oz*) *black pepper, coarsely crushed*
100 *g* (4 *oz*) *bunch of fresh dill including stalks*

(1) Cut the side of salmon across into two even halves.
(2) Sprinkle each half with equal amounts of a mixture of the salt, sugar and pepper.
(3) Place one half of the salmon on to a deep earthenware or stainless tray, flesh upward.
(4) Crush the thicker stalks of the dill and spread them evenly over this first half of the salmon. Then place the second half on top of the first, flesh downward.
(5) Cover with an oiled sheet of greaseproof paper and place into fridge for 24 to 72 hours. Turn the salmon frequently during this period.

(6) Serve gravad salmon cut into 2–3 thin slices as a starter on crisp leaves of lettuce. Garnish with a sprig of fresh dill and a quarter lemon. Offer dill mustard sauce (see below) and fresh hot toast separately.
(7) Alternatively, serve 4–5 thin slices as main fish course with new potatoes and small French beans. Offer dill mustard sauce separately.

Scandinavian Dill Mustard Sauce
(16–20 portions)

100 *g* (4 *oz*) (*large bundle*) *dill, finely chopped*
$\frac{1}{4}$ *l.* ($\frac{1}{2}$ *pint*) *light-coloured French mustard*
$\frac{1}{2}$ *l.* (1 *pint*) *vegetable or olive oil*
100 *g* (4 *oz*) *castor sugar*
$\frac{1}{8}$ *l.* ($\frac{1}{4}$ *pint*) *wine vegar*
1 *teaspoon mill pepper*
1 *teaspoon salt to taste*

(1) Place mustard, sugar, salt, vinegar and mill pepper into a bowl and mix well.
(2) Gradually stir in the oil with a whisk to obtain an emulsion not unlike mayonnaise.
(3) Add the finely chopped dill, and correct seasoning.
(4) Leave to stand for one to two hours before serving.

This sauce tends to separate after a while, but a good stir with a whisk should correct this easily.

7. *Chef du Froid*

The function and duties of the Chef du Froid are the preparation, dressing, and often the serving of cold buffets. These can range from the elaborate display buffet set out in the restaurant or grill room (in some establishments, both), to the buffet reception, the cocktail party, the cold luncheons for weddings or other functions, and the preparation of sandwiches for teas, dances, etc. The cold element on the daily Table d'Hôte menus are likewise his responsibility.

To carry out these duties efficiently, he must be familiar with the work concerned with Larder productions. These include the preparation of aspic, chaud-froid sauces, pies galantines, terrines, pâtés, mousses or cold soufflés, pressed beef, brawns, boar's head, etc., as well as the various fillings for sandwiches and cold savouries, canapés, etc. He must be skilled in the cooking and dressing of fish and shellfish, hams, tongues and other pickled meats, and in the dressing of smoked fish or meats.

He must maintain close liaison with other departments in the Larder, Kitchen and Pastry so as to obtain his various joints of meat, poultry, game etc., and his pastry cases, as and when required. He must be skilled in the use of aspic and have an artistic flair which will enable him to decorate and garnish the various dishes in the pleasant and eye-catching manner that is very important in this branch of Larder work. Some skill in carving fat, or ice, for socles is also desirable.

Finally, he must be a skilled carver, well able to use carving knives without handling the food with his fingers if he is to serve from a buffet in a dining room. His general appearance, smartness, cleanliness and manner, will also play an important part in this kind of work.

PREPARATIONS

He will start the day by dressing the various buffet dishes, carefully trimming where necessary, replacing stale items with fresh ones, re-glossing or glazing with aspic any pieces which have become 'tired' through contact with the atmosphere. Having dressed and decorated each dish, he will replace it in the refrigerator until such time as it is required for dressing the buffet in the restaurant. Just prior to sending the food onto the buffet, he will garnish each dish with its appropriate garnishes, e.g. parsley, watercress, hearts of lettuce, tomato, cucumber, horseradish, radishes, etc., to make it look fresh and appetizing. A record of the number of portions or weight of joints is desirable from the point of control, essential in a well-run Larder. This record is checked on return of the buffet at the end of service, against sales and number of portions or weight returned.

The rest of his time is spent in preparing any other cold dishes required for the day, sandwiches, canapés, etc., and in the preparation of the Larder productions already mentioned for the buffet on the following day.

He must of course ensure that such items as Hors d'Œuvre, salads, cold sauces, cold sweets, cheese board, display of fresh fruits for dessert, etc., are available to complement the cold dishes on the buffet.

The buffet will consist of a selection from the following items, if not all:

(1) Roast joints of meat, usually glossed over with a good clear aspic: e.g. ribs of beef or sirloin of beef, baron of lamb, saddle of mutton, leg or loin of pork, suckling pig, haunch of venison, leg or fillet of veal.

(2) Roast poultry: e.g. capon or chicken, duckling, turkey, goose.

(3) Game (when in season), e.g. pheasant, grouse, partridge, guinea fowl.

(4) Pickled and smoked meats, glossed with clear aspic, or red glaze, e.g., ham, ox-tongue, derby round, pressed beef, brawn, boar's head.

(5) Larder productions: e.g. veal and ham pie, chicken pie, pork pie, game pie, chicken, turkey or veal galantines, ballotines of chicken, lamb or veal, aspics of poultry or game, stuffed chickens or suprême of chickens in chaud-froid, lamb cutlets in chaud-froid, mousses of ham, poultry or game, ham cornets, liver pâté or pâté maison, salads and mayonnaises of meat or poultry.

(6) Fish and shellfish: e.g. salmon or salmon-trout, lobsters, crawfish, turbot or other white fish, stuffed and glazed, trout, salads or mayonnaises of fish or shellfish, dressed crab, etc.

(7) Appetizers, e.g. smoked salmon, smoked trout or eel, smoked ham (Bayonne or Parma), foie gras, oysters (in season), shellfish cocktail, canapés, or Russian Hors d'Œuvre, melon, grapefruit, various Hors d'Œuvre, salads, cold sauces, etc.

(8) Baskets or caskets of fruit, the cheese board and of course a good selection of cold sweets.

It is usual to set off the Display Buffet with an effective centrepiece. This can be a topical model made of gum paste and provided by the pastry department, or a carving in fat or ice, or an outstanding cold dish such as suckling pig, or a whole carcass of lamb or a boar's head, or a whole salmon, or a decorated ham or joint of meat, or even a large game pie.

ASPIC JELLY

A good aspic jelly is required to complement any cold dish. It is, in effect, what a good gravy is to hot meats. Whilst simple to prepare, all too often it is a badly neglected item; therefore some care should be taken in its preparation. It should have a pleasant aroma and flavour, a distinct savour matching the dish for which it is intended, be of a pale amber colour and completely transparent. The consistency must be neither too thick or rubbery, nor too thin.

Time was when aspic was served in a sauce-boat with cold dishes and had, therefore, to be of a 'pouring' consistency, but these days it is accepted that it should be firm enough to stand up to the temperature of the room without running.

Again, in days when meat was comparatively cheap, the 'setting' of aspic was obtained by using pieces of shin of beef or knuckle of veal to make a strongly gelatinous stock for the making of aspic; these days, whilst it is still desirable to make gelatinous stock using knuckle bones, calf's feet and pork rind, it is usual to use 'gelatine' to assist in the setting of the aspic. This should be of good quality, for preference sheet gelatine, and should be kept to the lowest possible quantity consistent with the desired result. In no circumstances should it exceed 25 g (1 oz) per pint of stock, if one is to avoid the distinctive fish glue flavour which is all too prevalent in this product.

There are many types of aspic, each suited to particular types of foodstuffs. The following are the most commonly used.

Ordinary Aspic – Gelée Ordinaire

3 *kg* (6 *lb*) *veal knuckle bones (chopped small)*
3–4 *calves' feet (boned and blanched)*
250 *g* (8 *oz*) *fresh pork rind (blanched)*
100 *g* (4 *oz*) *onions*
100 *g* (4 *oz*) *carrots*
25 *g* (1 *oz*) *bouquet garni (large)*
25 *g* (1 *oz*) *grey salt*
8 *l.* (1½ *gal*) *water*

(1) Lightly roast bones in oven without browning.
(2) Place in clean stock pot, add water and boil.
(3) Skin carefully and wipe side of pot with clean cloth.
(4) Simmer for 2 hours, skimming frequently.
(5) Add vegetables, bouquet garni and salt.
(6) Simmer for 1 hour, strain through muslin, test consistency by placing a little on ice, and adjust to requirement by adding gelatine well soaked in cold water and not exceeding 250 g (8 oz).
To produce 5 litres (1 gal).

Clarification

1 *kg* (2 *lb*) *minced shin of beef (cleared of all fat)*
juice of 2/3 *lemons*
6 *egg whites*

(1) Allow stock to cool overnight.
(2) Remove all fat from surface.

(3) Place shin of beef and whites in clean stock pot.
(4) Mix thoroughly, adding a little cold water $\frac{1}{4}$ l. ($\frac{1}{2}$ pint) to break up the eggs and beef.
(5) Add stock gradually, add lemon juice.
(6) Raise to boiling point quickly, stirring continuously to avoid burning.
(7) Simmer for 15-20 min, correct seasoning and strain carefully through double muslin or jelly bag.

Chicken Aspic – Gelée de Volaille

8 l. (1½ gal) clear chicken stock
1½ kg (3 lb) giblets and carcasses (lightly roasted)
25 g (1 oz) coarse salt
6 whites of egg
250 g (8 oz) gelatine (approx)

(1) Dissolve soaked gelatine in stock and test for consistency. Cool stock and skim off any fat.
(2) Break whites of egg in clean pot with a little cold water.
(3) Add remainder of ingredients and raise to boiling point quickly, stirring continuously.
(4) Simmer for $\frac{1}{2}$ hour and strain carefully through jelly bag or double muslin.
To produce 5 litres (1 gal).

Game Aspic – Gelée de Gibier

8 l. (1½ gal) clear game stock
1½ kg (3 lb) game trimmings and bones (lightly roasted)
6 whites of egg
500 g (1 lb) minced shin of beef
25 g (1 oz) coarse salt
1 bottle port or sherry
250 g (8 oz) gelatine (approx)

As for Chicken Aspic; the wine is added to the aspic when it is quite cool.

White Fish Aspic – Gelée Blanche de Poisson

5 l. (1 gal) white fish stock
4 egg whites
200 g (8 oz) gelatine (approx)
25 g (1 oz) coarse salt
½ bottle dry white wine

(1) Dissolve soaked gelatine in stock and test for consistency.
(2) Break whites in clean pot with little cold water.
(3) Add stock, salt; boil, quickly stirring continuously.
(4) Simmer for 5 mins.
(5) Strain carefully through jelly bag or double muslin.
(6) Add wine when quite cool.

Red Wine Fish Aspic – Gelée Rougeide de Poisson

5 l. (1 gal) red wine fish stock | *200 g (8 oz) gelatine (approx)*
4 whites of eggs

For salmon and fresh water fish. As for White Fish Aspic but, as the fish stock will have been used for cooking the fish, the colour will be faded; therefore, a little red colouring will need to be added to the finished aspic to make it a light pink colour.
All these Aspics should be tasted on completion: and the seasoning corrected before allowing them to set.

RED GLAZE

This is a gelatine coating which is put over pickled meats to protect the surface from the atmosphere and prevent them from discolouring.

Salt beef, ox tongue, boar's head, etc., are coated with red glaze. This will also improve the appearance of the piece of meat and provides a base for decoration.

As these meats will often require handling after glazing, the glaze must be much firmer than aspic and it will require 2 or 3 times as much gelatine added to the stock, as aspic. The colour should be reddish brown and this is obtained by using gravy browning and edible red colouring. The stock used is the stock in which the salt or pickled meat has been cooked.

Preparation is the same as for aspic, the colouring matter being added to the finished glaze.

CHAUD-FROID SAUCES

White

½ l. (1 pint) béchamel or velouté (chicken or veal)
4 dl (¾ pint) chicken aspic
¼ l. (½ pint) fresh cream

(1) Boil the velouté or béchamel in a sauteuse.
(2) Add the aspic and reduce quickly by about one third.
(3) Add the cream gradually, test for consistency, season.
(4) Strain through a tammy cloth into a clean bowl.
(5) Stir till cool to prevent skin forming on surface.

The sauce should be quite cold when used, so that it will coat foodstuffs immersed in it, or masked over it, and it must be liquid enough to allow the food to be easily steeped in it.

Fish or Lenten

Use fish velouté in place of chicken or veal, and white fish aspic in place of chicken. Quantities and method are the same. *Mayonnaise Colèe* is often used in case of fish.

Pink or 'Aurore'

Add a fine purée of fresh tomatoes or an infusion of paprika to white chaud-froid according to what it is intended for. The colour should be a very delicate rose pink.

Green or Vert Pré

Add a fine purée made of pounded and strained, blanched, fine herbs and spinach, and infused in a gill of white wine, to white chaud-froid. The colour should be a delicate pale green.

Brown

Use demi-glace flavoured with truffle essence and port wine, or madeira. No cream. For duck dishes, flavour with duck essence, orange juice and blanched fine Julienne of orange zest. For game dishes, flavour with game essence of the game the chaud-froid is intended for. For fish dishes, use fish espagnole in place of demi-glace, flavour with fish essence and use fish or lenten aspic. Chaud-froid sauces can be prepared in advance and need only be gently melted when required.

DECORATION AIDS AND DESIGNS

Decoration aids must at all times be edible and have a good natural colour. Their flavour should be as neutral as possible so as not to impair the taste of the food they are used to decorate. In most cases they must be blanched, or even cooked, to be limp and thus easily lie and take contact on the surface of the food, whether it is plain or covered with aspic or chaud-froid sauces.

Colours should be bright, and blanching and instant careful refreshing will assist in this; on the other hand, they must be kept firm so that one is able to cut the decoration aids into the desired shapes, and build them up to a picture, mosaic, or border.

The most common colours for food decoration in Cold Larder work are black, green, red and white.

Black Colours

The best known black decoration aid is truffle, the black mushroom/fungus imported fresh from France or, more commonly, in small tins. These can be sliced and cut into diamonds, squares, triangles, strips, etc., by hand, or with the help of a set of aspic cutters. Truffles are quite expensive. A black fungus paste in small tins, which has become available in the last few years, can easily be used for decoration purposes, very much like truffles.

Red Colours

The colour red, for decoration, is derived from several items of food, notably vegetables, such as red peppers and tomatoes. The red peppers when fresh should be opened and the seed removed, then blanched in a little salt and lemon water to become limp. Tomatoes are usually blanched and peeled, the pips being removed by cutting the tomato in halves across or quarters, then carefully washed. The flesh of firm red tomatoes can be most useful as a red decor. Both red peppers and tomatoes, prepared as above, can then again be easily cut into diamonds, petals, triangles, strips, etc., by a steady hand, or with a set of small aspic cutters. Beetroot, also of a good red colour, should never be used as its colour is not fast and will run into chaud-froid and aspics.

Green Colours

The colour green for decorating purposes can be had from a great number of green vegetables, notably, beans, cucumber peel, leeks, watercress and spinach. The latter two are very thin and soft and great care should be taken when blanching cress and spinach. A second or two in boiling salted water is usually sufficient and instant refreshing in cold water important. Thus prepared, the small leaf of the watercress and spinach will not tear or break and are most useful as natural leaves for flowers etc., when decorating a ham or galantine. Beans, cucumber peel and leeks, however, need slightly longer blanching time, carefully refreshed; the beam will separate into halves which can be cut into stems or diamonds. Even the leek-leaf will separate into two halves and experience tells that in most cases it is best used by separating the leaves. A set of aspic-cutters is of little use for cutting into different shapes because these vegetables are thin and tear easily, except cucumber peel. However, as green is usually used for leaves, stems and borders, these not too difficult designs can be cut with a sharp pointed knife into the desired shapes.

White Colours

Many white items of foods, such as turnips, the lower parts of leeks, and celeriac, have been tried as a decoration aid. In most cases they are not really satisfactory as they tend to lose their colour or are too soft and, as in the case of turnips, have too strong a flavour. Experience has shown that white of egg is still the best white decoration aid, usable with all foods such as meat, poultry, game and fish. The whites should be carefully separated from the yolks of very fresh eggs and placed in a slightly buttered or oiled dariol mould or similar container. Care should be taken when placing the whites into the mould to avoid air bubbles within the whites. Leave the whites in the mould to rest for one hour, piercing any air bubbles with a cocktail stick. The mould is then placed into a 'bain-marie' waterbath and the whites cooked in a very slow oven or even hot-plate. If the whites cook too quickly, it will rise within the mould and show little bubbles, as in a Gruyère cheese. In this condition they are not usable for decoration. Careful, slow cooking will set the white to a firm smooth white mass; slowly cooled and removed from the mould, it can be cut into almost any shape, either with a sharp knife or with the help of a set of aspic-cutters.

These 4 colours are used with other items, but the vegetables here described are really the best. Other colours for more varied decorations could and have been found, but these 4 should be quite sufficient.

Coloured Royale

Another decoration aid may be found in the use of a Royale in different colours. The Royale is made in the normal way, possibly slightly firmer. One part is kept to its natural yellow, another may be coloured with spinach and spinach juice to a pleasant green, and the third may be coloured with a tomato-purée of fresh tomatoes, gently poached in a waterbath and cooled slowly. The coloured Royales can then be cut and used very much like other colours of the given decoration aids.

Glace de Viande

A more modern method of decoration is the use of a good smooth *glace de viande*. Designs made with *glace de viande* will of course be of one colour only, i.e. a pleasant brown, but this can be most attractive with a good white background of chaudfroid sauce. Slightly warmed, the *glace* is put into small paper piping bags and is used following the principles of Royale icing. It needs, however, a very steady hand and only the more experienced should attempt to use this method.

Butters

Coloured butters have of late been much used in the decoration of cold foods, coloured with fast, edible colours or in the way described for Royale, but, many defenders of the classical decoration method will not use them as they consider it a too simple and unattractive method of decoration.

DECORATING TECHNIQUE AND METHOD

It has already been said that a set of aspic cutters are of very great help for the successful compilation of designs. These cutters come in 2 types: (1) A set of various shapes and forms, in one box, all of about the same size, (2) A set of one shape, or form, in one box, but of various sizes, usually between 6 to 8.

The shapes shown in Figure 90 ('A' to 'H') are those most commonly used and are, according to the type of set available in different sizes, ranging from about 1 cm ($\frac{1}{2}$ in.) sq to 4 cm (2 in.) sq, approximately.

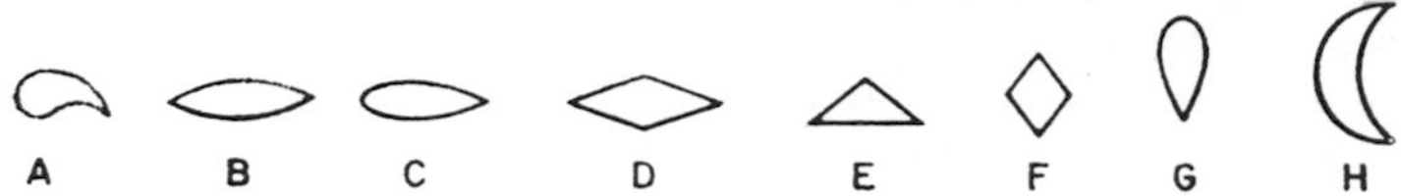

FIG. 90. *Commonly used shapes for classical decoration*

The designs in Figure 91 ('A' to 'H') show the use of each shape on its own, within one pattern, partly as a flower, or borders or parts of larger designs.

FIG. 91. *Typical designs made up from basic shapes*

The examples in Figure 92 ('I' to 'X') show the use of the same basic shapes with one another, as well as some simpler shapes, which can be cut by hand from the materials used.

The method of use of the above designs could be for the laying out of small dariol moulds with various fillings. These designs can, of course, be

FIG 92. *Further designs from basic shapes*

enlarged, or borders may be added when handling larger moulds, as in the case of mousses, galantines, fishes in aspic, or similar foods.

The foregoing layouts show very clearly the possibilities of the use of the basic shapes 'A' to 'H'. One can assemble quite easily whole designs of flowers first with one shape only and, in subsequent examples, by the use of several different shapes.

Two new shapes are added in the designs in Figure 93 – the shape of a heart and a star. Stems and the larger leaves have been cut free by hand, which can easily be done with a sharp pointed knife.

The larger flower in this illustration is, again a good example of the use of cutters of different shapes, as well as some pieces cut freehand, whereas the butterfly is solely cut by hand and, as shown, assembled in stages in one unit of design.

Another method of combination is the assembling of flowers with the use of cutters of one or more shape, as well as the freehand cuts of, e.g. a butterfly, as shown here with large flower and flower-peacock designs (Figure 94).

A simple, but very satisfying method of decoration is the laying of mosaics For this squares, triangles or diamonds can be used. In all 3 cases it is best to cut the shapes with a cutter of appropriate size, for even the most trained and steady hand will not be able to cut all the diamonds to the correct size all the time.

It is important to select the right size of shapes; a smaller item of food to be decorated will mean the use of a smaller size of diamond, whereas a larger piece will need the use of larger diamonds to show the mosaic to its best advantage. The cutter will ensure a correct size for the diamond used but care should be taken in getting the right thickness, otherwise the mosaic will not have a very even surface.

A truffle is quite easily cut into even slices and then into diamonds with a cutter, but the softer white of egg does not always make it easy.

FIG. 93. *Designs incorporating a heart and a star*

The examples in Figure 95 show the use of diamonds in a mosaic: (1) *Black and White* truffles and white of egg; (2) *Black and red* truffles and red peppers; (3) *Black, Red and White*, truffles, whites of egg and red peppers.

FIG. 94. *Large flower design*

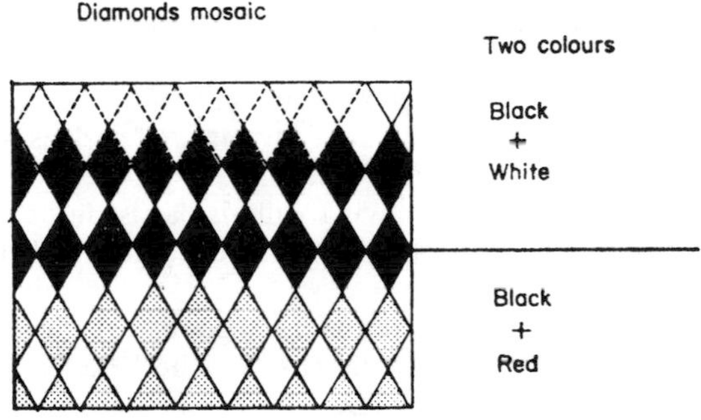

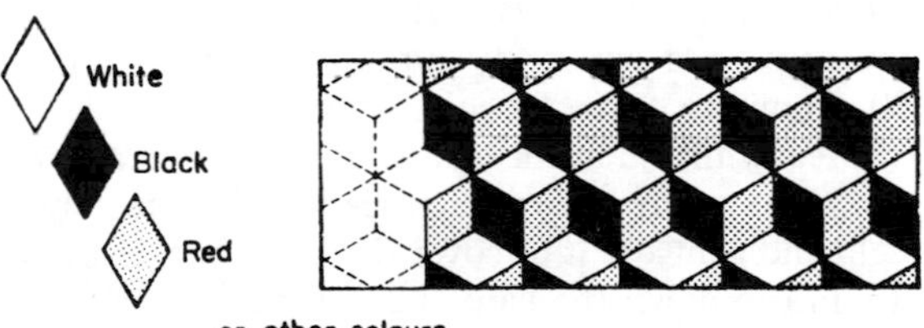

FIG. 95. *Decoration by mosaic*

Effective Decorating

Good effective decorating needs time. The normal accepted rush in the average hotel and restaurant kitchen does not always allow this complicated work to be executed effectively. The laying of a mosaic of tiny diamonds of truffles and whites of eggs on a chaud-froid coated ham needs time. It cannot and should not, be rushed. The diamonds must be cut evenly to 0.2 mm (a hundredth of an inch). The aspic in which the diamonds are dipped must be of the right temperature. The laying of this mosaic, or similar work, will need a steady hand, a keen eye, and uninterrupted attention.

The operator must prepare well for the decorating to be done. A good *mise en place* for this kind of work is vital to avoid undue running about and interruption.

Place the ham, for example, on a rack or, better still, a turntable; have a quiet place to work; have sharp knives and the correct tools at hand. Keep your working area clean all the time; have a clean cloth for wiping and drying when and where necessary.

Keep designs simple. The days when several chefs spent hours decorating only a few items on a cold buffet are long past except in very exceptional circumstances, say possibly for exhibition purposes.

Time nowadays is very costly; use it to the best advantage. A simple design will help; remember that the most beautiful design or picture elsewhere can look ghastly on a cold ham or salmon. One simple, single flower on a clean and smooth chaud-froid covered ham is often more effective than a whole bouquet.

It is advisable to have one design, drawn first on a piece of paper. Even the most experienced artist will make layouts and designs for his paintings. One is not normally an artist, hence there is all the more reason for the design to be predrawn. The drawing will also assist in deciding whether it will fit the size and shapes of the ham to be decorated and the best position in which to place it.

All this considered, make sure there is a good, clean, even surface (background) on which to place the design. The best designs look bad on an uneven or bumpy background. The ham, taking the same example, should be even and smooth even before the first layer of chaud-froid sauce is applied. The utmost care should be taken in removing the rind and excess fat so that the even, natural shape of the ham is retained. This done, place the ham on a wire rack and put on a tray in the refrigerator for at least 30-60 min to get really cold.

Meanwhile, melt the chaud-froid sauce in a waterbath; place it, with the pan, into a bowl of crushed ice, stirring steadily all the time. Just at the right moment use it to cover the cold ham. If the sauce is too warm (thin), it will run down the ham and will not give an effective cover. If it is too cold (thick), it will not run well and give an uneven and bumpy coat to the ham. Chaud-froid sauce which has run down the ham on to the tray can be returned to the pan, melted and strained; it can be used again and again. Before applying the second or subsequent layers of chaud-froid sauce, the ham, etc., should be placed into a refrigerator between each coating.

Having chosen the design, prepared the necessary *mise en place*, and having achieved a good surface to work on, the actual decorating can begin.

Diamonds, triangles and strips, or petals, leaves and stems for flowers, should be dipped into aspic before placing on to the ham. The larger items like leaves and stems can be easily picked up with one's fingers and placed in the desired position. Care should be taken here to find the right position first time; once placed on to the chaud-froid surface it should *never be removed*. This would only spoil the good shiny clean surface that has taken so much care to achieve.

The smaller items, like diamonds in a mosaic, or small petals for a flower are very difficult to pick up with one's fingers. The point of a small sharp knife, a trussing needle or even a cocktail stick will be ideal for transferring these small items to the desired postion within one's design.

Place the diamonds, triangles or petals on a plate with a little melted aspic; carefully pierce the small petal with a cocktail stick, lift and place into position. Use the index finger of your left hand, another cocktail stick or the point of a small knife to keep it there, and to withdraw the cocktail stick and so on. The aspic on the petal, etc., will act as a sort of adhesive, and will make it stay put. This may be of special importance when decorating on a sloping surface where otherwise these small items would easily slide off.

Aspic Finish

When the decoration on the ham has been finished, place the ham again into the refrigerator to let the decoration set. This will take usually about 1 hour and is of great importance, for in its present state the ham is not finished. It should always be covered by 1 or 2 layers of good clear aspic to give it a good clear shine and finish. As in the case of chaud-froid sauce, place some aspic in a sauteuse, melt it carefully, then place it into a bowl with crushed ice to cool. At just the right moment, not too warm and not too cold, use it to give the ham the finishing cover. This may have to be repeated 2 or 3 times. Much care should be taken to get a good result and finish. If the aspic is too warm it could rinse away the beautiful design when it is applied to the decorated ham. If it is too cold and thickening, it will not give a smooth, even finish.

GARNISHES

The basic difference between 'decoration' and 'garnish' is that decoration is usually placed on the food, whereas garnishes invariably loosely surround the cold foods. In contrast with the elaborate designs and much work needed to made a good decor, a garnish may consist of such simple things as a sprig of parsley or watercress, a crisp heart of lettuce, or a polished tomato. More advanced garnishes may consist of stuffed tomatoes or stuffed eggs, lemon or tomato baskets, as well as Russian or similar salads, set with aspic in small moulds (Figures 96 and 97). In the case of poultry and game, round, diamond or heart shaped croûtons with fillings of various pâtés, or jellies, are often used. A carefully emptied orange peel, filled with orange-flavoured aspic, set and cut into neat wedges is often used to garnish Duck *à l'orange*, or other roasted poultry or game dishes, when served cold.

Garnished eggs

Oranges filled

FIG. 96. *Garnishes*

Lemon baskets

Tomatoes garnished

FIG. 97. *Garnishes*

A simple but effective garnish can also be attained by the use of silver skewers (Figure 98); on these one may place small hearts of lettuce, small polished tomatoes, truffles, champignons, as well as various small shellfish. Skewers of this type can be most attractive and be of excellent use with a rib of beef, poultry, game, or even a cold fish dish. It is very important, when using garnishings, that these are compatible with the food they are used to garnish. A bright pink prawn may be an excellent garnish to a decorated salmon but should not be used, however attractive, when garnishing a ham or other meat, poultry or game dish. Here, more neutral garnishes such as egg, tomatoes, vegetables and salads can be used. A garnish should not disturb but complement the decoration, if any.

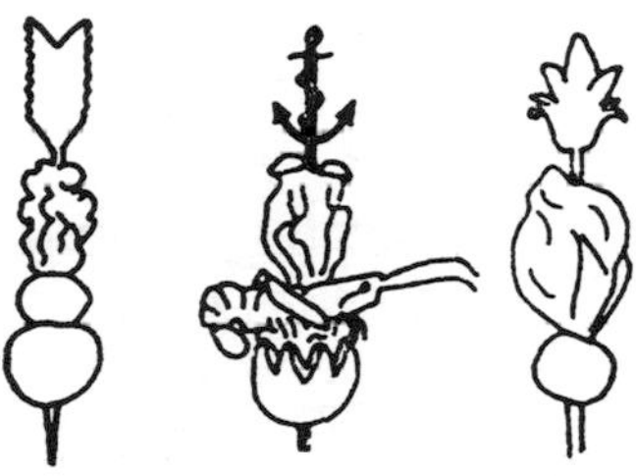

FIG. 98. *Decorated silver skewers*

A selection of buffet dishes is shown in Figures 99-102.

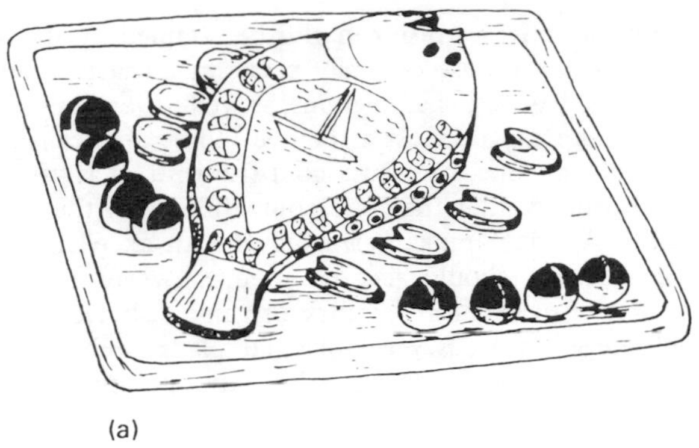

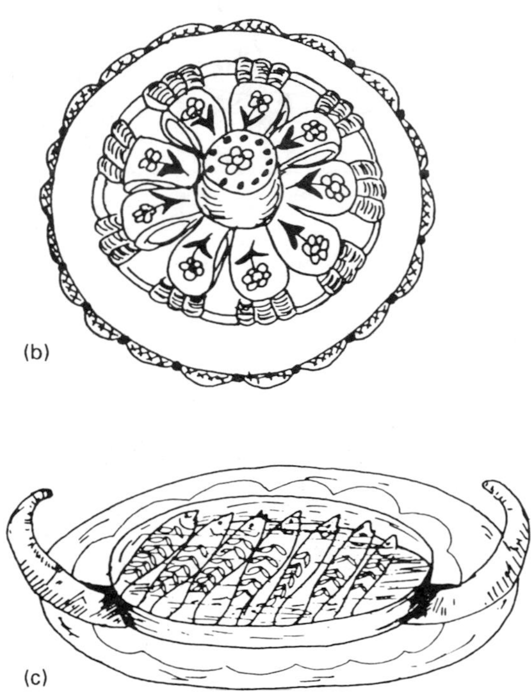

FIG. 99. (a) *Stuffed turbot surrounded by turbot steaks* (b) *Mousse and fillets of sole in gelée* (c) *Poached trout in gelée flavoured with tarragon*

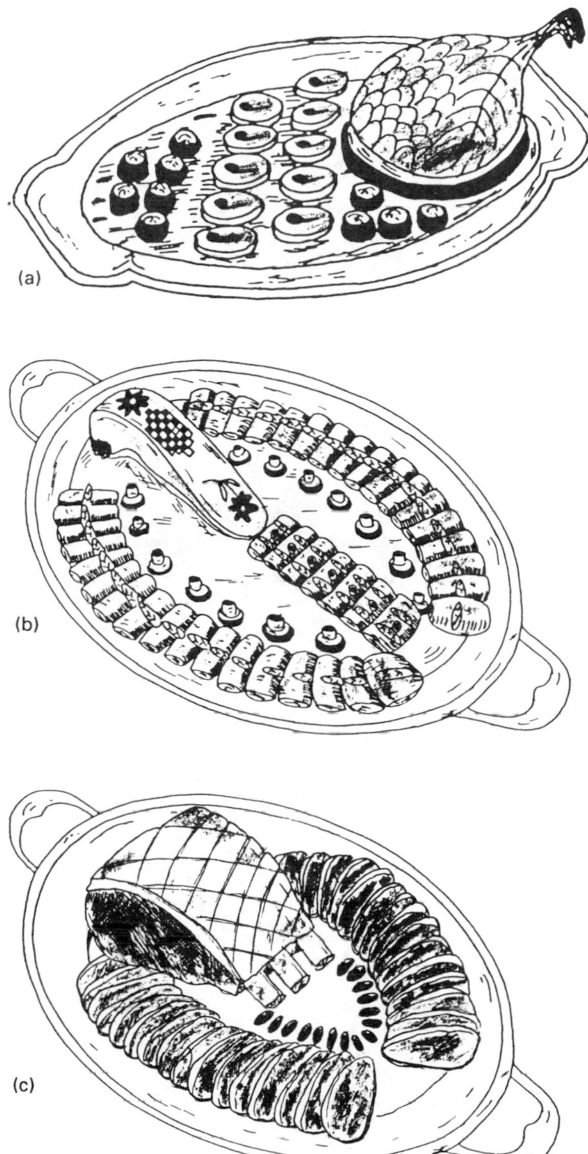

FIG. 100. (a) *Chicken mousselines and chaud-froid chicken* (b) *Glazed ox tongue garnished with asparagus tips* (c) *Roasted rib of beef with a sliced rib*

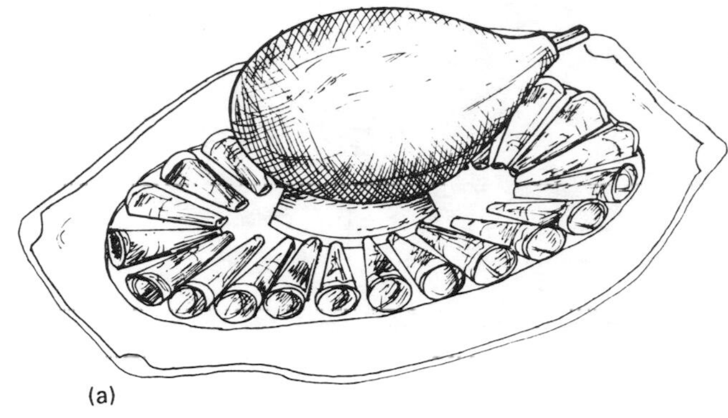

(a)

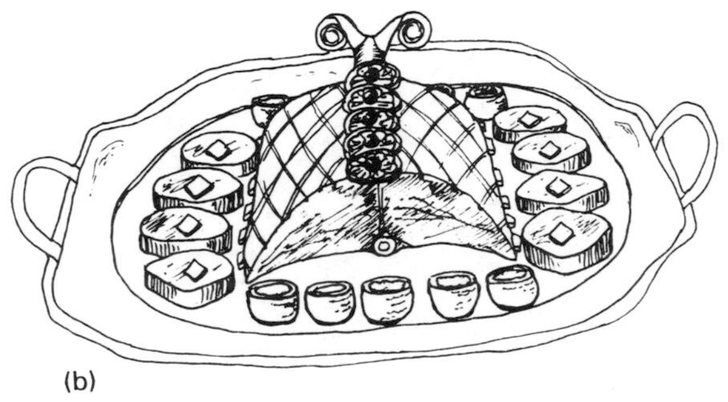

(b)

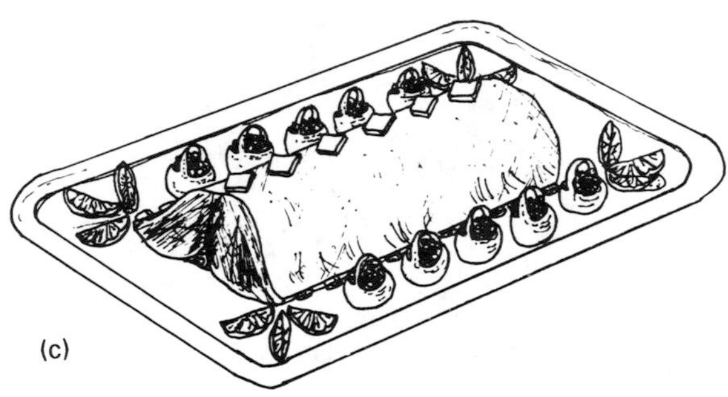

(c)

Fig. 101. (a) *Whole ham surrounded by filled cornets* (b) *Saddle of veal with noisettes of veal* (c) *Saddle of venison with cranberry-filled orange baskets*

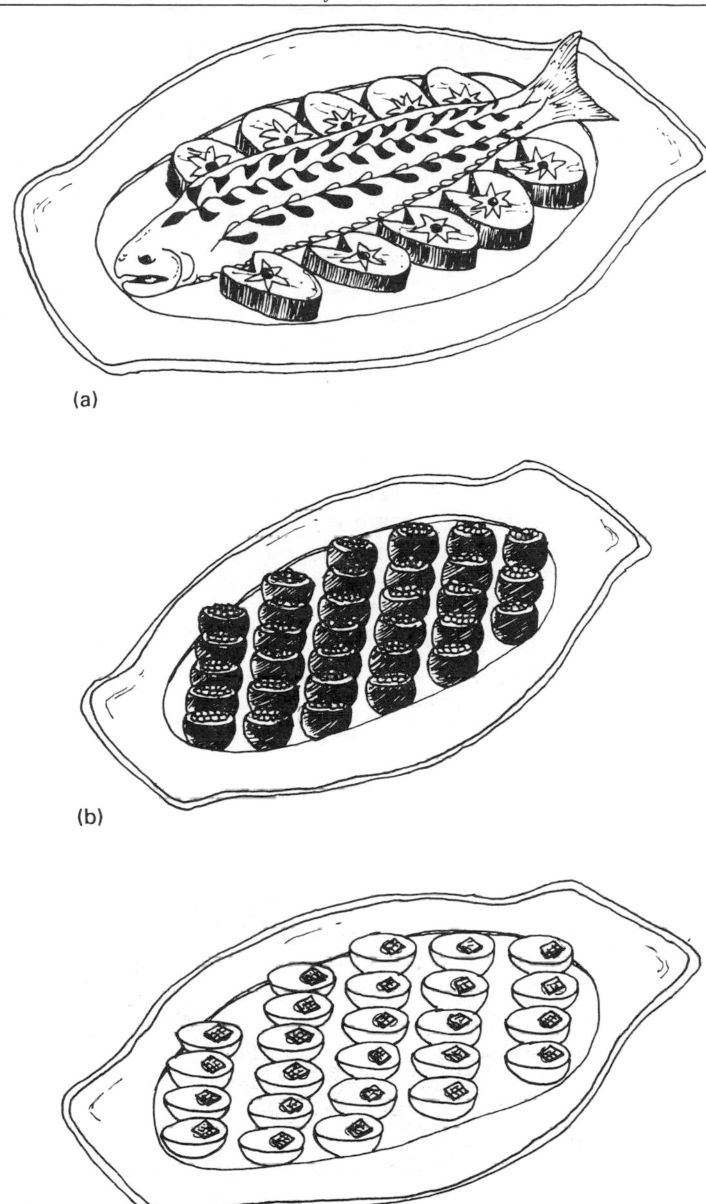

FIG. 102. (a) *Whole salmon surrounded by salmon steaks* (b) *Stuffed tomatoes* (c) *Stuffed eggs*

ASSEMBLING A COLD BUFFET

Once the different pieces for the cold buffet have been decorated and garnished, the assembly or layout of the cold buffet table takes place. It should be the concern of the Chef du Froid that this is done in an efficient and effective manner, not forgetting the various salads, cold sauces, breads and butter, which should not be missing on a cold buffet.

Although not directly his concern, the Chef du Froid should also assure himself that a sufficient number of plates and cutlery are on, or by, the cold buffet, as well as salts, pepper, various mustards and bottled sauces although these are usually the concern of the restaurant staff.

Most cold buffets are assembled on large oblong, square or round tables which in most cases have an elevation in the middle. This elevation, built up with boxes and a suitable board, or in some cases built especially for this purpose, will give more space and allows the food to be presented in a pleasant way. Some buffet table shapes are shown in Figure 103, and three examples of layout are given in Figure 104.

A cold buffet is best assembled around a *Pièce de Résistance* Centrepiece; this may be a boar's head, a decorated salmon or other such large decorated piece.

Around this Centrepiece are placed the different items of offered delicacies, alternating meats, fish, poultry and game, also such items as stuffed eggs, or tomatoes. Care should be taken to ensure that the customer can reach all foods without over-reaching himself and thus falling into the food.

Apple sauce should be conveniently placed with the roast pork, mint sauce with the roast lamb, cumberland with the venison, mayonnaise with shellfish and various dressings with the salads.

The biscuits should be near the cheese and breads and butter so placed that the customer does not have to go round the whole buffet to reach it.

Three examples are given of various sizes and shapes of cold buffets, allowing for different numbers, as well as types and quality. Cold buffet (a) is for normal buffets where the customer helps himself. For larger receptions and late night supper buffets, a system of service rendered by the Chef du Froid and some of his assistants is usual.

In this latter type of presentation, smart and very clean dressed chefs will serve the customer. They will carve the various joints, advise and generally help with the serving and presentation.

Remembering this, an elevation should be installed which will not hide the Chef but permit him to be easily seen and enable him to assist quite readily. A longer, narrower type of table situated along a wall, which allows the assisting chef (with his back to the wall) to face the customer, is advisable.

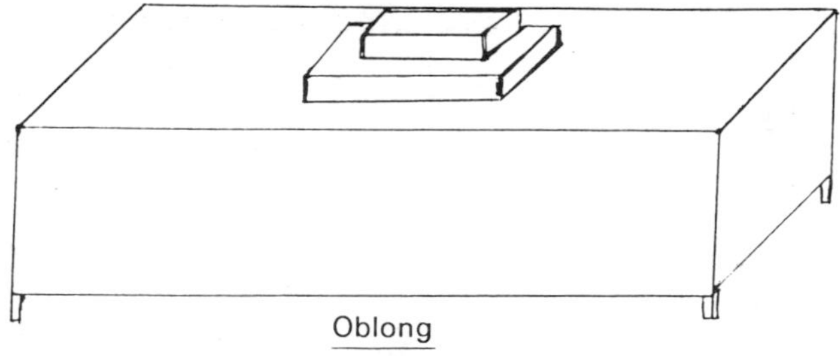

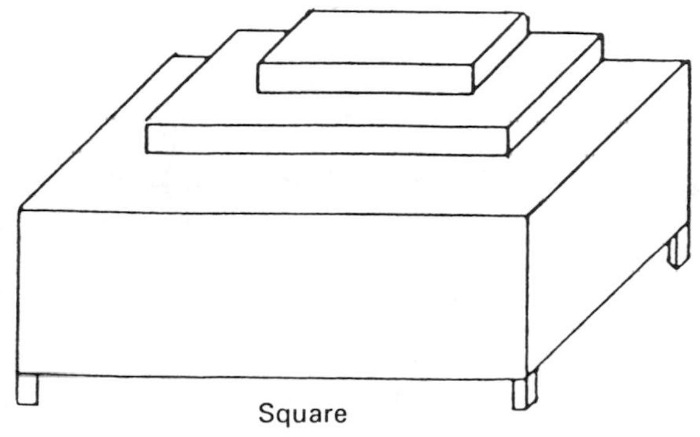

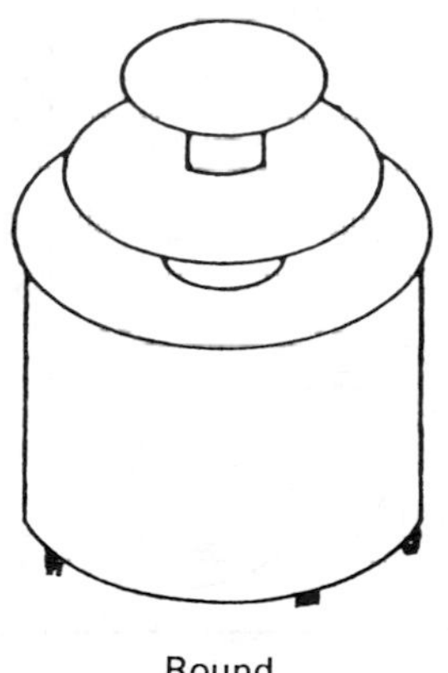

FIG. 103. *Buffet table shapes*

(a)

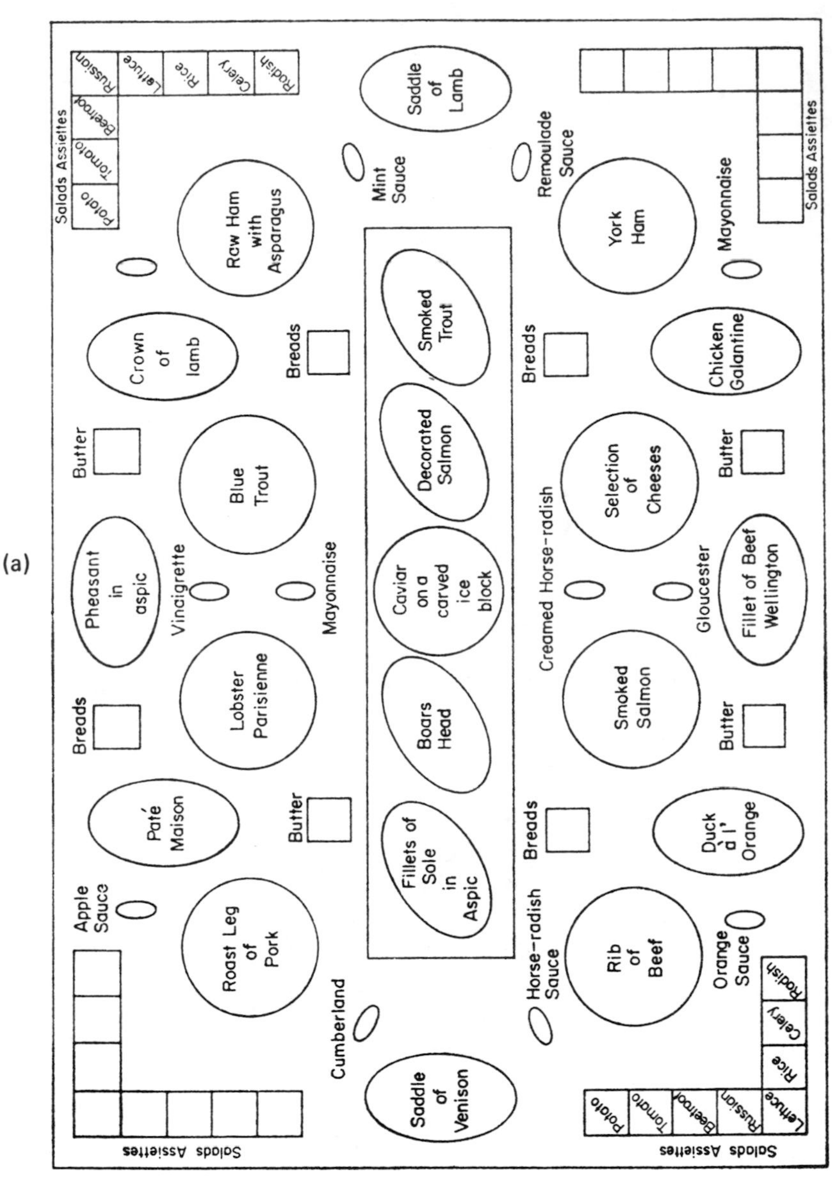

FIG. 104. *Examples of buffet layout*

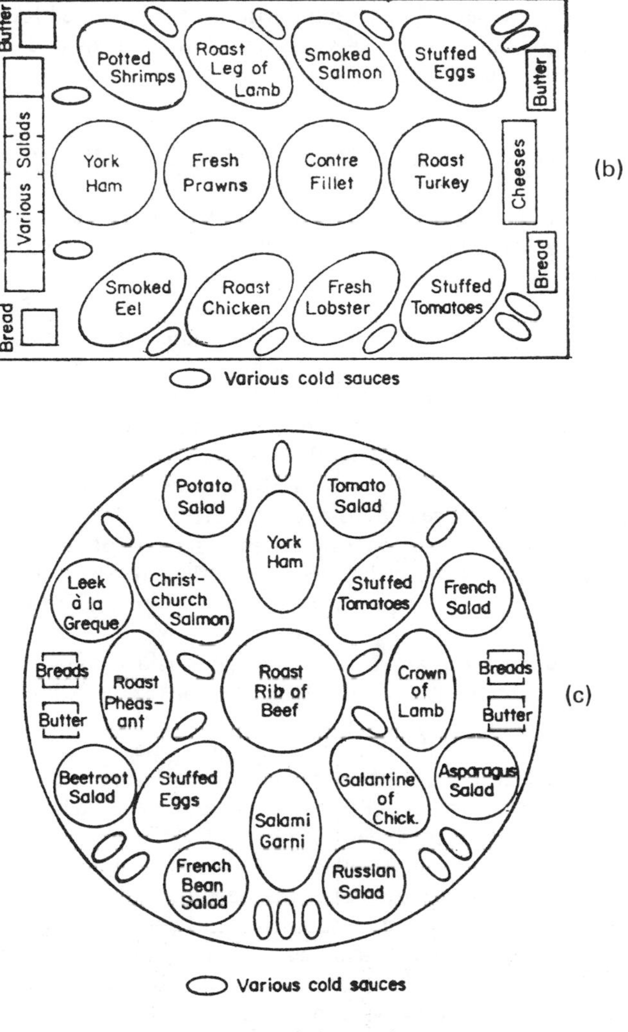

FIG. 104. (*contd.*)

Last but not least, there is one important factor in the assembling of a cold buffet. The best decorated salmon, or pheasant etc., looks bad when a piece or portion has been cut away. It is, therefore, advisable to surround a decorated salmon with small decorated steaks or portions of salmon. A decorated pheasant, with decorated suprêmes of slices of pheasant and so on, will allow the service of several portions of a decorated food before the attractive middle or centrepiece is cut into and spoiled. This applies especially to the busy cold buffet.

THE SCANDINAVIAN COLD BUFFET – SMÖRGASBORD

In most European countries a cold buffet is served for important receptions, dances, late night suppers or similar functions, and on such holidays as Easter, Whitsun and Christmas.

The Scandinavian Smörgasbord is a national heritage and a way of life. No outsider will ever quite understand its function nor grasp the respect and love with which the average Scandinavian views a good Smörgasbord.

Scandinavia's thousands of lakes, with an abundance of sweet water fish and shellfish of many types, makes the emphasis upon fish on a Smörgasbord understandable. Local feathered and furred game is also present, besides good poultry and meats – plain, brined and smoked as well as a vast selection of sausage and other charcuterie.

The buffet includes small Baltic herrings, served hot or cold and presented in various sauces and pickles, with such flavour as tomato, mustard and dill; the normal salted herring, dressed in a sweet-pickle of varying flavours, must never be omitted. Smoked and warm smoked salmons, as well as cod, herrings and Böckling, are a 'must' and raw pickled salmon (*Gravad Lax*) pickled in even amounts of salt and sugar, plus some pepper and dill, is a favourite speciality.

Many types of local game birds, various types of venison, as well as smoked reindeer or elk are also standard fare, together with local and foreign cheeses, as well as delicious plain and mixed salads.

Last but not least, the bread. At least a dozen or more varieties of bread are provided from an almost black, to a beautiful white, crisp or soft, and from a deep sour to an almost sweet in flavour.

The sight of a good Smörgasbord is mouth-wateringly attractive – the presentation simple by classical standards but most effective. The unique flavours and tastes of most dishes are known only to those who have sampled an actual Smörgasbord in Scandinavia.

The author has had the privilege of preparing and presenting a Smörgasbord in Sweden, in a small country town, at Christmas with not less than a hundred different dishes, hot and cold. The service opened at 11 a.m. and was served until 7 p.m. at night, with almost the whole population enjoying the proffered delicacies.

During this time, several dishes were emptied and replaced more than a dozen or so times, especially the hot ones. The provision of hot and cold dishes is the most striking difference between the Smörgasbord and the normal cold buffet. Since in most restaurants the Smörgasbord is a daily occurrence, it must also be understood that the presentation is very varied.

With this cold buffet, delicate, time-consuming decorations are omitted except in one or two special cases. For example, a whole poached cod is placed skinned on a silver flat, smothered with mayonnaise and only garnished with crisp lettuce leaves, parsley, dill, tomatoes and lemons.

A spare-rib of pork is studded with prunes, roasted and served cold, surrounded by prunes, lettuce, parsley, and polished tomatoes.

A *contre-filet* is brushed with *glace de viande*, or aspic, placed on a board and served with nothing more than 2 to 3 crisp lettuce leaves, a few polished tomatoes and some fresh, coarsely-grated horseradish.

Simplicity of presentation is the most important factor – only in this way will the chefs be able to present a Smörgasbord every day. But simplicity should not make it less attractive; on the contrary, the use of lettuce, tomatoes, parsley and dill makes a most attractive presentation possible, even if it is not comparable with the more classic type of buffet described in the previous chapter.

The Smörgasbord falls into 3 distinct sections and in the better type of hotel or restaurant is presented on specially built tables, invariably with one or more elevations. *See* Figure 105.

Section 'A'

This section is comparable with the normal Hors d'Œuvre service. It consists mainly of pickled or soused fish dishes, most of which are made from herring or Baltic herrings presented in various flavours. Also present are cheeses, bread and butter, as well as boiled potatoes. Here the guest will start his or her travels through the different adventures of new tastes and flavours.

The guest may place on his plate 4 or 5 different fish pickles, taking only a piece or two of each. With this he may take a little butter, a crisp piece of rye bread, a piece of cheese and 1 or 2 boiled potatoes. The guest will find himself a place in the restaurant, where he will be served by the waiter with an iced glass of schnapps, aquavite, or lager – an excellent beverage with this type of starter.

The boiled potatoes are eaten with the herrings almost at the end, to neutralize one's mouth for the other delicacies to come.

Leaving his used plate for the waiter to clear, the guest takes a clean plate and wanders along the main section to make his choice here.

Section 'B' (Main Section)

This section is the Main Course section and the nearest to the classic buffet. Students who wish to include typical Scandinavian dishes should study

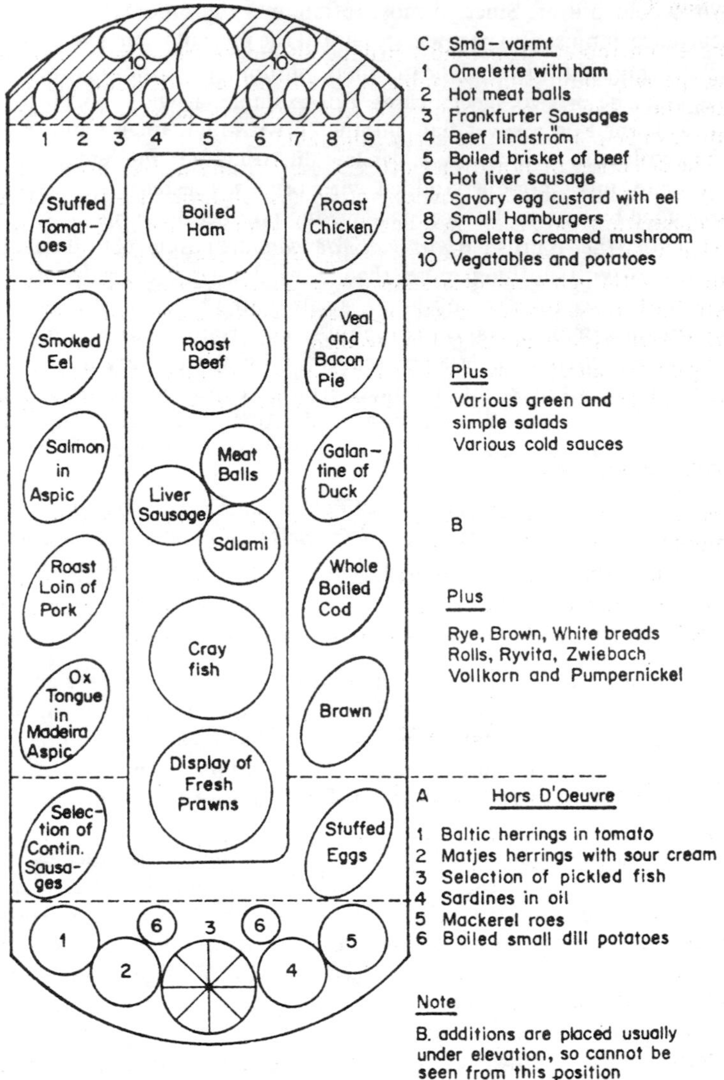

FIG. 105. *Scandinavian cold buffet*

relevant publications, of which *Scandinavian Cooking* (Elisabeth Craig) is a good example. The guest may refill his plate again and again from the many dishes offered. Leaving his plate again for the waiter to clear, he now takes a clean plate, this time hot, to make his selection from Section 'C'.

Section 'C'

This section represents the most striking difference from the normal buffet. The specially built Smörgas table is fitted with electrical hot-plates which allow the goods to be kept hot. When a normal table is used, separate hot-plates can be placed on one part of the table.

The selection of hot dishes offered, vary from one to a dozen or more. They are usually small in portion and consist of dishes like those shown in the illustration. Some of these are typical Scandinavian and their recipes, as well as others, will be found in publications dealing with Scandinavian cookery, although some dishes known in the British Isles are also included. From both these kinds of dishes it is easy to choose one's own selection of *Små Varmt*, as they are called in Swedish.

Again the guests may refill their plate several times, for it is the custom and good practice to take a little at a time but to help oneself more often.

Sweets and Desserts

These are seldom found on a Smörgasbord except for some fresh fruit, a compote, a simple cake or mousse.

All these three sections represent the Smörgasbord, and the customer pays a set charge. Extra charges are only made for drinks consumed and coffee or tea, with which the customers may finish their meal.

LARDER PRODUCTIONS

Chicken Chaud-Froid – Poulet Chaud-Froid

a 2 kg (4 lb) young chicken
1 l. (2 pints) chaud-froid blanc
$\frac{1}{4}$ *l.* ($\frac{1}{2}$ *pint*) *of chicken aspic*
decoration (invariably truffles)

(1) Select a nice pump chicken, prepare in the normal way.
(2) Carefully truss *en Entrée* to enhance the breast and have the legs nicely parallel.
(3) Gently simmer in a *Court Bouillon* (15 min per 500 g (per lb)).
(4) Cool slowly in the cooking liquor.
(5) Remove from liquor, drain and carefully remove all skin, drain again.
(6) Evenly mask the whole chicken with chaud-froid sauce 2 or 3 times, placing the chicken between each masking in a cool place.
(7) Finish with a neat decoration of personal design, using items suitable for chicken (Figure 106).
(8) Give a glaze with clear chicken aspic 2 or 3 times to attain a good finish.
(9) Present on a silver flat, with a mirror of aspic or chaud-froid sauce.

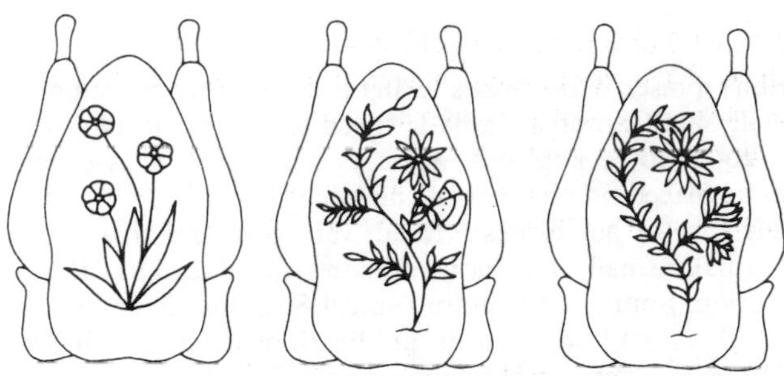

FIG. 106. *Decoration of chicken chaud-froid*

Stuffed Chicken Chaud-Froid – Poulet Farci en Chaud-Froid

For an added surprise, the breasts of chicken may be removed and a good chicken-mousse put in their place. Prepare and cook chicken as in the previous method, cool, and carefully remove both breasts. In their place, put a chicken mousse, carefully re-modelling the breasts. Application of chaud-froid sauce, decoration and chicken aspic, is the same as for the previous method.

For use of Suprêmes of Breasts see next recipe and method.

Cold Chicken Breast Chaud-Froid – Suprême de Volaille en Chaud-Froid

4 raw chicken breasts	$\frac{1}{2}$ *l. (1 pint) of chicken chaud-froid*
$\frac{1}{2}$ *l. (1 pint) of chicken aspic*	*8 slices of truffles or other decoration*

(1) Gently poach chicken breasts in a *Court Bouillon*.
(2) Cool and drain, remove all skin and gristle.
(3) Place on a rack; if too big cut into two, giving each a Suprême shape.

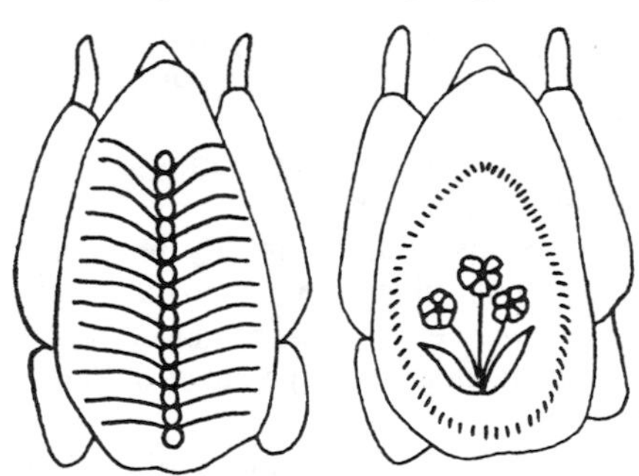

FIG. 107. *Decoration of cold chicken chaud-froid*

(4) Neatly coat 2 or 3 times with chicken chaud-froid.
(5) Use slices of truffles to apply a decoration (Figure 107).
(6) Glaze 2 to 3 times with chicken aspic.
(7) Place in cold place to set.
(8) Present on a silver flat with a mirror of aspic, often surrounding a whole chicken, as described in the previous 2 methods.

Cold Duck à l'Orange – Canard à l'Orange Froid

1 *medium duck*	$\frac{1}{2}$ *l.* (1 *pint*) *chicken or duck's aspic*
4 *to* 6 *oranges*	200 *g* (8 *oz*) *duck or chicken mousse*

(1) Select a very plump duck, prepare in the normal way.
(2) Carefully truss *en Entrée*, to enhance the breast, and have the legs nicely parallel.
(3) Roast carefully, cool well.
(4) Meanwhile, make an incision through the skin around the centre of each orange to obtain two halves of empty orange skins, and leaving the orange itself whole. The handle of a dessert-spoon will greatly assist with this.
(5) Cut orange-flesh into neat segments, drain and save the juice.
(6) Add strained orange juice to aspic, colour to a slight pink if necessary.
(7) Fill the halves of orange skins with part of this aspic, place in cool place to set like a jelly.
(8) Remove breast, but cutting just above the legs against the carcass on both sides.
(9) Now cut down from both sides of the breast-bone, to the incision previously made on the sides; this will allow the breasts to be lifted off quite easily.
(10) Spread a thin layer of mousse on the carcass bone, just freed, and place in a cool place.
(11) Now, cut your two duck's breasts into neat slices, slightly on the slant about $\frac{1}{2}$ cm ($\frac{1}{4}$ in.) thick, without disturbing the shape of the breasts.
(12) Replace the slices of breast on the carcass, with a slice of breast and 2 to 3 orange segments alternatively. The mousse on the carcass will help to keep orange and meat in place. Continue the building up, until the original nice shape of the breast is attained.
(13) Glaze the whole duck with the remainder of the orange flavoured aspic 2 or 3 times, and leave to set.
(14) Present duck on a silver flat with a mirror of aspic, surrounded by a neat wedge of orange jelly/aspic, set in orange skins.
Usually a showpiece on cold buffets or special parties and exhibitions (Figure 108).

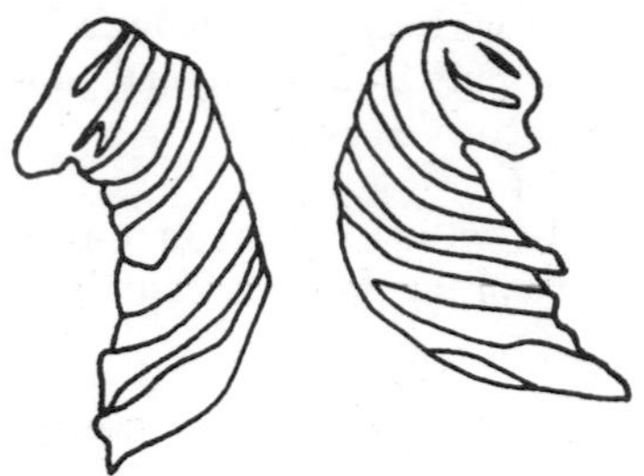

FIG. 108. *Cold duck à l'orange*

Galantine de Poulet

1 × 2 *kg* (4 *lb*) *chicken*	100 *g* ($\frac{1}{4}$ *lb*) *larding bacon*
250 *g* ($\frac{1}{2}$ *lb*) *fillet of veal*	50 *g* (2 *oz*) *truffles*
250 *g* ($\frac{1}{2}$ *lb*) *fillet of pork*	25 *g* (1 *oz*) *pistachio nuts*
500 *g* (1 *lb*) *fat bacon/speck*	40 *g* (2 *oz*) *spiced salt*
100 *g* ($\frac{1}{4}$ *lb*) *cooked lean ham*	2 *tablespoons brandy*
100 *g* ($\frac{1}{4}$ *lb*) *cooked pickled tongue*	4 *eggs*

The method (Figure 109) is as follows:

(1) Singe chicken, cut off winglets at 1st joint and legs at joint with drumstick.

(2) Bone out, taking care not to puncture skin.

(3) Remove all flesh from skin with tip of small knife.

(4) Scrape skin clean and soak in cold water. When required, dry well and spread out on clean cloth.

(5) Trim the breast fillets and cut into 5 mm ($\frac{1}{4}$ in.) strips. Cut ham, tongue and larding bacon to same size.

(6) Marinade the strips in brandy, together with diced truffles and peeled pistachio nuts, for at least 1 hour.

(7) Clear flesh from legs of all sinews and tendons, add trimmings from breast and use together with veal, pork and fat bacon to make forcemeat (see 'Forcemeats'). Season with spiced salt, flavour with marinade and bind with eggs.

(8) Spread a layer of forcemeat along centre of chicken skin. Set a layer of marinaded fillets neatly on top of this, sprinkle with truffles and pistachio nuts; repeat till all forcemeat and fillets have been used. Finish with layer of forcemeat.

(9) Draw the skin carefully around the forcemeat and roll the galantine, sausage shape, in the cloth, tie both ends securely; tie a string around the middle and poach in a good chicken stock made from the bones, for $1\frac{1}{4}$ hours.

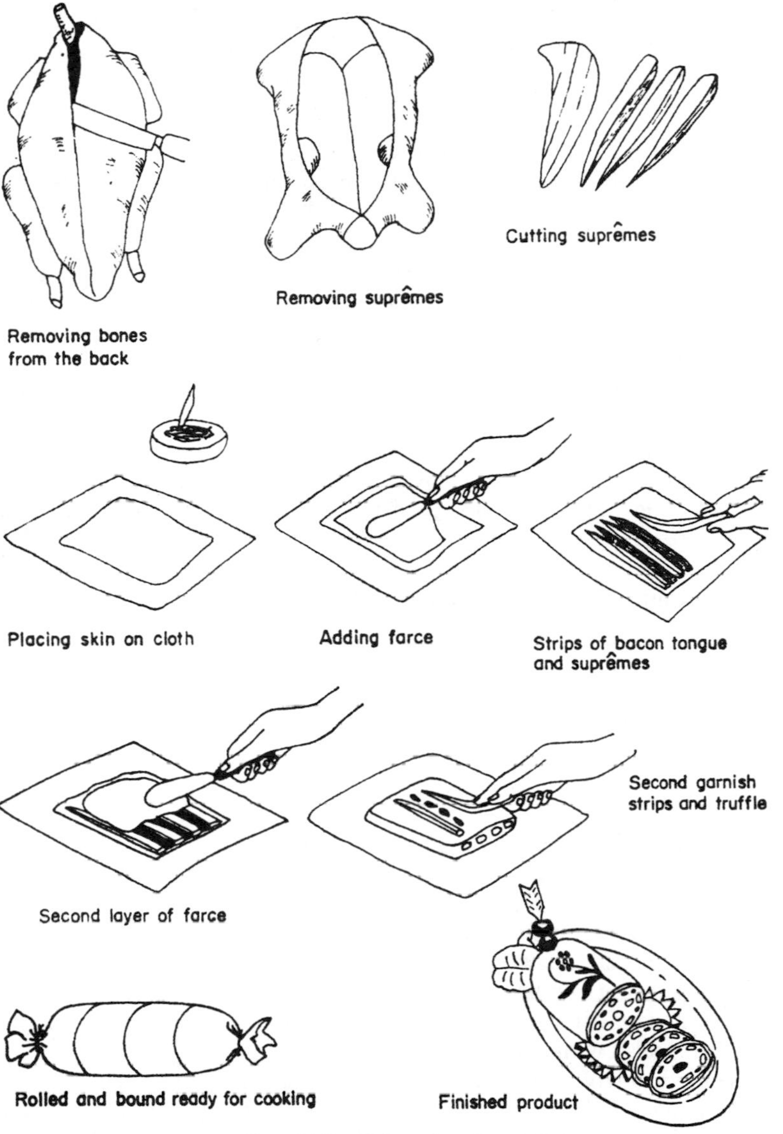

FIG. 109. *Galantine de poulet*

(10) Drain carefully, cool slightly, unwrap the cloth, re-roll and tie tightly; set to cool under a slight weight.
(11) When quite cold, remove cloth, decorate and coat with clear chicken aspic.

Cold Lobster – Homard Froid

1 medium lobster, cooked
1 heart of lettuce
8 slices of channelled lemon
1 peeled tomato
1 hard boiled egg
parsley or dill sprigs

(1) Remove claws and legs from lobster.
(2) Split body with a large knife into two even halves.
(3) Remove intestines, sac and coral from each half.
(4) Place the two halves on a silver flat with doily.
(5) In the empty sac cavity of each half, place a lettuce leaf,
(6) Remove flesh from claws and place on to this lettuce.
(7) Remove tail-flesh from each tail shell and place into the other.
(8) Now surround the two halves with lobster legs in a zig-zag fashion.
(9) Garnish with lettuce, quarters of tomatoes and eggs, parsley or dill, and sprinkle with lobster coral.
(10) Serve with hot toast, butter and mayonnaise sauce.
If a whole lobster is served, two halves of tail may be taken out of the shell and replaced in opposite shells, with the attractive markings of the tail uppermost.

Crawfish Beautiful View – Langouste en Belle Vue

1 *crawfish* 1-1½ *kg* (2-3 *lb*)
250-400 *g* (8-12 *oz*) *vegetable salad*
¼ *l.* (½ *pint*) *aspic* (*fish*)
6 *tomatoes, peeled*
6 *halves stuffed eggs*
2 *hearts of lettuce*
¼ *l.* (½ *pint*) *mayonnaise collée*
croûton of bread

Refer to Figure 110.

(1) Tie crawfish to a board with tail outstretched.
(2) Cook in a *Court Bouillon* (15 min per 500 g (lb)), cool in liquor.
(3) When cool, wipe off scum.
(4) With fish scissors, cut out a strip of shell, wide enough to remove tail, without breaking shell or tail.
(5) Cut flesh of tail into neat scallops, place on a rack, keep cool.
(6) Cut trimmings off, into dice, mix into vegetable salad.
(7) Bind this salad with a little aspic.
(8) Fill empty cavity of shell with most of the salad.
(9) Place in a cool place to set.
(10) Meanwhile, mask scallops of crawfish with mayonnaise collée, leave to set, neatly decorate to taste.
(11) Glaze with clear fish aspic.
(12) Place crawfish shell on a neat croûton on silver flat.
(13) Trim scallops if necessary.
(14) Place scallops slightly overlapping along the back of the shell, starting with the biggest near the head, and finishing with the smallest near the tail.

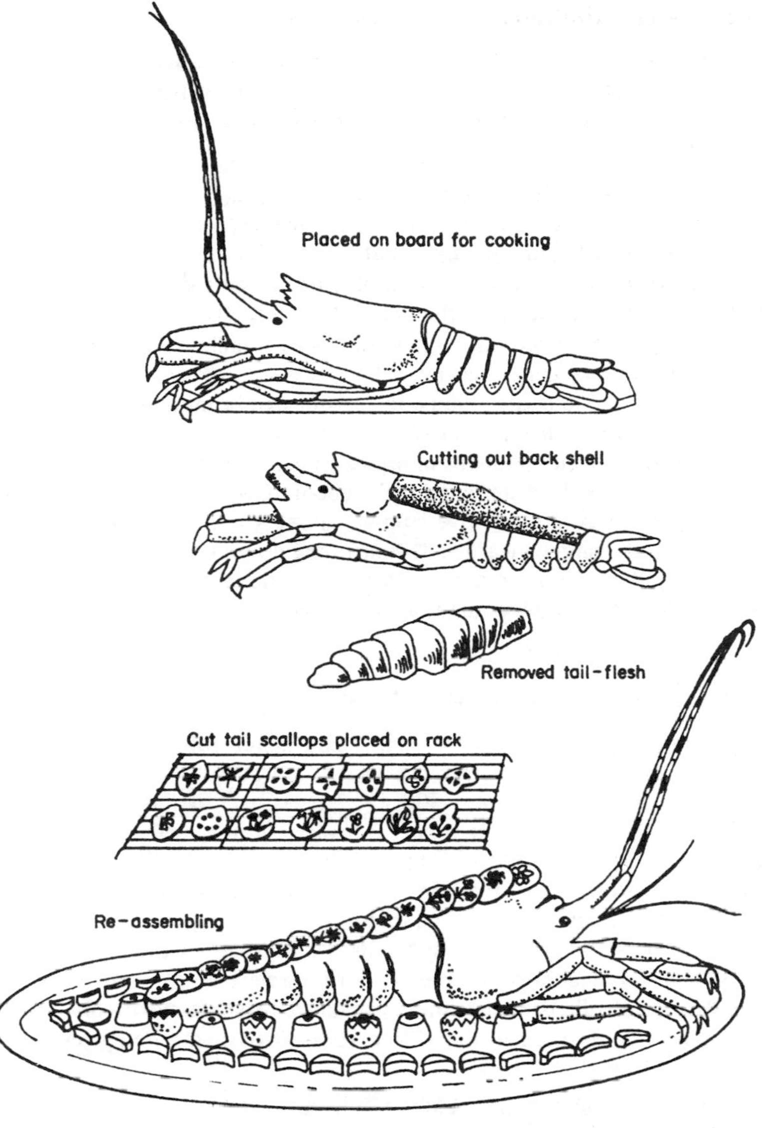

FIG. 110. *Crawfish*

(15) If necessary, make a slight groove in the salad, to prevent scallops slipping.
(16) Surround crawfish with mould of vegetable salad set in aspic, tomatoes filled with vegetable salad and stuffed eggs; garnish with hearts of lettuce.

Lobster (Parisienne Style) – Homard Parisienne

1 *medium lobster*	2 *hard boiled eggs*
8-10 *artichoke bottoms*	½ *l.* (1 *pint*) *of fish aspic*
250-400 *g* (8-10 *oz*) *vegetable salad*	4-8 *slices of truffles*

(1) Place lobster on a board and cook as for crawfish.
(2) Cool, remove from *Court Bouillon*, dry, and wipe.
(3) Remove claws, open and keep whole.
(4) With fish-scissors open tail from below, on both sides of softer shell. This will allow the removal of the tail.
(5) Cut tail and claws into neat scallops, place on rack.
(6) Cut lobster flesh trimmings into dice.
(7) Mix with vegetable salad, add a little aspic, set in moulds.
(8) Give a mirror of clear aspic to a large silver flat.
(9) Place lobster shell on mirror of aspic.
(10) Glaze scallop of lobster with aspic, decorate to taste.
(11) Place scallops slightly overlapping, along the back of lobster shell, starting with the largest near head, continuing down to the tail.
(12) Surround the lobster now with the artichoke bottoms, which have been filled with vegetable salad, as well as quarter of egg decorated with slices of truffles.

Fish Mayonnaise – Mayonnaise de Poisson

All the foregoing in respect of making fish salads applies to fish mayonnaise. The method of preparation as well as ingredients are the same as for lobster mayonnaise, using 400-500 g (12 to 16 oz) of flaked fish instead of the lobster flesh. Again, cucumber is invariably used with the pink fishes only.

Presentation. Recipes and methods given here are those most commonly in use, although individual tastes can undoubtedly make great improvements. Setting the bowls of salads or mayonnaise on crushed, or even socles of ice, surrounded by decoratively folded cloth serviettes, etc., are only two examples. Some allowance should be made for the classical recipes which may, in ingredients and method, differ from the basic method given here.

Cold Raised Pie and Terrine – Pâté et Terrine

The composition of these two preparations is the same, the only difference being the receptacle in which they are prepared and cooked and the actual cooking, which differs in some form.

The filling consists of a forcemeat prepared from the required meat, poultry or game, into which are set the marinaded fillets of the meat or flesh, together with seasoning, spices, herbs and whatever savoury garnishing, suitable to the particular Pâté or terrine.

In the case of pâté, this filling is then placed into a pie paste (pâté à pâté) which is set in a raised pie mould, or hand raised, and lined with thin slices of larding bacon and a coating of the forcemeat (Figure 111). The forcemeat and the fillets are placed in alternate layers, with the garnishing sprinkled, or laid on the fillets until the pie mould is filled, taking care to finish with a thick layer of forcemeat. The fillets can be wrapped in thin slices of larding bacon to enhance the appearance of the pie, when cut.

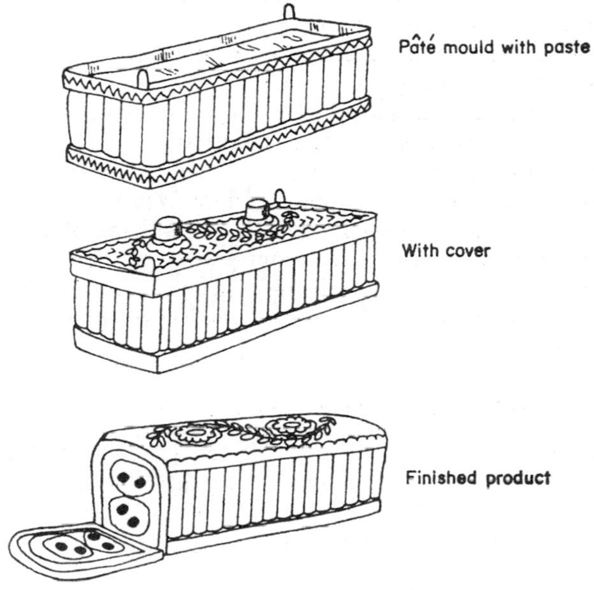

FIG. 111. *Pâté/Pie*

The top is then covered with thinly sliced larding bacon. A bay leaf is placed on the top of this and finally the pie is completely enclosed with paste which has been set aside for this purpose.

The edges should be well sealed and notched, the top being decorated with pastry leaves and flowers. One or more holes are made through the paste into which should be set oiled stiff paper funnels, to allow the steam to escape whilst cooking. Finally, the top should be well eggwashed and the pie baked in the oven for between $1\frac{1}{4}$ to $1\frac{1}{2}$ hours.

When quite cold, the pie is filled through the holes in the top with a good aspic, flavoured to suit the pie filling.

Veal and Ham Pie – Pâté de Veau et Jambon (French)

Filling:

400 *g* (12 *oz*) *fillet of veal*	200 *g* (8 *oz*) *larding bacon/speck*
400 *g* (12 *oz*) *fillet of pork*	20 *g* (¾ *oz*) *spiced salt*
250 *g* (8 *oz*) *lean ham or gammon*	3 *cl* (½ *gill*) *brandy or madeira*
500 *g* (1 *lb*) *veal forcemeat*	500 *g* (1 *lb*) *pie pastry*

Veal Forcemeat

125 *g* (¼ *lb*) *lean veal*	1 *egg*
125 *g* (¼ *lb*) *lean pork*	15 *g* (½ *oz*) *spiced salt*
250 *g* (½ *lb*) *fat bacon*	

Pork Pie (French) – Pâté de Porc

500 *g* (1 *lb*) *pork forcemeat*	20 *g* (¾ *oz*) *spiced salt*
125 *g* (¼ *lb*) *fillet pork*	250 *g* (½ *lb*) *larding bacon*
125 *g* (¼ *lb*) *pork fat*	5 *cl* (½ *gill*) *brandy or madeira*

Cut pork fillet and the fat into 5 mm (¼ in.) strips and marinade in brandy for 1 hour. Proceed as for *Pâté de Veau et Jambon.*

Poultry/Chicken Pie – Pâté de Volaille

500 *g* (1 *lb*) *chicken forcemeat*	200 *g* (8 *oz*) *larding bacon*
300 *g* (12 *oz*) *fillet of chicken*	5 *cl* (½ *gill*) *brandy*
100 *g* (4 *oz*) *foie gras*	20 *g* (¾ *oz*) *spiced salt*
50 *g* (2 *oz*) *truffle*	500 *g* (1 *lb*) *pie pastry*

Chicken Forcemeat

125 *g* (¼ *lb*) *boned chicken flesh*	200 *g* (½ *lb*) *fat bacon*
100 *g* (⅛ *lb*) *fillet of veal*	1 *egg*
100 *g* (⅛ *lb*) *fillet of pork*	15 *g* (½ *oz*) *spiced salt*

Pâté de Gibier

This is similar to *Pâté de Volaille*, fillets of game being used in lieu of chicken, and with the addition of 100 g (4 oz) of *Farce à gratin* (see farces) to the forcemeat, which is made from game flesh in place of chicken flesh.

Pie Pastry

(A) *Hot Water Paste:*

500 *g* (1 *lb*) *flour*	¼ *l.* (½ *pint*) *water*
150 *g* (¼ *lb*) *lard*	10 *g* (¼ *oz*) *salt*

(1) Sieve flour and salt in bowl.
(2) Boil water and lard.
(3) Pour into flour and mix well with a wooden spoon.
(4) Knead well, and use warm.

(B) *Pâté à Pâté:*

500 g (1 lb) flour
150 g (¼ lb) butter
150 g (¼ lb) lard
10 g (¼ oz) salt
⅛ l. (¼ pint) water
1 egg

(1) Sieve flour and salt.
(2) Rub in butter and lard.
(3) Add beaten egg and water.
(4) Mix well.
(5) Rest in cool place, before using.

Veal, Ham and Egg Pie (English)

250 g (½ lb) lean veal
250 g (½ lb) lean pork
250 g (½ lb) fat bacon
4 hard boiled eggs
zest of 1 lemon
20 g (¾ oz) spiced salt
12 cl (1 gill) stock or water
10 g (¼ oz) parsley and thyme
500 g (1 lb) pie paste

(1) Mince veal, pork and bacon.
(2) Add seasoning, lemon zest, water and herbs.
(3) Mix well and fill into pastry with eggs along centre.

Veal Ham Pie (Hot or Cold)

250 g (½ lb) fillet veal
250 g (½ lb) raw gammon
250 g (½ lb) streaky bacon
4 hard boiled eggs
25 g (1 oz) chopped onions
15 g (½ oz) chopped parsley
20 g (¾ oz) spiced salt
12 cl (1 gill) water
500 g (1 lb) puff pastry

(1) Cut veal into scallops and gammon into thin slices.
(2) Line pie dish with rashers of bacon.
(3) Fill alternate layers of veal and gammon.
(4) Season each layer and sprinkle with onion and parsley.
(5) Place eggs in centre or add coarsely chopped egg to each layer.
(6) Finish with layer of bacon.

Pork Pie (English) – Pâté de Porc

375 *g* (12 *oz*) *lean pork*
375 *g* (12 *oz*) *fat pork or green bacon*
Pinch powdered sage
10 *g* ($\frac{1}{4}$ *oz*) *chopped parsley*
20 *g* ($\frac{3}{4}$ *oz*) *spiced salt*
12 *cl* (1 *gill*) *water*
50 *g* (2 *oz*) *chopped, sweated onion*
500 *g* (1 *lb*) *pie pastry*

Mince pork coarsely; season, add water and herbs, and proceed as for Veal and Ham Pie.

Chicken Pie (English)

a 1 *kg* ($2\frac{1}{2}$ *lb*) *chicken*
125 *g* ($\frac{1}{2}$ *lb*) *streaky bacon rashers*
50 *g* (2 *oz*) *finely chopped onion*
15 *g* ($\frac{1}{2}$ *oz*) *chopped parsley*
pinch powdered thyme and bay leaf
125 *g* ($\frac{1}{4}$ *lb*) *sliced mushrooms (optional)*
500 *g* (1 *lb*) *puff pastry*
chicken stock

(1) Cut chicken as for sauté and season.
(2) Set in hot butter, without browning.
(3) Wrap each piece in a thin bacon rasher.
(4) Dress neatly in a pie dish and sprinkle with onion, parsley, herbs and mushrooms.
(5) Place remainder of bacon over the top and moisten with stock.
(6) Cover with pastry and bake approximately $1\frac{1}{4}$ hours.
(7) When cold, fill with good chicken aspic.

In the case of a terrine, the filling is placed into an earthenware, china or fireproof glass dish, which has a closely fitting lid. The same drill is carried out with regard to the lining and the filling. When full, the lid of the terrine is carefully sealed on, using a flour and water paste. The terrine is then cooked in the oven in a water bath (bain marie) for the same time and when cold is filled in the same way. In some instances, particularly if it is to be kept for any length of time, it is filled with melted bacon fat, or butter, to exclude air completely from the surface of the terrine. The terrine, or better still a pie dish, could be covered with a puff pastry top and baked in the oven as for a hot pie. This would be filled with aspic when cold, in the normal way. In fact, many 'hot' pies, set with the appropriate aspic, can be served cold from the buffet. Such traditional English pies as chicken pie, veal and ham, steak and kidney and game pie, are often served in this way instead of the French pâté or terrine.

Pâté Maison

500 *g* (1 *lb*) *chickens liver*
125 *g* ($\frac{1}{4}$ *lb*) *lean pork*
125 *g* ($\frac{1}{4}$ *lb*) *fat bacon*
100 *g* (4 *oz*) *larding bacon*
15 *g* ($\frac{1}{2}$ *oz*) *spiced salt*
1 *pinch thyme*

50 g (2 oz) *chopped onion*	1 *bay leaf*
10 g ($\frac{1}{4}$ *oz*) *parsley* (*chopped*)	100 g (4 *oz*) *butter*
1 *clove garlic*	3 *dl* ($\frac{1}{2}$ *pint*) *cream*

(1) Fry fat bacon, lightly in butter.
(2) Add livers and lean pork and set without browning.
(3) Add onions, herbs and garlic; season.
(4) Mince finely, and rub through fine wire sieve, add cream.
(5) Set in terrine, lined with larding bacon.
(6) Cook in oven in 'bain marie' till warm in centre and fat on surface is quite clear. Time – approximately 1-1$\frac{1}{4}$ hours.
(7) Cool under pressure.
(8) Serve from terrine, or turn out and slice.
The above could be cooked in pie pastry but is more commonly set in a terrine, so 'Pâté' is really a misnomer in this instance.

SANDWICHES

Sandwiches, so the story goes, came first on to the scene in the house of the 4th Earl of Sandwich. He was supposed to have been a compulsive gambler who so loved his gambling that he left himself no time for eating. One day he asked the butler to serve some bread and cheese, to be eaten while the Earl and his friends went on gambling.

His chef, knowing of his master's affliction, realized he would not stop gambling while the cheese and bread were eaten. To make eating easier, the chef placed the cheese between slices of buttered bread – thus the first sandwich was born. The story may or may not be true, but certainly sandwiches are named after the 4th Earl of that name.

In catering today there are many types of sandwiches, some of which are variations or improvements on the original above; others are imported from different countries, of which the open sandwich from Scandinavia is the most recent addition. Figure 112 shows some sandwich shapes.

(1) There is the so-called conventional, closed, lunch-box sandwich, which consists of 2 slices of white or brown bread with any filling of meat, poultry, game, fish, shellfish, cheese and eggs. It can be garnished with lettuce, cucumber, tomatoes, cress, mustard and cress. In the case of meat and fish, certain seasonings like made up English or French Mustard, salt, pepper and mayonnaise may be added where suitable. The sandwich is then cut into 2 triangles across, without removing the crust. Service: In bars, cafés, snack-bars and restaurants.

(2) The Tea sandwich. This has much lighter fillings, and again white or brown bread is used. The fillings may consist of any meat or fish spreads, made in one's own kitchen, or bought commercially: Marmite, tomatoes,

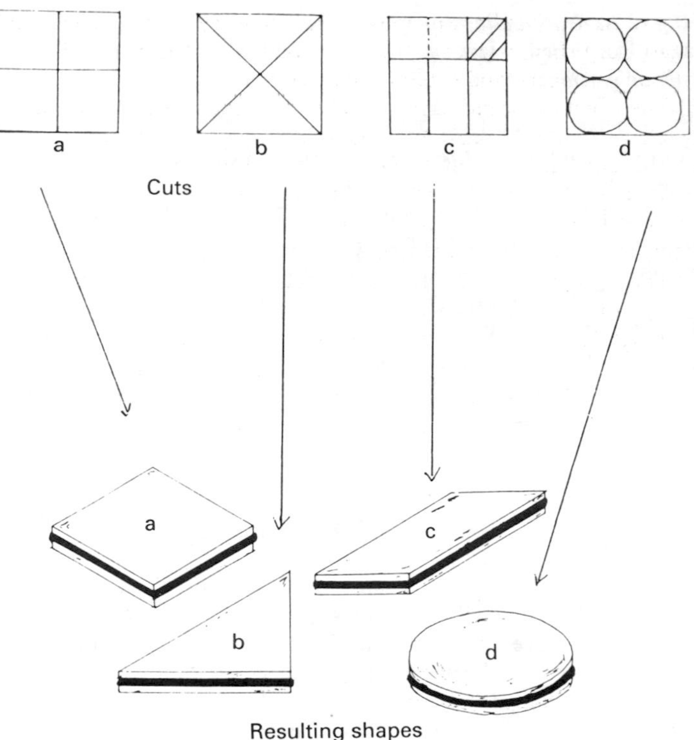

FIG. 112. *Sandwich cuts and shapes*

cucumber, jams and fruit, as well as mixtures of jam and fruit like bananas with strawberry jam, which are very good. The Tea sandwich is cut much smaller, into triangles, fingers, and squares and *the crust is always removed*.

(3) The Buffet sandwich. This sandwich is very much the same as the conventional sandwich No. 1, and similar fillings are used. The sandwich in this instance is cut much smaller, like the Tea sandwich, into neat triangles, fingers, or squares. With these sandwiches, a combination of white and brown bread is often used, which will give them the chessboard effect. At times these sandwiches are given fancy shapes by cutting them with different sizes and design of pastry cutters. This method is very wasteful and one should avoid using it, except for children who may find delight in the colourful shapes and designs of these sandwiches.

(4) The Continental or French sandwich. This usually consists of a crusty French stick, cut into half and well buttered with either a single savoury filling and garnished with lettuce, tomatoes, cucumber, mayonnaise, or a

mixture of savoury fillings of meats, fish, poultry, game, cheese and eggs, and again garnished as above. Cut into small strips, it can easily be picked up with one's fingers, and eaten in this manner.

(5) The open or Scandinavian sandwich is the more recent addition to sandwich variation, at least in England. Very much the same ingredients as for the conventional sandwich are used, but here the emphasis is put more on a very attractive and appetizing presentation and, as its name indicates, it is open and not covered with a second slice of bread (see notes on Smørrebrød later in this chapter).

(6) The canapé is not really a sandwich but small pieces of toast, white or brown, or biscuits or sheets of puff pastry, well buttered and covered with fillings of meat, game, poultry, fish, egg and cheese, decorated with flavoured or coloured butter; they are finished with a clear glaze of aspic jelly, according to their filling (see notes on *Canapés Russe*).

(7) Hot sandwiches do not really belong to this category since they are more a snack or even a meal, but as they are called sandwiches and bread is used they are included. Their number and variations are enormous. They range from the typical English 'bookmaker' sandwich to the French *Croûte Monsieur* and include such internationally famous sandwiches as the Club sandwich and the American Layer sandwiches, the German *strammer Max*, the Swedish *Lindström*, and the Dutch hot beef sandwich. Some of the Russian hot *Zakouskis* and French *Brioche*, as well as a late addition the 'Wimpy', (a fried Hamburger steak in a toasted roll) may also be included. The recipes of some of the better known are given later. There is quite a large number of these and if one is interested, through practical work and some private study, a more complete understanding of these hot sandwiches may be gleaned.

SANDWICH PREPARATION

Conventional Sandwich

Bread: Sandwich-bread, white or brown.

Butters: Plain, mustard, anchovy, tomato, onion or garlic flavoured.

Fillings: Bismark herring, smoked herring, sardines, smoked eel, smoked trout, smoked salmon, böckling, prawns, lobster, fresh salmon, shrimps, boiled ham, smoked ham, tongue, brisket, corned-beef, roast beef, pork or lamb, salami, mortadella, mettwurst, liver-sausage, blood-sausage, roast chicken, duck, game, turkey, chicken-liver, liver-pâté, gammon, eggs, as well as all dry and creamed cheeses.

Garnish: Lettuce, tomatoes, watercress, mustard and cress, spring onions, radishes, gherkins, pickled cucumber, fresh cucumber, pickles, chutneys, parsley, as well as mayonnaise, tartare sauce, and tomato ketchup.

Finish: Cut into a neat triangle (2), do not remove crust. Serve on a doily with a little watercress or mustard and cress.

Tea Sandwich

Bread: Sandwich-bread white or brown, thinly cut.
Butter: Creamy plain butter.
Fillings; Tinned and potted meats and fish, fish and meat pastes and spreads, Bovril, Marmite, fresh tomato purée, tomatoes, baked beans purée, cucumber, pickles, dry and creamed cheeses, fruit and jams, eggs, cress.
Garnish: As for conventional sandwiches.
Finish: Neatly remove crust; cut into even fingers, triangles or squares, or cut into fancy shapes, with a pastry cutter. Serve on a silver flat with doily or dish-paper; garnish with sprigs of parsley, water-cress or mustard and cress.

Buffet and Reception Sandwiches

Bread: Sandwich-bread white or brown, thinly cut.
Butter: As for conventional sandwich.
Fillings: As for conventional sandwich, plus tinned or potted meat and fish.
Garnish: As for conventional sandwich.
Finish: Neatly remove crust, cut into even fingers, triangles or squares, or cut with a fancy pastry cutter. Serve on a silver flat with doily or dish-paper; garnish with sprigs of parsley, watercress or mustard and cress.

Continental or French Sandwich

Bread: French stick or cottage loaf.
Butter: As for conventional sandwich.
Fillings: As for conventional sandwich, one single filling, or a selection of several.
Garnish: As for conventional sandwich.
Finish: Cut into even, neat strips. Serve on a silver flat with doily or dish-paper, garnish with sprigs of parsley, watercress, or mustard and cress.

The Open Sandwich (Smørrebrød)

Bread: French, sandwich, Vienna, rye, wholemeal, pumpernickle, vollkorn and rolls.

Butter: As for conventional sandwich.
Fillings: As for conventional sandwich.
Garnish: As for conventional sandwich.
Finish: Serve on a plate with doily or silver flat with doily or dish-paper, no garnish necessary, as open colourful presentation is sufficient.

Canapés

Bread: Thinly cut toast, sheets of puffpaste, luncheon crackers, Ritz or hotel biscuits.
Butter: As for conventional sandwich.
Fillings: As for conventional sandwich.
Garnish: As for conventional sandwich.
Finish: Piped with flavoured or coloured butter and glazed with aspic jelly. Serve on a silver flat, with doily or dish-paper.

Club Sandwich - Hot (4 Portions)

8 *slices of toast*
250 *g* (8 *oz*) *cooked boneless chicken*
8 *grilled bacon rashers*
1 *lettuce*
4 *peeled tomatoes*
2 *dl* ($\frac{1}{4}$ *pint*) *mayonnaise*
16 *cherry sticks*
100 *g* (4 *oz*) *butter*

(1) Toast bread, trim off crust and butter well.
(2) Place a leaf of lettuce on toast.
(3) Add chicken, grilled bacon, tomatoes and mayonnaise.
(4) Finish with another leaf of lettuce, and second slice of toast.
(5) Press, secure with 4 cherry sticks.
(6) Cut into 4 triangles.
(7) Serve upright on a plate or silver flat, with doily or dish-paper showing filling.

Bookmaker Sandwich - Hot (1 Portion)

2 *slices of toasted bread, crust French stick, or cottage loaf*
1 *minute stead*
English mustard
Springs of parsley, quarters of peeled tomatoes

(1) Season steak and grill in the normal way.
(2) Spread liberally with mustard.
(3) Place between bread which has been buttered.
(4) Press between 2 plates or boards.
(5) Cut in half or into strips.
(6) Serve on plate or silver flat with doily or dish-paper.
(7) Garnish with sprigs of parsley and quarters of tomatoes.

Croûte Monsieur - Hot (4 Portions)

50 g (2 oz) cooked ham, 4 slices
125 g (4 oz) Gruyère cheese, 8 slices
8 slices of slightly toasted thin bread

(1) Place each slice of ham between 2 slices of cheese.
(2) Now place ham and cheese between 2 slices of bread.
(3) Press firmly, remove crust and trim; cut into 2 large or 4 smaller triangles.
(4) Gently fry golden brown in clarified butter, so that cheese melts.
(5) Can also be dipped in batter and fried, as above.
(6) Serve on a plate or silver flat, with doily or dish-paper.
(7) Garnish with sprigs of parsley.

Strammer Max - Hot (1 Portion)

50 g (2 oz) lardons of bacon
1 slice of toasted bread
25 g (1 oz) of clarified butter
1 egg

(1) Fry bread golden brown, place on a warm plate.
(2) Sauté lardons of bacon, place on bread.
(3) Fry egg, place on top of bacon.
(4) Garnish with sprigs of parsley and quarters of tomatoes.

Sandwich Lindström - Hot (4 Portions)

100 g (4 oz) clarified butter
4 slices of toasted bread
25 g (1 oz) of finely chopped onions
25 g (1 oz) fine brunoise of beetroot
15 g ($\frac{1}{2}$ oz) capers
5 eggs
salt, pepper
250 g (8 oz) freshly minced beef-steak

(1) Mix minced beef, onions, beetroot, capers and 1 raw egg.
(2) Season with salt and pepper, shape into 4 steaks.
(3) Gently fry in butter.
(4) Toast and butter bread, place fried steaks on the bread.
(5) Fry remaining 4 eggs and place on the top of the steaks.
(6) Serve on warm plates, garnished with sprigs of parsley and quarters of tomatoes.

Danish Hot Tartare Sandwich (1 portion)

100 g (4 oz) freshly minced steak
1 slice of toasted butter
25 g (1 oz) clarified butter
2 gherkins
4 onion rings
a few capers
1 tomato

(1) Toast bread on one side.
(2) Spread the minced steak on the other.
(3) Fry golden brown on both sides in butter.
(4) Place on a warm plate.
(5) Garnish with onion rings, fans of gherkins, quarters of tomatoes and sprig of parsley.

OPEN SANDWICHES

This sandwich has gained great popularity in Great Britain in the last few years and they are most useful for several types of catering. Most of the open sandwiches originate from old Russia where, when nobility met for important and not so important dinners and dances, these sandwiches were served with drinks, especially vodka.

People attending these banquets often came from far away and the arrival of horsedrawn carriages with their important guests dragged on for hours with much pomp and ceremony. At first drinks only were served, but these receptions became longer and longer to give all guests time to arrive and many of them were, to put it politely, quite unsteady on their feet when it was time for the dinner to start.

Someone had the idea of serving something more substantial with the potent drinks and thus the open sandwich was born. At first it was only a simple slice of bread or toast with some cold meat, game, cheese and salads, to be eaten with one's fingers. Then, as the open sandwich became established, different chefs tried hard to outdo each other and only by their competition to do better than the next the sandwich grew to an enormous size, became very rich and often quite expensive. At times, in fact, it represented a meal before a meal.

French culture and language at that time were most prominent in Russia, as elsewhere in Europe, and many French chefs worked there. When they returned to France, they adopted and perfected the sandwich when and wherever possible. It became known in the *cuisine française* as Canapés or croûtons.

However, it was not France but the Scandinavian countries that adopted the open sandwich to such an extent that it became a real national food, in countries like Finland, Norway, Sweden, Northern Germany and especially in Denmark, where it is known as *Smørrebrød*. In Denmark there are shops selling *smørrebrød* in more than a hundred varieties and it is not uncommon for the busy housewife to walk away with a boxful for an easy tea or supper bought at the shop. These shops are open from early morning until late at night and *smørrebrøds* can be eaten on the premises with a glass of ice cool lager, as well as taken home.

Simplicity as well as combination of ingredients, decoration and expert presentation make all of these sandwiches very attractive and they represent in our hurried modern times a reasonable but excellent nourishing meal.

Besides being on sale in the special shops described, these open sandwiches can be found from the smallest café and public house bars, to the finest hotels and restaurants. In fact, some first class hotels serve these sandwiches in their bars, only smaller, more like canapés, as a sort of Hors d'Œuvre with a guest's drink. Many hotels and restaurants serve open sandwiches as a speciality and a typical *Smørrebrødssedde* open sandwich menu is shown translated into English. The menu is given to the guest, together with a pencil if necessary, and the customer fills in the menu according to his or her wishes, enumerating the required ingredients, garnishes, and breads.

The menu then goes into the kitchen where the sandwiches are freshly made, usually by people specially trained for this work.

When the sandwiches are made, the preparer puts the menu on to a silver flat of appropriate size, places over it a nicely folded paper or cloth serviette and expertly arranges the *Smørrebrød* on to the flat. Then the waiter takes it to the guest who can check whether his order corresponds with what is on the silver flat by looking at the menu he himself filled in.

The menu, at the same time, is also the bill to which the waiter only has to add the drinks the guest may have with his open sandwiches.

Open sandwiches fall into 3 types:

(1) *Large*
A normal slice of bread, with crust and fillings as described; this type is usually served in popular cafés, bars and restaurants, as well as *Smørrebrød* shops and restaurants.

(2) *Medium*
A half slice of bread with the crust removed, cut into oblongs, triangles, or cut round with a pastry cutter. Fillings are the same. This type is usually served in better type hotels and restaurants, usually as a speciality of the house and served as a Hors d'Œuvre. The medium size is also extensively used for reception buffets.

(3) *Small*
A quarter of a normal slice of bread with the crust removed, cut into oblong squares, triangles, or cut with a pastry cutter, representing the normal canapés. Fillings are as described below and this type is given at receptions, with drinks in bars and pubs, or as a Hors d'Œuvre before a meal where usually a selection of 6 of this small type is given. Contrary to the normal canapé, the *smørrebrød* canapé must be made to order or a very short time before service as they deteriorate very quickly in appearance.

Service
With the larger open sandwiches, a knife and fork must be given to the guest, who sits down. Where this is not possible, the open sandwich can be made much smaller, similar to a canapé, or the finished large open sandwich can be cut with a very sharp knife across, without doing damage to its appetizing looks.

In conclusion here is a condensed list of combinations and ingredients:
Breads:
French, sandwich, Vienna, rye, wholemeal, *pumpernickel, vollkorn*, rolls.
Butters:
Plain, mustard, anchovy, tomato, onion, or garlic flavoured.
Fillings:
Bismark herring, smoked herring, sardines, smoked eel, smoked trout, Böckling, prawns, lobster, salmon, soused mackerel, caviar, smoked salmon, shrimps, boiled ham, smoked ham, tongue, brisket, corned beef, salami, Mortadella, liver sausage, blood sausage, chicken, pheasant, duck, turkey, chicken-liver, gammon, eggs, all dry and creamed cheeses, etc., as well as combinations of these.
Garnishes:
Lettuce, tomatoes, watercress, mustard and cress, spring onions, radishes, mayonnaise, tartare sauce, tomato ketchup, gherkins, pickled cucumber, cucumber, pickles, chutney, and parsley.

Figure 113 shows a selection of open sandwiches.

Smørrebrødsseddel
Open Sandwich Menu

	White Bread	Brown Bread	Ryvita	Pumpernickel	Price
Caviar					
Smoked Goose Breast					
Goose Liver Pâté on toast					
Fish					
Smoked Salmon					
Smoked Eel					
Smoked Trout					
Smoked Herring		2			
Herrings, salad and egg					
Pickled Herrings					
Bismark Herring					
Rollmops		1			
Fillet Herring with sour cream					
Egg					
Hard Boiled Egg					
Egg with anchovy		1			
Egg with sardine					
Egg with caviar					
Egg with prawns					
Egg with smoked eel					
Scrambled egg and ham on toast HOT					
Fried egg and bacon on toast HOT					
Poultry and Game					
Chicken salad – boiled					
Breast of chicken – roasted					
Leg of chicken – roasted					
Turkey and chipolatas		3			
Roasted Goose on goose dripping					
Roast Pheasant					
Roast Duck					
Roast Pigeon					
Chicken liver and bacon					
Chicken Pâté					
Turkey Pâté					
Chicken liver pâté					

	White Bread	*Brown Bread*	*Ryvita*	*Pumper-nickel*	*Price*
Meats					
Beef Tartare with raw egg yolk					
Beef Tartare with onions					
Beef Tartare slightly grilled					
Minute steak					
Hamburger with fried onion rings					
Smoked Ham with pickles					
Boiled Ham with pickled gherkins	1			1	
Smoked tongue					
Boiled salted tongue					
Brisket of Beef					
Brined Brisket of Beef	1				
Danish Salami			2		
German Mettwurst					
Italian Salami					
Mortadella					
Liver Sausage					
Blood Sausage					
Roast beef with horseradish cream					
Roast beef with Sauce Remoulade					
Roast Pork with gherkins					
Roast Veal with Aspic Jelly					
Cheese					
Camembert				1	
Camembert with Cream and Onions				2	
Gervaise					
Gervaise Garni					
Harzer Cheese					
Gruyère					
Dutch					
Cheddar					
Limburger, Brie, Stilton					

Waiter No. .... Date ....
Bill No. .... Drinks ....
No. of Guests ...... Price ....

1 HANS ANDERSEN'S FAVOURITE

$1\frac{1}{2}$ *oz. liverpaté (1 slice)*
$\frac{1}{2}$ *oz. mushrooms (cooked, sliced)*
$\frac{1}{4}$ *oz. Danish bacon rasher (3" strip, cooked)*
1 tomato slice
1 gherkin fan
Lettuce
Danish buttered bread

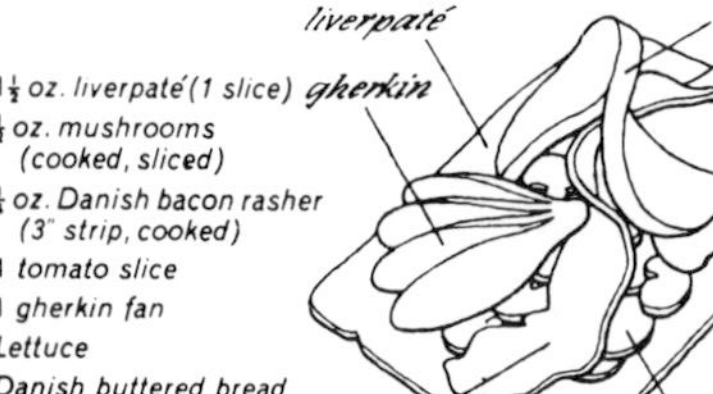

Place liverpaté slice on bread to cover it. Position small lettuce piece in one corner. Heap mushrooms in centre, securing lettuce. Add bacon strip diagonally. Twist tomato slice in position across bacon. Place gherkin fan to side of twist.

2 TIVOLI

4 hard-boiled egg slices
$\frac{1}{2}$ *oz. Danish-style caviar*
$\frac{1}{2}$ *oz. mayonnaise*
4 tomato slices
Lettuce
Danish buttered bread

Cover the bread with lettuce. Arrange egg and tomato slices in two rows lengthwise on the lettuce. Pipe mayonnaise down the centre. Spoon the caviar along the mayonnaise.

3 OLIVER TWIST

$1\frac{1}{2}$ *oz. pork luncheon meat (3 slices)*
2 prunes
1 orange slice
1 tablespoon horseradish cream
Lettuce
Parsley sprig
Danish buttered bread.

Fold meat slices one in front of the other onto bread. Spoon on horseradish cream. Cut and twist orange slice in position. Prunes go either side of twist. Tuck lettuce and parsley sprig into the cream.

4 CHEF'S SPECIAL

$1\frac{1}{2}$ *oz. home-cooked gammon (2 slices)*
$\frac{1}{2}$ *oz. scrambled egg strip*
2 tomato slices
1 cucumber slice
1 teaspoon chopped chives
Parsley sprig
Danish buttered bread

Arrange gammon slices neatly to cover bread. Position egg strip diagonally. Put cucumber slice between tomato slices. Cut through all three. Twist and position across scrambled egg. Sprinkle egg with chopped chives.

5 DANWICH INTERNATIONAL

2 oz. Danish canned ham ($1\frac{1}{2}$ slices)
1 dessertsp. (heaped) Russian Salad
1 tomato slice
2 cucumber slices
Lettuce
Parsley
Danish buttered bread

Fold ham neatly on the bread, getting a little height if possible. Place small piece lettuce on top. Spoon on Russian salad centrally securing but not covering lettuce. Place tomato slice between cucumber slices, cut through all, twist and position on Russian salad. Add parsley sprig.

6 THE EPICURE

$2\frac{1}{2}$ *oz. Danish chicken (boneless) weight*
$\frac{1}{4}$ *oz. Danish bacon roll or strip*
2 cucumber slices
1 tomato slice
Lettuce
Watercress sprig
Danish buttered bread

Cover buttered bread with crisp lettuce. Arrange chicken portion on top. Place tomato slice between cucumber slices, cut through all, twist and position on chicken. Tuck in bacon roll or strip. Add watercress sprig.

7 THE BEEFEATER

1 oz. roast beef, thinly sliced
1 dessertspoon Remoulade sauce
1 teaspoon fried onions
1 teaspoon grated horseradish
1 gherkin fan
1 tomato slice
Lettuce
Danish buttered bread

Arrange beef slices to cover bread. Put small piece lettuce at one end. Spoon on Remoulade sauce securing but not covering lettuce. Add scattering fried onion, and grated horseradish. Position gherkin fan to one side. Finish with tomato twist.

8 DANE'S DELIGHT

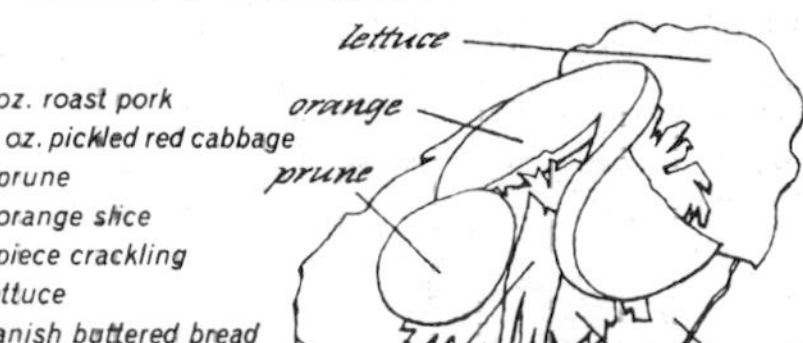

1 oz. roast pork
$1\frac{1}{2}$ oz. pickled red cabbage
1 prune
1 orange slice
1 piece crackling
Lettuce
Danish buttered bread

Arrange sliced pork to cover bread. Mound pickled red cabbage in centre. Place orange twist on top. Tuck small piece lettuce and stoned prune either side of the twist. Add crisp crackling if available.

9 PICNIC FANCY

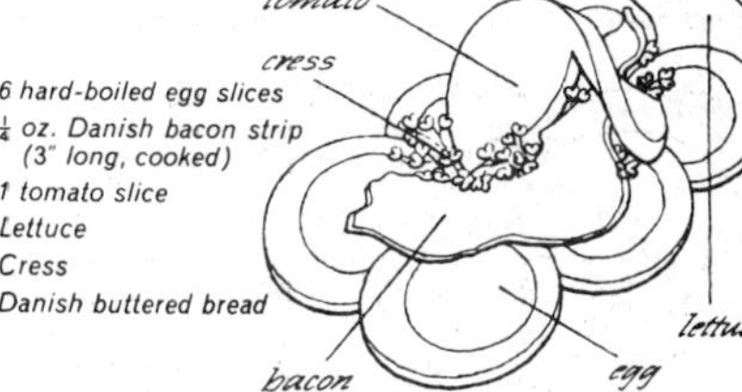

6 hard-boiled egg slices
$\frac{1}{4}$ oz. Danish bacon strip (3" long, cooked)
1 tomato slice
Lettuce
Cress
Danish buttered bread

Press small piece lettuce into butter at one end of bread. Arrange egg slices in two rows covering bread completely. Position bacon rasher on top. Cut and twist tomato slice across the bacon. Tuck cress in either side of twist

10 THE CONTINENTAL

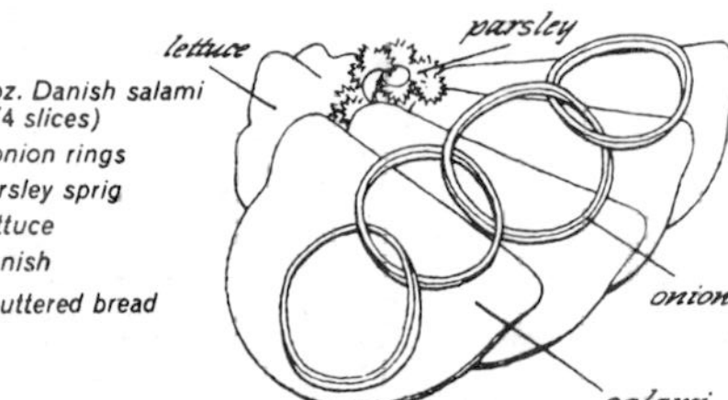

2 oz. Danish salami (4 slices)
4 onion rings
Parsley sprig
Lettuce
Danish buttered bread

Fold each slice of salami loosely in half. Press small piece of lettuce in one corner of bread. Arrange the salami pieces in fan shape to cover bread. Snip through two of the onion rings. Link all four together in a chain over salami slices. Decorate with parsley sprig.

11 SHRIMP CRUSH

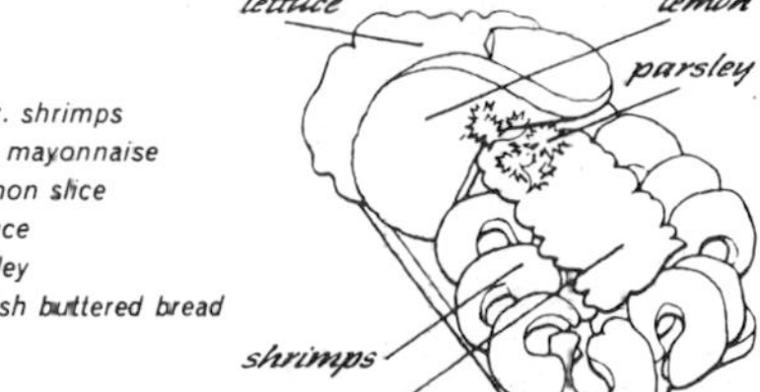

$1\frac{1}{2}$ oz. shrimps
$\frac{1}{3}$ oz. mayonnaise
1 lemon slice
Lettuce
Parsley
Danish buttered bread

Press small piece lettuce into one corner of bread. Pipe little mayonnaise down the centre to hold the topping. Drain shrimps well and pile neatly on the bread. Pipe mayonnaise along the top. Place lemon twist at one end. Garnish with parsley.

12 MASTER MARINER

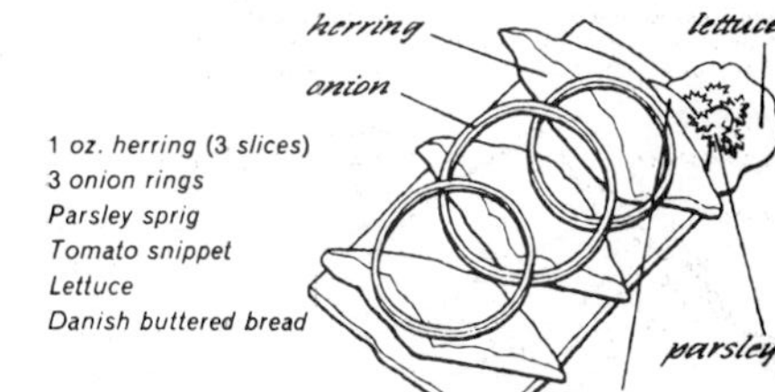

1 oz. herring (3 slices)
3 onion rings
Parsley sprig
Tomato snippet
Lettuce
Danish buttered bread

Press sprig lettuce into butter at one corner. Arrange the three strips of herring diagonally across each slice with the butter showing through. Garnish with three graduated onion rings across the herring, snippet of tomato and parsley sprig.

13 WEEKLY MEETING

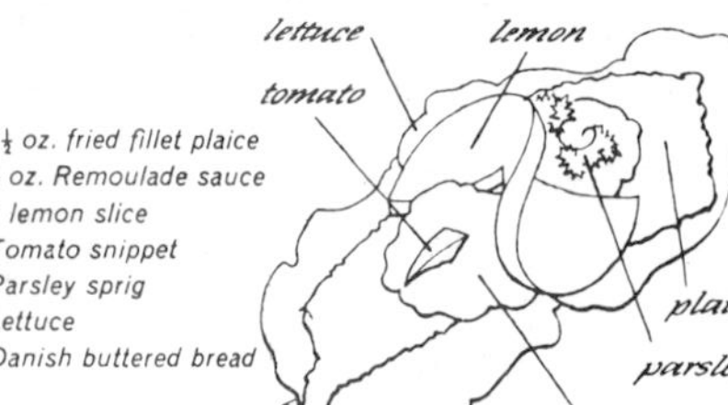

1½ oz. fried fillet plaice
¼ oz. Remoulade sauce
1 lemon slice
Tomato snippet
Parsley sprig
Lettuce
Danish buttered bread

Cover bread with lettuce. Place freshly cooked, but not hot plaice portion on top. Spoon on one dessertspoonful Remoulade Sauce. Fix lemon twist lightly in sauce. Add parsley sprig and tomato snippet on top.

14 BLUE BOY

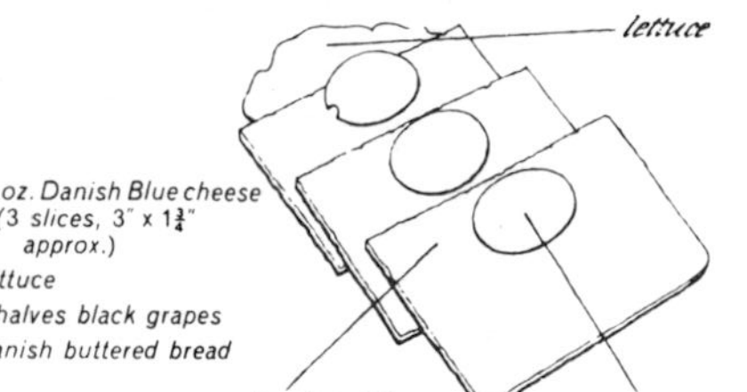

1½ oz. Danish Blue cheese (3 slices, 3" x 1¾" approx.)
Lettuce
3 halves black grapes
Danish buttered bread

Secure lettuce in butter at one end of bread. Cut cheese to shape. Arrange slices slightly overlappi , each other to cover the bread. Decorate with three halves de-seeded black grapes or a single radish rose.

15 HELLO HAVARTI DANWICH

2 oz Havarti cheese (3 neat slices)
Radish rose
Lettuce
Danish buttered bread

Cut cheese to 3 neat slices. Press lettuce leaf in one corner of bread. Arrange cheese slices to overlap each other to cover the bread. Decorate with radish rose.

16 MID-DAY SNACK

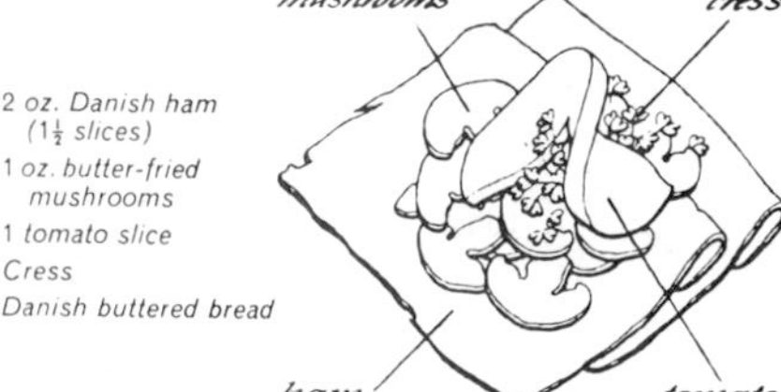

2 oz. Danish ham (1½ slices)
1 oz. butter-fried mushrooms
1 tomato slice
Cress
Danish buttered bread

Fold ham onto bread. Pile sliced mushrooms in centre. Cut tomato and twist in position on mushrooms. Garnish with cress either side of twist.

17 TIVOLI TONGUE

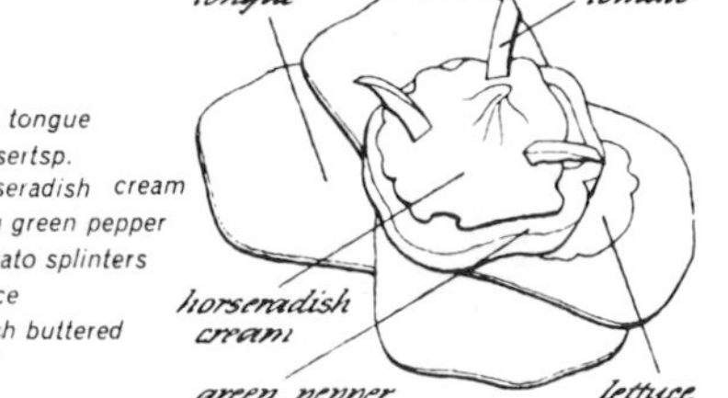

2½ oz. tongue
1 dessertsp. horseradish cream
1 ring green pepper
3 tomato splinters
Lettuce
Danish buttered bread

Arrange tongue slices on bread. Position lettuce and put green pepper on top. Pipe horseradish cream in centre of pepper. Add 3 tomato splinters.

18 COCKTAIL DANWICH

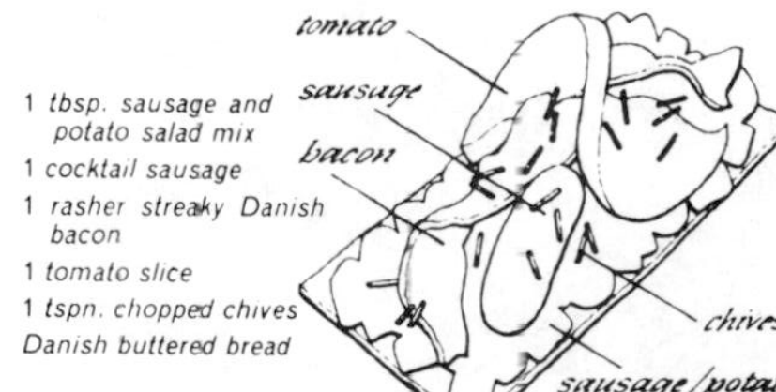

1 tbsp. sausage and potato salad mix
1 cocktail sausage
1 rasher streaky Danish bacon
1 tomato slice
1 tspn. chopped chives
Danish buttered bread

Spoon sausage and potato salad mix onto bread to cover. Place bacon rasher on top. Cut and twist tomato across rasher. Position whole cocktail sausage in front of twist. Sprinkle with chives.

19 HAM AND ASPARAGUS

1½ oz. Danish ham (3 half-slices)
3 asparagus spears
Lettuce
¼ oz. mayonnaise
1 tomato splinter
Danish buttered bread

Layer the 3 half slices of ham on the bread. Tuck lettuce under one corner of second slice. Place 3 asparagus spears across the ham. Pipe mayonnaise across base and between asparagus. Add tomato splinter.

20 HARLEQUIN

2 oz. chopped pork and ham (3 slices)
1 dessertsp. potato salad
Watercress sprig
Radish rose
Danish buttered bread

Layer meat slices on bread. Spoon potato salad on centre. Garnish watercress and radish rose.

21 TONGUE SAVOURY

2 oz. Tongue (thinly sliced)
½ oz. scrambled egg
1 strip aspic jelly
Parsley sprig
Tomato splinter
Danish buttered bread

Place the slices of tongue on the bread. Arrange scrambled egg strip across the tongue, and cross it with a strip of aspic jelly. Add parsley and tomato splinter.

22 SUNSHINE SALAMI

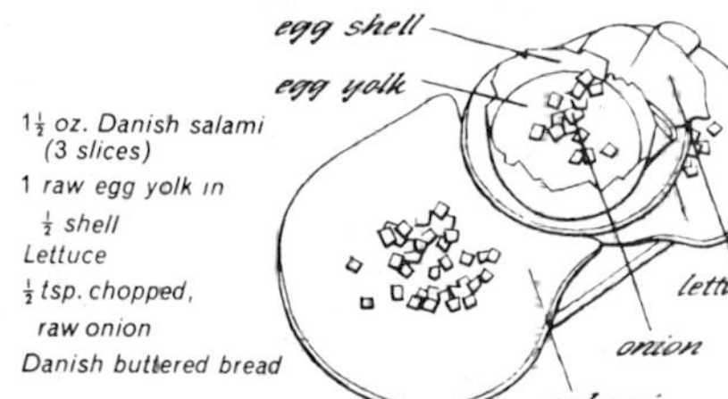

1½ oz. Danish salami (3 slices)
1 raw egg yolk in ½ shell
Lettuce
½ tsp. chopped, raw onion
Danish buttered bread

Fold 2 slices salami back to back on bread. Make third slice into cup shape and press between the slices. Place an egg yolk in the half-shell inside the cup and tuck small piece of lettuce in between salami and shell.

23 SALAMI SAVOURY

1½ oz. Danish salami (3 slices)
1 dessertsp. horseradish cream
3 onion rings
Sprig parsley
Danish buttered bread

Twist salami into cornet shapes, pressing well together. Position to cover bread. Pipe the centre of each cornet with horseradish cream. Cut through one onion ring, and link all three across top of salami. Place parsley sprigs in the centre of each cornet.

24 THE GUARDSMAN

1 oz. brisket of beef
1 dessertsp. horseradish cream
1 tomato slice
2 onion rings
Parsley sprig
Lettuce
Danish buttered bread

Place meat on bread to cover. Put small piece of lettuce on the meat. Heap the horseradish cream in the centre securing but not covering lettuce. Add the 2 onion rings. Cut and twist tomato slice on top. Add parsley sprig.

25 ROSKILDE SPECIAL

1 oz. Danish ham (1 slice)
1 oz. Cooked chicken in mayonnaise
1 cucumber slice
1 tomato slice
1 stuffed olive
Cress
Paprika pepper
Danish buttered bread

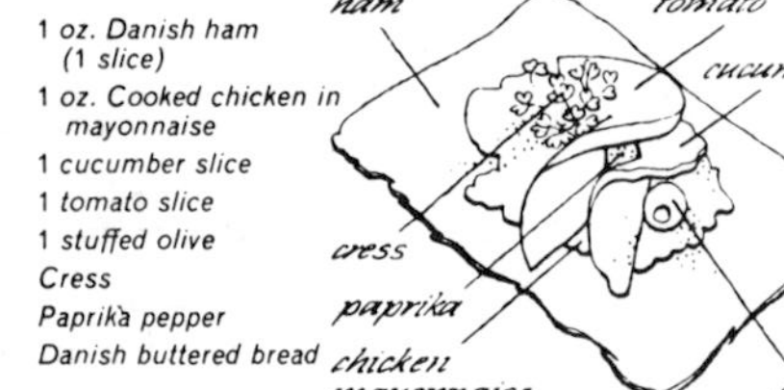

Place ham on bread to cover. Pile chicken mayonnaise centrally on top. Put tomato and cucumber slices together. Cut through, twist and place on mayonnaise mixture. Put olive one side of twist, with little cress opposite. Dust mayonnaise mixture with paprika.

26 HAM AND TONGUE DE LUXE

2 oz. thinly sliced tongue
$1\frac{1}{2}$ oz. Ham julienne in mayonnaise
$\frac{1}{2}$ oz. raw, sliced mushrooms
Lettuce
Cress
2 tomato splinters
Danish buttered bread

Place tongue slices on bread. Put piece of lettuce on tongue, slightly off centre. Secure but do not cover with the ham mixture. Place mushroom slices on top. Add tomato splinters and little cress.

27 KRONBORG SALAD

2 oz. Danish ham ($1\frac{1}{2}$ slices)
2 oz. Kronborg salad
3 onion rings
Parsley sprig
Danish buttered bread

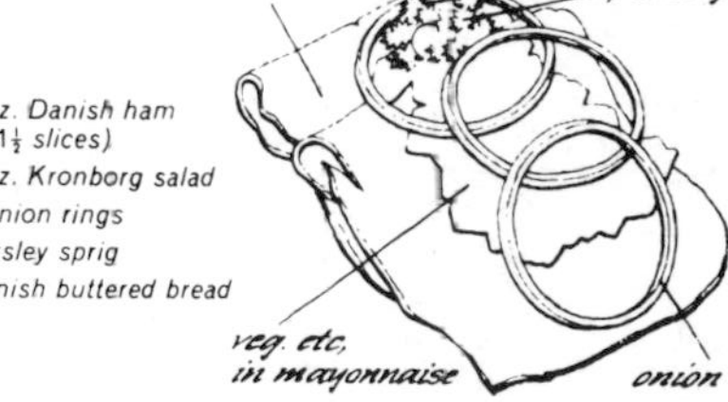

Fold ham slices on bread to cover. Pile salad mixture on centre of ham. Position 3 onion rings loosely across. Add parsley sprig.

28 MEAT SALAD

1 oz. Danish tongue
1 tbsp. chicken and ham in mayonnaise
Lettuce
2 onion rings
1 tomato splinter
Danish buttered bread

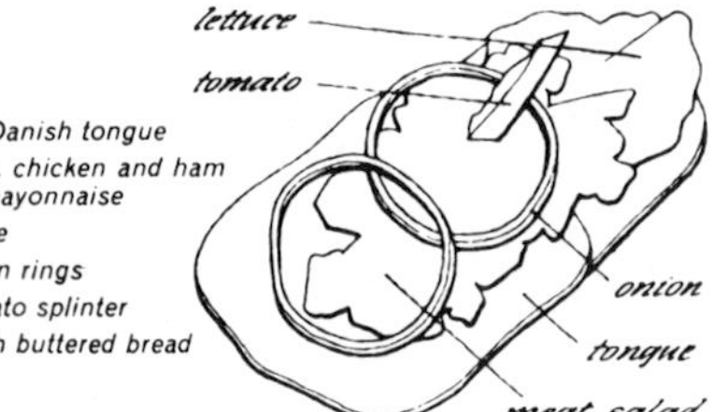

Put thinly sliced tongue on bread to cover. Place small piece lettuce, slightly off centre, on the tongue. Spoon on meat salad securing but not covering lettuce. Position 2 onion rings on top. Add tomato splinter.

29 COPENHAGEN SALAD

2 tbs. Copenhagen Salad
Lettuce
1 beetroot slice
2 slices hard-boiled egg
Danish buttered bread

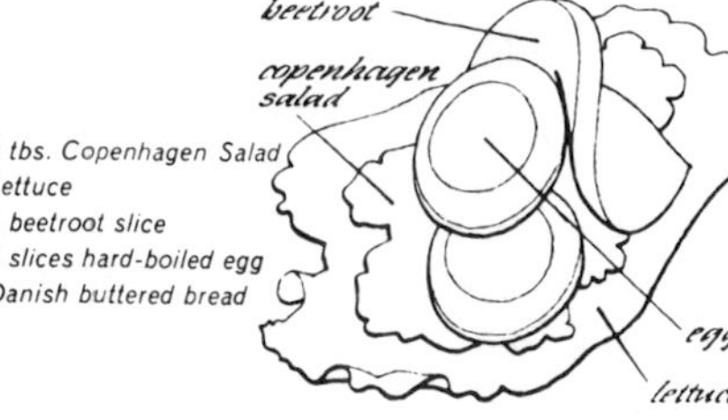

Cover bread with lettuce leaf. Spoon on salad. Cut and twist beetroot slice in position on top. Place egg slices in front of twist.

30 FRIKADELLER

2 oz. Frikadeller
(1 meat ball)
1 oz. red cabbage
Lettuce
1 gherkin fan
Danish buttered bread

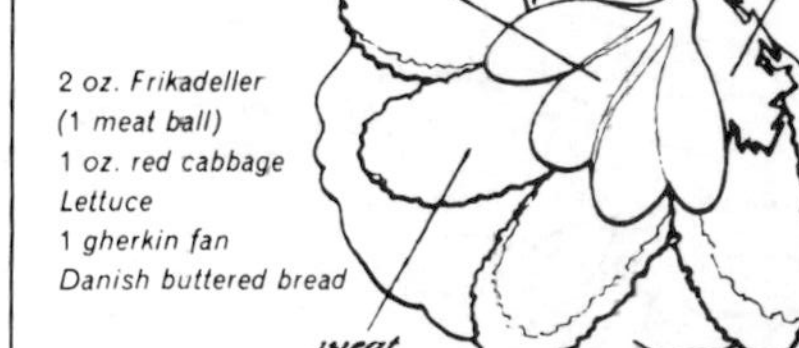

Cover bread with lettuce. Slice the meat ball and arrange slices on top, fanning out slightly. Spoon red cabbage to one end. Garnish with gherkin fan.

31 BACON AND APPLE

2 tbs. apple sauce
Lettuce
2 rashers streaky bacon
1 tomato splinter
Parsley
Danish buttered bread

Cover bread with lettuce leaf and spoon apple onto it. Place cooked bacon rashers diagonally across with the tomato splinter and parsley sprig to garnish.

32 BACON SNACK

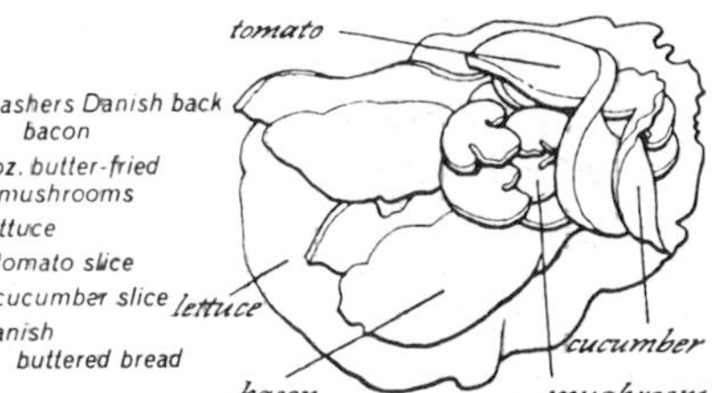

2 rashers Danish back bacon
½ oz. butter-fried mushrooms
Lettuce
1 tomato slice
1 cucumber slice
Danish buttered bread

Cover bread with lettuce leaf. Arrange cooked, cold bacon rashers across. Pile mushrooms on thin end of rashers. Cut through tomato and cucumber slices together, twist and position on mushrooms.

33 LOUISIANA

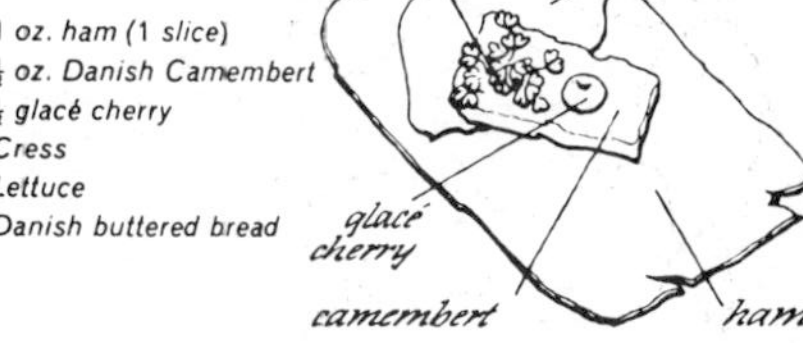

1 oz. ham (1 slice)
½ oz. Danish Camembert
½ glacé cherry
Cress
Lettuce
Danish buttered bread

Place ham on buttered bread. Position lettuce piece on top and hold in place with slice of cheese. Place cherry on cheese. Garnish cress.

34 BLUE BOY (with carrots)

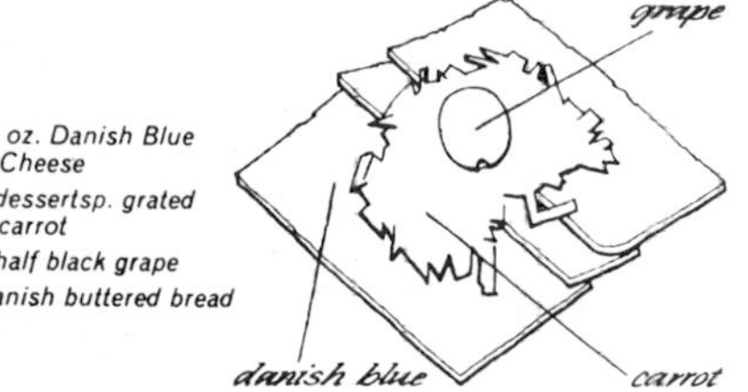

1½ oz. Danish Blue Cheese
1 dessertsp. grated carrot
1 half black grape
Danish buttered bread

Cut the cheese to give 3 slices. Place on bread to cover. Place grated carrot in the centre, and top with grape half.

35 BLUE DANWICH

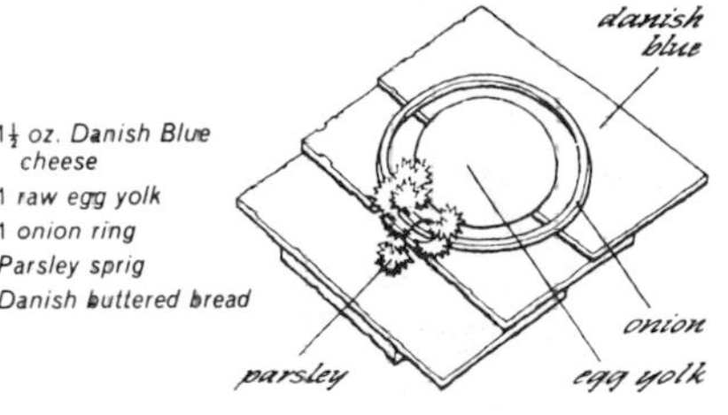

1½ oz. Danish Blue cheese
1 raw egg yolk
1 onion ring
Parsley sprig
Danish buttered bread

Place Danish Blue on buttered bread to cover. Put the onion ring on top in the centre. Carefully put egg yolk inside the ring. Garnish with parsley sprig.

36 THE MANDARIN

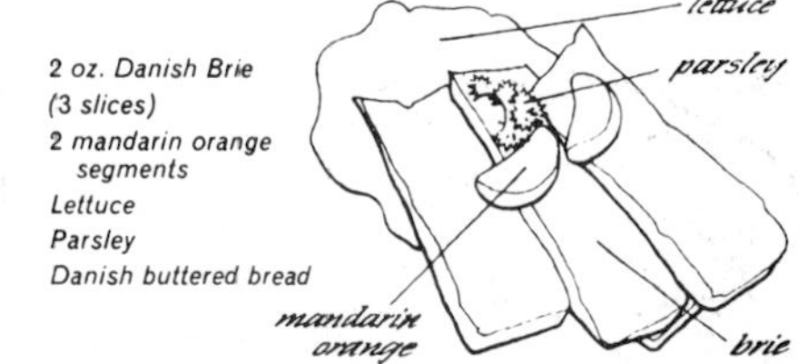

2 oz. Danish Brie
(3 slices)
2 mandarin orange segments
Lettuce
Parsley
Danish buttered bread

Place small piece of lettuce on bread. Arrange cheese on top, fanned out to cover bread. Put mandarin segments at narrow end of fan shape. Add parsley sprig.

37 CAMEMBERT DANWICH

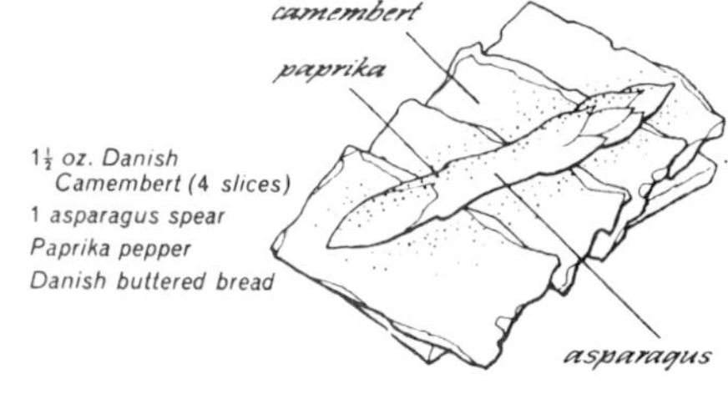

1½ oz. Danish Camembert (4 slices)
1 asparagus spear
Paprika pepper
Danish buttered bread

Arrange cheese slices to cover bread. Place asparagus at an angle across the cheese. Dust with paprika pepper.

38 VEGETARIAN DANWICH

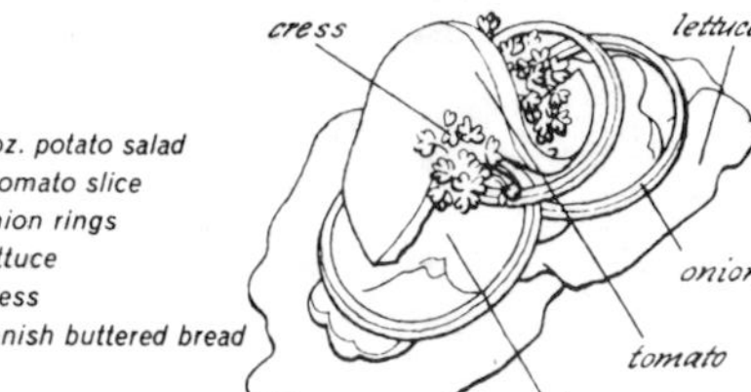

2 oz. potato salad
1 tomato slice
Onion rings
Lettuce
Cress
Danish buttered bread

Cover bread with lettuce leaf and pile potato salad generously on top. Garnish with onion rings, then cut and twist tomato slice on top of rings. Tuck cress either side of twist.

39 CAROUSEL

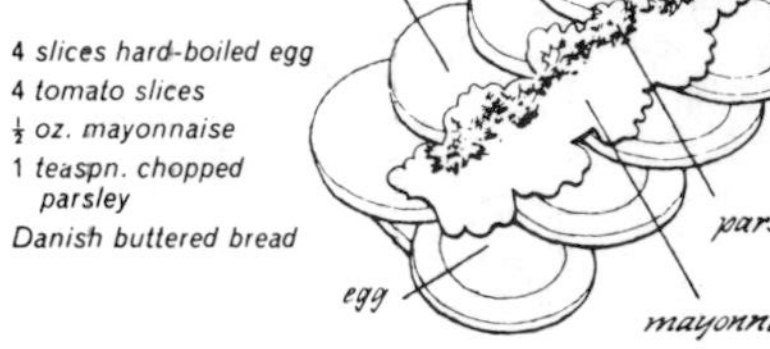

4 slices hard-boiled egg
4 tomato slices
½ oz. mayonnaise
1 teaspn. chopped parsley
Danish buttered bread

Place 4 slices of egg on one side of bread with the 4 slices of tomato opposite and slightly overlapping. Pipe the centre with mayonnaise and sprinkle with chopped parsley.

40 SARDINE SALAD

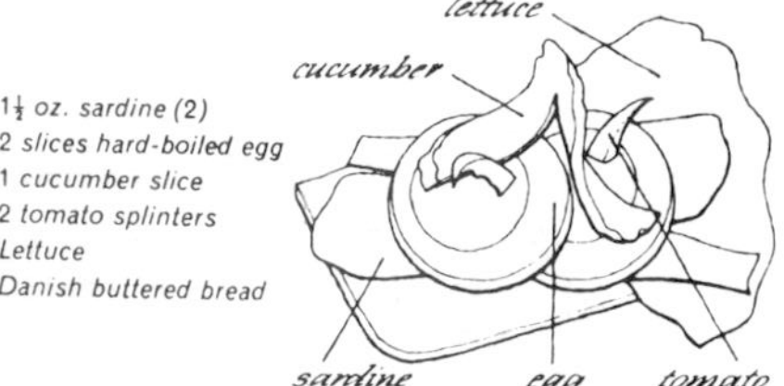

1½ oz. sardine (2)
2 slices hard-boiled egg
1 cucumber slice
2 tomato splinters
Lettuce
Danish buttered bread

Place lettuce on bread. Arrange sardines head to tail diagonally across the bread and overlapping the lettuce. Put two egg slices on top. Cut cucumber and twist in position on top of egg. Place tomato splinters either side.

41 ANCHOVY EGG

lettuce
olive
egg
anchovy

6 slices hard-boiled egg
2 anchovy fillets
Lettuce
1 stuffed olive
Danish buttered bread

Place small piece of lettuce at one end of bread. Arrange egg slices in two rows. Join two fillets, curve into the letter S, place on top of egg. Cut olive in half and place either side of S.

42 THE CAPTAIN'S BREAKFAST

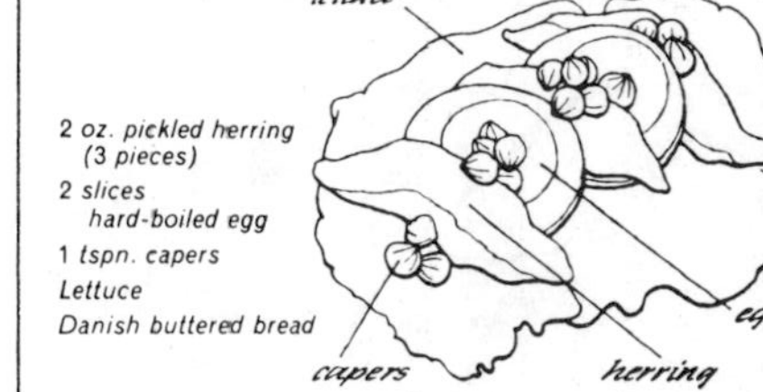

2 oz. pickled herring (3 pieces)
2 slices hard-boiled egg
1 tspn. capers
Lettuce
Danish buttered bread

Cover the bread with lettuce. Place alternate slices of hard-boiled egg and herring diagonally across the bread using 2 slices egg and 3 slices herring. Sprinkle with capers.

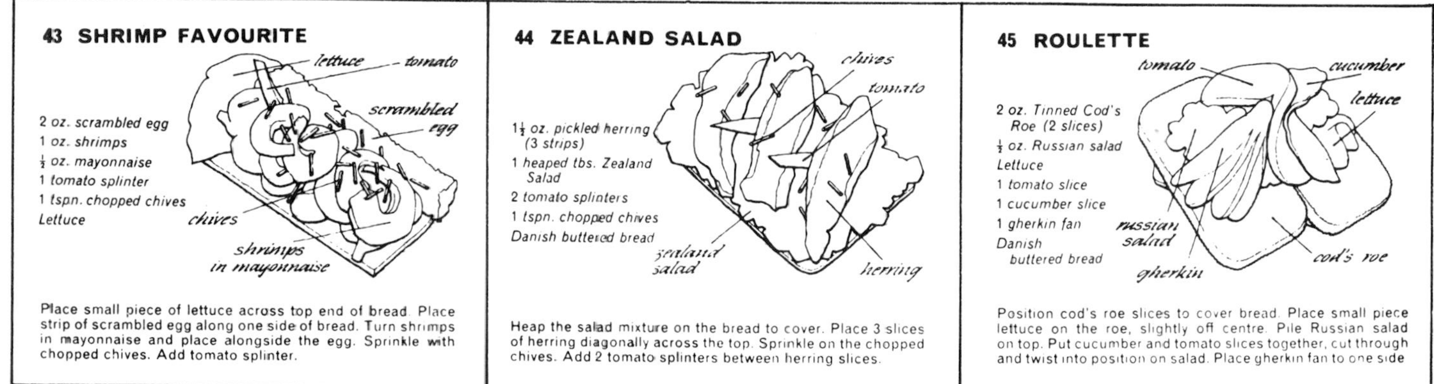

FIG. 113. *Selection of open sandwiches*
Reproduced by kind permission of the Danish Centre Ltd for Open Sandwiches, of which Danwich is the registered name

CANAPES

These canapés are usually made on toasted brown or white bread, or on sheets of puff paste. In the case of the various cheeses which might be used, small biscuits (Ritz) may be used or some of the darker continental breads like *pumpernickel* or *vollkornbrot*, which of course are *not* toasted. Fillings vary after time of year and foods in season may include: Caviar, sardines, shrimps, prawns, oyster, anchovy, etc.; smoked salmon, eel, trout or herring; pickled fish or meats; cold meats, game, poultry, sausages, pâtés, pâté de foie gras; ham, tongue, briskets, salami, fish, tomatoes, cucumbers, etc.; finely cut meats and fish-salads; all sorts of hard or creamed cheeses.

After the bread has been toasted, buttered and cooled, it is covered with the filling, then cut into neat canapés, in round, oblong, triangular, diamond or square shapes, according to the kind and suitability of the filling. This means to say that a large slice of toast with ham may be cut into any shape. A canapé which is to be filled with a sardine should be cut into a triangular shape, to the size of the sardine. A slice of egg, or salami, may be put on to a round canapé, a round piece of cheese may go on to a small round savoury biscuit. Once the canapés are cut into the shapes described, they are put on to a rack and neatly piped with a fine border or design of flavoured or coloured butter. Now the canapés go into the fridge to set and cool, and thereafter they are glazed with a fine clear aspic, according to filling. This may have to be repeated, to achieve a good finish and glaze.

Figure 114 shows cutting for canapé shapes.

Service of Canapés à la Russe

A large silver flat is covered with a simple or broken cloth-serviette or dish-paper, and a large grapefruit or small firm cabbage covered with silver paper is placed in the middle. Into this cocktail sticks are forced, like a hedgehog, on to which points olives, pieces of different cheese, celery, small chipolatas, gherkins etc. may be stuck. Around this middle piece the set canapés are now neatly arranged and garnished with sprigs of parsley, watercress, etc.

RECEPTION BUFFET SAVOURIES – LE DÉJEUNER À LA FOURCHETTE

Savouries for the reception-buffet should again be small and should represent not more than one or two mouthfuls. In this way they can easily be eaten from a small plate with a fork, or one's fingers, leaving the other hand free for a glass of sherry or champagne. There is already a very large number of savouries and each hotel or restaurant has its own specialities.

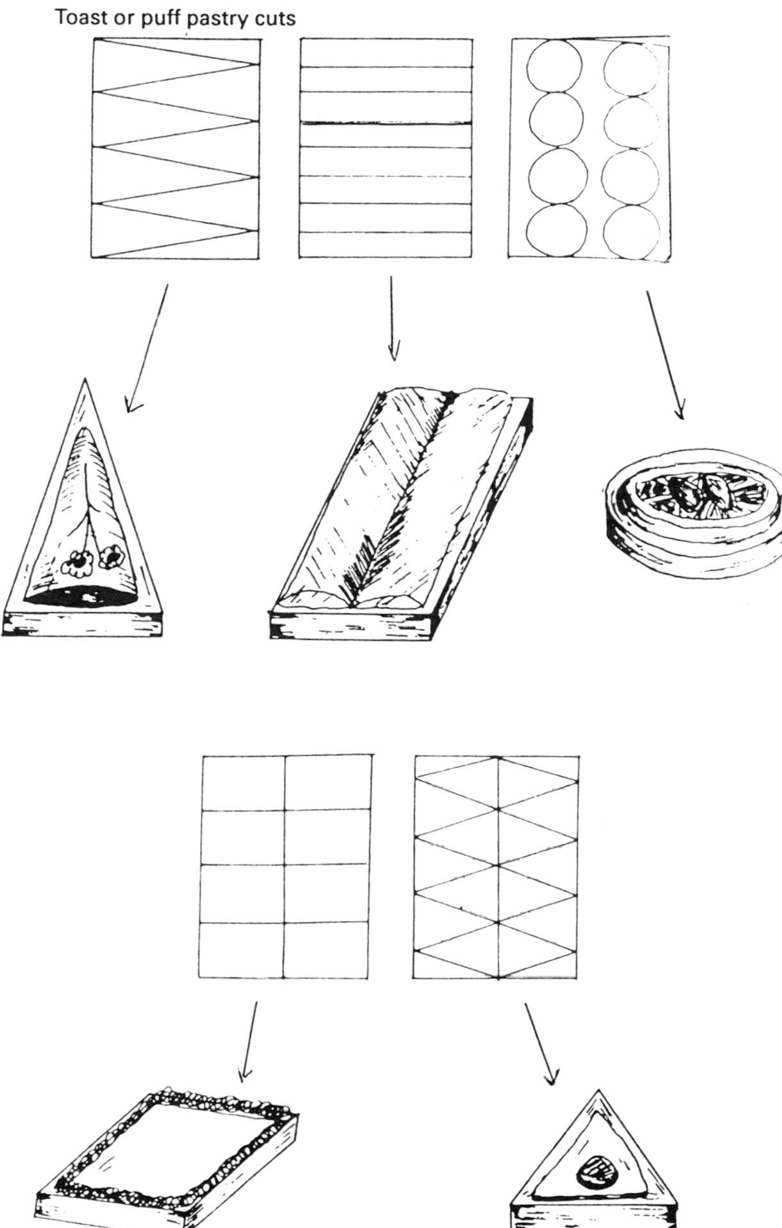

FIG. 114. *Canapé cuts and shapes*

Here is a list of the most commonly used savouries:
Small Sausage Rolls
Petit Bouches, filled with creamed fish, shellfish, meats, poultry and game.
Tartlettes, filled as above. Not necessarily creamed.
Barquettes, filled as above. Not necessarily creamed.
Carolines see Hors d'Œuvre Moscovite.
Duchesses, see Hors d'Œuvre Moscovite.
Cannelons, see Hors d'Œuvre Moscovite.
Croûtons, slices of bread or toast, hot or cold, garnished with meats.
Brioche, small bread rolls where the soft crumbs are removed and in this empty space some fillings of meats, poultry, game, fish or shellfish are placed. Some of these Brioche are already baked with the filling in the dough.
Sandwiches, a selection of buffet sandwiches.

Appendix A

CONVENIENCE FOODS

Before considering convenience foods it will be useful to define what we intend by the term, especially in the context of Larder Operations as outlined at the beginning of this book. The *Oxford Dictionary* defines the word 'convenience' as meaning 'ease of use in action' and broadly speaking we interpret it here to mean part-prepared, fully prepared, or prepared and processed food, with such preparations taking place in areas other than the kitchens of the catering establishment, nominally food factories or processing plants. These operations can save kitchen staff laborious routine preparation and in some instances replace certain sections of kitchen staff altogether. By the application of mass production techniques it is possible to provide a constant standardization of quality as well as the grading of size and weights, thus greatly facilitating portion control. These foods are particularly relevant to the operation of the 'Garde Manger' or cold larder, and can in fact revolutionize the routine work of such a department in a busy catering establishment.

Although convenience foods are often considered a comparatively recent innovation, they have been in many aspects in use over a number of years. Many interpretations of the term 'convenience food' have been applied and some taken to their logical conclusion could cause a considerable amount of confusion. As an example such items as sardines, anchovies, tunny fish, smoked or pickled fish and fish fillets, pickles of every kind and in some instances cooked hams, tongue, pâté de foie gras, and other meats as well as salad creams, canned fruit, and vegetables, to say nothing of fruit juices, have been accepted as conventional and have been in use in most catering establishments for many years.

Added to this, it has always been possible to obtain prepared or filleted fish. In some parts of the country, notably in the West End of London, joints or cuts of meat ready for cooking have been obtainable from butchers who specialize in supplying the hotel and restaurant trade. Poultry and game have also been available oven-ready from poulterers with a similar clientele. It is many years since the Larder staff had to pluck their chickens, although one still occasionally has to deal with pheasant, grouse or other game birds.

It will be observed, therefore, that convenience foods fall into a number of well-defined categories: e.g. part-prepared raw: dissected joints of meat, gutted fish, plucked and drawn poultry and game, washed and graded vegetables, etc.; also fully prepared raw oven-ready joints of meat, poultry and game, portioned meat, cuts and fillets of fish, trimmed and ready to cook, trimmed pared, cut, ready-to-cook vegetables, etc. For fully prepared and processed foods, this covers the whole range of the above, processed by canning, freezing, bottling, dehydrating, smoking, etc., in order to prolong shelf life, and would include ready cooked, ready mixes, and table ready foods.

The two most important aspects to consider in deciding whether to expand the use of convenience foods in any catering operation must surely be cost and quality. Savings in production time must and do result in some considerable cost savings, whilst good portion control means better management control, which in turn should lead to lower food costs. Some forms of processing or preserving – freezing as an example – can involve some capital expenditure on storage facilities, such as deep-freeze storage, and this has to be taken into account when computing any savings in a convenience-foods operation.

It is when applying the yardstick of quality that we are most apt to find convenience foods wanting. Cookery, and in particular the work of a good Larder Chef, is a craft which does not lend itself to mass production techniques. The conventional answer to large-scale quality catering has always been to employ adequate numbers of craftsmen aided by assistants or improvers (Commis), who learned their craft by constant practice under the watchful eye of the craftsman or Chef. Quality therefore rests not only in characteristics such as smell, colour, taste, texture, etc., but also in the more aesthetic pleasing appearance of foodstuffs well prepared and presented. Many cuts or dressings of meat, fish, poultry, etc., required for quality cuisine are still not obtainable from the mass production market and, as an example, any Larder Chef who attempts to prepare 'Suprême de Volaille' or 'Poulet Sauté' using chicken quarters will find that he could prepare them better and quicker from whole chicken. The same can be said of cuts of meat or fish in common use too numerous to list.

The advent of quick-freeze and deep-freeze storage cabinets, together with the expansion of the broiler industry and modern techniques in dehydration and packaging, have probably had the greatest impact on this type of food supply. We could therefore date the term convenience foods from this development which particularly in the field of frozen foods has increased by leaps and bounds in recent years, whereas the growth of canned, bottled, smoked, pickled food, etc., and the impact of ready mixes has had much less influence in Larder operations. It would be true to say at the same time that one should not overlook the storage of trained staff as a contributory cause for this revolution in food preparation in catering.

Whatever the trends or their causes, we firmly believe that there can be no substitute for fresh foods properly prepared and presented by skilled craftsmen. This must be the aim of the good caterer even if at times it is not very 'convenient'.

Appendix B

THE DEEP FREEZE

We should at the outset make a clear distinction between 'deep freeze storage' and 'quick freezing'. The basic purpose of storing food in deep freeze is to prolong its storage life. Under normal temperatures food will deteriorate rapidly through the action of micro-organisms and also enzymic and chemical reactions. By reducing the temperature it is possible to slow down the growth and multiplication of bacteria, such micro-organisms as moulds, yeasts, etc., and in particular the chemical and enzymic reactions. The lower the temperature, the slower the reactions until, at a temperature of about –20°C, or lower, all reactions cease. This will ensure that food storage is safe for long periods, that the natural flavours are maintained, and that off-flavours caused by these reactions are prevented.

Quick freezing, as the term implies, is the technique whereby the lowering of the temperature in the food to the level mentioned or below, is brought about in the shortest period of time possible. The reason for this quick freezing is the existence of a crucial point at which the water content of the food changes to the solid state (ice). At this point, known as the latent heat barrier, the temperature of the food remains static until the latent heat is removed from the food and the water is turned into ice. It is of the greatest importance that this stage be passed through as quickly as possible because, the longer the time taken, the larger will be the ice crystals formed in the intercellular structure of the food and, of course, vice versa. Large ice crystals cause rupture of the cell structure which causes drip when the food is thawed. Nutrients are drained away by drip which also results in moisture loss and thus poor texture in the food and in turn poor flavour. It will be seen, therefore, that food intended for deep freeze storage should be quick frozen first, then stored at a constant temperature of not more than –20°C, equal to –4°F.

The food processing industries have developed many sophisticated and expensive techniques of quick freezing but it is not appropriate to enter into a discussion of the comparative qualities of these, since they are not really relevant to the operation of the Garde-Manger, desirable as they might be.

It is sufficient to say that we should be wary of usurping the function of the food industries by attempting to freeze any large pieces or volume of food without the specialized know-how and the capital investment necessary, if we are to retain flavour, texture, and nutritional values, all necessary ingredients in good quality food.

There is no doubt that in the last ten years or so, the deep freeze has become ever more important in all types of catering establishments as well as in the home. Whether in a large hotel, or the large refectory with their enormous walk-in deep freezes, or whether in a guest house or small restaurant with only a deep freeze section within a normal refrigerator, all would find it difficult to do their work today without this most excellent long-term storage facility.

The reasons for this increased use of the deep freeze are many and may be placed under the following headings:

(a) Bulk-buying and subsequent need for storage.
(b) Special offer/seasonal buying and subsequent need for storage.
(c) Irregular supply or delivery and subsequent need for storage.
(d) Particular preparation requirements and *mise en place* storage.

To understand these four reasons let us look at each in turn and assess the respective reasons for use as well as possible advantages and disadvantages.

Bulk Buying

Experience shows that one can usually buy in bulk many foods at a reduction of 10-20 per cent and whenever possible one should take advantage of this. In larger establishments where usually the correct type of refrigeration and deep freezes are available, these foods should then be stored as and when they are delivered. Brought out of storage according to size and weight two or three days before they are required, they can then slowly defrost and be dissected and prepared for use and cooking over a number of days.

In smaller establishments where limited deep freeze storage is available, it is usually better to buy the foods fresh and after due dissection and preparation they are then placed into storage for use at a later date.

These smaller joints and cuts need only be taken out of deep freeze storage the day before use, as required for any particular function or dish. The removal of bones and carcasses from meat, fish, and poultry prior to storage will give more space and make the best possible use of the limited storage space available.

Special Offer Purchases

One is advised again and again as to the importance of good purchasing and there is no doubt that both bulk buying, special offer, or seasonal advantage purchasing fall into this category. We find that all suppliers make these offers from time to time for various reasons, and whenever possible one should take advantage of them.

Special or seasonal offers should, however, have a considerable reduction in price and one should make sure that correct and sufficient storage is available before consideration is given to the foods to be purchased and their relative saving. For all foods stored in the deep freeze cost money to keep, both in space and electricity.

In this way the purchase of six hindquarters of beef at 10-15 per cent reduction would be a more advantageous purchase than, say, twenty-four boxes of frozen vegetables at a reduction of 30 per cent on normal price. Both would take up the same space approximately in the deep freeze, but the very much higher cost of beef and subsequent higher saving in pounds and pence, would make beef the better buy for our purpose.

We purchased at one time a whole plane load of 5,000 pheasants and 6,500 partridges from Russia at a reduction of 50 per cent of the normal market price at the time. With the existence of a large deep freeze of the walk-in type, there was sufficient space to store this large purchase and the saving was considerable.

The saving was again emphasized when in the following year game prices rose by about 20 per cent and it thus paid for the interest of capital outlay of the purchase, the running cost of the deep freeze, together with many other items stored for several years.

One cannot of course always take inflation into consideration; it may work the other way, but in the last few years these types of purchase have proven to be useful.

Irregular Supply and Deliveries

In all parts of the country, catering establishments, particularly those a little out of the way or open only for a season, as well as those of small size, have experienced more and more irregular supplies and deliveries in recent years.

It may be because of the small amounts required thus making the cost of deliveries not worthwhile, or for reasons of distance or delivery patterns, but both small and large establishments will find a need for advanced buying under these circumstances.

The storage facilities of a deep freeze, as indeed all other storage space will be necessary, to be able to do normal business in a proper manner and with the necessary supplies available.

Particular Requirements

One thinks here in the first place of catering units of a specialist type whether it be in high class national or special catering of varying directions.

These places are usually small or medium establishments and sometimes only open at night and week-ends. With a small but highly skilled staff and often large and varied menus their special and particular need of all types of refrigerated storage, in particular the deep freeze, is easily understood.

Here the foods and dishes served need preparation and larder skill prior to and for cooking, and the mornings are usually given to this type of work preparing Hors d'Œuvres, salads, pâtés, mousses, cutlets, noisettes, escalopes, kebabs, fillets, and many many more such items. It may be said that most of these preparations can now be purchased by suppliers in these fields, on the normal market.

But although this is true to a great extent many items required here are in fact not available or if available are not of a sufficiently high enough standard or preparation and finish. Certain hotels and restaurants will not buy some of these preparations because they are afraid of losing the home cooking element which makes their food famous and particularly individual, a fact which must be encouraged for at least some hotels and restaurants in these days of mass production everywhere.

Whatever the reason, we can see here again the need for a deep freeze to hold the necessary prepared foods, which are vital for this type of skilled presentation of food.

It may be said that frozen uncooked foods, however fresh when frozen, are not really fresh foods when defrosted and freshly cooked. One may have a certain sympathy with this point of view, but it is a practice common all over the country, whether in the home or in the catering industry, and it will we are sure continue on these lines. The lack of the right staff, lack of the right skills, the fact that most foods can only be stored in a normal fridge for two or three days before they are wasted, make the deep freeze a most important aid for all, as no one today can let any foods go to waste or spoil.

As long as the food is well prepared and freshly cooked when the guest gives his order and then well presented it is to all intents and purposes fresh food. Even if it is only freshly cooked, it must still be better than some foods we are eating today or indeed those which are served to us after some two or three days in a normal fridge.

TYPES OF DEEP FREEZE

There are three types of deep freezers. Their difference, however, is only one of shape, size, and possibly make, for all work by the same principle of compressor, condenser, evaporator, and a refrigerant.

Built-in Walk-in Type

This type of deep freeze is usually found in larger catering units, such as hospitals, refectories, canteens, and large hotels and restaurants. It is also used in the main by hotels and restaurants which have not normally a large volume of business, but which do a high-class type of work, with large and varied menus and need for this reason the space and type of deep freeze storage.

The size of these built-in walk-in deep freezes vary from the smallest of about 1.5 x 1.5 x 1.5 x 2.25 metres (4 x 4 x 7 feet), and giving about 5 cubic metres (100 cubic feet) of storage space, to as big as a football pitch if that is the size required.

The average size normally found in catering establishments is 2 x 2 x 2.25 metres (6 x 6 x 7 feet). Should a larger space be required it is advisable to build, shall we say, three deep-freezes of 2 x 2 x 2.25 metres rather than one at 6 x 6 x 2.25 metres.

With the normal division available with the three deep freezes we can now separate meat from fish and possibly even vegetables from meat and fish, and the three doors will allow us a quick and easy access; this would be most important in a busy establishment and for the last reason alone makes it a worthwhile extra expense.

Deep-freeze Cabinet

Here we have two types. Firstly the box or chest type which is the most popular deep freeze and the cheapest to buy with some having the advantage of a built in quick-freeze section, which is separate from the storage section and which allows one to freeze foods quite quickly.

These types of deep freeze have, however, one big disadvantage in that even with some divisions in the form of plastic-coated wire baskets, foods are mixed and often lie on top of one another. Quick access to the food is often difficult, and usually what one is looking for is found on the bottom of the freezer. One has to remove many things before the item one is looking for can be found, even if well marked as to content and amount.

The second type of cabinet is the so-called upright cabinet. It is usually a little more expensive to buy, but by its design and inner shelving allows easy and quick access to foods required, which is most useful in a busy establishment. Its disadvantage is in the opening of the upright door, which allows in a lot of warm air, and which warms the inside of the freezer very easily and so it therefore needs more electricity for this reason than the box type freezer. Manufacturers have of late gone over to fitting two or three doors, which allow for the division of foods from one another and of course only lets hot air into one of several compartments of the freezer, thus reducing the excessive use of electricity for this type.

Some of these upright freezers have freeze-cooled shelves which help in the quick freezing of items to be home frozen, similar to the separated quick-freeze section as described in the box deep freezer.

Multi-cabinet Freezer

The last type of deep freeze is that of a combination of normal fridge and freezer in one unit. Originally intended for the larger household, they have been readily bought by small catering units, and have also found good use in back-bar cooking, floor-service cooking, and ward-service cooking storage in hospitals. They are available in two types, with two doors over one another, the top being usually the fridge and the lower door being the deep freeze. They are also available with four doors as a complete unit for the smaller establishment, where one door is intended to hold Hors d'Œuvres and salads, one to hold fish and shell fish, and another to hold meats and poultry under normal refrigeration. The fourth door is the deep freeze with three or four shelves for various separate foods.

DEEP FREEZE MANAGEMENT

Whatever the type of freezer it needs a good organization of use to give the best possible service. This organization must at all times follow three basic rules, which are:

(a) Food to be frozen must be sealed in moisture or vapour-free material, and as much air as possible excluded (ideally a vacuum if possible).
(b) Only fresh and sound foods should be placed into a deep freeze.
(c) Frozen food, once defrosted must never be refrozen.

These three basic rules for deep freezing have certain implications and a guide to this may be given under the following headings:

Amounts

Weights, numbers, and size must always be of the correct amount for the volume and type of business for which intended. It is not easy to find the right amounts at first, but experience and time will show the right quantities needed. If for example we use on the average 2 kg (4 lb) of diced beef for about 16-20 portions of beef goulash as one of our courses regularly, we should, when dissecting and cutting beef, package our diced meats in that amount. Any residue which will not make a full 2 kg can be packed in $\frac{1}{2}$ or 1 kg lots, should we wish to increase portions on the odd occasion. Should this occasion not arise we can then use up on a normal day one 1 kg and two $\frac{1}{2}$ kg before it gets too old and is kept in the freezer too long.

If for an average meal we need 24 chicken suprêmes, for example, we should after preparation of these suprêmes put them in packs of 6, 12, 18 or 24 and place them like this in the freezer. One or two of the smaller packets may even have small pieces of oiled greaseproof paper between each portion, so that we can easily break away a further portion or portions should this be necessary. In this way we do not defrost more than we actually need.

If a 3 kg (6 lb) joint of meat is needed for roasting, boiling or braising we should again after necessary preparation package and freeze joints of that weight.

A long list of examples could be given here, but from the examples already given the principle is easily understood. The larger the volume of business the larger the number of portions to be frozen and vice versa.

Another good reason for the use of a deep freeze in this connection is that of collection. Small amounts of fresh foods not sufficient for a dish or meal can be placed into the deep freeze until sufficient for a given meal or dish, e.g. chicken livers may be collected over a period, until there are enough to make pâté, or skewers of chicken liver and bacon.

Packages and Packaging

Most frozen foods bought on the market are packed in plastic bags or plastic bags plus cardboard boxes. This is ideal for most foods of the manufacturers' and free-flow frozen types of food. But it can be very wasteful in space, and one is advised to remove the outer wrapping which then makes it easier to recognize the food in a deep freeze filled to the brim.

For foods of one's own preparation to be placed into the deep freeze (in particular meats, poultry, and fish) plastic bags are not always the best suited packing material. Contrary to the free-flow frozen manufactured foods, where the food is placed into plastic bags after blast freezing, the use of plastic bags in one's own production of freezing food is more difficult, especially as some types of plastic bags do not give sufficient coverage and protection and expose the foods to frost freeze burns. This will make the food, at least in parts, unsuitable for consumption.

Certain types of plastic bag, and certain plastic papers of the right gauge, are better than others, especially if we force out – or if possible vacuum out – any excess air and moisture.

For the average catering establishment experience shows that oiled greaseproof paper is usually the best packaging material. It will make contact with the food to be frozen, and by this fact alone forces out any air, and the oil will usually give good protection against freeze burns. If we then wrap this again in a generous sheet of normal kitchen paper a good result is usually assured.

As one can seldom write the contents of the package to be frozen on greased or oiled greaseproof paper, the extra sheet of kitchen paper not only gives added protection but enables one to write the contents, weight, amounts, and date on each packet. The latter is *most* important for two reasons:

(a) It is quickly recognized for use and stocktaking purposes.
(b) The written date will ensure that older stocks are used first.

Storage and Shelving

Most deep freezes are supplied with a number of shelves according to size, or they are equipped with shelves or baskets as in the case of box deep freezes.

To place frozen items well one should if possible reserve one shelf for each item or type of food, e.g.

one shelf for beef
one shelf for lamb
one shelf for veal
one shelf for poultry, and so on.

Smaller cuts and portions are best stored in shelf baskets as they do not stack very well and fall out when the doors are opened forcefully.

Stock Control

One should always know what foods and how much of each food is found in the deep freeze. This is best done with a stock list on or near the freezer, where staff can easily cross off or add items which are removed or placed from or into it. Thus at a glance one is aware of the stock in hand, and this can be taken into consideration when placing new orders. This stock list should be well laid out and simple to use. If the working of the stock list gets too complicated any additions or subtraction will not be recorded and in the atmosphere of a busy kitchen, incorrect stock will be shown. This could be disastrous and result in either too much or too little stock.

Once every three or four weeks all the stock should be removed from the deep freeze, excess ice scraped out, and the deep freeze thoroughly cleaned. Every two or three months the deep freeze should be switched off and defrosted, if it is not of the self-defrosting type, and thoroughly cleaned. The guidance given on pages 6 and 7 with regard to cleaning an ordinary refrigerator may be applied equally well to a deep freeze.

Withdrawal

When foods are required from the deep freeze it takes good timing to place them outside the deep freeze for defrosting. The best place for defrosting meats, poultry, and fish is of course a normal fridge where the food can defrost slowly and without sudden temperature change. Various weights and sizes need different times, and the amount of bone left in some cuts of meat or fish (as in the case of a rib of beef or halibut steaks) will have some delaying effect on the defrosting.

Foods of any kind should never be defrosted by applying either dry heat or hot water, as they will always lose flavour and appearance. Of late the microwave ovens have been used in the defrosting of larger cuts or joints of meat, but not very successfully, as it needs some experience and good timing so that the food is only defrosted and does not actually begin to cook. A guide for defrosting in a normal fridge may be as follows:

Small cuts and portions	overnight
Small joints/poultry	12-24 hours
Small carcasses (lamb)	12-24 hours
Larger carcasses/quarters (beef)	48-72 hours

In the case of small or medium packages, especially those of one's own production and preparation, all wrapping should be removed and food placed on to trays or into bowls.

In some cases it may be advisable to place foods to be defrosted on a perforated tray or colander, with a receiving tray or bowl underneath. This will avoid the defrosting item lying in its own defrosting liquid or causing drip on shelving and floor.

The slower the defrosting cycle the better the results, especially with red meats like beef and game. These should be defrosted slowly, otherwise they bleed excessively and much of the goodness and blood will be found on the defrosting tray.

Marinading

However carefully we freeze foods they lose some of their flavour and sometimes appearance, and we would do well to put some of this back. It is best done in the form of marinades or by some seasonings.

A bag of defrosted prawns is much improved by the following method: when defrosted, wash and drain, then add a little lemon juice, oil, salt and pepper, and let them marinade for 1-2 hours before using. Both flavour and colour will return and make these prawns much more pleasant to use for both hot and cold dishes.

When it is necessary to freeze sirloins for steaks always freeze whole or possibly in two pieces if a large strip-loin, for individual steaks bleed much more excessively in proportion than the whole or piece of sirloin. When the piece for entrecôtes has been defrosted, cut the steaks and place them on a tray for grilling or frying with the addition of a little red wine, oil, garlic, salt and pepper marinade. The flavour and appearance will greatly improve and render the entrecôtes ready for grilling or frying at the same time.

The same is the case for fish. If left for an hour or so before cooking in a little seasoning and lemon juice marinade for boiling or poaching fish or seasoning, lemon juice, and oil for all grilling or frying fish it will improve both in appearance and flavour and much will be added to its final presentation when cooked.

Never force foods when defrosting: give them time. Hanging foods to defrost in a hot kitchen, or leaving them outside in a kitchen overnight will cause deterioration especially in appearance, and there are also some dangers in respect of contamination. Many scientists will advise, for various reasons, not to freeze food oneself as normal deep freezes are only intended for storing frozen food, and are not made to freeze fresh foods. This should be done by blast freezing only. This advice has surely much base and scientific reason behind it, but there is no law in Great Britain against home freezing in a normal deep freeze except the rules and regulations applying to ice creams, which are well known.

The practice of doing our own freezing is widespread both in the home as well as in our industry and manufacturers of deep freezes have even supplied various types with special quick-freeze sections or coils for quick contact freezing to help us in this, but they are not as effective as the proper blast-freeze units which few can afford to install.

If we only freeze smaller joints and packages, if we only freeze good fresh and sound foods, if we keep our freezers and equipment absolutely clean, and cook our food properly and well, most deep freezes are a most valuable aid in the preparation of food in our industry.

Appendix C

GLOSSARY OF FRENCH TERMS USED IN COLD LARDER WORK

Abatis	Chicken giblets
Abats	Offal
Agneau	Lamb
Aiguille à brider	Trussing needle
Aiguille à piquer	Larding needle
Ail	Garlic
Aile	Wing
Aileron	Winglet
Airelles	Cranberries
Aloyau	Sirloin
Arêtes	Fish bones
Aromates	Herbs for flavouring
Barbue	Brill
Barde de lard	Thin slice of fat salt bacon
Baron	Legs with loins attached
Barquette	Boat-shaped tartlet
Bavette	Flank, skirt
Blinis	Buckwheat pancake
Bœuf	Beef
Bonne-bouche	Savoury tit-bit
Bouchée	Pastry casing
Brider	Truss
Brie	Cheese
Brin	Sprig
Briser	Break (bones)
Broché	Trussed
Brochet	Pike
Broyé	Bruised
Buisson	Cluster of small fish
Camembert	Cheese
Carapace	Shell
Carcasse	Carcass
Carré	Best end
Carrelet	Plaice, dab
Casser	Break (bones)
Caviar	Caviar, caviare
Cerfeuil	Chervil

Cervelle	Brain
Chair	Flesh
Chapelure	Brown crumbs
Châteaubriand	Double fillet steak
Chaufroiter	Coat with chaud-froid sauce
Chipolata	Small pork sausage
Clou de girofle	Clove
Clouter	Stud
Cochon de lait	Suckling pig
Contrefilet	Boned sirloin
Corbeille	Basket
Cornichon	Gherkin
Côtelette	Cutlet
Couronne	Crown
Court-bouillon	Cooking liquor
Crapaudine	Spatchcock (birds split and trussed to look like a toad)
Crémeux	Creamy
Crépine	Pig's caul
Cromesquis	Croquette in caul
Croquant	Crisp, crackling
Croûte	Crust
Cru	Raw
Cuillère	Spoon
Cuissot	Thigh, leg of veal or pork
Culinaire	Applying to cookery
Culotte	Rump, aitchbone
Cumin	Caraway seed
Darne	Slice of round fish on bone
Découper	Carve
Dégorger	Whiten by soaking
Demi-deuil	Poultry studded with truffle
Dénerver	Remove sinews
Dénoyauter	Stone (olives)
Dépouiller	Skin, skim
Dessaler	Remove salt
Doré	Golden
Douilles	Piping tubes
Ébarber	Beard, trim
Écailler	Scale
En croûte	Wrapped in pastry
En papillote	Wrapped in paper
Enlever	Remove
Épaule	Shoulder
Épice	Spice
Éplucher	Peel, skin
Escaloper	Scallop

Escarole	Endive salad
Estomac	Stomach
Faisander	Ripen game
Farcir	Stuff
Farine	Flour
Fendre	Split
Flambé	Flamed, singed
Flétan	Halibut
Foie	Liver
Foie gras	Goose liver
Foncer	Line
Fondre	Melt
Fouetter	Whisk
Frappé	Iced, chilled
Fricandelle	Steaklet minced
Fumé	Essence, smoked
Garde-Manger	Cold larder
Garniture	Garnish
Gelinotte	Grouse
Gervais	Cheese
Gigot	Leg of lamb or mutton
Gingembre	Ginger
Glacière	Ice box
Godiveau	Forcemeat
Goût	Taste
Graisse	Fat, grease
Gras	Plump, fat
Gras-double	Tripe
Gratter	Scrape
Grenadin	Larded veal steak
Grillade	Grilling meat
Grosse-pièce	Joint
Gruyère	Cheese
Hacher	Chop, mince
Hanche	Haunch
Hareng	Herring
Harenguets	Sprats
Haut-goût	Fine taste
Hirondelle	Swallow
Huile	Oil
Huître	Oyster
Jambon	Ham
Jarret	Shin, knuckle

Lait	Milk
Laitance	Soft roes
Laitue	Lettuce
Lamproie	Lamprey
Langouste	Crawfish, shellfish
Langue	Tongue
Lapereau	Young rabbit
Lapin	Rabbit
Larder	Lard with bacon
Laver	Wash
Levraut	Young hare
Lièvre	Hare
Limon	Lime
Lingue	Ling
Longe	Loin
Lustrer	Gloss or glaze with aspic
Macérer	Steep in flavouring liquor
Mâche	Salad
Macreuse	Scoter, scoter-duck
Maïs	Sweetcorn
Maquereau	Mackerel
Marinade	Wine pickle
Mariné	Pickled
Marquer	Prepare marinade
Masquer	Coat with sauce
Médaillon	Round steak
Mélange	Mixture
Melon	Melon
Menthe	Mint
Mie de pain	White, fresh crumbs
Mignon	Small fillet
Moelle	Bone marrow
Monter	Emulsify sauce
Mortifier	Hang meat or game, tenderize
Moule	Mould, mussel
Moutarde	Mustard
Mouton	Mutton
Muscade	Nutmeg
Navarin	Lamb or mutton stew
Nettoyer	Clean
Noisette	Hazel nut, boneless chop
Noix	Nut, cushion veal
Oeuf	Egg
Oeuf farci	Stuffed egg
Oie	Goose

Oiseau	Bird
Oison	Gosling
Olive	Olive
Oreille	Ear
Os à moelle	Marrow bone
Ouvrir	Open
Pain	Bread
Pain bis	Brown bread
Pain de volaille	Mould of finely pounded poultry
Pamplemousse	Grapefruit
Panaché	Mixed
Panade	Binding paste for forcemeats
Pané	Breaded, crumbed
Paner	Crumb
Passoire	Colander, strainer
Pâte	Paste
Pâté	Raised pie, savoury pasty
Paupiette	Stuffed meat or fish olive
Perdreau	Young partridge
Perdrix	Partridge
Petits pains fourrés	Filled rolls or bridge rolls
Pièce montée	Centrepiece
Pieds	Feet, trotters
Pintade	Guinea fowl
Piquant	Sharp
Piquer	Stud with bacon, truffle, etc.
Pistache	Pistachio nut
Plie	Plaice
Pluvier	Plover
Poissonnière	Fish kettle
Poitrine	Breast
Poivre	Pepper
Pomme	Apple
Pomme de terre	Potato
Porc	Pork
Pré-salé	Mutton raised on salt meadows
Printanier	Selection of spring vegetables
Printemps	Spring
Quartier	Quarter of carcass
Queue	Tail
Râble	Saddle of hare or rabbit
Racines	Roots
Rafraîchir	Refresh or cool
Ragoût	Meat stew
Raie	Skate

Râper	Grate, scrape
Ravigote	Cold sauce
Réchauffé	Reheated cooked food
Réduire	Reduce
Réforme	Garnish
Refroidir	Chill
Renverser	Turn out
Repasser	Re-strain
Rillettes	French potted meats
Ris de veau	Calf's sweetbread
Rognon	Kidney
Rognures	Trimmings
Romaine	Cos lettuce
Roquefort	French cheese
Rouget	Red mullet
Roulade	Meat roll
Rouler	Roll
Royan	Sardine-type fish
Saignant	Bloody, underdone
Saindoux	Hog's lard
Salamandre	Toasting grill
Salipicon	Diced foodstuffs for *bouchées*, etc.
Saucière	Sauce boat
Saucisse	Sausage
Saucisson	Garlic sausage, smoked sausage
Sauge	Sage
Saumon	Salmon
Saumure	Brine
Sauter	Toss
Sautoire	Sauté pan
Sec, sèche	Dried
Selle	Saddle
Socle	Base, ornamental stand
Spatule	Spatula
St. Pierre	John Dory
Suif	Mutton suet, tallow
Suprême	Best cut, most delicate
Tailler	Cut
Tamis	Fine sieve
Tamiser	Sieve or rub through tammycloth
Tarte	Open tart
Tartelette	Round tartlet
Tartine	Bread slice, sandwich
Tasse	Cup
Terrine	China pie dish
Tête	Head

Thon	Tunny
Timbale	Round china mould
Tourner	Cut barrel shape, turn
Tournedos	Round fillet steak
Tranche	Slice
Trancher	Carve
Tronçon	Flat fish steak (on bone)
Tronçonner	Cut into steaks
Truite	Trout
Turbot	Turbot
Turbotière	Turbot kettle
Veau	Veal
Viande	Meat, viands
Vider	Draw poultry, empty
Vinaigrette	Salad dressing
Volaille	Poultry
Vol-au-vent	Puff pastry case
Volière	Birds with plumage
Zeste	Rind of orange or lemon without pith

Index